NEW FIRST
SPANISH COURSE

E. C. HILLS
FORMERLY UNIVERSITY OF CALIFORNIA

AND

J. D. M. FORD
HARVARD UNIVERSITY

NEW EDITION PREPARED WITH
THE COLLABORATION OF

GUILLERMO RIVERA
HARVARD UNIVERSITY

GEORGE G. HARRAP & CO. LTD
LONDON   TORONTO   WELLINGTON   SYDNEY

First published 1942

Reprinted: 1944; 1946; 1947; 1948; 1950;
1952; 1955; 1956; 1957; 1960; 1961;
1963; 1965; 1967; 1969; 1971

ISBN 0 245 56944 8

Reproduced and Printed in Great Britain by
Redwood Press Limited, Trowbridge & London

PREFACE

THE original edition of *First Spanish Course* was published in 1917. The authors aimed to present to English-speaking students the essential facts of Spanish grammar and to illustrate them by means of abundant material for oral and written exercises. The amount of formal grammar given in each lesson was small, and in the early lessons there were almost no exceptions to the general rules. At the end of each lesson the rules of grammar were repeated in Spanish.

The continuing success of *First Spanish Course* led the authors to bring out a new edition in 1925. The grammar presentation had proved so satisfactory that few modifications were required in the order and wording of the rules. A new and complete set of Alternative English-Spanish Exercises was added at the end. The new exercises, like the old, illustrated the grammatical material of the respective lessons and repeated with variants the subject matter of the Spanish reading texts. The 1925 edition contained also a list of Classroom Expressions and fourteen Topical Illustrated Charts with numbered objects designed to provide additional material of a practical nature for oral direct-method exercises.

The present edition is a complete revision of the entire book. The emphasis on the spoken language is maintained, with due recognition of the present demand for early and abundant reading. The grammatical presentation and the basic vocabularies, essential features of the book, have been carefully revised in the light of these objectives. The vocabulary is smaller and is used more frequently in the exercises. The *Resúmenes gramaticales* and the Illustrated Charts have been replaced by fifty *lecturas*, one for each lesson. These readings are carefully graded, and they contain in story form considerable factual and cultural information on the life of the Spanish-speaking peoples. Another feature is the review lesson, of which there are five with abundant and varied exercises. The Verb Appendices, feature of the older editions, have been preserved in the present one.

Grateful acknowledgment of indebtedness is made to Professor Guillermo Rivera, who assisted the authors in the preparation of the original edition and who has assumed the major share of the work in this one.

J. D. M. F.

CONTENTS

FIRST SPANISH COURSE

INTRODUCTION

Pronunciation

1. Castilian forms the basis of both the spoken and the written language of cultivated Spaniards and Spanish Americans.

2. *The Alphabet.* The following list gives the signs comprised in the Spanish or Castilian alphabet with the usual Castilian names for them:

a (*a*)	f (*efe*)	l (*ele*)	p (*pe*)	u (*u*)
b (*be*)	g (*ge*)	ll (*elle*)	q (*cu*)	v (*ve* or *uve*)
c (*ce*)	h (*hache*)	m (*eme*)	r (*ere*)	[w (*doble ve*)]
ch (*che*)	i (*i*)	n (*ene*)	rr (*erre*)	x (*equis*)
d (*de*)	j (*jota*)	ñ (*eñe*)	s (*ese*)	y (*i griega*)
e (*e*)	k (*ka*)	o (*o*)	t (*te*)	z (*zeta* or *zeda*)

NOTE: **Ch, ll, ñ,** and **rr** figure as distinct signs in the Spanish alphabet. In the dictionary, words and syllables beginning with **ch, ll,** and **ñ** are found after those beginning with **c, l,** and **n** respectively.

VOWELS

3. **a** = *a* of *father:* **padre.**

e = (1) *a* of *mate:* **mesa,** *table;* (2) *e* of *met,* before a consonant (except *n* or *s*) in the same syllable, before **rr,** and in the diphthong **ei** (or **ey**): **papel,** *paper;* **ser,** *to be;* **muerto,** *dead;* **defecto,** *defect;* **perro,** *dog;* **ley,** *law.*

i = *ee* of *meet:* **libro,** *book.*

o = (1) *o* of *note:* **todo,** *all;* (2) *o* of *not* before a consonant

in the same syllable, before **rr,** and in the diphthong **oi** (or **oy**):
sol, *sun;* **señor,** *sir;* **con,** *with;* **gorra,** *cap;* **soy,** *I am.*
u = *u* of *boot:* **pluma,** *pen.*

The vowels are of medium length or short; they never have
the diphthongal sounds heard in the English long *a* (*fate*), long *o*
(*no*), etc. There should not be prefixed to **u** the *y* element
which it has in such English words as *tube, pure,* etc. In the
conjunction **y,** *and,* the sound is that of the simple vowel **i**
(*ee*); approximately the same sound is given to final **y,** as in
muy, *very;* in other positions the **y** has nearly the sound of
English *y* in *yet.*
In the western countries of South America, especially in Chile,
the final **y** of Castilian is frequently supplanted by **i,** as in
mui for **muy,** *very,* **i** for **y,** *and,* etc.

4. *Vowel Combinations.* When two adjacent vowels in a word
combine into a single syllable, they form a diphthong; when
three do so, they form a triphthong.

5. *Diphthongs.* These are constituted when one of the strong
vowels, **a, e, o,** combines with one of the weak vowels, **i, u;**
thus:

ai	ei	oi	au	eu	ou
ia	ie	io	ua	ue	uo

or when the two weak vowels combine; thus:

iu   ui

If the second element is **i** and occurs at the end of a word, it
is written **y,** as in **muy, soy,** etc.
When the syllable containing the diphthong is accented, the
stress falls on the strong element, if there be one; otherwise it
falls on the second of the two weak vowels.
The various combinations, in an accented syllable, may be illustrated by these words:

baile, *dance;* **hay,** *there is* (*are*)	**principiamos,** *we begin*
flauta, *flute*	**cuatro,** *four*
reina, *queen;* **rey,** *king*	**bien,** *well*
deuda, *debt*	**fuerte,** *strong*
oigo, *I hear;* **doy,** *I give*	**naciones,** *nations*

bou (*Catalonian mode of fishing*)   **cuota,** *quota*
triunfo, *triumph*   **cuita,** *grief*

NOTE: No diphthong, but two distinct syllables, will be the result,
(1) when two strong vowels come together, as in **Saavedra** (a proper
name), **faena,** *task,* **caoba,** *mahogany,* etc.; (2) when the accent falls
on a weak vowel adjacent to a strong vowel, as in **traído,** *brought,* **oído,**
heard, etc.; or (3) when two adjoining weak vowels are pronounced
separately, as in **flúido,** *fluid;* **huída,** *flight;* **construído,** *constructed.*
In the last two cases the accent is always written on the stressed
vowel.

6. *Triphthongs.* There are but four of these; they are formed
when a stressed strong vowel stands between two weak vowels.
Final **i** of a word is written **y.** The combinations are

    iai, as in **principiáis,** *you begin*
    iei, as in **principiéis,** *may you begin*
    uai (uay), as in **averiguáis,** *you ascertain;* **guay,** *woe*
    uei (uey), as in **continuéis,** *may you continue;* **buey,** *ox*

CONSONANTS

7. Of the consonants, **f, m,** and **p** may be said to have practically
the same values as in English. **Ch** has the sound of English
ch in *church:* **mucho,** *much.* **H** is silent: **hora,** *hour;* but **h**
from **f** was pronounced as late as the sixteenth century: **hacer**
(from *fazer*). **K** has the English sound and occurs only in
foreign words. **Q** never occurs except with a following **u,** and
the two together mean **k;** moreover they can appear only before
e or **i,** as in **aquel,** *that,* **quitar,** *to take away.* **W** is found only
in foreign words and has the foreign value; the sound of the
English *w,* as in *well,* etc., is possessed by the Spanish unaccented **u** in hiatus before another vowel, as in **cuestión,** *question,* **cuando,** *when,* etc. The other consonants need special
consideration.

8. **B, v.** These have one and the same value. It is given to
neither of them in English, and is produced by bringing the
lips quite close to each other and allowing the air to pass out
constantly between them; there is no stoppage of the air as
in the case of the English *b.* The sound of the English *v* does
not exist in Spanish. In a measure the Spanish sound in ques-

tion may be realized by trying to utter *b* and *v* in the same breath: cf. **cuba,** *vat,* **uva,** *grape.* Initial **b** or **v** more nearly resembles English *b,* as in **basta,** *enough,* **brazo,** *arm,* etc. After **m** or **n** (within a word or at the end of a preceding word), both **b** and **v** acquire the full value of the English *b,* as in **también,** *also,* **en verdad,** *in truth,* **envidia,** *envy.* (In these cases the **n** becomes **m** in pronunciation.)

9. **C, z.** **C** has two values. Before **a, o,** or **u,** or before a consonant (except in **ch**) it is pronounced *k,* as in **calle,** *street,* **codo,** *elbow;* **clase,** *class,* etc. Before **e** or **i** it has approximately the value of *th* in English *thin,* as in **cena,** *supper,* **cinco,** *five.* **Z,** which is ordinarily used only before **a, o,** or **u,** has also the value of *th.*

NOTE: In Spanish America and in parts of Spain (especially southern Spain) the **c** before **e** or **i** and the **z** before **a, o,** or **u** are pronounced like the English *ss.* There should be consistency in the use of either of these sounds, that is, they should not be mixed.

10. **D, t, l, n.** These differ from the English sounds in that they are produced farther forward in the mouth: when making them, the tongue touches the upper teeth, or at least the roots of the upper teeth.

In most positions the sound of **d** somewhat resembles that of English *th* in *father.* It may be compared to a prolonged English *d,* but pronounced with the tongue farther forward: cf. **todo,** *all,* **madre,** *mother.* Initial **d** more nearly resembles English *d,* as in **dámelo,** *give it to me.* After **l** and **n** Spanish **d** acquires the full value of English *d:* cf. **espalda,** *back,* **tienda,** *shop.* At the end of a word **d** is sometimes pronounced like the *th* of *thin,* or is omitted altogether, but neither course is sanctioned by the best usage. There is a tendency for it to disappear in pronunciation between vowels, especially in the ending –**ado.**

Aside from the fact that they should be produced well to the front in the mouth, **t, l,** and **n** are not unlike the English sounds.

11. **Ll, ñ.** These are palatalized modifications of **l** and **n.** The sign **ll** does not mean double **l** at all; it simply denotes an **l** pronounced in that part of the mouth in which a **y** is regularly

produced. In the endeavor to make an l the tongue is arched toward the palate (near which a **y** has its place of enuncia‹ tion); hence it is a palatalized l. The sound, as in Spanish **millón,** is rendered in a measure by that in English *million.* The ñ is, similarly, a palatalized variety of **n,** that is, an n produced in the **y** place in the mouth: the *ny* in the English *canyon* is an approximate rendering of the ñ in the Spanish **cañón.** The mark over the ñ is called a **tilde** (a word derived ultimately from the Latin "titulus," *title, sign*).

NOTE: In a good part of Spanish America, as in certain parts of Spain, the ll has become simply a **y** in pronunciation (which shows how strong the **y** element is in the ll), so that **caballo,** *horse,* is pronounced **cabayo.** In Chile it is **dz** and in the Argentine **dz** and **ts.**

12. **G, j.** Before **a, o,** or **u** and before a consonant **g** has the so-called "hard" sound, as in **gato,** *cat,* **gota,** *drop,* **gusto,** *taste.* Before **e** or **i** this sound is rendered by **gu** (in which the **u** has no pronounceable value of its own), as in **guerra,** *war,* **guisar,** *to cook.* Intervocalic "hard" **g** tends to become an indistinct spirant, as in **hago,** *I make,* **sigue,** *he follows.* **G** followed immediately by **e** or **i,** and **j,** wherever it occurs, have the "velar" sound given to *ch* in the Scotch-English "loch" or in the German "noch," as in **gente,** *people,* **jardín,** *garden.* While the sound indicated is the correct Castilian one, many Spanish speakers pronounce this **g** like a strong form of the *h* in English *hat.*

NOTES: 1. A diaeresis is placed over **u** when it is pronounced in **gue-** or **gui-,** as in **lingüístico,** *linguistic.*
2. **J** is silent at the end of a word, as in **reloj,** *watch.*

13. **R, rr.** The Spanish **r** is carefully pronounced with an unmistakable trill of the tongue. It has a well-defined utterance, which resembles that of a carefully enunciated English *r,* as in **caro,** *dear,* **grande,** *large,* **amar,** *to love.* When initial in a word and when it immediately follows **l** or **n,** it has a re-enforced value of this sound, as in **roto,** *broken,* **Enrique,** *Henry,* **alrededor,** *about.* The **rr** is like a carefully uttered English *r,* but much prolonged, as in **perro,** *dog,* **barra,** *bar.*

14. **S.** In most cases of its occurrence, between vowels and else-where, the Spanish **s** has the sound of the English *ss*, but it is hissed less: cf. **ser,** *to be,* **casa,** *house,* **más,** *more.* It should not receive between vowels the *z* sound which it often has in English. Nowadays, however, there is a tendency to voice it, that is, pronounce it like English *z*, before a voiced consonant (**b, d, g, l, r, m, n**), and many speakers aspirate it or fail to pronounce it at all before a consonant or at the end of a word. The better rule for foreigners is to pronounce it like English *ss* wherever it occurs.

15. **X.** This is a sound of infrequent occurrence in Spanish. Be-tween vowels it has ordinarily the English value (that is, *ks*, as in **nexo,** *knot,* or *gz*, as in **examen,** *examination*). Before consonants it may be pronounced like the English *x* (that is, as *ks*) or as *s*; both **sexto** and **sesto** are found as spellings for the word meaning *sixth.*

16. **Y.** This sound has been treated in part under the heading *Vowels.* At the beginning of a word or syllable it has a value comparable to that of the English *y.* However, when it is initial in a word, it is uttered strongly, and, in dialectal Spanish in Spain and rather generally in Spanish America, it acquires the sound of the English *j*, so that **yo,** *I;* becomes **jo** and **ya,** *already,* becomes **ja.** For Castilian a forcible **y** pronunciation suffices.

17. *Double Letters.* When Spanish letters are written double, each is pronounced separately. Of the vowels, **a, e,** and **o** may appear as doubled; and of these double **e** is the com-monest, as in **leer,** *to read,* **creer,** *to believe.* Of the consonants, only two are doubled in writing; these are **cc** and **nn.** **Cc** can occur only before **e** or **i,** and then the first **c** is *k* in sound and the second is the spirant *th*, as in **acceder,** *to accede,* **acción,** *action.* Careless speakers are prone to neglect the first **c** in such cases. Double **n** is found only where the first **n** belongs to a prefix, as in **innoble,** *ignoble.* **Ll** and **rr** are not con-sidered double letters in Spanish. They are pronounced as single signs and, as also in **ch,** the component parts must not be separated in writing.

ACCENTUATION

18. Many Spanish words reveal the place of their accent by their very form; for a considerable number, however, a written accent is thought necessary. The leading rules are these:

a) Words ending in a vowel, or in the consonants **n** or **s**, stress regularly the next to the last syllable and require no written accent, as in

habla, *he speaks*	**especie,** *species*
dulce, *sweet*	**paraguas,** *umbrella*
examen, *examination*	

NOTE: S and n are often inflectional endings or a part of inflectional endings. Usually their presence does not vary the accent which the particular word would have without them; thus:

carta, *letter;* **cartas,** *letters*
ama, *he loves;* **amas,** *thou lovest;* **aman,** *they love*

b) Words ending in a consonant except **n** or **s** stress regularly the last syllable and take no written accent, as in

libertad, *liberty* **amar,** *to love*

NOTE: For accentual purposes final **y** is treated as a consonant.

c) A written accent is required for words not obeying the two rules just given and for all words whose stress comes more than two syllables from their end. (This means that a written accent is needed by all words ending in a vowel and stressing it, by words ending in **n** or **s** and stressing the last syllable, by all those ending in a consonant — except **n** or **s** — and not stressing their last syllable, and by all words not stressed on either the last or the next to the last syllable). Examples:

papá, *papa*	**lápiz,** *lead pencil*
sofá, *sofa*	**mármol,** *marble*
razón, *reason*	**ejército,** *army*
interés, *interest*	**telégrafo,** *telegraph*

NOTES: 1. The addition of the plural sign –es sometimes involves the use of a written accent not needed in the singular; thus, **crimen,** *crime,* but **crímenes;** on the other hand, it may mean the omission of an accent required in the singular, as in **razón,** *reason,* **razones.**

2. In general, the addition of a plural sign has no effect upon the place of accent in any particular word; however, two words advance the place of stress one syllable toward the end; these are **carácter**, *character*, **caracteres** (for which word no written accent is necessary), and **régimen**, *rule of conduct*, **regímenes** (for which the written accent is still necessary, as the stress occurs more than two syllables from the end of the word).

19. Accents are also used merely to indicate different parts of speech. Certain monosyllables (which, of course, need no written accent to indicate the place of stress), and certain demonstrative, interrogative, and exclamative words require an accent to distinguish them from other words spelled and pronounced like them. Compare:

mí	*me, myself*	**mi**	*my*
sí	*himself*, etc.; *yes*	**si**	*if*
más	*more*	**mas**	*but*
éste	*this one* (pron.)	**este**	*this* (adj.)
ése	*that one* (pron.)	**ese**	*that* (adj.)
aquél	*that one* (pron.)	**aquel**	*that* (adj.)
qué	*what, which* (interrog. and exclam.)	**que**	*who, whom, which* (rel.)
quién	*who, whom* (interrog. and exclam.)	**quien**	*who, whom* (rel.)

NOTES: 1. An accent is written on **o**, *or*, between Arabic numerals, as in **2 ó 3**.

2. The written accent of a verb form must not be omitted even though, by the addition of an object pronoun to it, the place of the accent is clear enough, thus, **hablé**, *I spoke*, **habléle**, *I spoke to him*. A verb form which does not take an accent when it stands alone may require one, if the addition of object pronouns to it throws the stress of the compounded form on a syllable preceding the next to the last; thus, **diciendo**, *saying*, **diciéndomelo**, *saying it to me*; **traer**, *to bring*, **traértelo**, *to bring it to thee*; **escriba Vd.**, *write*, **escríbalo Vd.**, *write it*.

SYLLABIFICATION

20. A single consonantal character and the digraphs **ch, ll, rr** (these three being inseparable combinations) are, in a syllabic division, passed over to the following vowel; so, also, are most combinations of a consonant with an ensuing **l** or **r** (except **rl, sl, tl, nr**, and **sr**, which are separable):

la-bio, *lip*	cu-brir, *to cover*	no-ble, *noble*
ja-ca, *pony*	su-frir, *to suffer*	mo-fle-tu-do, *chubby-*
la-do, *side*	re-pri-mir, *to repress*	*cheeked*
ne-xo, *knot*	la-cre, *sealing wax*	su-plir, *to supply*
mu-cho, *much*	ma-gro, *meager*	te-cla, *key*
bu-llir, *to boil*	ma-dre, *mother*	si-glo, *century*
pa-rra, *vine*	cua-tro, *four*	

Cf. mer-lu-za, *cod;* es-la-bón, *link;* At-lán-ti-co, *Atlantic;* En-ri-que, *Henry;* Is-ra-e-li-ta, *Israelite.*

a) With the exception of the inseparable combinations mentioned in the foregoing rule, two consonants between vowels are so divided that one remains with the preceding, the other goes with the following vowel:

ap-to, *fit*	más-til, *mast*	in-no-ble, *ignoble, etc.*
cor-te, *court*	ac-ci-den-te, *accident*	

b) Where the combination of consonants between vowels is of more than two, there is a tendency to pass over to the second vowel only a single consonant or one of the inseparable combinations mentioned at the beginning of §20; e.g.:

> par-che, *plaster*   cons-truc-ción, *construction*
> pers-pi-ca-cia, *perspicacity*

c) Prefixes felt as such are usually kept intact contrary to the rules given above; e.g.:

> des-es-pe-rar, *to despair* (cf. esperar, *to hope*)
> sub-le-var-se, *to rebel* (cf. levar, *to raise*)
> ab-ro-ga-ción, *abrogation* (cf. rogar, *to ask*)

Punctuation

21. The only notable points here are: (1) the double use of question marks and exclamation points, which not only end their clause, but in an inverted form usually precede it (e.g. ¿ **Cómo está Vd. ?** *How are you?* ¡ **Qué hermosa mujer !** *What a beautiful woman!*); (2) the frequency of suspension points (. . .) in narrative or dramatic style; and (3), in dialogue, the use of a dash (—) to indicate that there is a change of speaker.

Capitalization

22. Capitals are less commonly used in Spanish than in English.
Unless they begin a sentence, a line of verse, or a quotation,
proper adjectives and the pronoun **yo**, *I*, are not capitalized.
National or other locative adjectives used as nouns may take
a capital when they denote persons (although usage varies in
this respect); when they denote languages, they usually take
no capital, even though used substantively: **los franceses
(or Franceses) hablan francés,** *Frenchmen speak French.*
In the titles of books and in the headings of chapters, paragraphs, etc., it is customary in Spanish either to use capital
letters exclusively, or to capitalize only the first letter of the
title or heading and use small letters elsewhere, as in **RE-
SUMEN GRAMATICAL** or **Resumen gramatical, GÉ-
NERO DE LOS NOMBRES** or **Género de los nombres,**
etc.

23. *Drill.*

I. Pronounce:

alquilar, *to hire, rent*	**escuela,** *school*	**martes,** *Tuesday*
bastante, *enough*	**feliz,** *happy*	**mío,** *mine*
billete, *ticket*	**gente,** *people*	**oficina,** *office*
ciudad, *city*	**grande,** *large*	**paquete,** *package*
continuar, *to continue*	**guerra,** *war*	**pequeño,** *small*
cuarto, *room*	**hielo,** *ice*	**perro,** *dog*
diploma, *diploma*	**hombre,** *man*	**reloj,** *watch*
distinguir, *to distinguish*	**José,** *Joseph*	**volver,** *to return*
edificio, *building*	**lección,** *lesson*	**yerba,** *grass*
Enrique, *Henry*		

II. Pronounce, and then explain the reason for the use of the
accent:

aquí, *here*	**lástima,** *pity*	**pájaro,** *bird*
árbol, *tree*	**lección,** *lesson*	**papá,** *papa*
café, *coffee*	**María,** *Mary*	**periódico,** *newspaper*
después, *afterwards*	**médico,** *physician*	**reunión,** *meeting*
difícil, *difficult*	**millón,** *million*	**sábado,** *Saturday*
fácil, *easy*	**número,** *number*	**sillón,** *armchair*
jardín, *garden*	**página,** *page*	**teléfono,** *telephone*
lápiz, *pencil*	**país,** *country*	**útil,** *useful*

III. Pronounce, and then divide into syllables:

aprender, *to learn*

biblioteca, *library*

bicicleta, *bicycle*

caballo, *horse*

catorce, *fourteen*

construir, *to build*

costumbre, *custom*

demasiado, *too much*

diciembre, *December*

distintamente, *distinctly*

ejercicio, *exercise*

febrero, *February*

interesante, *interesting*

lápices, *pencils*

libro, *book*

mañana, *tomorrow*

muchacho, *boy*

multiplicar, *to multiply*

perro, *dog*

pluma, *pen*

programa, *program*

sabroso, *tasty*

trabajador, *industrious*

ventana, *window*

LESSON I

24. *Gender of Nouns (1).*

a) Nouns ending in **−o** are usually masculine.

muchacho *boy*   **libro** *book*

b) Nouns ending in **−a** are usually feminine.

muchacha *girl*   **pluma** *pen*

25. *Indefinite Article.* **Un,** *a, an,* is used with masculine nouns, and **una,** *a, an,* with feminine nouns.

un muchacho *a boy*   **una pluma** *a pen*

26.   **yo tengo,** *I have*
       usted tiene, *you have*
       un muchacho (una muchacha) tiene, *a boy (a girl) has*

NOTES: 1. **Yo,** *I,* may be omitted (see § 51).
2. The same form of the verb is used when **usted** is the subject that is used when the subject is a singular noun.

EXERCISES

un libro *a book*	**tiene** *have, has*
un muchacho *a boy*	**un, una** *a, an*
una muchacha *a girl*	**usted** *you*
un perro *a dog*	**y** *and*
una pluma *a pen*	**yo** *I*
tengo *I have*	

A. *Study:* 1. Yo tengo un libro.   2. Usted tiene un perro. 3. Un muchacho tiene una pluma.   4. Yo tengo un libro y una

14

pluma. 5. Usted tiene una pluma. 6. Una muchacha tiene un libro. 7. Yo tengo un perro. 8. Usted tiene un libro. 9. Un muchacho tiene un libro y una pluma. 10. Yo tengo una pluma. 11. Un muchacho tiene un libro. 12. Usted tiene un libro y una pluma.

B. *Write in Spanish:* 1. You have a pen. 2. A girl has a dog. 3. I have a book. 4. A girl has a book and a pen. 5. A boy has a dog. 6. I have a pen. 7. You have a book. 8. A boy has a book and a pen. 9. You have a dog. 10. A boy has a pen. 11. A girl has a book. 12. I have a book and a pen.

LECTURA

Yo tengo un libro de [1] lectura.[2] Me gusta [3] la [4] lectura. El [4] libro tiene anécdotas * españolas.[5] Me gustan [3] las [4] anécdotas españolas. El libro tiene también [6] selecciones. Tiene selecciones sobre [7] la vida [8] y las costumbres [9] españolas. Las selecciones son [10] cortas.[11] Yo leo [12] el libro en [13] la [14] escuela.[15]

LESSON II

27. *Gender of Nouns* (2). If nouns do not end in –o or –a, it is usually best to learn the gender of each one separately.

    un lápiz *a pencil*   **papel** (m.) *paper*

28. *The Regular Conjugations.* Spanish verbs are divided into three conjugations. The infinitive ending for the first conjugation is –ar.

    compr-ar *to buy*

NOTE: The part of the verb which precedes the ending –ar is called the radical.

[1] *of.*   [2] *reading;* **libro de lectura,** *reader.*   [3] *I like.*   [4] *The.*   * Cognates, that is, words of like derivation in both languages, and those which are easily recognized, are not translated.   [5] *Spanish.*   [6] *also, too.*   [7] *about.* [8] *life.*   [9] *customs.*   [10] *are.*   [11] *short.*   [12] *(I) read.*   [13] *in.*   [14] Omit. [15] *school.*

29. *Present Indicative.* The inflectional endings of the present indicative are:

SINGULAR	PLURAL
1 −o	1. −amos
2. −as	2. −áis
3. −a	3. −an

NOTE: These endings are added to the radical.

30. *Present Indicative of* **comprar.**

SINGULAR

1. **compro**	*I buy, do buy, am buying*
2. **compras**	*thou buyest, dost buy, art buying*
3. **compra**	{ *you buy, do buy, are buying*
	{ *he, she* (or *it*) *buys, does buy, is buying*

PLURAL

1. **compramos**	*we buy, do buy, are buying*
2. **compráis**	*ye buy, do buy, are buying*
3. **compran**	*you* or *they buy, do buy, are buying*

NOTE: With **usted** and **ustedes,** *you,* as the subject, the third person singular and plural are used (see § 26, note 2): **usted compra, ustedes compran,** *you buy, do buy, are buying.*

EXERCISES

comprar *to buy*	papel m. *paper*
en *in*	una tienda *a store*
un lápiz *a pencil*	ustedes pl. *you*

A. *Study:* 1. Yo tengo papel y un lápiz. 2. Usted tiene un lápiz y una pluma. 3. Yo tengo papel y un libro. 4. Usted tiene papel y una pluma. 5. Compro un libro y un lápiz. 6. Compro una pluma en una tienda. 7. Un muchacho tiene papel y un lápiz. 8. Una muchacha tiene un lápiz y una pluma. 9. Compramos un libro y un lápiz. 10. Compramos papel en una tienda. 11. Compro un lápiz y una pluma en una tienda. 12. Un muchacho compra papel. 13. Una muchacha compra un libro y un lápiz en una tienda. 14. Un muchacho compra una pluma y un lápiz en una tienda. 15. Compramos papel y un lápiz en una tienda.

B. *Translate:* 1. I have a pencil. 2. I have paper. 3. You have paper. 4. You have a pencil. 5. I buy a book. 6. I buy a pencil. 7. I buy a pen. 8. I buy paper. 9. A boy has a pencil. 10. A boy has paper. 11. A girl has a pencil. 12. A girl has paper. 13. We buy a pencil. 14. They buy a book. 15. We buy a pen.

C. *Write in Spanish:* 1. I have a pencil and a pen. 2. I have paper and a pen. 3. You have paper and a book. 4. I buy paper and a pen. 5. I buy a book in a store. 6. A boy has a book and a pencil. 7. A girl has paper and a pen. 8. A boy buys a book. 9. A girl buys a pen in a store. 10. A boy buys paper. 11. A boy buys a pencil in a store. 12. I buy paper in a store. 13. We buy a pen and a pencil. 14. We buy a book in a store. 15. We buy a pencil and a book in a store.

LECTURA

Antonio [1] tiene un libro de lectura. Tiene también un cuaderno.[2] No lee [3] en el cuaderno. Escribe [4] anécdotas en el cuaderno. Pone [5] láminas [6] en el cuaderno. El maestro [7] dicta [8] y Antonio escribe. Escribe anécdotas y selecciones. Yo también escribo [9] las anécdotas y selecciones. Voy [10] a [11] copiar [12] algunas [13] de ellas [14] ahora.[15]

LESSON III

31. *Plural of Nouns (1).*

a) Nouns ending in an unstressed vowel add –s to form the plural.

libro	*book*	**pluma**	*pen*
libros	*books*	**plumas**	*pens*

[1] *Anthony.* [2] *notebook.* [3] *No lee, He does not read.* [4] *He writes.*
[5] *He puts.* [6] *pictures.* [7] *teacher.* [8] *dictates.* [9] *(I) write.* [10] *I am going.*
[11] Omit. [12] *to copy.* [13] *some.* [14] *them.* [15] *now.*

b) Nouns ending in a consonant add –es to form the plural.

papel	*paper*	**lección**	*lesson*
papeles	*papers*	**lĕcciones**	*lessons*

NOTES: 1. The plural form **lecciones** does not have the accent mark.

2. The plural of **lápiz** is **lápices**.

32. *Definite Article (1).* The forms of the definite article are:

	SINGULAR	PLURAL	
Masculine	**el**	**los**	
Feminine	**la**	**las**	*the*

el libro	*the book*	**los libros**	*the books*
la pluma	*the pen*	**las plumas**	*the pens*

33. *Negative Sentences.* In negative sentences, **no**, *not*, is placed before the verb.

no compro   *I do not buy*   **usted no tiene**   *you haven't*

NOTES: 1. The auxiliary forms *do*, *does*, used in the English negative, are not translated into Spanish.

2. **Yo no tengo, usted no tiene** are translated by *I haven't (any)*, *you haven't (any)*, or by *I have no . . ., you have no . . .*

EXERCISES

el *the*	**la lección** *the lesson*
la escuela *the school*	**los** *the*
estudiar *to study*	**no** *not*
la, las *the*	

A. *Study:* 1. Yo tengo los libros. 2. Usted tiene los lápices. 3. El muchacho tiene las plumas. 4. Compramos un perro. 5. No compramos el perro en la tienda. 6. Compramos plumas y lápices en la tienda. 7. Yo no tengo lápices. 8. Usted no tiene plumas. 9. El muchacho no tiene libros. 10. La muchacha estudia la lección. 11. El muchacho no estudia la lección. 12. Las muchachas no estudian las lecciones en la escuela. 13. Los muchachos no compran libros. 14. No estudian la lección. 15. Compran lápices y plumas.

B. *1. Conjugate* **estudiar** *in the present indicative.*

Sí, me castigó.

II. Translate, and then repeat, changing each sentence to the negative form: 1. I have a book. 2. You have a dog. 3. I have the pen. 4. The girl has the pencil. 5. The boy has a book. 6. You have paper. 7. I buy books. 8. They buy pens. 9. We buy pencils. 10. I study the lesson.

C. *Write in Spanish:* 1. The boy has a dog. 2. You have the pen. 3. The girl hasn't any books. 4. We study the lessons. 5. The boy does not study. 6. We do not study in the school. 7. The girl does not buy the pens. 8. The boy buys the pens and (the)[1] pencils. 9. He buys the pens and (the) pencils in the store. 10. You do not study the lesson. 11. They study in (the) school. 12. The boy does not buy paper. 13. I buy paper, pens, and pencils in the store. 14. The girls are studying the lessons. 15. The boys are buying the books.

LECTURA

El muchacho está[2] triste[3] y el padre[4] le[5] pregunta[6]:
— ¿ Te[7] castigó[8] el maestro ?
— Sí,[9] me castigó.

[1] Words in ( ) are to be supplied. Words in [ ] are to be omitted.   [2] *is.*
[3] *sad.* [4] *father.* [5] *him.* [6] *asks.* [7] *You.* [8] *(he) punished, did punish.* [9] *Yes.*

— ¿ Te castigó porque [1] no estudias las lecciones ?

— No, yo estudio las lecciones. Me castigó porque yo dije [2] que [3] Dios [4] no está en la tienda de Antonio.

— ¿ No sabes [5] que Dios está en todas [6] partes ? [7]

— Sí, Dios está en todas partes, pero [8] Antonio no tiene tienda.

LESSON IV

34. *Second and Third Conjugations.* The infinitives of all verbs of the second and third conjugations end in –er and –ir respectively.

aprend–er *to learn*   viv–ir *to live*

NOTE: The part of the verb which precedes the endings –er and –ir is called the radical.

35. *Present Indicative.* The inflectional endings of the present indicative in the second and third conjugations are:

	SINGULAR		PLURAL	
	II	III	II	III
1.	–o	–o	–emos	–imos
2.	–es	–es	–éis	–ís
3.	–e	–e	–en	–en

NOTES: 1. These endings differ only in the first and second persons of the plural.

2. These endings are added to the radical.

36. *Present Indicative of* **aprender** *and* **vivir.**

Aprender, *to learn*   **Vivir,** *to live*

(*I learn, do learn, am learning, etc.*)   (*I live, do live, am living, etc.*)

SINGULAR	PLURAL		SINGULAR	PLURAL
1. aprend–o	aprend–emos		1. viv–o	viv–imos
2. aprend–es	aprend–éis		2. viv–es	viv–ís
3. aprend–e	aprend–en		3. viv–e	viv–en

[1] because.   [2] I said.   [3] that.   [4] God.   [5] Don't you know?   [6] all.
[7] parts; **en todas partes,** *everywhere.*   [8] but.

37. *Interrogative Sentences.* In questions, the subject, if it is expressed, usually follows the verb.

compramos	*we buy*	¿ compramos?	*do we buy?*
usted tiene	*you have*	¿ tiene usted?	*have you?*
el muchacho aprende		¿ aprende el muchacho?	
the boy learns		*does the boy learn?*	

NOTES: 1. In interrogation, as in negation, the auxiliary forms *do*
and *does* are not translated into Spanish.
2. In writing, an inverted interrogation mark is placed at the beginning of a question.

EXERCISES

aprender *to learn*	el maestro *the teacher*
la casa *the house, home;* en —, *at*	la mesa *the table*
home	qué interrog. *what*
con *with*	quién(es) interrog. *who, whom*
el dinero *the money*	la silla *the chair*
dónde interrog. *where*	vivir *to live*
enseñar *to teach*	

A. *Study:* 1. ¿ Vive el maestro en la escuela ? 2. El maestro
no vive en la escuela. 3. Vive en una casa. 4. En la casa tiene
libros. 5. En la escuela tiene papel, pluma y lápices. 6. El
maestro enseña y los muchachos aprenden. 7. ¿ Estudia usted
en la escuela ? 8. No estudio en la escuela. 9. Estudio en casa
y aprendo las lecciones. 10. En casa tengo una mesa y una silla.
11. En la mesa tengo libros, papel y lápices. 12. ¿ Tiene usted
dinero ? 13. No tengo dinero. 14. Compro papel con dinero.
15. No compro papel en la tienda.

B. *Answer in Spanish:* 1. ¿ Dónde vive el maestro ? 2. ¿ Quién
vive en una casa ? 3. ¿ Qué tiene en la casa ? 4. ¿ Dónde tiene
papel ? 5. ¿ Quién enseña ? 6. ¿ Dónde estudia usted ?
7. ¿ Quién aprende las lecciones ? 8. ¿ Qué tiene usted en casa ?
9. ¿ Qué tiene usted en la mesa ? 10. ¿ Con qué compra usted
papel ?

C. *Translate, and then change to the interrogative form:* 1. We•
buy pencils. 2. The teacher teaches. 3. The boy learns. 4. I
have a chair. 5. You have money. 6. You buy a house. 7. The

boy buys a dog. 8. The girl studies the lesson. 9. The teacher
lives in the school. 10. The girl has a chair and a table.

D. *Write in Spanish:* 1. I have books and pencils. 2. Where
do you buy the books? 3. I buy the books and (the) pencils
in the store. 4. What does the teacher buy in the store? 5. He
buys books and pencils in the store. 6. The girls buy paper and
pens. 7. We buy books and paper. 8. Who teaches the lessons?
9. The teacher teaches the lessons. 10. We do not teach. 11. We
study and learn the lessons. 12. The boys study and learn.
13. The girls do not study. 14. Where do they live? 15. They
live in the school.

LECTURA

El maestro de Antonio vive en la casa de un amigo.[1] El maestro quiere [2] comprar una casa y el amigo le dice [3]:

— Me gusta la casa. Te prestaré [4] el dinero pero con nueve [5]
por [6] ciento [7] de interés.

— ¡ Nueve por ciento!

— ¿ No sabes que el negocio [8] es [9] el negocio ?

— Sí. ¿ Pero no temes [10] la cólera [11] del [12] cielo ? [13]

— Desde [14] el cielo el nueve parece [15] seis.[16]

LESSON V

38. *Inflection of Adjectives (1).*

a) An adjective that ends in –o in the masculine singular has
four forms.

	SINGULAR	PLURAL	
Masculine	blanco	blancos	white
Feminine	blanca	blancas	

perro blanco   *white dog*
casas blancas   *white houses*

[1] *friend.* [2] *wishes.* [3] *says (tells).* [4] *I'll lend.* [5] *nine.* [6] *per.*
[7] *cent(um).* [8] *business.* [9] *is.* [10] *you fear.* [11] *wrath.* [12] *of [the].* [13] *Heaven.*
[14] *From.* [15] *seems (is like).* [16] *six.*

b) Other adjectives have, as a rule, only two forms of the ending, one for the singular and one for the plural.

	SINGULAR	PLURAL	
Masculine	fácil	fáciles	*easy*
	grande	grandes	*big, large*
Feminine	fácil	fáciles	*easy*
	grande	grandes	*big, large*

perro grande *large dog*   **casas grandes** *large houses*

39. *Plural of Adjectives.* The plural of adjectives is formed like that of nouns.

SINGULAR	PLURAL	
blanco	**blancos**	*white*
grande	**grandes**	*big, large*
fácil	**fáciles**	*easy*

40. *Position of Adjectives (1).*

a) Limiting adjectives (articles, possessives, demonstratives, numerals, etc.) usually precede their noun.

un libro *a book*   **la casa** *the house*
muchos lápices *many pencils*

b) Descriptive adjectives usually follow their noun.

un libro fácil *an easy book*   **la casa blanca** *the white house*
muchos lápices rojos *many red pencils*

41. *Present Indicative of* **tener,** *to have.*

SINGULAR		PLURAL	
yo tengo	*I have*	**tenemos**	*we have*
tienes	*thou hast (you have)*	**tenéis**	*ye (you) have*
usted tiene	*you have*	**ustedes tienen**	*you have*
tiene	*he (she, it) has*	**tienen**	*they have*

NOTE: This verb is irregular in all forms of the present indicative except the first and second persons of the plural.

EXERCISES

blanco, –a *white*	**muchos, –as** *many*
es *is*	**quiénes** interrog. pl. *who (whom)*
fácil *easy*	**rojo, –a** *red*
grande *big, large*	**tener** *to have*

A. *Study:* 1. Los muchachos tienen lápices rojos. 2. ¿ Tienen ustedes papel blanco ? 3. Tenemos plumas y lápices. 4. No tenemos papel blanco. 5. Tenemos muchos libros. 6. El maestro tiene papel. 7. ¿ Qué tienen las muchachas ? 8. Las muchachas tienen libros rojos. 9. ¿ Dónde viven las muchachas ? 10. Las muchachas viven en una casa grande. 11. ¿ Viven ustedes en una casa roja ? 12. Vivimos en una casa blanca. 13. No vivimos en una casa roja. 14. ¿ Qué estudia usted ? 15. Estudio una lección en el libro rojo. 16. La lección no es fácil.

B. *Answer in Spanish:* 1. ¿ Qué tienen los muchachos ? 2. ¿ Tiene usted papel ˋblanco ? 3. ¿ Qué tienen ustedes ? 4. ¿ Quiénes tienen muchos libros ? 5. ¿ Qué tiene el maestro ? 6. ¿ Quiénes tienen libros rojos ? 7. ¿ Quiénes viven en una casa grande ? 8. ¿ Dónde viven ustedes ? 9. ¿ Estudia usted la lección ? 10. ¿ Es fácil [1] la lección ?

C. *Read rapidly, supplying the proper forms of articles and adjectives in parentheses:* (*white*) papel ——, perros ——, casas ——;

[1] Note this order.

(*many*) —— libros, —— mesas, —— lápices; (*easy*) lección ——,
lecciones ——; (*red*) lápiz ——, silla ——, libros ——; (*a, white*)
—— perro ——, —— casa ——; (*the, red*) —— libro ——, ——
casa ——, —— lápices ——; (*many, easy*) —— lecciones ——.

D. *Write in Spanish:* 1. I live in the white house. 2. Who
lives in the red house? 3. The teacher and a boy live in the red
house. 4. The red house is not large. 5. Have they many books?
6. They have many books in (the) school. 7. Have you the pen
and the white paper? 8. I have the pen and the red pencil.
9. Who studies the lessons? 10. The boys study. 11. They do
not learn the lessons. 12. I buy white paper in the store. 13. I
have many red pencils. 14. We learn the easy lessons. 15. They
have money and many houses.

LECTURA

Antonio no tiene esta [1] anécdota en su [2] cuaderno.

Un muchacho quiere estudiar en la ciudad [3] y su padre le dice:
— No gastes [4] mucho [5] porque no tengo mucho dinero.

[1] *this.*   [2] *his.*   [3] *city.*   [4] *spend* (imperative form).   [5] *much*, or *too much*.

En una tienda el muchacho pregunta:

— ¿ Cuánto [1] vale [2] una vaca ? [3]

— Ochenta [4] dólares.

— Es mucho.[5] ¿ Cuánto vale un cerdo ? [6]

— Veinte [7] dólares.

— Es mucho. ¿ Cuánto vale una gallina ? [8]

— Dos [9] dólares.

— Eso [10] es lo que [11] mi [12] padre quiere. Comeré [13] gallinas.

LESSON VI

42. *Agreement of Adjectives (1).*

a) An adjective that modifies two or more masculine nouns or pronouns is in the masculine plural.

Muchos libros y lápices rojos.   *Many red books and pencils.*

El maestro y el muchacho son altos.   *The teacher and the boy are tall.*

b) An adjective that modifies two or more feminine nouns or pronouns is in the feminine plural.

Las puertas y las ventanas grandes.   *The large doors and windows.*

La casa y la tienda son blancas.   *The house and the store are white.*

c) An adjective that modifies both a masculine and a feminine noun or pronoun is usually in the masculine plural.

El árbol y la casa son altos.   *The tree and the house are tall.*

NOTE: A noun in the masculine plural may refer to both men and women: **los maestros,** *the teachers* (men and women); **muchos muchachos** *many boys* or *many boys and girls.*

---

[1] *How much.* [2] *is worth.* [3] *cow.* [4] *Eighty.* [5] *much,* or *too much.* [6] *pig.*
[7] *Twenty.* [8] *hen (chicken).* [9] *Two.* [10] *That.* [11] **lo que,** *what.* [12] *my.*
[13] *I shall eat.*

43. *Genitive (or Possessive) Case.* Possession is denoted in Spanish by the preposition **de,** *of.*

> **el cuarto de Juan**   *John's room*
> **la madre de María**   *Mary's mother*

NOTE: Spanish nouns have no ending which corresponds to the English *'s.*

44. Del. **De + el** is contracted to **del;** but **de la, de los, de las** are not contracted.

> **el libro del muchacho**   *the boy's book*

But:

> **el dinero de la muchacha**   *the girl's money*
> **los lápices de los maestros**   *the teachers' pencils*
> **el dinero de las muchachas**   *the girls' money*

EXERCISES

alto, –a *high, tall*	**Juan** *John*
el árbol *tree* [1]	**la madre** *mother*
el cuarto *room*	**María** *Mary*
de *of*	**la puerta** *door*
del (de + el) *of the*	**son** *(they) are*
en *on*	**la ventana** *window*

A.[2] 1. La madre de Juan tiene muchas casas. 2. Tiene una casa blanca. 3. La casa blanca es alta. 4. La madre de Juan vive en la casa blanca. 5. Juan no vive en la casa blanca. 6. Vive en la casa del maestro. 7. El cuarto de Juan no es grande. 8. Las puertas y las ventanas no son altas. 9. ¿Dónde vive María? 10. María no vive en una casa grande. 11. La casa de María no es blanca. 12. El cuarto de María es grande. 13. María tiene muchas sillas y una mesa en el cuarto. 14. Tiene muchos libros y lápices en la mesa. 15. Tiene los lápices de los muchachos. 16. La mesa y las sillas no son altas. 17. María no es alta. 18. La madre de María es alta.

B. 1. ¿Quién tiene muchas casas? 2. ¿Dónde vive la madre de Juan? 3. ¿Dónde vive Juan? 4. ¿Dónde vive usted?

---

[1] Hereafter the English definite article will be omitted from the special vocabularies. [2] In this and succeeding lessons, the directions for Exercise C alone will be given. For A, B, and D they will be the same as in Lesson V.

5. ¿ Es grande el cuarto de Juan ? [1] 6. ¿ Tiene ventanas altas el cuarto de Juan ? [1] 7. ¿ Vive usted en una casa grande ? 8. ¿ Quién no vive en una casa grande ? 9. ¿ Qué tiene María en el cuarto ? 10. ¿ Qué tiene María en la mesa ?

C. *Translate:* tall trees, high rooms, many dogs, many doors; the teacher's chair, Mary's table, the girl's mother, the boys' money; the books are red, the lessons are easy, John is tall.

D. 1. The boy has a white dog. 2. You have the girl's pen. 3. We do not study the easy lessons. 4. The boy buys the books with the girl's money. 5. The girls have red books and pencils. 6. I have the teacher's red pencil. 7. I buy many books in John's store. 8. John's store is large. 9. It has many doors and windows. 10. They buy white paper and red pencils. 11. Do you live in a red house ? 12. Have you Mary's large book ? 13. The girls' rooms are large. 14. The doors and (the) windows are high. 15. Do they live in a white house ?

LECTURA

Un rey [2] pregunta a [3] un señor [4] de su corte [5]:
— ¿ Sabe usted el [3] español ?
— No, señor.
— Es lástima.[6]

El señor cree [7] que el rey quiere nombrarle [8] embajador [9] si [10] aprende el español, y lo [11] estudia. Un día [12] le [3] dice al [13] rey:
— Señor, ahora sé [14] el español.
— ¿ Y lo sabe usted bien ? [15]
— Sí, señor, lo sé bien.
— Ahora usted puede [16] leer [17] el *Don Quijote* en el original.

---

[1] Note this order.　　[2] *king.*　　[3] *Omit.*　　[4] *sir, gentleman.*　　[5] *court.*　　[6] *a pity.*　　[7] *believes, thinks.*　　[8] *appoint (name) him.*　　[9] *ambassador.*　　[10] *if.* [11] *it.*　　[12] *day.*　　[13] *to the.*　　[14] *I know.*　　[15] *well.*　　[16] *(you) can.*　　[17] *(to) read.*

LESSON VII

45. *Personal Subject Pronouns.*

SINGULAR		PLURAL	
1.	yo *I*	nosotros, –as	*we*
2.	{ tú *you (thou)*	vosotros, –as	*you (ye)*
	usted *you*	ustedes	*you*
3.	{ él *he*		
	ella *she*	ellos, –as	*they*

46. *Use of the Pronouns.*

a) **Tú,** *thou,* is used in familiar speech, as between the members of a family or between intimate friends and when speaking to small children and animals (the dog, the horse, etc.).

> La madre: **María, tú no estudias mucho.**
> The mother: *Mary, you don't study hard.*

NOTE: **Tú** is also used in poetry and in prayers to the Deity.

b) **Usted,** *you,* is required in more formal speech. It must be used in addressing a stranger or mere acquaintance.

> **¿ Dónde vive usted ?**   *Where do you live?*

NOTE: **Usted** and **ustedes** are abbreviated to **Vd.** and **Vds.** and also to **Ud.** and **Uds.** or **V.** and **VV.**

c) **Nosotros,** *we,* **vosotros,** *you* (*ye*), and **ellos,** *they,* have feminine forms: **nosotras, vosotras, ellas.**

> **Nosotras enseñamos.** *We teach.*   **Ellas aprenden.** *They learn.*

NOTES: 1. **Nosotros, –as** is the plural of **yo, vosotros, –as** is the plural of **tú, ellos** the plural of **él,** and **ellas** the plural of **ella.**
2. In Spanish America, **ustedes,** *you,* is used more frequently than **vosotros, –as.**
3. **Él,** *he,* is distinguished by the accent mark from **el,** *the:* **Él tiene el libro,** *He has the book.*

47. Tener que means *must, to have to.*

> **Yo tengo que trabajar.**   *I must (have to) work.*
> **Ella tiene que estudiar.**   *She has to study.*

EXERCISES

él *he*

ella *she*

ellos, –as *they*

la flor *flower*

la hija *daughter*

el hijo *son*

    mucho, –a *much;* mucho adv. *much, hard*

nosotros, –as *we*

el padre *father*

pero *but*

que: tener —, *must, to have to*

trabajar *to work*

tú *you (thou)*

vosotros, –as *you (ye)*

A. 1. El muchacho tiene que estudiar mucho. 2. Pero él no tiene libros. 3. Él tiene que comprar muchos libros. 4. Pero él no tiene mucho dinero. 5. ¿Tiene dinero la madre del muchacho? 6. Ella no tiene dinero. 7. El padre tiene dinero. 8. ¿Dónde compra el hijo los libros? 9. Él compra los libros en la tienda de Juan. — 10. Yo tengo que comprar un libro. 11. Pero no tengo mucho dinero. 12. ¿Tiene usted que estudiar mucho? 13. Las lecciones no son fáciles. — 14. La madre de María trabaja en la casa. 15. María no trabaja. 16. Ella estudia mucho. 17. El padre y el hijo no estudian. 18. Ellos tienen que trabajar en la tienda de Juan.

B. 1. ¿Quién tiene que estudiar mucho? 2. ¿Quién tiene que comprar muchos libros? 3. ¿Tiene usted dinero? 4. ¿Qué tiene el padre del muchacho? 5. ¿Qué compra en la tienda de Juan? 6. ¿Qué tiene usted que comprar? 7. ¿Qué tiene usted que aprender? 8. ¿Quién trabaja en la casa? 9. ¿Quién no trabaja? 10. ¿Quiénes tienen que trabajar en la tienda de Juan?

C. *I. Continue:* 1. yo estudio la lección, tú estudias la lección, etc. 2. yo no tengo dinero, etc.

II. Translate: 1. I work. 2. You buy. 3. He learns. 4. She studies. 5. We live. 6. You have. 7. They teach. 8. I do not learn. 9. Do you work? 10. He does not study. 11. Have we? 12. They do not buy flowers.

D. 1. John's father has a large house. 2. But he hasn't much money. 3. Who has money? 4. The teacher has money, but he doesn't have to buy a house. 5. Do they have to buy many books? 6. I have many books in (the) school and in the room. 7. The white house is high. 8. The red house has many rooms. 9. Mary's mother is buying the red house. 10. Who is buying the white house ? 11. Has the teacher's father much money ? 12. He hasn't much money, but he has to buy a house. 13. What is the mother buying ? 14. She is buying flowers and books. 15. She has no flowers in the house. 16. The daughter has no books.

LECTURA

Mi maestro le [1] pregunta a [1] Juan:

— ¿ Sabes cuáles [2] son algunas de las cualidades [3] del pueblo [4] español ?

Juan no contesta [5] pronto [6] y Antonio dice:

— Yo sé. Es democrático, individualista y ama [7] la [1] independencia.

Entonces [8] Juan dice:

— Tiene un ingenio [9] vivo [10] y una imaginación exuberante.

— ¿ Y qué sabes de su lengua ? [11]

— La lengua de Cervantes es rica [12] y sonora.

— ¿ Quién es Cervantes ?

— Es el autor del *Don Quijote.*

LESSON VIII

48. *Possessive Adjectives (1).* The forms of the possessive adjectives are:

SINGULAR		PLURAL	
mi		mis	*my*
tu		tus	*your (thy)*
(Corresponding to **tú**)			
su		sus	*your*
(Corresponding to **usted**)			
su		sus	*his, her, its*

[1] *Omit.* [2] *what.* [3] *qualities.* [4] *people.* [5] *answer.* [6] *quickly.* [7] *loves.* [8] *Then.* [9] *mind.* [10] *keen.* [11] *language.* [12] *rich.*

SINGULAR	PLURAL	
nuestro, nuestra	**nuestros, nuestras**	*our*
vuestro, vuestra	**vuestros, vuestras**	*your*
(Corresponding to **vosotros**)		
su	**sus**	*your*
su	**sus**	*their*

49. *Agreement of Possessives.* Possessive adjectives agree in gender and number with the nouns with which they are used, not with the possessor.

su libro	*his (her, your, their) book*
sus libros	*his (her, your, their) books*
nuestro abuelo	*our grandfather*
nuestras familias	*our families*

NOTE: Possessive adjectives are usually repeated before each noun to which they refer: **mi padre y mi madre,** *my father and mother.*

50. *Present Indicative of* **ser,** *to be.*

SINGULAR		PLURAL		
yo soy	*I am*	**nosotros** / **nosotras**	**somos**	*we are*
tú eres	*you are (thou art)*	**vosotros** / **vosotras**	**sois**	*you (ye) are*
usted es	*you are*	**ustedes son**		*you are*
él / **ella** **es**	*he* / *she* *is*	**ellos** / **ellas** **son**		*they are*

51. *Omission of the Subject Personal Pronouns.*

a) In Spanish the subject pronoun is usually omitted.

soy *I am*	**somos** *we are*

b) Sometimes the subject pronoun is needed for emphasis or to make the meaning clear.

Yo estudio, pero él tiene que trabajar.
I am studying, but he has to work.

Él estudia, pero ella no estudia.
He studies, but she doesn't study.

c) **It is** usually more polite to express **usted** or **ustedes,** but this pronoun need not be repeated within a sentence.

Usted estudia y aprende. *You study and you learn.*

d) *It* as a subject is ordinarily not expressed.

tiene *it has* **es** *it is*

EXERCISES

el abuelo *grandfather*	**nuestro, −a, −os, −as** *our*
la calle *street*	**rico, −a** *rich*
Carlos *Charles*	**ser** *to be*
diez *ten*	**su(s)** *his, her, your* (sing.), *its;*
dos *two*	*your* (pl.), *their*
la familia *family*	**tres** *three*
el hombre *man*	**tu(s)** *your* (*thy*)
mi(s) *my*	**vuestro, −a, −os, −as** *your*

A. 1. ¿Dónde vive Juan? 2. Juan vive en la calle Wáshington. 3. Vive con su abuelo, su padre y su madre. 4. Su casa tiene diez cuartos. 5. El cuarto del abuelo es grande. 6. Tiene dos puertas y tres ventanas. 7. El abuelo es un hombre rico. 8. Tiene una tienda y muchas casas. — 9. Mi padre trabaja mucho, pero no es rico. 10. Nuestra familia no es rica. 11. Vivimos en una casa blanca. 12. María tiene una familia grande. 13. Su padre y su madre son ricos. 14. Carlos es el padre de María. 15. Tienen una hija, María, y dos hijos. 16. El abuelo vive con la familia. 17. El abuelo es el padre de Carlos. 18. Carlos no tiene madre.

B. 1. ¿En qué calle vive Juan? 2. ¿Con quién vive Juan? 3. ¿Qué tiene la casa? 4. ¿Quién tiene un cuarto grande? 5. ¿Quién es rico? 6. ¿Quién trabaja mucho? 7. ¿Dónde vive usted? 8. ¿Quién es el padre de María? 9. ¿Quiénes son ricos? 10. ¿Quién vive con la familia?

C. *I. Continue:* 1. yo tengo mi pluma, tú tienes tu pluma, etc. 2. yo aprendo mi lección, etc.

II. Translate: 1. It is John's school. 2. They are the teacher's daughters. 3. He is John's son. 4. She is Charles' mother. 5. Charles is the teacher.

Don Quijote y Sancho Panza.

D. 1. I have to work in my room. 2. You have to study in (the) school. 3. Has the school many rooms ? 4. The school has ten large rooms. 5. Are you Mary's teacher ? 6. I am not Mary's teacher. 7. John's father is her teacher. — 8. Mary's mother is not rich. 9. But she has two houses. 10. Do you live in the red house ? 11. We live in the white house. 12. Our house has ten rooms, but [it] is not large. — 13. I am tall, but Charles is not tall. 14. We buy our books in John's store. 15. We are not rich. 16. The flowers are white. 17. Charles is Mary's father. 18. He has a daughter and two sons. 19. The family is not rich. 20. The father works in a store.

LECTURA

Tenemos que leer algunas selecciones del *Don Quijote* en la [1] clase [2] y yo tengo algunos apuntes [3] en mi cuaderno.

En casa mi padre lo lee en inglés. [4] Mi padre dice que Don Quijote parece loco. [5] Pero dice también que él merece [6] nuestra simpatía [7] por [8] sus ideales.

---

[1] Omit.　[2] *class.*　[3] *notes.*　[4] *English.*　[5] *mad.*　[6] *deserves.*　[7] *sympathy.*　[8] *because of.*

En la [1] literatura universal Don Quijote representa el tipo de persona que no logra [2] su propósito [3] porque cree que todos tienen ideales tan [4] sublimes como [4] los [1] suyos.[5]

LESSON IX

52. *Past Participles (1).*

I. Comprar:	comprado	*bought*
II. Aprender:	aprendido	*learned*
III. Vivir:	vivido	*lived*

Like these are formed the past participles of all regular verbs.

NOTES: 1. The past participles of **ser** and **tener** are regular: **sido, tenido**, *been, had*.

2. The past participle of **escribir** is irregular: **escrito**, *written*.

53. **Tener** *and* **haber**.

a) Spanish has two verbs meaning *to have:* **tener** and **haber**. *To have*, meaning *to possess*, is expressed by **tener**.

> **Tengo dinero.** *I have money.*
> **Tienen una casa.** *They have a house.*

b) The auxiliary **haber** is combined with the past participle to form the perfect tenses.

> **he comprado** *I have bought*

NOTE: When used with **haber**, the past participle is invariable in form: **hemos comprado**, *we have bought*.

54. *Present Indicative of* **haber**.

SINGULAR		PLURAL	
he	*I have*	hemos	*we have*
has	*you have (thou hast)*	habéis	*you (ye) have*
usted ha	*you have*	ustedes han	*you have*
ha	*he (she, it) has*	han	*they have*

---

[1] Omit. [2] *attain.* [3] *end.* [4] *as.* [5] *his own.*

55. *Present Perfect Indicative.*

I have bought (learned, lived), etc.

he comprado (aprendido, vivido)
has comprado (aprendido, vivido)
ha comprado (aprendido, vivido)

hemos comprado (aprendido, vivido)
habéis comprado (aprendido, vivido)
han comprado (aprendido, vivido)

56. **Haber** is also used impersonally.

    hay   *there is, there are*
    ha habido   *there has (have) been*

NOTES: 1. The impersonal form in the present indicative is **hay** and not **ha.** The **y** is an old adverb meaning *there.*
2. The third person singular alone is used.

EXERCISES

a *to;* ¿ — **quién(es)?** *whom?* *to whom?*

el amigo, la **–a** *friend;* los **–os** *friends* (men, or men and women)

  beber *to drink*

el café *coffee*

la carta *letter*

doce *twelve*

escribir *to write*

escrito irreg. past part. **of escribir**

  haber *to have*

el hermano *brother*

el jardín *flower garden*

la leche *milk*

A. 1. Hemos comprado papel, pero no tenemos plumas. 2. ¿Dónde compran ustedes papel y plumas? 3. Compramos papel, plumas y lápices en la tienda de Carlos. 4. Carlos tiene una tienda en la calle Wáshington. 5. Su tienda es grande, pero él no es rico. — 6. ¿Ha estudiado usted sus lecciones? 7. Las lecciones no son fáciles. 8. He aprendido tres de mis lecciones. 9. He tenido que estudiar mucho. 10. Pero no he escrito a mi madre. — 11. Mi amiga María vive en Wáshington. 12. Vive con su padre y su hermano Juan. 13. Mi padre ha escrito una carta al padre de Juan y María. 14. Mi madre ha escrito a María. 15. Yo tengo que escribir a Juan. 16. No tenemos café en la casa. 17. ¿Quiénes beben café en su casa? 18. Mi hermano y yo be-

bemos café. 19. Mi madre y María beben leche. 20. Mi padre
bebe leche y café.

B. 1. ¿Qué han comprado ustedes? 2. ¿Quién tiene una
tienda? 3. ¿Qué ha aprendido usted? 4. ¿A quién no ha escrito
usted? 5. ¿Dónde vive su amiga María? 6. ¿Quién es el hermano de María? 7. ¿A quién ha escrito su madre? 8. ¿Qué
no tenemos en la casa? 9. ¿Quiénes beben café? 10. ¿Quiénes
beben leche?

C. *I. Continue:* 1. he escrito, has escrito, etc. 2. he bebido,
etc.

II. Translate, and then repeat with all the nouns in the plural:
1. The girl's book. 2. The boy's table. 3. The girl's father.
4. The teacher's pencil. 5. The boy's mother.

D. 1. Our mother has bought flowers. 2. There are many trees
in our garden. 3. But there are not many flowers. 4. The trees
in our garden are tall. 5. But our house is not tall. 6. On Washington Street there are tall trees. 7. There are many houses,
but [they] are not large. 8. We live in a large house. 9. [It]
has twelve rooms. 10. The rooms are large, and [they] have
many windows. 11. Charles has a daughter and a son. 12. His
daughter is tall. 13. The son is not tall. 14. John is Charles'
son. 15. Mary is Charles' daughter. 16. My brother doesn't
drink coffee. 17. We have to write to our mother. 18. I have
many friends in Washington.

LECTURA

Hay un refrán [1] español que dice: « Quien [2] no ha visto [3] a [4]
Granada no ha visto nada ».[5]

Y aquí [6] tenemos una conversación entre [7] un hombre de [8] Roma
y otro [9] de Granada.

— Tú dices que tus antepasados [10] han hecho [11] maravillas.[12]
¿ Sabes lo que han encontrado [13] en una excavación en Roma?
— No. ¿Qué?

---

[1] *proverb.* [2] *He who.* [3] *seen.* [4] *Omit.* [5] *nothing;* **no . . . nada,**
not . . . anything. [6] *here.* [7] *between.* [8] *from.* [9] *another.* [10] *forefathers.*
[11] *done.* [12] *wonders.* [13] *found.*

— Alambres.[1] Eso quiere decir [2] que los romanos son los inventores de la [3] telegrafía.[4]

— ¿ Y sabes tú lo que han encontrado en una excavación en Granada ?

— No. ¿ Qué ?

— Nada. Eso quiere decir que mis antepasados son los inventores de la telegrafía sin [5] hilos.[6]

LESSON X

57. *Radical-changing Verbs (1).* Many verbs of the first and second conjugations change the radical vowel **e** to **ie,** or the radical vowel **o** to **ue,** whenever the stress falls on the root.

PRESENT INDICATIVE

Cerrar	cierro,	cierras,	cierra,	(cerramos, cerráis),
to close			cierran
Contar	cuento,	cuentas,	cuenta,	(contamos, contáis),
to count			cuentan
Perder	pierdo,	pierdes,	pierde,	(perdemos, perdéis),
to lose			pierden
Volver	vuelvo,	vuelves,	vuelve,	(volvemos, volvéis),
to return			vuelven

NOTE: The past participle of **volver** is irregular: **vuelto.**

58. *Demonstrative Adjectives.*

este, —a, —os, —as   *this, these*

ese, —a, —os, —as

aquel, aquella, —os, —as   *that, those*

59. **Ese** usually denotes that which is near or which refers to the person addressed. **Aquel** denotes that which is more remote.

---

[1] *Wires.* [2] **quiere decir,** *means.* [3] Omit. [4] *telegraphy.* [5] *without.*
[6] *threads, wires;* **sin hilos,** *wireless.*

esa silla   *that chair* (near you or on which you are seated)
aquella mesa   *that table* (at a distance from you)

NOTE: A demonstrative adjective is repeated before each noun to which it refers: **este hombre y esta mujer,** *this man and* (*this*) *woman.*

60. *Cardinal Numerals (1).*

un(o), –a	*one*	**nueve**	*nine*
dos	*two*	**diez**	*ten*
tres	*three*	**once**	*eleven*
cuatro	*four*	**doce**	*twelve*
cinco	*five*	**trece**	*thirteen*
seis	*six*	**catorce**	*fourteen*
siete	*seven*	**quince**	*fifteen*
ocho	*eight*	**diez y seis**	*sixteen*

61. *a*) **Uno** loses the final **o** of the masculine singular when it precedes its noun.

uno *one*   **un libro** *one book*

b) **Un(o), –a** has both a masculine and a feminine form, but the other numerals given above have only one form each for both genders.

un árbol	*one tree*	**una flor**	*one flower*
dos árboles	*two trees*	**dos flores**	*two flowers*

NOTE: **Un árbol** may mean either *one tree* or *a tree*, and **una flor** may mean either *one flower* or *a flower.*

EXERCISES

aquel, aquella, –os, –as *that,*
   those
bien *well*
catorce *fourteen*
cerrar *to close*
cinco *five*
contar *to count*
cuántos, –as *how many*
cuatro *four*
de *from* (**del** *from the*)

el dólar *dollar*
ese, –a, –os, –as *that, those*
este, –a, –os, –as *this, these*
mucho *a great deal*
no *no*
nueve *nine*
ocho *eight*
once *eleven*
perder *to lose*
quince *fifteen*

seis *six*	**un(o), -a** *one*
sí *yes*	**vender** *to sell*
siete *seven*	**volver** *to return, go (come) back*
trece *thirteen*	**vuelto** irreg. past part. of **volver**

A. 1. La familia de Carlos es rica. 2. Tiene tres casas en esta calle. 3. Viven en aquella casa alta. 4. Su casa tiene doce cuartos. 5. Hay muchos árboles en el jardín. — 6. ¿ A quién escribe usted ? 7. Escribo una carta a mi hermano. 8. He escrito a Carlos. 9. La madre de Carlos vive en mi casa. 10. No son ricos. — 11. En la escuela aprendo mucho. 12. El maestro enseña bien las lecciones. 13. Yo vuelvo a la casa y estudio mucho. 14. ¿ No estudia usted en la escuela ? 15. Sí, estudio en la casa y en la escuela. — 16. Juan no estudia mucho. 17. Cuenta su dinero. 18. Ha perdido cuatro dólares. 19. Tiene once dólares. 20. Once y cuatro son quince.

B. 1. ¿ Cuántas casas tiene la familia de Carlos ? 2. ¿ Dónde vive su familia ? 3. ¿ Cuántos cuartos tiene su casa ? 4. ¿ Qué hay en el jardín ? 5. ¿ A quién escribe usted ? 6. ¿ Ha escrito usted a Carlos ? 7. ¿ Dónde vive la madre de Carlos ? 8. ¿ Quién enseña en la escuela ? 9. ¿ No estudia usted mucho ? 10. ¿ Estudia usted en la escuela ? 11. ¿ Quién no estudia mucho ? 12. ¿ Qué cuenta Juan ? 13. ¿ Cuántos dólares tiene ? 14. ¿ Cuántos son cuatro y once ? 15. ¿ Cuántos dólares tiene usted ?

C. *I. Continue:* 1. Cuento mis libros, cuentas tus libros, etc. 2. He escrito esta carta, has escrito esa carta, etc. 3. No bebo café, etc.

II. Translate: 1. Two, four, six, eight, ten. 2. One, three, five, seven, nine. 3. Fifteen, fourteen, thirteen, twelve, eleven. 4. Two and two are four. 5. Five and ten are fifteen. 6. This lesson is easy. 7. That pencil is red. 8. Those tables are high. 9. We sell these chairs. 10. They close those doors.

D. 1. That man lives in this house. 2. He returns to the house and closes the windows. 3. He doesn't close the doors. 4. I return to the house and I close the doors. 5. I do not close the windows. — 6. John has to write to his father. 7. He has not returned from the store. 8. He is counting the money. 9. He

loses mon,y in his store. 10. He doesn't sell much in his store. —
11. Where do those men work? 12. They work in my grandfather's garden. 13. There are many flowers in the garden.
14. There are many high trees. 15. We have not counted the
trees. — 16. Have you much money? 17. No, I haven't much
money. 18. I have eight dollars. 19. How many has your
brother? 20. He has nine, and I have six.

LECTURA

La animación en las calles de algunas ciudades españolas es
cosa [1] que interesa [2] al turista. Pero no hay animación durante [3]
todo [4] el día. En las ciudades donde hace [5] mucho sol [6] tienen la
costumbre de la siesta. Cierran muchas tiendas y oficinas [7] entre
la una [8] y las cuatro.[8] Las calles están desiertas.[9] Es casi [10] imposible comprar nada o [11] atender [12] a ningún [13] negocio. Pero más
tarde [14] vuelven el negocio y la animación y es como [15] el despertar [16]
de otro día.

[1] *a thing.* [2] *interests (is of interest).* [3] *during.* [4] *all.* [5] *lit. 'it makes':*
it is. [6] *sun;* **hace mucho sol,** *it is very sunny.* [7] *offices.* [8] *one (four) o'clock.*
[9] *deserted.* [10] *almost.* [11] *or.* [12] *to attend.* [13] *any.* [14] *late;* **más tarde,**
later. [15] *like.* [16] *awakening.*

REVIEW LESSON A

I. *A.* Use the definite article with the following nouns:

café	dinero	lápiz	leche
calles	flores	lecciones	papeles

B. Use both the indefinite and the definite article with each of the following nouns:

árbol	escuela	jardín	padre
dólar	hombre	madre	puerta

II. *A.* Supply the subject pronoun, where needed, and the possessive adjective in the following sentences:

1. María tiene —— lápiz. 2. —— compro —— libros en la tienda. 3. —— estudiamos —— lecciones. 4. —— viven en —— casa. 5. —— cierra —— cuarto. 6. —— no trabajo en —— cuarto. 7. —— estudian —— lecciones.

B. Supply a cardinal number and the demonstrative or possessive adjective in the following sentences:

1. —— muchacho tiene —— dólares. 2. —— hombre tiene —— tiendas. 3. —— casa tiene —— puertas. 4. Hay —— mesas en —— cuarto. 5. —— cuarto tiene —— ventanas.

III. *A.* Give the present indicative of the following verbs:

beber	enseñar	escribir	trabajar	vender

B. Give the past participles of the following verbs:

aprender	contar	haber	trabajar
beber	enseñar	perder	vender
cerrar	escribir	ser	vivir
comprar	estudiar	tener	volver

IV. *A.* Translate, and then repeat in the plural:

the easy lesson	the teacher's letter
the large table	my grandfather's chair
the red pencil	the window of that room

that rich man	her brother's garden
our teacher and his friend	this man's daughter

B. Translate, and then repeat in the negative:

1. The boy has a dog. 2. You have the pen. 3. We study the lessons. 4. He buys the books in the store. 5. The boys are buying the pens.

C. Translate, and then repeat, changing all possible forms to the plural:

1. I live in the red house. 2. This room is large. 3. The white house is not large. 4. The tree is tall. 5. I have the red pencil. 6. You are my brother. 7. The boy writes the letter. 8. The book is red. 9. He learns the lesson. 10. I am his son.

V. Translate:

1. She doesn't study hard. 2. He has to work. 3. She has a son. 4. They are not rich. 5. My father has a store. 6. He lives with his father. 7. I don't drink coffee. 8. What has he learned? 9. Who is that man? 10. His family is rich. 11. Where do you live? 12. Has he returned? 13. Have you a dollar? 14. We have to study. 15. I have written a letter.

LESSON XI

62. *Imperfect Indicative.*

a) Spanish has in the indicative mood two simple past tenses where English has one. These Spanish tenses are the imperfect (or past descriptive) and the preterite (or past absolute).

b) The inflectional endings of the imperfect are:

FIRST CONJ.		SECOND AND THIRD CONJ.	
−aba	−ábamos	−ía	−íamos
−abas	−abais	−ías	−íais
−aba	−aban	−ía	−ían

c) The imperfect of **comprar, aprender, vivir.** ·

I bought, did buy, was buying, used to buy, etc.

compraba	comprábamos
comprabas	comprabais
compraba	compraban

I learned, did learn, was learning, used to learn, etc.

aprendía	aprendíamos
aprendías	aprendíais
aprendía	aprendían

I lived, did live, was living, used to live, etc.

vivía	vivíamos
vivías	vivíais
vivía	vivían

63. *Uses of the Imperfect.*

a) When the English simple past tense expresses an action or state as of indefinite duration, it is equivalent to the Spanish imperfect.

> **Él estudiaba, pero no aprendía bien las lecciones.**
> *He studied, but he did not learn his lessons well.*

b) The Spanish imperfect is also used to tell what was customary or habitual.

> **Cuando yo vivía aquí tenía un caballo.**
> *When I lived here I had a horse.*

NOTE: In this use the imperfect is often best translated by **used to** or *would* and the infinitive.

64. *Omission of the Indefinite Article (1).*

a) The indefinite article is usually omitted before an unqualified predicate noun.

> **Mi amigo es maestro.** *My friend is a teacher.*

b) The indefinite article is not used with **otro,** *other, another.*

> **otro hombre** *another man*   **el otro hombre** *the other man*

65. *Dative Case.* The indirect object requires the preposition **a,** *to.*

> **¿ A quién escribe usted esa carta ?**
> *To whom are you writing that letter?*
>
> **Doy el pan a Juan.**
> *I give the bread to John* (or *I give John the bread*).

NOTE: The preposition *to* is omitted in English if the indirect object precedes the direct. The Spanish preposition **a** cannot be omitted before a noun.

66. **Al.** **A** + **el** is contracted to **al.**

> **Escribimos una carta al maestro.**
> *We are writing a letter to the teacher.*

EXERCISES

ahora *now*	**aquí** *here*
al *to the*	**el caballo** *horse*
amarillo, –a *yellow*	**caro, –a** *dear, expensive, costly*

cuando *when*
doy *I give*
español, –ola *Spanish;* n. *Spaniard, Spanish woman*
inglés, –esa *English;* n. *Englishman, Englishwoman*

la librería *bookstore*
otro, –a *other, another*
el pan *bread*
pobre *poor*
quién(es): ¿ **de —?** *whose?*

A. 1. Cuando Juan vivía aquí no estudiaba mucho. 2. Pero escribía mucho. 3. Escribía cartas en español a una muchacha española. 4. No escribía cartas en inglés. 5. Él tenía siete libros españoles. 6. Su hermano tenía ocho. 7. ¿ Cuántos tenían ? 8. Siete y ocho son quince. — 9. Yo compraba mis libros en esa librería. 10. La librería es del amigo de Juan. 11. Tenía muchos libros en español. 12. Pero sus libros son caros. 13. No compro muchos libros ahora. 14. Compro mis libros en otra librería. — 15. Cuando yo vivía aquí estudiaba con Carlos. 16. Él vivía en la casa amarilla. 17. Él compraba leche y yo compraba pan. 18. Comprábamos la leche y el pan en aquella tienda. 19. Él bebía mucha leche. 20. Ahora él no bebe leche, bebe café.

B. 1. ¿ Quién no estudiaba mucho ? 2. ¿ Qué escribía ? 3. ¿ A quién escribía ? 4. ¿ Cuántos libros españoles tenía ? 5. ¿ Cuántos son siete y ocho ? 6. ¿ Qué compraba usted en esa librería ? 7. ¿ De quién es la librería ? 8. ¿ Qué tenía la librería ? 9. ¿ Qué no compra usted ahora ? 10. ¿ Con quién estudiaba usted ? 11. ¿ En qué casa vivía él ? 12. ¿ Qué compraban ustedes ? 13. ¿ Qué bebía él ? 14. ¿ Qué bebe ahora ?

C. *I. Conjugate the imperfect of the following verbs:* 1. cerrar (cerraba, etc.). 2. contar (contaba, etc.). 3. perder (perdía, etc.). 4. volver (volvía, etc.).

II. Translate: 1. His grandfather is a Spaniard. 2. Our friend is an Englishman. 3. My brother is a teacher. 4. I give money to the boy. 5. We sell the book to the man.

D. 1. Have you written a letter to Charles' brother ? 2. I have written two letters. 3. I have written a letter to Charles, and another to Mary. 4. But I have not written to Charles' brother. 5. He doesn't write to his friends. 6. He and Charles work now in their father's store. 7. I don't work, but I have to study. — 8. That boy is writing a letter to his grandfather. 9. His grandfather used to live in this house. 10. But he and his family live in another house now. 11. Their house is large and they have many horses. 12. His son is that boy's father. 13. He is a teacher in our school. 14. How many teachers are there in your school ? 15. There are five teachers in our school. — 16. What do you buy in that store ? 17. I buy bread and milk. 18. I give the bread and the milk to a poor family.

LECTURA

Cuando Antonio volvía a su casa de la escuela algunas veces [1] jugaba [2] y otras leía o escribía. Siempre [3] aprendía bien sus lecciones. Su padre estaba [4] muy [5] contento [6] con él [7] por su conducta durante la semana.[8] Los [9] domingos [10] le llevaba [11] al campo [12] o a otras partes. Si su padre no le llevaba al campo Antonio visitaba [13] a [9] sus tías.[14] Ellas siempre le daban [15] dinero. Cuando visitaba a sus tías Antonio iba [16] algunas veces con su padre y otras con su madre.

LESSON XII

67. *Present Indicative of* **estar,** *to be.*

SINGULAR	PLURAL
estoy	estamos
estás	estáis
está	están

68. *Use of* **estar.** **Estar,** *to be,* is used instead of **ser,** *to be:*

a) To express position.

Mi padre está en Chile. — *My father is in Chile.*
Madrid está en España. — *Madrid is in Spain.*

[1] *times.* [2] *played.* [3] *Always.* [4] *was.* [5] *very.* [6] *pleased.* [7] *him.* [8] *week.* [9] *Omit.* [10] *(on) Sundays.* [11] *took.* [12] *country.* [13] *visited.* [14] *aunts.* [15] *gave.* [16] *went.*

b) **To express an accidental or temporary condition.**

> **Juan está cansado.**   *John is tired.*
> **María está enferma.**   *Mary is ill.*

69. *Adjectives with* **ser** *and* **estar.** Some adjectives have one meaning when used with **ser,** and another meaning when used with **estar.**

> **ser bueno**   *to be good*   **ser malo**   *to be bad*
> **estar bueno** *to be well*   **estar malo** *to be ill*

70. *Imperfect Indicative of* **ser, haber, estar, tener.**

> **Ser:** era, eras, era, éramos, erais, eran
> **Haber:** había, habías, había, habíamos, habíais, habían
> **Estar:** estaba, estabas, estaba, estábamos, estabais, estaban
> **Tener:** tenía, tenías, tenía, teníamos, teníais, tenían

EXERCISES

bueno, –a *good;* **estar —,** *to be well*
cansado, –a *tired*
cómo interrog. *how*
cuándo interrog. *when*
enfermo, –a *ill, sick*
España *Spain*
estar *to be*

malo, –a *bad;* **estar —,** *to be ill, sick*
también *also, too*
la verdad *truth;* **es —,** *it is true;* **¿ no es —?** *or* **¿ verdad?** *isn't it true? isn't it so? (don't you, doesn't he? etc.)*

A. 1. Mi hermano tenía diez caballos.   2. Ha vendido cuatro al padre de María.   3. Ahora tiene seis.   4. Dos de sus caballos son blancos.   5. Tenía también tres perros.   6. Los perros no eran grandes. — 7. Cuando yo estaba malo no estudiaba. 8. Ahora estoy bueno y estudio.   9. Tengo que aprender mis lecciones.   10. Uno de mis maestros es inglés.   11. Otro es español. 12. Estos dos maestros viven en aquella casa blanca. — 13. Aquel hombre era pobre.   14. Trabajaba en el jardín de mi abuelo. 15. Cuando no trabajaba en el jardín estudiaba.   16. También vendía flores a sus amigos.   17. Ahora no es pobre.   18. Tiene dinero y tres casas.

B. 1. ¿ Quién tenía diez caballos ?   2. ¿ Cuántos ha vendido al padre de María ?   3. ¿ Cuántos caballos son blancos ?   4. ¿ Qué tenía también ?   5. ¿ Cuándo no estudiaba usted ?   6. ¿ Cómo está usted ahora? 7. ¿Qué tiene que aprender? 8. ¿Quién es inglés? 9. ¿Dónde viven los dos maestros? 10. ¿Quién era pobre? 11. ¿Dónde trabajaba? 12. ¿Cuándo estudiaba? 13. ¿Qué vendía a sus amigos? 14. ¿Qué no es ahora? 15. ¿Qué tiene?

C. *Translate:* 1. The tree is tall. 2. I was good. 3. This garden was large. 4. We are tired. 5. They were poor. 6. Where was he? 7. She is tall. 8. You were ill. 9. That man is an Englishman. 10. Was she ill? 11. My pencil is red. 12. Was the house white? 13. Are they here? 14. His mother was poor. 15. Their father is rich.

D. 1. John was in his room. 2. But he is now in the room of one of his friends. 3. His friend has been ill. 4. This friend is a Spaniard. 5. He has worked hard, and is sick. 6. When he is sick he doesn't work. — 7. Those boys are not bad. 8. But they have not studied their lessons. 9. They were in the store, weren't they? 10. Mary and I were not in the store. 11. We were in [1] school. 12. Mary is in her room now. — 13. Who is in John's room? 14. He has not returned from the bookstore. 15. He is counting the books now. 16. He has to work hard. 17. He doesn't sell many books, and is losing money. 18. But his family is rich, isn't it?

LECTURA

Carlos encuentra [2] a [3] uno de sus amigos en la calle.

— Buenos días.[4] ¿Cómo estás?

— Bien, muy bien, gracias.[5] ¿Y tú?

— Yo también estoy bien, gracias. Tú pareces muy contento.

— Sí, estoy muy contento. ¿Y por qué [6] no? Desde ahora no tengo preocupaciones [7] en mis negocios.[8]

— ¿No tienes preocupaciones en tus negocios? ¿Y cómo has arreglado [9] eso?

— He nombrado un apoderado.[10]

— ¿Cuánto le pagas? [11]

— Seis mil [12] dólares al [13] año.[14]

---

[1] Supply the article. [2] *meets.* [3] Omit. [4] **buenos días,** *good morning.*
[5] *thank you.* [6] **por qué,** *why.* [7] *worries.* [8] *affairs.* [9] *managed.*
[10] *attorney.* [11] *pay.* [12] *thousand.* [13] *a.* [14] *year.*

— ¡ Seis mil dólares! Es mucho. ¿ Cómo vas [1] a pagar [2] tanto [3] dinero ?

— Ésa [4] es la primera [5] de sus preocupaciones.

LESSON XIII

71. *Accusative Case.* The direct object does not, as a rule, require a preposition, but the preposition **a** is required before the direct object if the object is a proper noun, or any noun or pronoun that denotes a *definite* person or personified thing.

	Hallé el libro.	*I found the book.*
But:	**Hallé al hombre.**	*I found the man.*
	Hallé a mi amigo.	*I found my friend.*
	Desea ver a Madrid.	*He wishes to see Madrid.*

72. *The Preterite.*

a) The inflectional endings of the preterite (past absolute) are:

FIRST CONJ.		SECOND AND THIRD CONJ.	
–é	–amos	–í	–imos
–aste	–asteis	–iste	–isteis
–ó	–aron	–ió	–ieron

b) The preterite of **comprar, aprender, vivir.**

I bought, did buy, etc.

compré	compramos
compraste	comprasteis
compró	compraron

I learned, did learn, etc.

aprendí	aprendimos
aprendiste	aprendisteis
aprendió	aprendieron

[1] *are you going.* [2] *pay.* [3] *so much.* [4] *That.* [5] *first.*

I lived, did live, etc.

viví	vivimos
viviste	vivisteis
vivió	vivieron

73. *Uses of the Preterite.*

a) When the English simple past tense expresses an action or state as definitely past, it is equivalent to the Spanish preterite.

Él estudió sus lecciones ayer.   *He studied his lessons yesterday.*

b) In narrations, the Spanish imperfect is used to describe the conditions or circumstances which prevailed when something happened, while the preterite is used to tell what happened.

Él estudiaba cuando nosotros entramos.
He was studying when we entered.

NOTE: In this use the imperfect is best translated by *was*, etc., and the present participle, as in the above sentence.

74. *Idioms.*

había	*there was, there were*
hubo	*there was, there were*
¿ Qué hora es (era)?	*What time is (was) it?*
Es (era) la una.	*It is (was) one o'clock.*
Son (eran) las cuatro.	*It is (was) four o'clock.*
Son (eran) las cinco y media.	*It is (was) half past five.*

EXERCISES

allí *there*	la **hora** *hour, time (of day)*
el **año** *year*	**medio, -a** *half*
ayer *yesterday*	**que** rel. pron. *that*
el **campo** *country*	**veo** *I see*
la **ciudad** *city*	**ver** *to see*
desear *to wish*	**vieron** *you saw*
entrar (**en**) *to enter* (*into*)	**vimos** *we saw*
hallar *to find*	

A. 1. Mi padre vivió muchos años en esta casa. 2. Su cuarto era grande. 3. Tenía tres mesas y muchas sillas. 4. En las mesas

y sillas había muchos libros. 5. Mi padre estudiaba y escribía
mucho. — 6. ¿ Dónde estaba usted ? 7. Estaba en la librería
con Juan. 8. Vimos a María y a su amigo. 9. Pero no vimos a
Carlos. 10. Carlos no ha vuelto del campo. 11. Escribió ayer a
su madre. — 12. Mi abuelo tenía una casa en el campo. 13. Ahora
desea vivir en la ciudad. 14. Vendió la casa que tenía en el campo.
15. Compró una casa en la ciudad. 16. Yo estaba con mi abuelo
cuando compró la casa. 17. La casa no es alta pero tiene muchos
cuartos. 18. Es una casa blanca y está en la calle Wáshington.

B. 1. ¿ Quién vivió en esta casa ? 2. ¿ Qué tenía en su cuarto ?
3. ¿ Qué había en las mesas y sillas ? 4. ¿ Quién estudiaba y escribía ? 5. ¿ Quién estaba en la librería ? 6. ¿ A quién vieron
ustedes ? 7. ¿ Dónde está Carlos ? 8. ¿ A quién escribió Carlos ?
9. ¿ Quién tenía una casa en el campo ? 10. ¿ Qué quiere el
abuelo ? 11. ¿ Qué vendió ? 12. ¿ Qué compró ? 13. ¿ Con quién
estaba usted ? 14. ¿ Qué tiene la casa ? 15. ¿ Dónde está la
casa ?

C. *I. Continue:* 1. Veo a mi amigo, ves a tu amigo, etc.
2. Escribí la carta, etc. 3. Hallé el dinero, etc.

II. Translate: 1. There was a pencil on the table. 2. There
were three pens. 3. We learned the lesson. 4. She was tired.
5. Who closed the door ? 6. He used to teach [1] English. 7. I
lost my book. 8. They returned yesterday.

D. 1. Did the boy drink the milk ? 2. Yes, he was ill and he
didn't wish to drink milk. 3. But he is well now, and he drinks
much milk. 4. When he was ill he didn't study. 5. He studies
hard now, and he learns his lessons. — 6. When I entered (into)
the room John was writing. 7. He was writing a letter to his
friend Mary. 8. Mary's father has been ill, hasn't he (= isn't it
so) ? 9. Yes, but he is well now. 10. He is in the country with
his family. 11. Mary's family is not rich. — 12. My brother returned from the country yesterday. 13. He was there with our
grandfather. 14. What time was it when he returned ? 15. It
was three o'clock. 16. What time is it now ? 17. It is half past
eight. 18. I have to see Mary.

[1] Supply the article.

La señora de aquella casa estaba muy enfadada.

LECTURA

Cuando Carlos era pequeño [1] sus padres [2] le llevaron un día a un concierto.[3] El niño [4] vió a una señora [5] bien vestida [6] y a un hombre vestido de [7] negro.[8] Carlos había visto al mayordomo [9] de su casa vestido de negro. La señora cantaba [10] muy fuerte [11] y el hombre tocaba [12] el piano. Cuando volvió a casa Carlos le dijo [13] a su hermano: « La señora de aquella casa estaba muy enfadada.[14] Gritaba [15] y amenazaba [16] al mayordomo y él tocaba el piano sin cesar. » [17]

[1] *small.* [2] *parents.* [3] *concert.* [4] *child.* [5] *lady.* [6] *dressed.* [7] *in.* [8] *black.* [9] *butler.* [10] *sang.* [11] *loud.* [12] *played.* [13] *said.* [14] *angry.* [15] *shouted.* [16] *threatened.* [17] **cesar,** *to cease;* **sin cesar,** *unceasingly.*

LESSON XIV

75. *Personal Object Pronouns (1).* The following **personal pronouns** are used as objects of verbs:

SINGULAR		PLURAL	
me	*me, to me*	nos	*us, to us*
te	*thee, to thee*	os	*you, to you*

NOTES: 1. **Te** corresponds to **tú** and **os** to **vosotros, –as.**

2. The preposition **a** is not used with these object pronouns.

76. *Position of Personal Pronouns (1).* The personal pronoun objects usually precede their verb (but see § 192).

Me ve.	*He sees me.*
No me ve.	*He doesn't see me.*
Me vende el libro.	{ *He sells me the book.* *He sells the book to me.* }

77. *Radical-changing Verbs of the Third Conjugation.*

a) Some verbs of the third conjugation change **e** to **ie** and **o** to **ue** in the present indicative whenever the stress falls on the root.

Preferir, *to prefer*		**Dormir,** *to sleep*	
SINGULAR	PLURAL	SINGULAR	PLURAL
prefiero	**preferimos**	**duermo**	**dormimos**
prefieres	**preferís**	**duermes**	**dormís**
prefiere	**prefieren**	**duerme**	**duermen**

b) Other verbs of the third conjugation change the radical **e** to **i** whenever the stress falls on the root.

Pedir, *to ask (for)*

SINGULAR	PLURAL
pido	**pedimos**
pides	**pedís**
pide	**piden**

NOTES: 1. The negative precedes the object pronouns: **no me ve,** *he doesn't see me.*

2. In the present indicative the radical vowel does not change in

the first and second persons plural. In these forms the stress falls on the inflectional ending and not on the root.

3. With the exception of regularly recurring changes in the radical vowels, the radical-changing verbs are inflected like regular verbs.

4. There is no rule by which all radical-changing verbs can be recognized (but see § 258). Whenever a verb is radical-changing, this fact will be indicated in the vocabularies, thus: **preferir (ie), pedir (i), dormir (ue)**. See also the list of verbs in § 286.

78. *Preterite of* **ser, haber, estar, tener.**

fuí, fuiste, fué, fuimos, fuisteis, fueron
hube, hubiste, hubo, hubimos, hubisteis, hubieron
estuve, estuviste, estuvo, estuvimos, estuvisteis, estuvieron
tuve, tuviste, tuvo, tuvimos, tuvisteis, tuvieron

79. *Idioms.*

Es la una y media.	*It is half past one.*
Son las dos menos cuarto.	*It is a quarter to two.*
¿ A qué hora ?	*At what time ?*
A la una y cuarto.	*At a quarter past one.*
A las ocho menos diez.	*At ten minutes to eight.*

NOTE: **La una** agrees with **hora** understood, and **las dos, las tres**, etc., agree with **horas**. **Media** (*half*) is an adjective and agrees with **hora**, while **cuarto** (*quarter, fourth*) is a noun and therefore does not agree.

EXERCISES

a *at*	**nos** *us, to us*
el **cuarto** *quarter, fourth*	**ochenta** *eighty*
dejar *to leave*	**os** *you, to you*
dormir (ue) *to sleep*	**pedir (i)** *to ask* (*for*)
me *me, to me*	**preferir (ie)** *to prefer*
menos *less*	**te** *thee, to thee*

A. 1. Mi amigo no está aquí ahora. 2. Está en Wáshington con su padre. 3. Ayer me escribió una carta. 4. Me pide un libro que dejó en su cuarto. 5. Hallé el libro en una silla. — 6. Mi hermano no desea comprar esta pluma. 7. Prefiere el lápiz rojo. 8. Escribe en papel blanco con lápiz rojo. 9. Tenía una pluma y dos lápices. 10. Me vendió la pluma y un lápiz. — 11. El muchacho no está en la escuela. 12. Ayer trabajó mucho en la

3

tienda. 13. Está cansado y ahora duerme. 14. Él duerme mucho. 15. Yo no duermo cuando tengo que estudiar. — 16. Nuestro hermano nos escribió de Chicago. 17. No tiene mucho dinero. 18. Nos pide ochenta dólares. 19. Estuvo enfermo pero ahora está bueno. 20. Pero no duerme bien.

B. 1. ¿Quién no está aquí? 2. ¿Quién te escribió una carta? 3. ¿Qué te pide? 4. ¿Dónde estaba el libro? 5. ¿Quién no desea comprar una pluma? 6. ¿Qué prefiere usted, una pluma o un lápiz? 7. ¿Quién escribe con lápiz rojo? 8. ¿Qué te vendió tu hermano? 9. ¿Quién no está en la escuela? 10. ¿Dónde trabajó ayer? 11. ¿Quién duerme mucho? 12. ¿Duerme usted mucho? 13. ¿De dónde nos escribió nuestro hermano? 14. ¿Cuánto dinero tiene? 15. ¿Cuánto nos pide?

C. *Translate:* 1. He teaches us. 2. We entered the house at three o'clock. 3. She wrote to me. 4. There were four boys here. 5. He found me in the room. 6. She sees us. 7. We prefer coffee. 8. They drink milk. 9. Are they sleeping now? 10. I ask for a book. 11. They are asking for money. 12. I see you.

D. 1. At what time did you return from [1] school? 2. I returned at half past three. 3. I went into my room at a quarter to four. 4. We didn't see you in the house. 5. I returned from school with John. 6. He is in the house now. — 7. Do you prefer the pencil to the pen? 8. No, I prefer the pen. 9. That pencil is not red. 10. I prefer to write on white paper with a red pencil. 11. I bought this pen in Charles' store. 12. Charles sold me the pen and the paper. — 13. How is your sister Mary? 14. She is in the country now. 15. She was ill, but she is well now. 16. She has written many letters to us. 17. In one letter she asks for money. 18. She wishes to buy a horse.

LECTURA

Refrán español: Más [2] vale poco [3] que [4] nada.

Un hombre que comía [5] mucho entró en un restaurant con un amigo. Era tarde y en el restaurant había sólo [6] tres huevos [7] y café.

---

[1] Supply the article.　　[2] *more;* **más vale,** (*it*) *is better.*　　[3] *a little.*　　[4] *than.*
[5] *ate.*　　[6] *only.*　　[7] *eggs.*

— Hay bastante [1] café — dijo el hombre que comía mucho — porque mi amigo no bebe café. Pero me parece que no hay bastantes huevos.

Trajeron [2] el café y los huevos y los [3] pusieron [4] en la mesa. El hombre tomó [5] dos huevos y dijo a su compañero [6]:

— Ahora usted puede escoger.[7]

— ¿ Escoger ? Hay sólo un huevo.

— Bien. Puede escoger entre ese huevo y nada.

LESSON XV

80. *Personal Object Pronouns* (2).

a) The personal pronouns of the third person used as objects of the verb are:

	DIRECT OBJECT		INDIRECT OBJECT	
Sing.	le	*him*		*him, to him*
	la	*her, it*	le	*her, to her*
	lo	*it*		*it, to it*
Pl.	los	} *them*		
	las		les	*them, to them*

NOTES: 1. La, las and los are used both as articles and as object pronouns, but the article el differs in form from the corresponding object pronouns le and lo.

2. Lo is also used with the meaning *him* or *you* (masc.), but le is generally considered preferable.

Escribo la carta. La escribo.	*I write the letter. I write it.*
Cuenta los libros. Los cuenta.	*He counts the books. He counts them.*
Vendió la casa a mi abuelo. Le vendió la casa.	*He sold my grandfather the house.* *He sold him the house.* *He sold the house to my grandfather.* *He sold the house to him.*

[1] *enough.* [2] *They brought.* [3] *them.* [4] *they placed.* [5] *took.* [6] *companion.* [7] *choose.*

Enseña el español a los mucha-chos. Les enseña el español.	*He teaches the boys Spanish. He teaches them Spanish.* *He teaches Spanish to the boys. He teaches Spanish to them.*

b) All the pronouns given above serve also as the object pronouns corresponding to **usted** and **ustedes.**

Le hallé.	*I found him* or *you* (m. sing.).
La hallé.	*I found her* or *you* (f. sing.).
Los hallé.	*I found them* or *you* (m. pl.).
Las hallé.	*I found them* or *you* (f. pl.).

Le vende la casa.	*He sells him (her, you) the house.* *He sells the house to him (her, you).*
Les vende la casa.	*He sells them (you) the house.* *He sells the house to them (to you).*

c) English *it* (dir. obj.) is expressed in Spanish by **la** when it refers to a feminine noun, and by **lo** when it refers either to a masculine noun or to a mere idea or statement.

Tengo la pluma. La tengo.	*I have the pen. I have it.*
Tengo el libro. Lo tengo.	*I have the book. I have it.*
Creo eso. Lo creo.	*I believe that. I believe it.*

81. *Pluperfect and Preterite Perfect.* These tenses are formed by combining the imperfect and preterite of **haber** with the past participle (see § 53*b*).

PLUPERFECT (or PAST PERFECT)

I had bought (learned, lived), had been buying (learning, living), etc.

Sing.	**había comprado (aprendido, vivido)** **habías comprado (aprendido, vivido)** **había comprado (aprendido, vivido)**

Pl.	**habíamos comprado (aprendido, vivido)** **habíais comprado (aprendido, vivido)** **habían comprado (aprendido, vivido)**

PRETERITE PERFECT (or SECOND PAST PERFECT)

(*when*) *I had bought* (*learned, lived*), *etc.*

Sing. {
hube comprado (aprendido, vivido)
hubiste comprado (aprendido, vivido)
hubo comprado (aprendido, vivido)
}

Pl. {
hubimos comprado (aprendido, vivido)
hubisteis comprado (aprendido, vivido)
hubieron comprado (aprendido, vivido)
}

82. *Use of Pluperfect and Preterite Perfect.*

a) *I had* (*you had, etc.*) with the past participle is usually expressed in Spanish by the pluperfect, **había** (**habías,** etc.) and the past participle.

Yo había comprado el libro.   *I had bought the book.*
Ella había aprendido la lección.   *She had learned the lesson.*

b) The preterite perfect, **hube** (**hubiste,** etc.) and the past participle, is used after the temporal conjunctions **cuando,** *when,* **luego que,** *as soon as,* and the like. But with these conjunctions the simple preterite is the more common in colloquial Spanish.

Luego que hube comprado el libro estudié la lección.
As soon as I had bought the book I studied the lesson.

Or more commonly: **Luego que compré el libro,** etc.

83. *Idioms.*

Eso no me gusta.   { *I do not like that.*
                            { *That does not please me.*

Nos gustan esas flores. { *We like those flowers.*
                             { *Those flowers please us.*

EXERCISES

anoche *last night*
el **billete** *bill*
el **bolsillo** *pocket*
la **casa** *house, home;* **a —,** (*to, at*) *home*
contestar *to answer, reply*

creo *I believe, think*
da *he* (*she*) *gives*
diez y ocho (or **dieciocho**) *eighteen*
eso neut. pron. *that*
fresco, –a *fresh*

gustar *to please*	**lo** *it, him, you*
los **hijos** *children*	**los** *them, you*
la *her, you, it*	**luego que** *as soon as*
largo, –a *long*	**llegar** *to arrive*
las *them, you*	**por qué** *why*
le *him, to him, her, to her, you,*	**porque** *because*
to you, it, to it	**ví** *I saw*
les *them, to them, you, to you*	

A. 1. Mi hermano llegó ayer a las cuatro y media. 2. Yo le había escrito una carta. 3. Pero él no me había contestado. 4. Cuando mi hermano llegó a casa entró en su cuarto. 5. Mi padre entró en el cuarto también. 6. Juan y yo no entramos. 7. Luego que hubieron entrado cerraron la ventana. 8. ¿ Por qué no cerraron la puerta ? — 9. Anoche tuve que estudiar mis lecciones. 10. Cuando las hube estudiado escribí a María. 11. Le escribí una carta larga. 12. Ella estuvo en Wáshington con su padre. 13. Ahora está en Nueva York con una amiga. 14. Yo le había escrito cuando estaba en Wáshington. 15. Pero ella no me había escrito. 16. En mi carta le pido un libro español. — 17. Usted estaba en la tienda ayer ¿ no es verdad ? 18. Yo la ví cuando usted entró. 19. Sí, había comprado leche. 20. Pero no había pan fresco en la casa y volví a la tienda. 21. Mis hijos comen mucho pan y beben mucha leche. 22. Les gusta el pan fresco.

B. 1. ¿ A qué hora llegó su hermano ? 2. ¿ Quién le había escrito ? 3. ¿ Dónde entró su hermano ? 4. ¿ Quién entró también ? 5. Luego que hubieron entrado ¿ qué cerraron ? 6. ¿ Qué tuvo usted que estudiar anoche ? 7. ¿ Cuándo escribió usted a María ? 8. ¿ Dónde estuvo ella ? 9. ¿ Dónde está ahora ? 10. ¿ Qué le pide usted en su carta ? 11. ¿ Dónde estaba usted ayer ? 12. ¿ Cuándo le (la) ví yo ? 13. ¿ Qué había comprado usted ? 14. ¿ Qué no había en la casa ? 15. ¿ Qué les gusta a los niños ?

C. *I. Continue:* 1. No me (te, etc.) gusta esta casa. 2. No me gustan las flores. 3. Juan me enseña. 4. Mi (tu, etc.) hermano me (te, etc.) halló. 5. Yo entro en la casa.

II. Translate, and then repeat, using the personal pronoun instead of the last noun in each sentence: 1. She drinks milk. 2. They

close the door. 3. We buy the house. 4. I count the books.
5. She found the boy. 6. He loses his pencils. 7. They sell the
pens. 8. I prefer the dollar. 9. They ask for the money. 10. She
left the chair here.

D. 1. Are you counting the money ? 2. Yes, I am counting it
because I have lost a bill. 3. I think (that) I have lost five dollars.
4. Last night I had eighteen dollars. 5. Now I have thirteen.
6. Where did you have the bills ? 7. I had them in this pocket.
8. But I found them on the table in my room. — 9. That woman
is poor. 10. She has two sons. 11. I give her money when I see
her. 12. She sells flowers in the street. 13. She sells them and
buys milk and bread. 14. She gives the milk and the bread to
her sons. — 15. My brother had worked hard. 16. He had to
write many letters. 17. As soon as he had written them he
worked in the garden. 18. He is tired now and is sleeping.
19. When he is tired he sleeps long (= much). 20. I don't sleep
long when I am tired.

LECTURA

Un muchacho rico quería [1] comprar un caballo. Preguntó a [2]
uno de sus amigos si había manera [3] de [2] conocer [4] la edad [5] de
los [2] caballos.

— La edad de un caballo — le dijo el amigo — se conoce [6] en [7]
los dientes.[8]

Un día le trajeron un caballo de mucho valor [9] que [10] tenía
treinta [11] y dos dientes.

— Tréinta y dos años es mucho — dijo el muchacho y no compró el caballo.

Otro día le trajeron uno muy viejo.[12] Examinó la boca [13] del
caballo y halló sólo cuatro dientes.

— Este caballo es bueno — dijo. — Es un caballo de cuatro
años. Está flaco, [14] pero comiendo [15] mucho engordará.[16]

[1] *wanted.* [2] Omit. [3] *a way.* [4] *to know.* [5] *age.* [6] **se conoce,** *is
known.* [7] *by.* [8] *teeth.* [9] *value.* [10] *which.* [11] *thirty.* [12] *old.* [13] *mouth.*
[14] *lean.* [15] *by eating.* [16] *he will get fat.*

LESSON XVI

84. *Personal Object Pronouns (3).*

a) When a verb has two personal pronoun objects, the **indirect object precedes the direct.**

Me lo da.	*He gives it to me.*
Te lo da.	*He gives it to you.*
Nos la da.	*He gives it to us.*
Os las da.	*He gives them to you.*

b) If both pronouns are in the third person, the form **se** is used as the indirect object instead of **le** or **les**.

Se lo da. *He gives it to him (her, it, them, you).*

NOTE: In this sentence **se** has all the possible meanings of both **le** (ind. obj.) and **les**.

85. *Prepositional Forms of the Personal Pronouns (1).* The personal pronouns governed by a preposition are the same in form as the subject pronouns, except that **mí** and **ti** are used instead of **yo** and **tú**.

para mí	*for me*	**para nosotros, –as**	*for us*
para ti	*for you (thee)*	**para vosotros, –as**	*for you (ye)*
para usted	*for you*	**para ustedes**	*for you*
para él	*for him (it)*	**para ellos, –as**	*for them*
para ella	*for her (it)*		

NOTE: **Mí**, *me*, is distinguished from **mi**, *my*, by the accent mark.

86. *Emphatic Use of the Prepositional Forms.* When a personal pronoun is the object of a verb, the meaning may be made clear or emphatic by adding **a mí, a ti,** etc.

Me gusta a mí.	*I like it.*	**Se lo da a él.**	*He gives it to him.*
Le gusta a ella.	*She likes it.*	**Se lo da a usted.**	*He gives it to you.*

NOTES: 1. One may say with still more emphasis on the pronoun: **a mí me gusta,** etc.

2. With a noun the corresponding personal pronoun object is often used thus, even though it is not required to make the meaning clear

or emphatic: **Le gusta a Juan,** *John likes it;* **Se lo da a María,** *He gives it to Mary.*

87. De él, de ella, *etc.* The definite article with **de él, de ella,** etc., may be used instead of **su,** to make the meaning clear or emphatic.

su libro	or **el libro de él**	*his book*
su casa	or **la casa de ella**	*her house*
su cuarto	or **el cuarto de usted**	*your room*
su padre	or **el padre de ellos**	*their father*

NOTE: With these expressions compare **el libro de Juan,** *John's book;* **la casa de María,** *Mary's house.*

88. *Idiom.*

volver a + infinitive, *to . . . again*

Volvió a perder el dinero. *He lost the money again.*
Volvieron a entrar en la casa. *They went in the house again.*

EXERCISES

antes *before, formerly*
cuánto, -a interrog. *how much*
da *he (she) gives; you give*
él *him, it*
ella *her, it*
ellos, -as *them*
hermoso, -a *beautiful, handsome*
mí *me*
muy *very*
nosotros, -as *us*

para *for;* before inf. *in order to*
quinientos, -as *five hundred*
se *to him, to her, to it, to them, to you*
ti *you (thee)*
la tía *aunt*
el tío *uncle*
volver a + inf. *to . . . again*
vosotros, -as *you (ye)*

A. 1. Mi tío Juan compró un caballo blanco. 2. Lo compró cuando estaba en el campo. 3. A él le gusta mucho el campo. 4. Pero a mi tía no le gusta. 5. Han vivido diez años allí. 6. Pero ahora viven en la ciudad. — 7. Carlos le vendió un lápiz a María. 8. Se lo vendió en la escuela. 9. ¿Cuándo se lo vendió? 10. Se lo vendió ayer. 11. María había perdido la pluma de ella y dos lápices. 12. Luego que María hubo comprado el lápiz le escribió una carta a su hermano. 13. Le escribió una carta muy larga. — 14. ¿Por qué le pidió usted ese dinero a su tía? 15. Se lo pedí

3*

porque deseo comprar papel y flores. 16. El papel es para mí y las flores son para mi madre. 17. Anoche yo tenía ocho dólares. 18. Cuando volví a casa conté el dinero. 19. Había perdido un billete de cinco dólares. 20. A mí no me gusta perder dinero.

B. 1. ¿Quién compró un caballo blanco? 2. ¿Cuándo lo compró? 3. ¿A quién le gusta mucho el campo? 4. ¿A quién no le gusta el campo? 5. ¿Cuántos años han vivido allí? 6. ¿Qué le vendió Carlos a María? 7. ¿Qué había perdido María? 8. ¿A quién le escribió María? 9. ¿Cuándo le escribió? 10. ¿A quién le pidió usted dinero? 11. ¿Qué quiere usted comprar? 12. ¿Para quién es el papel? 13. ¿Para quién son las flores? 14. ¿Cuánto dinero tenía usted anoche? 15. ¿Cuándo contó usted el dinero? 16. ¿Qué había perdido usted?

C. *I. Continue:* 1. Me enseña la lección. 2. Me la enseña. 3. Me da el libro. 4. Me lo da a mí. 5. A mí no me gusta el campo. 6. Hay una carta para mí.

II. Translate: 1. He has her book. 2. She has his book. 3. I have your pencil. 4. Have you my letter? 5. He gives the paper to me. 6. He gives it to me. 7. He doesn't give the chairs to you. 8. He doesn't give them to you. 9. I like the country, but you do not like it. 10. Mary likes the country, but John doesn't like it.

D. 1. My brother again asked for money yesterday. 2. Whom did he ask for it? 3. Before he had asked our father (for it). 4. Yesterday he asked me (for it). 5. He asked for it in order to buy a book. 6. The book was not for him. — 7. That boy's father is not rich. 8. But he has bought that house. 9. My uncle sold it to him. 10. My aunt liked the house. 11. But she didn't like the garden. 12. She didn't like it because there weren't many trees in it. — 13. This city is very large. 14. It has many beautiful streets. 15. This street is very long. 16. There are large and beautiful houses in it. 17. Yes, and there are many trees also. 18. I think (that) there are five hundred trees. 19. Have you counted them? 20. No, John and Mary counted them.

El Cid fué un guerrero intrépido y altivo.

LECTURA

Anoche copié en mi cuaderno algunas selecciones que nuestro maestro nos había dictado.

Hallamos en la historia del mundo [1] muchos personajes [2] interesantes [3] y osados [4] que son héroes de extensas [5] leyendas. Muchas veces en el fondo [6] de una tradición hallamos un hombre de carne [7] y hueso.[8] Uno de ellos es el Cid,[9] Rodrigo Díaz de Bivar. Nació [10] en el pueblecillo [11] de Bivar cerca de [12] Burgos en el norte [13] de España. Fué un guerrero [14] intrépido y altivo.[15] Pero fué generoso con el enemigo [16] vencido [17] y frecuentemente fué defensor [18] de los pobres.

LESSON XVII

89. *Imperfect and Preterite of Radical-changing Verbs.* In the imperfect (past descriptive) and preterite (past absolute) indicative, radical-changing verbs are inflected like regular verbs, without change in the radical vowel, except in the preterite of the third conjugation. Here the radical vowels **e** and **o** are changed to **i** and **u** respectively, in the third person singular and plural.

PRETERITE

Preferir (*I preferred, did prefer, etc.*)

  preferí, preferiste, prefirió, preferimos, preferisteis, prefirieron

Pedir (*I asked, did ask, etc.*)

  pedí, pediste, pidió, pedimos, pedisteis, pidieron

Dormir (*I slept, did sleep, etc.*)

  dormí, dormiste, durmió, dormimos, dormisteis, durmieron

world. [2] characters. [3] interesting. [4] daring. [5] extensive. [6] background. [7] flesh. [8] bone. [9] Lord. [10] He was born. [11] little village. [12] near. [13] north. [14] warrior. [15] haughty. [16] enemy. [17] conquered. [18] a defender.

90. *Future and Conditional.* The future and the conditional (or past future) indicative of all regular verbs are formed by adding the following endings to the infinitive:

FUTURE		CONDITIONAL	
–é	–emos	–ía	–íamos
–ás	–éis	–ías	–íais
–á	–án	–ía	–ían

91.

FUTURE		CONDITIONAL	
I. *I shall buy, shall be buying, etc.*		*I should buy, should be buying, etc.*	
compraré	compraremos	compraría	compraríamos
comprarás	compraréis	comprarías	compraríais
comprará	comprarán	compraría	comprarían
II. *I shall learn, shall be learning, etc.*		*I should learn, should be learning, etc.*	
aprenderé	aprenderemos	aprendería	aprenderíamos
aprenderás	aprenderéis	aprenderías	aprenderíais
aprenderá	aprenderán	aprendería	aprenderían
III. *I shall live, shall be living, etc.*		*I should live, should be living, etc.*	
viviré	viviremos	viviría	viviríamos
vivirás	viviréis	vivirías	viviríais
vivirá	vivirán	viviría	vivirían

92. *Use of the Definite Article (1).* The definite article is required:

a) Before a noun used in a general sense to denote all of the thing or kind it names.

Las mujeres aman a los niños.	*Women* (as a rule) *love children* (generally speaking).
But: **Compramos flores.**	*We are buying (some) flowers.*

b) Before a proper noun modified by a title or a descriptive adjective, except in direct address.

el señor García	*Mr. García*
la pequeña Isabel	*little Elizabeth*
But: **Buenos días, señor García.**	*Good day, Mr. García.*

NOTES: 1. **Don** and **doña** (used before given names only) are exceptions in that they never require the definite article: **Doña Emilia no está en casa,** *Doña Emilia is not at home.*

2. The definite article is usually repeated before each noun to which it refers: **la pluma y la tinta,** *the pen and (the) ink.*

EXERCISES

amar *to love*
dar *to give*
el **día** *day*
don (doña) *Mr. (Mrs.)*
dónde interrog. *where;* a —, *where* (= *whereto, whither*)
Emilia *Emily*
ganar *to earn*
hoy *today*
mañana *tomorrow*
Méjico *Mexico*
el **mes** *month*
la **mujer** *woman*

el **niño** *small boy, child;* la **niña** *small girl, child;* los **niños** *children*
pequeño, –a *little, small*
que conj. *that*
querer (ie) *to wish, want*
señor *Mr., Sir, gentleman;* **señora** *Mrs., madam (ma'am), lady;* **señorita** *Miss, young lady;* **señores** *Messrs., Sirs, gentlemen, Mr. and Mrs.*
si *if*
la **tinta** *ink*

A. 1. Creo que la señorita García volverá mañana. 2. Ha escrito que le gustaría ver a su tía. 3. Su tía está en el campo, pero volverá hoy. 4. ¿ Dónde ha estado la señorita García ? 5. Ha vivido un año en Cuba y dos en Méjico. 6. Estará aquí cinco meses. 7. De aquí volverá a Méjico. 8. Allí estudiará y trabajará. — 9. La pequeña Emilia vivirá con nosotros. 10. Es una niña muy buena y muy hermosa. 11. Antes vivía con la señora García. 12. A ella le gustaría vivir con su tía. 13. Pero su tía es pobre y tiene que trabajar mucho. · 14. Ha perdido el dinero que tenía. — 15. Buenos días, don Juan. 16. ¿ Ha vendido usted la casa al señor Castro ? 17. Se la venderé a él si la quiere. 18. Pero no se la vendería al hermano de él. 19. Su hermano no tiene dinero ahora. 20. Tenía dinero, pero lo ha perdido.

B. 1. ¿ Quién volverá mañana ? 2. ¿ Qué ha escrito ella ? 3. ¿ Dónde está su tía ? 4. ¿ Cuándo volverá su tía ? 5. ¿ Dónde ha vivido la señorita García ? 6. ¿ Cuántos años ha vivido en Méjico ? 7. ¿ Cuántos meses estará aquí ? 8. ¿ A dónde volverá ? 9. ¿ Con quién vivirá la pequeña Emilia ? 10. ¿ Con quién vivía antes ? 11. ¿ Con quién le gustaría vivir ? 12. ¿ Por qué tiene que trabajar su tía ? 13. ¿ Qué ha perdido ella ? 14. ¿ A quién

venderá la casa don Juan ? 15. ¿ A quién no se la vendería ?
16. ¿ Qué no tiene el hermano del señor Castro ?

C. *I. Continue:* 1. Cerraré la puerta. 2. No beberé leche.
3. Dormiré aquí. 4. Estudiaré mi lección. 5. Me gustaría volver
a casa.

II. Translate: 1. Who will drink this milk ? 2. Will he count
the money ? 3. When will you write ? 4. I'll find the street.
5. We shall work hard. 6. They slept here. 7. Did he prefer the
dog ? 8. What did he ask ? 9. He wrote that he would sell the
house. 10. She replied that she would teach the child.

D. 1. Charles wishes to live in the country with his uncle.
2. His uncle has three dogs and many horses. 3. Charles likes
horses. 4. But he doesn't like dogs. 5. He prefers horses to dogs.
6. I think that Charles will work hard. 7. But he will not earn
much money. — 8. Who wrote to you yesterday ? 9. I saw a
letter on the table. 10. It is from Elizabeth. 11. She writes to
me that she will return tomorrow. 12. She would return today,
but she has to work. 13. She will arrive at half past four o'clock.
14. Her family is here now. — 15. That woman asked me for one
dollar. 16. I shall give it to her because she is poor and has
three children. 17. Her children are small. 18. She asked me
for it in order to buy bread and milk. 19. The bread and milk
are not for her. 20. She works in a store, but she doesn't earn
much money.

LECTURA

Uno de los héroes de la independencia de los países [1] hispanoamericanos [2] fué Francisco Miranda. Nació en Caracas, Venezuela. Luchó [3] bajo [4] Wáshington por [5] la independencia de los
Estados Unidos.[6] Luego [7] trabajó en su país por la independencia
de los países hispanoamericanos. Tuvo que huir [8] y vino [9] a los
Estados Unidos. Fué luego a Inglaterra,[10] Francia, Austria, Rusia
y otros países de Europa. En ellos buscó [11] pero no halló apoyo [12]
material para la revolución hispanoamericana. Gastó [13] su propia [14]

---

[1] *countries.* [2] *Spanish American.* [3] *He fought.* [4] *under.* [5] *for.*
[6] *United States.* [7] *Then.* [8] *to flee.* [9] *he came.* [10] *England.* [11] *he
sought.* [12] *support.* [13] *He spent.* [14] *own.*

Miranda, el Quijote de la libertad, en prisión.

fortuna en dos tentativas.[1]　Dos veces proclamó la república, pero fracasó.[2]　Por sus esfuerzos[3] ha sido llamado[4] « el Quijote de la libertad ».

LESSON XVIII

93. *Inflection of Adjectives* (2).　(Review §§ 38, 39.)　By exception, the following adjectives ending in consonants add –a to form the feminine:

a) Adjectives in **–án, –ón,** and **–or** (not including comparatives in **–or**).

> **un muchacho haragán, preguntón y hablador**
> *an idle, inquisitive, talkative boy*

> **una muchacha haragana, preguntona y habladora**
> *an idle, inquisitive, talkative girl*

b) Adjectives of nationality.

> **un muchacho español**　　*a Spanish boy*
> **una muchacha española**　*a Spanish girl*

[1] *attempts.*　[2] *he failed.*　[3] *efforts.*　[4] *called.*

94. *Adjectives of nationality.*

a) When an adjective of nationality denotes the language, it is masculine and usually takes the definite article.

El español no es fácil.	*Spanish is not easy.*
Estudiamos el español.	*We are studying Spanish.*

b) The definite article may be omitted when the name of a language immediately follows **hablar,** or is used with **en.**

¿ **Habla usted español** (or **castellano**)?	*Do you speak Spanish?*
Está escrito en español (or **en castellano**).	*It is written in Spanish.*

NOTE: The article is not used in certain idiomatic expressions: **una lección de francés,** *a French lesson;* **un ejercicio de español,** *a Spanish exercise.*

95. *Apocopation of Adjectives (1).* The following adjectives lose the final –o of the masculine singular when they immediately precede their noun:

buen(o), –a	*good*	**un(o), –a**	*one*
mal(o), –a	*bad*	**algún(o), –a**	*some*
primer(o), –a	*first*	**ningún(o), –a**	*none*
tercer(o), –a	*third*		

	el tercer ejercicio	*the third exercise*
But:	**el tercero**	*the third (one)*

NOTE: When **alguno** and **ninguno** drop the **o,** the accent must be used: **algún, ningún.**

96. *Future and Conditional of* **haber, querer, tener.**

FUTURE		CONDITIONAL	
habré	habremos	habría	habríamos
habrás	habréis	habrías	habríais
habrá	habrán	habría	habrían
querré	querremos	querría	querríamos
querrás	querréis	querrías	querríais
querrá	querrán	querría	querrían
tendré	tendremos	tendría	tendríamos
tendrás	tendréis	tendrías	tendríais
tendrá	tendrán	tendría	tendrían

97. *Idioms.*

diez dólares al mes	*ten dollars a month*
en la escuela	*in (at) school*

EXERCISES

alguno, -a *some*	**hablador, -ora** *talkative*
castellano, -a *Castilian, Spanish*	**hablar** *to speak*
	haragán, -ana *idle, lazy*
el edificio *building*	**ninguno, -a** *none*
el ejercicio *exercise*	**partir (de)** *to leave, depart (from)*
Enrique *Henry*	**preguntón, -ona** *inquisitive*
la esposa *wife*	**primero, -a** *first*
Felipe *Philip*	**tercero, -a** *third*
francés, -esa *French*	**trabajador, -ora** *industrious*

A. 1. Don Felipe y su esposa doña Isabel eran españoles. 2. Don Felipe era un hombre trabajador y ganaba mucho dinero. 3. Doña Isabel era una mujer muy hermosa. 4. Tenían dos hijos, Carlos y Emilia. 5. Carlos tenía quince años y Emilia doce. 6. Carlos era un buen muchacho, pero era haragán y no quería estudiar. 7. Emilia era habladora y preguntona. 8. Don Felipe y doña Isabel los amaban mucho. — 9. Somos ingleses y hablamos inglés bien. 10. Ahora queremos aprender el español. 11. Nuestra lección para hoy no es fácil. 12. Tenemos que escribir los ejercicios con tinta. 13. El primer ejercicio es largo. 14. A mí no me gusta el tercer ejercicio. — 15. ¿ Cuánto dinero hay aquí ? 16. Hay quinientos dólares. 17. Juan y yo los contamos. 18. Le daré ochenta a mi tío. 19. Quince son para mí. 20. Y diez son para la pequeña María.

B. 1. ¿ Quiénes eran españoles ? 2. ¿ Es usted español ? 3. ¿ Quién era trabajador ? 4. ¿ Cuántos hijos tenían don Felipe y doña Isabel ? 5. ¿ Cuántos años tenía Carlos ? 6. ¿ Cuántos años tenía Emilia ? 7. ¿ Quién no quería estudiar ? 8. ¿ Era Emilia haragana ? 9. ¿ Quiénes amaban mucho a los muchachos ? 10. ¿ Habla usted español ? 11. ¿ Qué quiere usted aprender ? 12. ¿ Es fácil la lección de español ? 13. ¿ Cuántos ejercicios tiene que escribir usted ? 14. ¿ Con qué escribe usted los ejercicios ? 15. ¿ Cuánto dinero tiene usted ? 16. ¿ Ha contado usted su dinero ?

C. *I. Continue:* 1. No soy español (española). 2. Yo no hablaba inglés. 3. Tendré algún dinero. 4. Yo no había escrito la carta. 5. Yo no querría eso.

II. Translate: 1. He is a good teacher. 2. It is the third day. 3. I should write the letter. 4. He would have money. 5. We should have to work. 6. Where are the children ? 7. Mrs. García loves little Elizabeth. 8. He preferred it. 9. They did not sleep well. 10. I lost the book again.

D. 1. I saw Miss García yesterday. 2. She had written to me that she would return to this city. 3. She has been in Cuba and in Mexico. 4. She has studied Spanish and speaks it well. 5. I think that she likes Spanish. 6. I like it a great deal too. 7. I shall study it in school. — 8. John and I shall leave for New York tomorrow. 9. We shall arrive in ¹ that city at half past five. 10. I should sleep here, but I prefer to return home. 11. I shall see John tomorrow at eight o'clock. 12. In New York we shall live with John's aunt. 13. John will want to see his friends. 14. I shall prefer to see the buildings of New York. — 15. Henry will leave for Mexico tomorrow. 16. There he will work in his uncle's store. 17. He will earn eighty dollars a month. 18. He is an industrious boy, and soon he will earn more. 19. Some day he will earn a great deal of money. 20. I should like to go with him.

LECTURA

En Caracas nació también el más ² conocido de los héroes hispanoamericanos. Simón Bolívar, hijo de padres nobles y ricos, estudió en Madrid. Luego viajó ³ por diferentes partes de Europa y también en los Estados Unidos donde estudió el gobierno ⁴ del país y conoció hombres de ideas liberales. En Roma había prometido ⁵ dedicar ⁶ su vida a la libertad de Venezuela. Fué ⁷ a Londres ⁸ como ⁹ representante ¹⁰ del gobierno revolucionario de Venezuela para obtener ¹¹ el apoyo de Inglaterra. De allí volvió con Miranda para luchar en la guerra ¹² de independencia. Bolívar tomó parte en más de ¹³ doscientas ¹⁴ batallas ¹⁵ en Venezuela,

¹ **a.**   ² *best.*   ³ *traveled.*   ⁴ *government.*   ⁵ *promised.*   ⁶ *to devote.*
⁷ *He went.*   ⁸ *London.*   ⁹ *as.*   ¹⁰ *representative.*   ¹¹ *obtain.*   ¹² *war.*
¹³ *than.*   ¹⁴ *two hundred.*   ¹⁵ *battles.*

Simón Bolívar.

Colombia, Ecuador y el Perú, liberando [1] estos países del dominio [2] de España.

LESSON XIX

98. *Commands.*

 a) To express a direct command with **usted** or **ustedes** as subject, the following forms of the regular verbs are used:

I. **Comprar:**	compre usted	compren ustedes	*buy*
II. **Aprender:**	aprenda usted	aprendan ustedes	*learn*
III. **Vivir:**	viva usted	vivan ustedes	*live*

 b) Radical-changing verbs change **e** to **ie** or **i,** and **o** to **ue,** as
in the third person of the present indicative.

Cerrar:	cierre usted	cierren ustedes	*close*
Pedir:	pida usted	pidan ustedes	*ask (for)*
Volver:	vuelva usted	vuelvan ustedes	*return*

[1] *freeing.* [2] *rule.*

c) Some irregular verbs:

Dar:	dé usted	den ustedes	*give*
Ser:	sea usted	sean ustedes	*be*
Tener:	tenga usted	tengan ustedes	*have*
Ver:	vea usted	vean ustedes	*see*

NOTES: 1. If **usted** or **ustedes** is expressed once in a command as in the examples given above, it is not usually repeated in the same sentence. 2. The command form of **dar** with **usted** is accented to distinguish it from the preposition **de**.

99. *Position of Personal Object Pronouns* (2).

a) Personal pronoun objects precede the verb in a negative command, according to the general rule for the position of these pronouns (§ 192).

No me dé usted ese libro. *Do not give me that book.*
No me lo dé usted. *Do not give it to me.*

b) In an affirmative command the personal pronoun objects follow the verb and are attached to it so that the verb and the pronoun form one word.

Déme usted ese libro. *Give me that book.*
Démelo usted. *Give it to me.*

NOTE: When a pronoun is thus attached to one of these verb forms having two or more syllables, the verb requires the accent mark: **beba usted,** *drink;* **bébalo usted,** *drink it.*

100. *Numerals* (2).

diez y siete	*seventeen*	veintidós	*twenty-two*
diez y ocho	*eighteen*	veintitrés	*twenty-three*
diez y nueve	*nineteen*	veinticuatro	*twenty-four*
veinte	*twenty*	veinticinco	*twenty-five*
veintiun(o), –a	*twenty-one*		

NOTES: 1. Before a noun **veintiún** is used with the accent written. 2. An optional spelling is **diecisiete,** etc., **veinte y uno,** etc.

101. *Future and Conditional Perfect.* These two compound tenses are formed with the future and conditional of **haber** and the past participle.

FUTURE PERFECT

I shall have bought, shall have been buying, etc.

habré comprado	habremos comprado
habrás comprado	habréis comprado
habrá comprado	habrán comprado

CONDITIONAL PERFECT

I should have bought, should have been buying, etc.

habría comprado	habríamos comprado
habrías comprado	habríais comprado
habría comprado	habrían comprado

EXERCISES

la **cosa** *thing*

el **cuidado** *care;* **tener —**, *to be careful*

diecinueve (diez y nueve) *nineteen*

diecisiete (diez y siete) *seventeen*

dijo *he (she) said*

más *more*

tan *so*

veinte *twenty*

veintiuno (veinte y uno) *twenty-one*

veintidós (veinte y dos) *twenty-two*

veintitrés (veinte y tres) *twenty-three*

veinticuatro (veinte y cuatro) *twenty-four*

veinticinco (veinte y cinco) *twenty-five*

A. 1. Felipe es hijo del señor García. 2. Es un muchacho haragán. 3. Duerme mucho y no estudia sus lecciones. 4. Ayer el maestro le dijo: 5. Felipe, estudie la lección diez y nueve. 6. Escriba el primer ejercicio. 7. Escríbalo con tinta. 8. Pero Felipe no aprendió su lección. 9. Cuando volvió a la escuela hoy el maestro le dijo: 10. Entre en ese cuarto. 11. Cierre la puerta, pero no cierre las ventanas. 12. Estudie las lecciones diez y nueve y veinte. 13. Si no las aprende bien, le escribiré a su padre. — 14. ¿Quiere usted un buen libro? 15. Déme el dinero y lo compraré en la ciudad. 16. Tenga cuidado y no pierda el dinero. 17. Compre un libro y una pluma. 18. Quiero un libro francés y una buena pluma. 19. El libro es para la esposa de don Juan. 20. La pluma es para mi tío.

B. 1. ¿Quién es el padre de Felipe? 2. ¿Quién es haragán? 3. ¿Duerme usted mucho? 4. ¿Quién no estudia sus lecciones?

5. ¿ Qué le dijo el maestro a Felipe ? 6. ¿ Cuántas lecciones hemos estudiado ? 7. ¿ Cuántos ejercicios hemos escrito ? 8. ¿ Escribe usted sus ejercicios con tinta ? 9. ¿ Quién no aprendió bien su lección ? 10. ¿ Quién volvió a la escuela ? 11. ¿ Qué cerró Felipe ? 12. ¿ Ha estudiado usted la lección veintiuna ? 13. ¿ A quién escribirá el maestro ? 14. ¿ Dónde compra usted sus libros ? 15. ¿ Ha perdido usted algún dinero ? 16. ¿ Para quién es el libro ?

C. *I. Give the command forms, affirmative and negative, of the following verbs:*

| aprender | contar | ganar | partir | vender |
| beber | enseñar | hablar | pedir | ver |

II. Translate, and then repeat with the verbs in the negative:
1. Learn it (*f.*). 2. Drink it (*m.*). 3. Close them (*f.*). 4. Buy them (*m.*). 5. Count it (*m.*). 6. Study it (*f.*). 7. Find them (*f.*). 8. Sell it (*m.*). 9. He preferred it (*m.*). 10. He asked for it (*f.*)

D. 1. John, how many hours a day do you work ? 2. I work seven hours and sleep eleven. 3. Eleven and seven are eighteen, aren't they ? 4. And the day has twenty-four hours. 5. Don't be so lazy. 6. Sleep less and work more. 7. If you work more you will earn more. — 8. Do you see that white building ? 9. Henry has a store in it. 10. He sells books, pens, pencils, and other things. 11. Yesterday I asked him for twenty-five dollars. 12. He didn't have much money, and he answered me: 13. Come back tomorrow, and I'll give it to you. 14. I think that if he has it now he will give it to me. — 15. Leave the books on that chair. 16. Answer the letter that Charles wrote to us. 17. He will have arrived in New York. 18. He left last night at nine o'clock. 19. I like him a great deal because he is a good boy. 20. He is inquisitive, but he is industrious.

LECTURA

El argentino [1] José de San Martín, como Bolívar, estudió en Madrid. Tomó parte en la guerra contra [2] Napoleón y luego ofreció [3] sus servicios al gobierno de Buenos Aires. Después que [4] hubo logrado la independencia de Argentina y Chile marchó [5] al

---

[1] *Argentine.*   [2] *against.*   [3] *offered.*   [4] *After.*   [5] *went.*

El paso de los Andes por San Martín.

Perú. El paso [1] de los Andes por el ejército [2] de San Martín es una de las más [3] grandes [4] hazañas [5] en la historia militar. Luchó en el Perú y ganó [6] batallas muy importantes. Comprendiendo [7] que sólo un jefe [8] era necesario, renunció [9] el mando [10] de su ejército después de [11] una entrevista [12] con Bolívar. San Martín fué el más abnegado [13] de los héroes hispanoamericanos.

LESSON XX

102. *Infinitives.*

a) Some verbs require a preposition before a subordinate infinitive, but many do not.

Juan aprende a leer.	*John is learning to read.*
Empieza a escribir.	*He is beginning to write.*
Me enseña a hablar español.	*He teaches me to speak Spanish.*
Tratamos de estudiar.	*We try to study.*
No pienso entrar.	*I do not intend to go in.*
No quiero almorzar.	*I do not wish to breakfast.*
¿ Prefiere usted tomar café ?	*Do you prefer to take coffee?*

[1] *crossing.* [2] *army.* [3] *most.* [4] *great;* **(las) más grandes,** *greatest.*
[5] *feats.* [6] *won.* [7] *Realizing.* [8] *leader.* [9] *resigned.* [10] *command.*
[11] *after.* [12] *interview.* [13] *unselfish.*

José de San Martín.

b) Personal pronoun objects follow an infinitive and are attached to it, so that the verb and the pronoun or pronouns form one word. If there are two pronoun objects, the final syllable of the infinitive requires the accent mark.

¿ **Quiere usted dármelo?** *Are you willing to (Will you) give it to me?*

c) After a preposition the infinitive is regularly used in Spanish instead of the present participle (gerund).

antes de (después de) comer *before (after) eating*
Estoy cansado de estudiar esta lección. *I am tired of studying this lesson.*

d) Spanish **al** + an infinitive is equivalent to English *on* + a present participle (gerund).

al entrar en la casa *on going into the house*
al leer la carta *on reading the letter*

103. **Ir,** *to go.*

a)

PAST PART.	ido
PRES. INDIC.	voy, vas, va, vamos, vais, van
IMPERFECT	iba, ibas, iba, íbamos, ibais, iban
PRETERITE	fuí, fuiste, fué, fuimos, fuisteis, fueron
COMMAND FORMS (with **usted, ustedes**)	vaya usted vayan ustedes
FUTURE	iré, irás, irá, iremos, iréis, irán
CONDITIONAL	iría, irías, iría, iríamos, iríais, irían

b) **Vamos,** used in commands, means *let us go.*

> **Vamos a la escuela.**   *Let us go to school.*
> **Vamos a trabajar.**   *Let us go to work.*

NOTE: When followed by an infinitive, **vamos a** often means no more than *let us:* **vamos a hablar con él,** *let us speak with him.*

104. *Idioms.*

> **Acaba (acababa) de hablar.**   *He has (had) just spoken.*
> **Vaya usted a comprarlo.**   *Go and buy it.*

EXERCISES

acabar *to finish;* — **de** + inf. *to have just* + past part.
al before inf. *on*
almorzar (ue) *to breakfast* (late), *have breakfast, lunch*
antes de *before*
el **centavo** *cent*
después de *after*
empezar (ie) *to begin*

ir *to go*
leer *to read*
pensar (ie) *to think;* before inf. *intend*
salir *to go* (*come*) *out*
tomar *to take, drink*
tratar (de) *to try* (*to*)
varios, –as *several*

A. 1. Yo iba a casa ayer cuando ví a Juan. 2. Él iba a ver a su amiga María. 3. Quería verla para darle un libro. 4. Pero ella no estaba en casa. 5. El hermano de ella le dijo a Juan: 6. María acaba de salir. 7. Ha ido a comprar varias cosas. 8. Vuelva usted mañana si quiere. — 9. Doña Emilia acaba de llegar del campo. 10. Al entrar en la casa me dijo: 11. Enrique y yo no hemos almorzado. 12. Vaya usted a la tienda a comprar café. 13. Compre también pan y leche. 14. Enrique prefiere tomar leche. — 15. María enseña a mis niños. 16. Han aprendido a leer. 17. Ahora empiezan a escribir. 18. Creo que aprenderán mucho con ella. 19. ¿ No están cansados de estudiar ? 20. No, les gusta mucho porque aman a María.

B. 1. ¿ A dónde iba usted ? 2. ¿ A quién vió usted ? 3. ¿ A quién iba a ver Juan ? 4. ¿ Qué quería darle a María ? 5. ¿ Dónde no estaba ella ? 6. ¿ Qué le dijo el hermano a Juan ? 7. ¿ Qué había ido a comprar María ? 8. ¿ Cuándo volverá Juan ? 9. ¿ De dónde acababa de llegar doña Emilia ? 10. ¿ Quiénes no han almorzado ? 11. ¿ Qué prefiere Enrique ? 12. ¿ Quién enseña a

sus niños ? 13. ¿ Qué han aprendido ? 14. ¿ Qué empiezan ahora ?
15. ¿ Con quién aprenderán mucho ? 16. ¿ Por qué les gusta
estudiar ?

C. *I. Continue:* 1. Acabo de leer el libro. 2. Vuelvo a leerlo.
3. Voy a verla. 4. Aprendo a hablar español. 5. Trato de estudiar. 6. Pienso trabajar mucho.

II. Translate: 1. Let us have breakfast. 2. They went to the
country. 3. She preferred to go out. 4. They have learned to
write. 5. Read that. 6. They tried to give it to him. 7. They
don't wish to work. 8. We intend to go out. 9. We taught them
to read. 10. He is tired of writing. 11. On entering the room
we saw him. 12. We were going to the country.

D. 1. Yesterday I went to the city with Philip. 2. We went
to a store to buy coffee. 3. In another store we bought milk and
bread. 4. The bread was not fresh. 5. My father doesn't like
fresh bread. 6. Before buying these things I had two dollars.
7. I returned home with one dollar. 8. Philip had twenty cents.
— 9. We study our lessons. 10. We wish to learn to speak Spanish. 11. We shall learn to speak it well. 12. Mr. García is teaching us. 13. He is a good teacher. 14. Don't you wish to study
with him ? — 15. Do you intend to go to the city today ? 16. No,
I was ill last night. 17. I am not going to work today. 18. I
shall try to sleep three or four hours. 19. After having breakfast
I shall drink much milk. 20. If there is no milk in the house I
shall go to the store.

LECTURA

Un hombre creía [1] que su criado [2] era simple y le dijo un día:
— Vaya usted a la tienda y compre una docena de huevos y
otra de ayes. [3]

El criado salió de la casa, pensó un poco y comprendió que su
amo [4] quería burlarse de [5] él. Con esta idea compró los huevos y
los puso [6] en una cesta. [7] Salió luego al campo, cogió [8] un buen
manojo [9] de hojas [10] de cardo [11] y las puso encima de [12] los huevos.

---

[1] *believed.*   [2] *servant.*   [3] *laments* ('*ouches*').   [4] *master.*   [5] *to make fun of.*
[6] *put.*   [7] *basket.*   [8] *picked.*   [9] *bunch.*   [10] *leaves.*   [11] *thistle.*   [12] *on top of.*

— ¿ Ha comprado usted lo que le dije ? — le preguntó el amo esperando [1] reír.[2]

— Sí, señor, aquí lo tiene.

El hombre puso la mano en la cesta, agarró [3] las hojas de cardo y gritó:

— ¡ Ay ! [4] ¡ Ay ! ¡ Ay !

— Los huevos están debajo de los ayes — dijo el criado.

[1] *hoping.*   [2] *to laugh.*   [3] *grasped.*   [4] *Ouch!*

REVIEW LESSON B

I. *A.* Use forms of **ser** or **estar,** both in the present and imperfect indicative:

1. El árbol no —— alto. 2. Aquel jardín —— grande. 3. Mi amigo —— pobre. 4. El lápiz no —— amarillo. 5. ¿ Dónde —— su hermana ? 6. María —— enferma. 7. Las mujeres —— en su cuarto. 8. Mi hermana —— cansada. 9. Juan no —— aquí. 10. ¿ Cómo —— la hermana de Juan ? 11. Mi padre no —— en la tienda. 12. Mi tía —— en la ciudad.

B. Use the preposition **a** where it is needed:

1. Escribo —— una muchacha. 2. Vendió la casa —— una mujer. 3. Mi tío tiene —— un caballo. 4. No he estudiado —— mi lección. 5. ¿ Quién escribió —— la carta ? 6. Había dado —— dinero —— la mujer. 7. Ví —— una carta aquí. 8. ¿ Vieron —— la señorita García ? 9. Felipe ama —— Isabel. 10. Hallé —— perro; no hallé —— muchacho.

II. *A.* Give the first and third persons singular of the preterite of the following verbs:

cerrar	estar	partir	perder	ser
contar	haber	pedir	preferir	tener
dormir	ir	pensar	salir	volver

B. Give both the future and conditional forms of the following verbs in the persons indicated in parentheses:

SINGULAR

(1) contestar	(2) dormir	(3) hallar
(2) dejar	(3) entrar	(2) pedir
(3) desear	(1) estar	(1) preferir

PLURAL

(3) acabar	(1) gustar	(2) partir
(1) amar	(2) hablar	(1) querer
(2) dar	(3) llegar	(3) volver

III. *A.* Supply the object pronoun that corresponds with the noun in parentheses:

1. (lección) —— aprendí. 2. (leche) —— bebe. 3. (puerta) —— cierro. 4. (libro) —— compró. 5. (carta) —— escribí. 6. (al muchacho)

—— enseño. 7. (horas) —— cuento. 8. (lecciones) —— estudiamos.
9. (lápiz) —— perdí. 10. (dólar) —— tiene. 11. (caballos) —— vendimos. 12. (árbol) —— ví. 13. (al hombre) —— pedimos. 14. (casa)
—— preferimos. 15. (dinero) —— dejé.

B. Supply in the proper order and form the equivalents of the
words in parentheses:

1. (*book, Spanish, yellow*) el —— —— es ——; los —— —— son ——.
2. (*English, industrious*) El hombre —— es ——; la mujer —— es ——;
los hombres —— son ——; las mujeres —— son ——. 3. (*that, French,
talkative*) —— muchacho —— es ——; —— muchacha —— no es ——.
4. (*my, lazy*) —— tío es ——; —— tía no es ——; —— hermanos son
——. 5. (*long, first, third*) Los ejercicios son ——; me gusta el ——
ejercicio; no me gusta ——.

IV. *A.* Translate, and then repeat, changing all verb forms to
the imperfect:

1. When he lives here he works hard. 2. I buy pens and he buys
pencils. 3. This girl has fifteen books. 4. What are you buying in this
store ? 5. There are ten boys here. 6. I have written to my English
friend.

B. Translate, and then repeat, changing the preterite to the
present:

1. I had to see the city. 2. He asked me for the money. 3. He entered
at three o'clock. 4. When did he leave ? 5. Where did you go ?

V. Translate:

1. His uncle is a teacher. 2. Are there many boys in school ? 3. Who
is tired ? 4. Were you ill ? 5. He is a good boy. 6. It is half past seven.
7. Has he any money ? 8. Do you prefer coffee ? 9. I don't like that
man. 10. He had written to me. 11. We had closed the window.
12. The coffee is for you. 13. The milk is for her. 14. Do you like
flowers ? 15. When will he return ? 16. Where will you go tomorrow ?
17. She will return today. 18. We don't want to speak. 19. I have
written the first exercise. 20. Does he earn much ? 21. Give me the
money. 22. Don't close the door. 23. Study the first lesson. 24. He
tried to see her. 25. Give the boy ten cents.

LESSON XXI

105. *The Feminine Article* **el.** (Review § 32.) Before a feminine noun with initial **a–** (or **ha–**) and with the stress on the first syllable, **el** is used instead of **la.**

el agua	*the water*	**el hacha**	*the ax*
But: **las aguas**	*the waters*	**las hachas**	*the axes*

106. *The Neuter Gender.* There are no neuter nouns in Spanish; but pronouns and adjectives are called neuter when they do not refer to masculine or feminine nouns.

Eso es bueno. *That is good.*

107. *The Neuter Article* **lo.** The neuter article **lo** is required before the masculine form of an adjective when the adjective is used substantively with the force of an abstract noun. **Lo** cannot be used with a noun.

lo bueno *the good* (that which is good)
lo malo *the bad* (that which is bad)

108. Dar, *to give.*

PAST PART.	**dado**
PRES. INDIC.	**doy, das, da, damos, dais, dan**
IMPERFECT	Regular
PRETERITE	**dí, diste, dió, dimos, disteis, dieron**
FUTURE	Regular
CONDITIONAL	Regular
COMMAND FORMS	See § 98*c*, and note 2.

109. *Idioms with* **dar.**

dar a, *to face*
La ventana da a la calle. *The window faces the street.*

dar de comer, *to feed, give something to eat*
Ella le dió de comer. *She fed him.*

dar los buenos días, *to say good morning (good day)*
Les damos los buenos días. *We say good morning to them.*

EXERCISES

el **agua** f. *water*
el **apetito** *appetite*
la **carne** *meat*
  comer *to eat, dine*
la **comida** *meal, dinner*
  dice *he (she) says*
la **ensalada** *salad*
  fresco, –a *cool*
la(s) **fruta(s)** *fruit*
el **hacha** f. *ax*
  lo neut. art. *the*
la **papa** (Span. Amer.) *potato*

la **patata** (Spain) *potato*
  pedir *to order*
el **pescado** *fish* (after being caught)
los **postres** *dessert*
  primero adv. *first*
  pronto *soon*
el **queso** *cheese*
el **restaurant** *restaurant*
  sabroso, –a *savory;* **ser —,** *to taste good*
  servir (i) *to serve*
la **sopa** *soup*

A. 1. Vamos a aquel restaurant a comer. 2. Sí, allí sirven buenas comidas. 3. Y hoy yo tengo buen apetito. 4. ¿A qué hora almorzó usted? 5. A las doce, pero no comí mucho. 6. Vamos a aquella mesa pequeña. 7. La ventana da a la calle. 8. Primero pediremos sopa y pescado. 9. ¿Le gusta a usted el pescado? 10. Sí, me gusta, pero en casa no lo comemos mucho. 11. Después de comer el pescado pediremos ensalada, carne y papas (patatas). 12. La ensalada que sirven aquí es buena y la carne es sabrosa. 13. ¿Piensa usted tomar postres? 14. Sí, tomaré queso o frutas. 15. Después de los postres, si usted quiere, tomaremos café. 16. No, yo prefiero leche hoy. 17. Usted ha bebido mucha agua. 18. Sí, el agua que tienen aquí es muy fresca. 19. ¿Quién es aquella señora que acaba de salir? 20. Es la esposa de don Juan.

B. 1. ¿A dónde vamos a comer? 2. ¿Dónde sirven buenas comidas? 3. ¿Tiene usted buen apetito? 4. ¿A qué hora al-

muerza usted ? 5. ¿ A qué hora quiere almorzar hoy ? 6. ¿ A
dónde dan las ventanas de este cuarto ? 7. ¿ Qué pedirán primero en el restaurant ? 8. ¿ Comen pescado en su casa ? 9. ¿ Qué
pedirán después de comer el pescado ? 10. ¿ Le gustan a usted
las papas ? 11. ¿ Dónde sirven buena ensalada ? 12. ¿ Qué toma
usted después de los postres ? 13. ¿ Prefiere usted la leche al
café ? 14. ¿ Bebe usted mucha agua ? 15. ¿ Ha bebido usted
mucha agua hoy ?

C. *I. Continue:* 1. Almuerzo a la una. 2. Empiezo a escribir.
3. Voy a casa. 4. No le doy el dinero a él. 5. Le dí de comer.

II. Translate: 1. He took milk. 2. Give me twenty-two cents.
3. Who tried to go ? 4. Do you read much ? 5. They have just
gone out. 6. She was going to the country. 7. He intends to
write to her. 8. Why doesn't he go ?

D. 1. I have just found this letter on the table. 2. My father
tells me in it that Henry will arrive today. 3. Yes, he has arrived.
and is in your room now. 4. Henry is not a good boy. 5. I think
that he prefers what is bad to what is good. 6. But he is tired.
and has not eaten today. 7. Let us give him something to eat.
8. We have meat, potatoes, and milk. — 9. I went to don Carlos
restaurant today. 10. On entering I said good morning to him.
11. But he didn't answer me. 12. He was reading a red book.
13. I ordered soup, fish, and cheese. 14. I didn't eat much and
came out soon. — 15. Go to Mr. García's store. 16. Buy bread,
meat, fruit, and milk. 17. Have you money for that ? 18. Yes,
but give me eighty cents more. 19. I want to buy several things
for Mary. 20. Try to come back soon.

LECTURA

Un hombre entró en un restaurant y le dijo al mozo [1]:

— Tráigame [2] un plato [3] de sopa antes de la batalla.

El mozo se sorprendió [4] pero sirvió la sopa. Después de algunos
minutos [5] el hombre le dijo al mozo:

— Tráigame biftec [6] y papas fritas [7] antes de la batalla.

---

[1] *waiter.* [2] *Bring me.* [3] *plate.* [4] *was surprised.* [5] *minutes.* [6] *beef-*
steak. [7] *fried.*

4

El mozo se sorprendió más, pero sirvió el biftec y las papas. Después de algunos minutos el hombre le dijo al mozo:

— Tráigame café y un cigarro [1] antes de la batalla.

El mozo trajo [2] el café y el cigarro. Después de algunos minutos le preguntó al hombre:

— ¿ Por qué dice usted antes de la batalla ?

— La batalla va a comenzar [3] ahora porque yo no tengo dinero.

LESSON XXII

110. *Reflexive Pronouns.*

a) The object pronouns of the first and second persons (see § 75) may also be used as reflexive. The reflexive pronoun of the third person, singular or plural, is **se.**

[1] *cigar.*   [2] *brought.*   [3] *begin.*

yo me engaño	*I deceive myself*
tú te engañas	*you deceive yourself*
usted	*you deceive yourself*
él } se engaña	*he deceives himself*
ella	*she deceives herself*

nosotros, (–as) nos engañamos	*we deceive ourselves*
vosotros, (–as) os engañáis	*you deceive yourselves*
ustedes	*you deceive yourselves*
ellos, –as } se engañan	*they deceive themselves*

b) Many verbs are used reflexively in Spanish, but not in English.

Me acuesto.	*I lie down, go to bed.*
Ella se desayuna.	*She breakfasts, has (early) breakfast.*
Él se levantó.	*He rose, got up.*

NOTE: Se is used also with the infinitive: **engañarse,** *to deceive oneself;* **acostarse,** *to go to bed.*

111. *Definite Article for the Possessive.*

a) When speaking of parts of the body or articles of clothing, the definite article is generally used instead of the possessive adjective.

Los niños abrieron los ojos.	*The children opened their eyes.*
Perdí el sombrero.	*I lost my hat.*

b) To avoid ambiguity, an indirect object pronoun may be used also.

Me corté el dedo.	*I cut my finger.*
Me puse el sombrero.	*I put on my hat.*

NOTE: The possessive is generally used before the subject of a sentence: **Su sombrero es nuevo,** *His hat is new.*

c) In some idiomatic expressions **tener** is used with names of parts of the body.

Tengo los ojos cansados.	*My eyes are tired.*
Tiene las manos frías.	*His hands are cold.*

112. *Distributive Construction.* When speaking of similar objects one of which belongs to each member of a group, the singular is generally used in Spanish.

> **Los niños se lavaron la cara y las manos.**
> *The children washed their faces and hands.*

NOTE: **Cara** is singular, since each child has one, while **manos** is plural, since each child has two.

113. **Venir,** *to come.*

PAST PART.	venido
PRES. INDIC.	vengo, vienes, viene, venimos, venís, vienen
IMPERFECT	Regular
PRETERITE	vine, viniste, vino, vinimos, vinisteis, vinieron
FUTURE	vendré, vendrás, vendrá, vendremos, vendréis, vendrán
CONDITIONAL	vendría, vendrías, vendría, vendríamos, vendríais, vendrían
COMMAND FORMS	venga usted vengan ustedes

114. *Idioms.*

por lo común, *usually*

la semana
el mes   } que viene, *next* { week / month / year
el año

EXERCISES

abrir *to open*
acostarse (ue) *to lie down, go to bed*
la cara *face*
común *common;* por lo —, *usually*
cortar *to cut*
debajo de *under*
el dedo *finger*
desayunarse *to breakfast, have (early) breakfast*
encontrar (ue) *to find, meet*
engañar *to deceive*
frío, -a *cold*

lavar *to wash*
levantarse *to rise, get up*
la mano *hand*
la mañana *morning*
el médico *physician*
nuevo, -a *new*
el ojo *eye*
ponerse *to put on* (clothes)
se *himself, herself, yourself, itself, oneself, themselves, yourselves*
la semana *week*
el sombrero *hat*
temprano *early*
venir *to come*

A. 1. Ayer encontré a Carlos en la calle. 2. Él iba a comprar un libro de español en la librería. 3. Entramos en un restaurant. 4. Él pidió sopa y pescado. 5. Yo pedí sopa pero no pescado. 6. Pedí carne, papas y ensalada. 7. Él pidió postres y yo pedí café. 8. Después de almorzar salimos del restaurant. — 9. El hombre vino a cortar el árbol. 10. Tomó el hacha con cuidado. 11. Pero al cortar el árbol se cortó un dedo. 12. Me dijo que había perdido tres dedos. 13. Pero se engañó; había perdido uno. 14. Ahora va a ver al médico. — 15. Los niños se levantaron hoy a las cinco. 16. Anoche se acostaron muy temprano. 17. Se lavaron las manos y la cara. 18. Después de desayunarse salieron con Enrique. 19. Fueron al campo a ver a su abuelo. 20. Al salir me dieron los buenos días.

B. 1. ¿A quién encontró usted en la calle? 2. ¿Qué iba a comprar Carlos? 3. ¿Ha comprado usted un libro de francés? 4. ¿En dónde entraron ustedes? 5. ¿Qué pidió Carlos? 6. ¿Qué pidió usted? 7. ¿Quién pidió café? 8. ¿Cuándo salieron del restaurant ♭ 9. ¿ Quién vino a cortar el árbol ♭ 10. ¿ Qué tomó con cuidado el hombre ♭ 11. ¿ Cuántos dedos dijo que había perdido ♭ 12. ¿ A quién va a ver ahora ♭ 13. ¿ A qué hora se levantaron los niños ♭ 14. ¿ Cuándo se acostaron anoche ♭ 15. ¿ Con quién salieron después de desayunarse ♭ 16. ¿ A quién fueron a ver ♭ 17. ¿ Dónde vive el abuelo de los niños ♭

C. *1. Continue:* 1. Iré el mes que viene. 2. Vengo a verle. 3. Vine con mi amigo. 4. Me desayuno a las ocho. 5. Me lavé la cara. 6. Tengo las manos frías.

II. Translate, and then repeat with the verb in the plural of the same person: 1. I deceived myself. 2. I open my eyes. 3. Her eyes are tired. 4. I wash my face. 5. I get up at seven o'clock.

D. 1. John was coming from the country with his friend. 2. They were tired and they lay down under a tree. 3. They slept three or four hours. 4. When they opened their eyes it was six o'clock. 5. They got up and returned soon to the city. 6. They reached (= arrived at) home at half past nine. 7. John had lost his hat. 8. But his hat was not new. — 9. Have you a good appetite now ♭ 10. Yes, I want to go to don Felipe's restaurant. 11. They serve good meals there, don't they ♭ 12. Yes, the meat tastes good. 13. Let us go, because I, too, wish to eat. 14. Do you wish to wash your hands before going out ♭ — 15. At what time did you go to bed last night ♭ 16. I went to bed at twelve o'clock. 17. Usually I go to bed at ten or eleven. 18. This morning I got up at half past seven. 19. I had breakfast at eight. 20. I came to this building at half past eight.

LECTURA

En una noche [1] de invierno [2] llegó un viajero [3] a una posada.[4] Vió que había mucha gente [5] y que no había sitio [6] para él al rededor del [7] fuego.[8]

— Mozo — dijo en voz [9] alta [10] al criado — llévale un par [11] de huevos fritos a mi caballo.

— ¿ A su caballo ♭ ¿ Su caballo come huevos fritos ♭

— Llévele usted los huevos y verá.

---

[1] *night.*   [2] *winter.*   [3] *traveler.*   [4] *inn.*   [5] *people.*   [6] *place.*   [7] *al rededor de, about.*   [8] *fire.*   [9] *voice.*   [10] *loud.*   [11] *couple.*

En el patio de una posada.

El mozo le llevó los huevos al caballo. Los demás ¹ huéspe-
des,² sorprendidos, fueron a ver el caballo que comía huevos fritos.
Entonces el viajero se sentó ³ cómodamente ⁴ frente al ⁵ fuego.
Después de algunos minutos volvieron el mozo y los huéspedes.

— Su caballo no quiere comer los huevos.

— ¿ No ? — dijo el hombre — Entonces yo me ⁶ los comeré.

LESSON XXIII

115. *Negative Pronouns and Adverbs.*

a)

nadie	*no one, nobody*
nada	*nothing*
ninguno (ningún), –a	*no, none*

¹ *other.* ² *guests.* ³ *sat down.* ⁴ *comfortably.* ⁵ **frente a,** *before.* ⁶ Omit.

nunca	*never*
ni; ni . . . ni	*nor; neither . . . nor*
tampoco; ni . . . tampoco	*neither; nor . . . either*
¿ Quién vino ? — Nadie.	*Who came? No one.*
Nadie vino.	*No one came.*
Nada tengo.	$\left\{\begin{array}{l}\textit{I have nothing.}\\ \textit{I haven't anything.}\end{array}\right.$

b) When such negatives follow the verb, **no** must precede it. This means that then they are really affirmative in force.

No conozco a nadie en Nueva York. $\left\{\begin{array}{l}\textit{I know no one}\\ \textit{I do not know any-}\\ \textit{one}\end{array}\right\}$ *in New York.*

No tengo nada. $\left\{\begin{array}{l}\textit{I have nothing.}\\ \textit{I haven't anything.}\end{array}\right.$

No tengo ni pluma ni papel. $\left\{\begin{array}{l}\textit{I have neither pen nor paper.}\\ \textit{I haven't either pen or paper.}\end{array}\right.$

116. *Act or State in Continued Time.*

a) To express an act or state that continues from the past into the present, the present tense is used in Spanish, while in English the present perfect is used.

Hace tres semanas que él está aquí.
 He has been here for three weeks.

Hace dos años que vivimos en esta casa.
 We have lived, or *we have been living, in this house for two years* (and we are still here, hence the present tense).

But:

Hemos vivido dos años en esta casa.
 We lived in this house for two years. (We do not live here now, hence the perfect tense.)

b) Similarly, if the act or state continues from one period in the past into another less remote, the imperfect tense is used in Spanish, while in English the pluperfect is used.

Cuando Carlos vino hacía dos horas que estábamos aquí.
 When Charles came we had been here for two hours.

117. *Idioms with* **haber.** Review §§ 53, 54, 56, 70, 74, 78, 96.

Hay (había, etc.**) luna (sol).** *The moon (sun) is (was,* etc.*) shining.*
Hay (había, etc.**) lodo (neblina, polvo).** *It is (was,* etc.*) muddy (foggy, dusty).*

Haber de + infinitive
  Él ha de venir hoy. *He is to (He will) come today.*

Hay . . . que and **hay que** + infinitive
  Hay mucho que estudiar. *There is much to study.*
  Hay que estudiar mucho. *One has (It is necessary) to study much.*
  ¿ Qué hay? *What is the matter?*

EXERCISES

conozco *I know (am acquainted)*
la **gente** *people*
  haber: — **de** + inf. *to be to;*
    hay que + inf. *one must, it is necessary;* **hay . . . que** +
    inf. *there is . . . to;* **¿qué hay?**
    what is the matter?
hace 3rd pers. sing. pres. indic.
  of **hacer** *to do, make*
hacía 1st and 3rd pers. sing.
  imperf. indic. of **hacer** *to do, make*
limpiar *to clean*
el **lodo** *mud;* **hay —,** *it is muddy*
la **luna** *moon;* **hay —,** *the moon is shining*
nada *nothing;* **no . . . —,** *not . . . anything*

nadie *no one, nobody;* **no . . . —,** *not . . . any one*
la **neblina** *fog;* **hay —,** *it is foggy*
ni *nor;* **ni . . . ni** *neither . . . nor;* **no (ni) . . . tampoco**
  not (nor) . . . either
ninguno (ningún), -a *no, none;*
  no . . . —, *not . . . any*
nunca *never;* **no . . . —,** *not . . . ever, never*
Pedro *Peter*
el **polvo** *dust;* **hay —,** *it is dusty*
preguntar *to ask (questions)*
el **sol** *sun;* **hay —,** *the sun is shining*
tampoco *neither;* **no (ni) . . . —,** *not (nor) . . . either*
visto irreg. past part. of **ver** *to see*

A. 1. En la calle había mucha gente. 2. Enrique estaba allí con su amigo. 3. Le pregunté a Enrique: « ¿ Qué hay ? » 4. Me contestó: « Hace una hora que estoy aquí. 5. Pero no he visto nada. 6. Creo que un niño se cortó la mano. 7. Está en esa casa con el médico. 8. Pronto han de salir de la casa. » — 9. No hay nadie en este cuarto. 10. ¿ De quién es el sombrero que está debajo de la mesa ? 11. Hace varios días que está allí. 12. María

4*

tendrá que trabajar mucho aquí. 13. Hay que limpiar el cuarto bien. 14. Abrá la puerta y cierre las ventanas. 15. Hay mucho polvo en la calle. — 16. ¿ Por qué no viene usted nunca a verme ? 17. Hace varios meses que vivo en esta ciudad y no ha venido a mi casa. 18. Pero usted no va a mi casa tampoco. 19. Iré la semana que viene con mi hermano. 20. Ahora hay mucho lodo y a él no le gusta salir.

B. 1. ¿ Dónde había mucha gente ? 2. ¿ Quién estaba allí ? 3. ¿ Qué le preguntó usted a Enrique ? 4. ¿ Qué contestó Enrique ? 5. ¿ Qué había visto Enrique ? 6. ¿ Quién se cortó la mano ? 7. ¿ Dónde estaba el niño ? 8. ¿ Con quién estaba el niño ? 9. ¿ Dónde estaba el sombrero ? 10. ¿ Cuántos días hacía que el sombrero estaba allí ? 11. ¿ Quién tendrá que trabajar mucho ? 12. ¿ Qué hay en la calle ? 13. ¿ Cuántos meses hace que vive en la ciudad ? 14. ¿ Cuándo irá a verle ? 15. ¿ Con quién irá a verle ? 16. ¿ Por qué no le gusta salir ?

C. *I. Continue:* 1. Pienso venderla. 2. No pedí nada. 3. No encontré a nadie. 4. Yo no voy tampoco. 5. He de partir para Nueva York.

II. Translate: 1. Come early. 2. Go to bed now. 3. Open your eyes. 4. I know no one here. 5. It was foggy last night. 6. He never comes to this house. 7. He has nothing now. 8. I have been here two days. 9. The moon is shining now. 10. He had been working for ten hours.

D. 1. At what time do you have breakfast ? 2. Usually I have breakfast at eight o'clock. 3. But I got up early today. 4. I had breakfast at seven and I went out at half past seven. 5. I met my friend Peter on the street. 6. He had been ill for several weeks. 7. But he says that he is well now. — 8. I had six pencils yesterday. 9. But today I haven't any. 10. I gave them to the children this morning. 11. They came to see me at seven o'clock. 12. That is very early. 13. At what time did they get up ? 14. I believe that they got up at five o'clock. — 15. Will you give me some money to buy a hat ? 16. How much money do you want ? 17. I want three dollars for the hat and two for other things. 18. I have a dollar in my hand. 19. In this pocket I have twenty cents. 20. And in the other pocket I haven't anything.

LECTURA

Un predicador [1] tenía la costumbre de copiar de los libros de
oratoria [2] cuando preparaba [3] sus sermones. Un día un anciano [4]
se sentó cerca del púlpito. Apenas [5] hubo comenzado el predicador, el anciano dijo en voz alta:

— ¡ Eso es de Santander ! [6]

El predicador miró [7] al anciano pero continuó su sermón. Poco
después [8] el anciano dijo:

— ¡ Eso es de Pardo ! [6]

El predicador volvió a mirar al anciano pero continuó su sermón
después de una pequeña pausa. Pero después de algunos minutos
el anciano interrumpió [9]:

— ¡ Eso es de Manterola ! [6]

Esto [10] era demasiado.[11] La paciencia del predicador estaba
agotada.[12] Muy enfadado miró al anciano y le gritó:

— Si usted no se calla [13] tendrá que marcharse [14] de aquí. ¿ Me
oye [15] usted, necio ? [16]

— Eso . . . eso es de usted.

LESSON XXIV

118. *Future and Conditional of Probability.* The future indicative
is often used to denote probability or conjecture in present
time, and the conditional to denote probability or conjecture in past time.

> ¿ **Qué hora es ?** — **Será la una.**
> *What time is it? — It is probably about one o'clock.*
>
> ¿ **Qué hora era ?** — **Sería la una.**
> *What time was it? — It was probably about one o'clock.*
>
> ¿ **Dónde estará ?** { *Where can he (she, it) be?*
>   *I wonder where he (she, it) is.*

[1] *preacher.* [2] *oratory.* [3] *he prepared.* [4] *old man.* [5] *Hardly.* [6] Fathers
Miguel de Santander (1744–1831), Venancio Pardo (1838–1908), and Vicente
Manterola (1833–1891), famous Spanish preachers. [7] *looked at.* [8] **Poco
después,** *Soon afterwards.* [9] *interrupted.* [10] *This.* [11] *too much.* [12] *exhausted.* [13] *keep silent.* [14] *go away.* [15] *hear.* [16] *fool.*

119. *Use of the Definite Article* (2). The definite article is required before expressions of time modified by **próximo**, *next*, **pasado**, *past*, *last* (= *past*), and the like.

> **el lunes próximo**   *next Monday*
> **la semana pasada**   *last week*
> **el mes que viene**   *next month*

NOTE: There are many expressions for *next* when referring to time. Thus *next month* may be translated by **el mes que viene, que entra**, etc. In referring to a specific date **próximo** may be used, but **próximo** really means *nearest*, either in the past or in the future. **El mes próximo pasado** means *the last month past*.

120. *Names of the Months of the Year.*

enero	abril	julio	octubre
febrero	mayo	agosto	noviembre
marzo	junio	septiembre	diciembre

All are of the masculine gender.

> **el próximo mayo**   *next May*

121. *Days of the Month.* The cardinal numbers are used to express the days of the month, with the one exception of **primero**, *first*.

> **El primero, el dos, el tres**, etc., **de enero.**
> *The first, the second, the third, etc., of January.*

122. **Poner,** *to put, place, put on.*

PAST PART.	puesto
PRES. INDIC.	pongo, pones, pone, ponemos, ponéis, ponen
IMPERFECT	Regular
PRETERITE	puse, pusiste, puso, pusimos, pusisteis, pusieron
FUTURE	pondré, pondrás, pondrá, pondremos, pondréis, pondrán
CONDITIONAL	pondría, pondrías, pondría, pondríamos, pondríais, pondrían
COMMAND FORMS	ponga usted pongan ustedes

123. *Idioms with* **poner.**

> **ponerse,** *to become, turn;* *put on* (clothes)
>> **Se puso enfermo.** *He became ill.*
>> **Se puso el sombrero.** *She put on her hat.*
>
> **ponerse a,** *to begin*
>> **Nos pusimos a limpiar el cuarto.** *We began to clean the room.*

EXERCISES

abril *April*	**octubre** *October*
agosto *August*	**pasado, –a** *last, past*
ciento *one (a) hundred*	**pasar** *to pass, spend* (time)
diciembre *December*	**poner** *to put, place;* **—se** *become,*
enero *January*	*turn, put on* (clothes); **—se a**
febrero *February*	*begin*
julio *July*	**próximo, –a** *next*
junio *June*	**septiembre** *September*
el **lunes** *Monday*	**tanto** adv. *so much*
marzo *March*	el **tiempo** *time*
mayo *May*	**treinta** *thirty*
noviembre *November*	**veintiocho** *twenty-eight*

A. 1. ¿ A dónde piensa usted ir el mes de julio ? 2. El año pasado fuí a Nueva York en junio. 3. Mi abuelo tiene una casa allí. 4. En julio fuí al campo con mi hermano. 5. Este año pasaré el mes de julio en la ciudad. 6. Iré al campo el dos de agosto. 7. Volveré a casa el cuatro de septiembre. — 8. ¿ Ha visto usted a mi tío Pedro ? 9. Estará en su cuarto. 10. Se levantó temprano pero no ha salido de la casa. 11. Después de desayunarse se puso a escribir. 12. Hace dos horas que escribe. 13. ¿ A quién escribirá tanto ? 14. Ha escrito varias cartas muy largas. — 15. Hemos de ir a Nueva York el quince de mayo. 16. Hoy es el primero de febrero. 17. Vamos a contar los días. 18. Febrero tiene veintiocho días este año. 19. Marzo tiene treinta y uno y abril treinta. 20. Son ciento cuatro días.

B. 1. ¿ A dónde piensa usted ir el mes próximo ? 2. ¿ A dónde fué en junio del año pasado ? 3. ¿ Quién tiene una casa en Nueva York ? 4. ¿ Con quién fué usted al campo en julio ? 5. ¿ Dónde pasará usted el mes de julio este año ? 6. ¿ A dónde irá usted el dos de agosto ? 7. ¿ Cuándo volverá a casa ? 8. ¿ Dónde está

La rendición de Granada.

don Pedro ? 9. ¿ Cuándo se levantó don Pedro ? 10. ¿ Cuántas horas hace que escribe ? 11. ¿ Qué ha escrito don Pedro ? 12. ¿ A dónde hemos de ir el quince de mayo ? 13. ¿ Cuántos días tiene febrero este año ? 14. ¿ Cuántos días tiene marzo ? 15. ¿ Cuántos días tiene abril ?

C. *I. Continue:* 1. Me puse el sombrero. 2. Partiré el primero de octubre. 3. Hace tres semanas que vine. 4. Volveré el veinticinco de septiembre. 5. Me pondré a cortar el árbol con el hacha.

II. Translate: 1. Where have you put it ? 2. Are there many people here ? 3. One must work hard. 4. He drinks neither milk nor coffee. 5. I have not seen him either. 6. I asked him if she had returned. 7. It was about five o'clock when he came. 8. I saw him last week. 9. He will come next month. 10. He said that he would put it here.

D. 1. When did he arrive from New York ? 2. He arrived the eighth of last month. 3. He has been here for five days. 4. He says that he will leave next Monday. 5. He wishes to work, but he has not found anything. 6. Ask him if he has gone to Henry's store. 7. He tried to go one day, but he became ill. — 8. I'll put my hat here today. 9. I don't wish to lose it again. 10. Last month I lost one. 11. Didn't any one find it ? 12. No, there were many people where I left it. 13. I put my hat with others on a chair. 14. On going out I didn't find any on the chair. — 15. I saw

La rendición de Granada.

Mr. García this morning. 16. It was about seven o'clock when I met him. 17. He wrote to me in January that he would come to see me. 18. Who is Mr. García? I don't know him. 19. He is Charles' and Mary's father. 20. I think that you have never seen him.

LECTURA

— Un día en la clase — nos dijo ayer el maestro — hablamos del héroe español El Cid y luego de tres héroes hispanoamericanos. Para la semana próxima escriban en sus cuadernos algunos trozos [1] sobre el descubrimiento [2] de América.

Yo he copiado los siguientes [3]:

Algunos meses antes de la rendición [4] de Granada llegó al campamento [5] cristiano de Santa Fe un extranjero [6] que tendría cuarenta [7] y seis años de edad. Era de noble porte [8] y de cabello [9] que fué dorado [10] en su juventud,[11] pero blanqueado [12] ahora por el sufrimiento.[13] Tenía el aspecto triste y su mirada [14] grave expresaba entusiasmo y ansiedad.

Largos años había ido de corte en corte solicitando [15] apoyo para una empresa [16] inmortal: la de [17] hallar una nueva ruta [18] para ir al Asia o a las Indias, como entonces se decía.[19]

---

[1] *selections.* [2] *discovery.* [3] *following.* [4] *surrender.* [5] *camp.* [6] *stranger.* [7] *forty.* [8] *bearing.* [9] *hair.* [10] *golden.* [11] *youth.* [12] *whitened.* [13] *suffering.* [14] *look.* [15] *seeking.* [16] *undertaking.* [17] *that of.* [18] *route.* [19] *was said.*

LESSON XXV

124. *Past Participles* (2). If the infinitive of a verb ends in –ar, the past participle ends in –ado; if the infinitive ends in –er or –ir, the past participle ends in –ido (see § 52).

Estar:	**estado**	*been*
Haber:	**habido**	*had*
Venir:	**venido**	*come*

125. *Irregular Past Participles.* The following verbs are among those that have irregular past participles:

a) Otherwise regular verbs:

Abrir:	**abierto**	*opened, open*
Escribir:	**escrito**	*written*

b) Radical-changing verbs:

Volver:	**vuelto**	*returned*

c) Irregular verbs:

Decir:	**dicho**	*said, told*
Poner:	**puesto**	*put, placed*
Ver:	**visto**	*seen*

d) Verbs of the second or third conjugation whose stems end in a vowel (**a, e, o**), and which must have the accent mark on the ending –**ido**:

Leer:	**leído**	*read*

126. *Inflection of the Participle.* A past participle used as an adjective is inflected like an adjective.

un libro bien escrito	*a well written book*
una carta bien escrita	*a well written letter*

127. *Names of the Days of the Week.*

domingo	**miércoles**	**viernes**
lunes	**jueves**	**sábado**
martes		

All are of the masculine gender. They usually take the definite article if **próximo** or **pasado** is expressed or understood, or if used in a general sense (see § 92). Those ending in —**es** have the same form in the plural as in the singular.

Llegó el martes pasado.	*He arrived last Tuesday.*
Yo trabajo los sábados.	*I work on Saturdays.*
Pero no trabajo los viernes.	*But I do not work on Fridays.*

128. Decir, *to say, tell.*

PAST PART.	**dicho**
PRES. INDIC.	**digo, dices, dice, decimos, decís, dicen**
IMPERFECT	Regular
PRETERITE	**dije, dijiste, dijo, dijimos, dijisteis, dijeron**
FUTURE	**diré, dirás, dirá, diremos, diréis, dirán**
CONDITIONAL	**diría, dirías, diría, diríamos, diríais, dirían**
COMMAND FORMS	**diga usted** **digan ustedes**

EXERCISES

abierto *opened, open*	**el jueves** *Thursday*
el banco *bank*	**el martes** *Tuesday*
como *as*	**el miércoles** *Wednesday*
decir *to say, tell*	**el sábado** *Saturday*
el domingo *Sunday*	**el viernes** *Friday*
el huevo *egg*	

A. 1. Hace doce días que estamos aquí. 2. Llegamos el lunes de la semana pasada. 3. Y hoy es jueves o viernes ¿ no es verdad ? 4. Tenemos que volver a casa pronto. 5. No me gusta mucho esta ciudad. 6. No conozco mucha gente aquí. 7. Póngase el sombrero y vaya a la calle y a las tiendas. 8. Allí verá muchas cosas y encontrará amigos. — 9. Carlos ha ganado mucho dinero este año. 10. Me dijo en enero que no tenía ninguno. 11. Se puso a vender café, huevos y otras cosas. 12. Como no es haragán, trabajaba muchas horas al día. 13. En marzo tenía ciento veinticinco dólares en el banco. 14. Ahora tendrá mucho más. — 15. Juan le ha dicho a don Felipe que vendrá el lunes. 16. Quiere empezar a trabajar con él. 17. Ha de ganar veinte dólares a la semana. 18. Trabajará los sábados pero no los domingos. 19. Va a vivir con un amigo de su familia. 20. Irá a su casa los domingos.

B. 1. ¿ Cuánto tiempo (= *How long*) hace que estamos aquí ?
2. ¿ Cuándo llegamos ? **3.** ¿ Qué día es hoy ? **4.** ¿ Cuándo tenemos que volver a casa ? **5.** ¿ Se ha puesto ella el sombrero ?
6. ¿ Ha salido usted hoy ? **7.** ¿ Qué verá en las tiendas ? **8.** ¿ Qué
ha ganado Carlos este año ? **9.** ¿ Cuánto dinero tenía en enero ?
10. ¿ Qué se puso a vender ? **11.** ¿ Cuántas horas al día trabajaba ? **12.** ¿ Cuánto dinero tenía Carlos en marzo ? **13.** ¿ Dónde
tenía el dinero ? **14.** ¿ Qué le ha dicho Juan a Felipe ?
15. ¿ Cuánto ha de ganar ? **16.** ¿ Cuándo irá a su casa ?

C. *I. Continue:* 1. Le diría la verdad. 2. Vendré a las diez.
3. Me pondré el sombrero. 4. No he dicho nada. 5. He leído
la carta.

II. Translate: 1. He gave. 2. They went. 3. She would
come. 4. I would put. 5. We shall say. 6. They say. 7. Monday, Wednesday, and Friday. 8. Did they put it there ? 9. I
have not seen him. 10. Who has returned ?

D. 1. What did you tell your brother ? 2. I told him that I
would come today with Mary. 3. She and I left her house early.
4. But we met her uncle in the street. 5. We went to several
stores with him. 6. We had to return to his house with him.
7. We didn't come to see John, as we had told him. 8. We shall
have to come next Tuesday. — 9. Tell your brother that we are
not going to see him tomorrow. 10. I have written to him that
we shall go next Thursday. 11. We shall have to leave here on
Wednesday. 12. How long are we going to be with him ? 13. We
shall spend five days in his house. 14. We shall return next Tuesday. — 15. Get up, Peter, it is half past seven. 16. You have
to go to the store before going to the bank. 17. It is necessary
to buy several things. 18. We have neither milk nor coffee.
19. We haven't eggs either, and you like them. 20. Yes, but I
don't want to eat eggs today.

LECTURA

El viaje[1] inmortal de Cristóbal Colón fué preparado después
de la rendición de Granada. Los reyes[2] Fernando e[3] Isabel le
dieron el dinero necesario y le nombraron almirante[4]:

[1] *royage.* [2] *monarchs,* i.e. king and queen. [3] *and.* [4] *admiral.*

El día dos de agosto había mucha animación en el pequeño puerto [1] de Palos. En todas partes había grupos [2] de gente que comentaba [3] el asunto [4] del día. El pueblo, [5] por lo común tranquilo y desierto, estaba agitado por la fiebre [6] del gran [7] acontecimiento. [8] En todas las casas, en todas las esquinas [9] discutían [10] la loca aventura de un grupo de hijos del pueblo. Guiados [11] por Colón, iban a abrir una nueva ruta en el vasto océano desconocido. [12] Tres naves [13] estaban listas [14] para el viaje. Todos los tripulantes, [15] menos [16] uno, eran españoles. Español era también el apoyo moral y material para la expedición.

LESSON XXVI

129. *The Passive Voice.*

a) The past participle is used with **ser** to form the tenses of the passive voice when an agent is expressed.

> **Este libro fué escrito por un amigo de mi padre.**
> *This book was written by a friend of my father.*

b) The past participle agrees in gender and number with the subject.

> **La puerta es abierta por el criado.**
> *The door is opened by the servant.*

c) If the subject is inanimate, the reflexive construction (see § 110) is generally preferred in Spanish to the passive voice.

Aquí se habla español.	*Spanish is spoken here.*
No se sabe nada de él.	*Nothing is known about him.*
Se dice que habrá guerra.	*It is said that there will be war.*

[1] *harbor.* [2] *groups.* [3] *commented on.* [4] *subject.* [5] *town.* [6] *excitement.* [7] *great.* [8] *event.* [9] *street corners.* [10] *they discussed.* [11] *Led.* [12] *unknown.* [13] *vessels.* [14] *ready.* [15] *sailors.* [16] *except.*

130. **Por.** With passive verbs, *by* is expressed by **por;** but it may be expressed by **de** (instead of **por**) after some verbs that denote mental action.

<table>
<tr><td>La carta fué escrita por mi amigo.</td><td>*The letter was written by my friend.*</td></tr>
<tr><td>Él es amado de todos.</td><td>*He is loved by all (beloved of all).*</td></tr>
</table>

131. *Past Participle with* **estar.** When used with **estar,** a past participle has the force of an adjective and simply denotes a resultant state, rather than the passive voice.

<table>
<tr><td>El libro está escrito en inglés.</td><td>*The book is written in English.*</td></tr>
<tr><td>La puerta estaba abierta.</td><td>*The door was open.*</td></tr>
</table>

132. *Future and Conditional of* **salir,** *to go (come) out, leave.*

FUTURE		CONDITIONAL	
saldré	saldremos	saldría	saldríamos
saldrás	saldréis	saldrías	saldríais
saldrá	saldrán	saldría	saldrían

133. **Saber,** *to know, know how, can* (= *know how*).

PAST PART.	sabido
PRES. INDIC.	sé, sabes, sabe, sabemos, sabéis, saben
IMPERFECT	Regular
PRETERITE	supe, supiste, supo, supimos, supisteis, supieron
FUTURE	sabré, sabrás, sabrá, sabremos, sabréis, sabrán
CONDITIONAL	sabría, sabrías, sabría, sabríamos, sabríais, sabrían
COMMAND FORMS	sepa usted sepan ustedes

EXERCISES

costar (ue) *to cost*	la **luz** *light*
el **criado,** la **criada** *servant*	el **minuto** *minute*
de *about, by*	**mirar** *to look*
descansar *to rest*	la **oficina** *office*
la **guerra** *war*	**por** *by*

el **primo**, la **prima** *cousin*
   saber *to know, know how, can*
   (= *know how*)
   salir (**de**) *to leave*
el **teatro** *theater*

todavía *yet, still*
todo, –a *all*
viajar *to travel*
ya *already*

A. 1. Les he dicho a mis amigos que saldré para Cuba pronto.
2. Quería ir en mayo con mi primo. **3.** Pero él se puso enfermo.
4. El médico dijo que estaba muy malo. **5.** Yo no sé hablar español bien. **6.** Como mi primo lo habla muy bien yo quiero ir con él. **7.** Ahora está bueno y hoy vendrá a nuestra casa. **8.** Mi primo es un buen muchacho y es amado de todos. — **9.** Llegamos anoche a las once y media. **10.** Al entrar en la casa vimos una luz en el cuarto de mi padre. **11.** La puerta de la calle no había sido cerrada por el criado. **12.** Una de las ventanas estaba abierta. **13.** Mi padre me dijo que Juan no había vuelto todavía. **14.** Juan había ido al teatro con varios amigos. — **15.** Vamos al edificio donde mi hermano tiene su oficina. **16.** Creo que no está abierto todavía. **17.** Las puertas se abren a las ocho. **18.** Pero ya son las ocho y cinco minutos. **19.** Mi hermano llega a su oficina por lo común a las ocho y cuarto. **20.** Mire, allí está con don Felipe.

B. 1. ¿ Qué les ha dicho usted a sus amigos ? **2.** ¿ Cuándo quería usted ir a Cuba ? **3.** ¿ Por qué no fué usted ? **4.** ¿ Qué dijo el médico ? **5.** ¿ Sabe usted hablar español ? **6.** ¿ Cómo está su primo ahora ? **7.** ¿ Quién es un buen muchacho ? **8.** ¿ A qué hora llegaron ustedes a su casa anoche ? **9.** ¿ Qué vieron al entrar en la casa ? **10.** ¿ Qué no había sido cerrada ? **11.** ¿ Cuántas ventanas estaban abiertas ? **12.** ¿ Qué dijo su padre ? **13.** ¿ A dónde había ido Juan ? **14.** ¿ A qué hora se abren las puertas del edificio ? **15.** ¿ A qué hora llega su hermano a la oficina ? **16.** ¿ Con quién está él ?

C. *I. Continue:* **1.** Estoy cansado (–a). **2.** No sé mi lección. **3.** Yo saldría ahora. **4.** Me acosté temprano. **5.** Me levantaré a las seis.

II. Translate: **1.** He will not come out now. **2.** They know nothing. **3.** He will arrive on Monday. **4.** They cleaned the room. **5.** How many weeks did you spend here ? **6.** He began to study. 7. They washed their faces. 8. The child doesn't know how to count. 9. They served the meal. 10. He tried to cut the tree.

D. 1. Do you know who put this chair here ? 2. No, I don't know; I asked the servant if he knew. 3. He told me that Charles didn't want it in his room. 4. I don't want it here either. 5. Let us put it in another room. 6. Leave it here; you haven't many chairs. — 7. I have to buy a book for my mother. 8. She says that it was written by her grandfather. 9. She wants to give it to my cousin. 10. She doesn't know how much it costs. 11. And I haven't much money now. 12. I shall have to go to the bank. 13. Do you know at what time it opens ? 14. It must be open already; it is nine o'clock. — 15. We intend to go to California next month. 16. We shall leave here on [1] the eleventh. 17. We should leave on [1] the fifth but my cousin is going with us. 18. He is in New York now. 19. He will come on [1] the eighth with John. 20. He wants to rest before traveling again.

LECTURA

El trozo siguiente es una adaptación de lo que [2] dice Romera-Navarro en su *Historia de España*:

El once de octubre, después de setenta [3] días de navegación, vieron señales [4] de la proximidad de la costa. Hacía más de un mes que navegaban [5] por [6] mares [7] desconocidos. El día doce temprano resonó [8] un disparo [9] en la nave que iba delante [10] y todos comenzaron a gritar: ¡ Tierra! [11] ¡ Tierra!

Colón y los españoles que iban con él habían hallado el Nuevo Mundo. Pero la obra [12] del descubrimiento de un continente cuatro veces más grande que Europa no fué la obra de un hombre; fué la obra de miles de hombres, de miles de españoles que descubrieron [13] sus ríos, [14] sus cordilleras, [15] sus bosques [16] y sus desiertos. [17]

---

[1] *Omit.*   [2] **lo que,** *what.*   [3] *seventy.*   [4] *indications.*   [5] *they had been sailing.*   [6] *through.*   [7] *seas.*   [8] *resounded.*   [9] *shot.*   [10] *ahead.*   [11] *Land!*   [12] *work.*   [13] *discovered.*   [14] *rivers.*   [15] *(ranges of) mountains.*   [16] *forests.*   [17] *deserts.*

LESSON XXVII

134. *Possessive Adjectives* (2).

a) See § 48.

mío, −a, −os, −as	*my, (of) mine*
tuyo, −a, −os, −as	*your, (of) yours (thy, of thine)*
suyo, −a, −os, −as	*your, (of) yours, (of) his, her, (of) hers, its*
nuestro, −a, −os, −as	*our, (of) ours*
vuestro, −a, −os, −as	*your, (of) yours*
suyo, −a, −os, −as	*your, (of) yours, their, (of) theirs*

b) These longer forms follow the noun in direct address, and in indefinite expressions.

querido amigo mío	*my dear friend*
Padre Nuestro	*Our Father* (in the Lord's prayer)
una amiga suya	*a friend of his*

c) They are also used as predicate adjectives.

Esa pluma es mía.   That pen is mine.

NOTE: *Your, (of) yours* is often best expressed by **de usted: Este lápiz es de usted,** *This pencil is yours.*

135. *Demonstrative Pronouns.*

a)   éste, −a, −os, −as   *this (one), these*

ése, −a, −os, −as
aquél, aquélla, −os, −as   } *that (one), those*

esto   *this*

eso
aquello } *that*

Este libro es mío y ése es de usted.
   This book is mine, and that one is yours.

b) **Esto, eso,** and **aquello** are neuter. They are used to denote a thing not mentioned by name, or a mere idea. They can-

not represent a noun, since there are no neuter nouns in
Spanish.

> ¿ Qué es esto ?   *What is this?*
>
> ¡ Eso es!   *That's it!   That's right!*

NOTE: The masculine and feminine demonstrative pronouns are
distinguished by the accent mark from the demonstrative adjectives.
The neuter demonstratives are never used as adjectives, and therefore the neuter demonstrative pronouns do not need the accent
mark.

136. **Hacer,** *to do, make.*

PAST PART.	**hecho**
PRES. INDIC.	**hago, haces, hace, hacemos, hacéis, hacen**
IMPERFECT	Regular
PRETERITE	**hice, hiciste, hizo, hicimos, hicisteis, hicieron**
FUTURE	**haré, harás, hará, haremos, haréis, harán**
CONDITIONAL	**haría, harías, haría, haríamos, haríais, harían**
COMMAND FORMS	**haga usted hagan ustedes**

137. **Poder,** *to be able, can.*

PAST PART.	**podido**
PRES. INDIC.	**puedo, puedes, puede, podemos, podéis, pueden**
IMPERFECT	Regular
PRETERITE	**pude, pudiste, pudo, pudimos, pudisteis, pudieron**
FUTURE	**podré, podrás, podrá, podremos, podréis, podrán**
CONDITIONAL	**podría, podrías, podría, podríamos, podríais, podrían**

EXERCISES

algo *something*

aquél, aquélla, –os, –as *that
(one), those*

aquello *that*

ése, –a, –os, –as *that (one),
those*

éste, –a, –os, –as *this (one),
these*

esto *this*

gracias *thanks, thank you*

hacer *to do, make*

mío, –a, –os, –as *my, (of) mine*

la noche *night;* **esta —,** *tonight*

nuestro, –a, –os, –as *our, (of) ours*

poder *to be able, can*

querido, –a *dear, beloved*

si *whether*

suyo, –a, –os, –as *your, (of) yours,*

(of) his, her, (of) hers, its, their,
(of) theirs
tuyo, –a, –os, –as *your, (of) yours*
(thy, of thine)

unos, –as *some*
visitar *to visit*
vuestro, –a, –os, –as *your, (of)*
yours

A. 1. La carta fué escrita por aquel muchacho. 2. Sé que no
fué escrita por éste. 3. Este muchacho no haría eso. 4. Le
conozco bien. 5. Es hijo de un amigo mío. 6. Hace dos años
que vive aquí. 7. Él no sabe escribir bien todavía. 8. Aprende
a escribir ahora. — 9. Esa muchacha es prima mía. 10. Ha
viajado mucho y está cansada. 11. Dice que quiere descansar.
12. No podrá ir al teatro esta noche con nosotros. 13. ¿ Por qué
no se acuesta temprano? 14. Sí, lo hará después de comer algo.
— 15. María ha escrito a unas amigas suyas. 16. Pensaba visi-
tarlas este mes. 17. Ahora les dice que no podrá hacerlo. 18. Sus
amigas viven en Wáshington. 19. Y ellas no pueden venir a
esta ciudad. 20. Pero creo que María podrá ir el mes próximo.

B. 1. ¿ Por quién fué escrita la carta? 2. ¿ Qué no haría el
muchacho? 3. ¿ De quién es hijo? 4. ¿ Cuánto tiempo hace
que vive aquí? 5. ¿ Qué no sabe bien todavía? 6. ¿ Qué aprende
ahora? 7. ¿ De quién es prima esa muchacha? 8. ¿ Por qué
está cansada? 9. ¿ Qué quiere ella? 10. ¿ A dónde no podrá
ir con nosotros? 11. ¿ Cuándo se acostará? 12. ¿ Qué pensaba
hacer ella? 13. ¿ Qué les dice ahora? 14. ¿ Dónde viven sus
amigas? 15. ¿ Qué no pueden hacer ellas?

C. *I. Continue:* 1. El billete es mío (tuyo, etc.). 2. La casa
es mía. 3. Éste es bueno. 4. Saldré a las tres. 5. Fuí visitado
por mis amigos.

II. Translate, and then repeat in the plural: 1. The horse is
mine. 2. This one is easy. 3. The bank is ours. 4. That one
is fresh. 5. The table is theirs. 6. That one (yonder) is rich.

D. 1. Do you see (= ve) this? Do you want it? 2. I don't
know whether it is good or bad. 3. Look, it is a pencil. 4. Pencils
are not expensive. 5. But this one cost me three dollars. 6. Give
it to me. I should like to have it. 7. Take it, you are a good
friend of mine. 8. Thank you, I am going to give you a book
that you will like. — 9. Do you know whose are those two houses?
10. Yes, the white one is ours, but that one (yonder) is Philip's.

11. I did not know that.   12. A friend of mine had told me that that one was his.   13. Yes, but Philip bought it last month. 14. But he doesn't live in it yet. — 15. We wanted to go into that room.   16. There was a light in that one but not in this one. 17. We could not go in without [a] light.   18. My friend told me that he would not do it.   19. The room was his, not mine. 20. Why doesn't he want to do it ?

LECTURA

Tenemos que copiar y luego traducir [1] al inglés varios trozos sobre diferentes asuntos.

Alonso Alonso vive en Madrid.

Su Musa [2] (porque todo [3] poeta tiene su Musa, y Alonso Alonso es poeta) lo encontró un día en la calle de Fuencarral.

— Adiós, [4] Alonso . . . — dijo la Musa.

— Adiós, muchacha . . . — contestó él.

— ¿ A dónde vas ?

— A cualquier [5] parte.

— ¿ Qué tienes ? [6]

— Voy [7] muy triste.

— ¿ Por qué ?

— Porque me aborrezco. [8]

— Siempre lo mismo. [9]

— ¡ Hoy más que nunca ! [10]   Vengo de estar solo [11] en el Paseo [12] del Prado entre dos o tres mil personas.

— ¿ En qué trabajas ?

— En nada.

— ¿ Por qué ?

— Porque no tengo dinero.

— Razón [13] demás [14] para que [15] trabajes. [16]

— No tengo tiempo.

— Pues ¿ qué haces ?

— Pensar en que no tengo dinero.

P. A. DE ALARCÓN, *Narraciones inverosímiles.*

[1] *translate.*   [2] *Muse (inspiration).*   [3] *every.*   [4] *Greetings.*   [5] *any;* **cualquier parte,** *anywhere.*   [6] *What is the matter with you?*   [7] *I am.*   [8] *hate.* [9] *same.*   [10] *ever.*   [11] *alone.*   [12] *Promenade.*   [13] *Reason.*   [14] *extra, another.* [15] *in order that.*   [16] *you should work, (for) you to work.*

La calle de Alcalá, Madrid.

LESSON XXVIII

138. *Present Participles.*

a) Regular verbs:

Comprar: comprando
Aprender: aprendiendo
Vivir: viviendo

b) Radical-changing verbs of the third conjugation:

Dormir:	**durmiendo**	**Preferir:**	**prefiriendo**
Pedir:	**pidiendo**	**Servir:**	**sirviendo**

NOTES: 1. The radical vowels **e** and **o** are changed to **i** and **u** respectively.
2. The present participles of radical-changing verbs of the first and second conjugations are regular.

c) Some irregular verbs:

Decir:	**diciendo**	**Poder:**	**pudiendo**
Ir:	**yendo**	**Venir:**	**viniendo**

NOTE: Many irregular verbs form their present participles regularly.

d) If the stem of a verb of the second or third conjugation ends in a vowel, **-iendo** becomes **-yendo** (see § 246).

Creer: creyendo   **Leer: leyendo**

139. *Invariability of the Present Participle.* The present participle is invariable in form.

Ví a un muchacho (una muchacha) leyendo un libro.
I saw a boy (girl) reading a book.

NOTE: Review § 102*c*, *d*.

140. *Progressive Forms of Verbs.* English *to be* + present participle often equals Spanish **estar** or **ir** + present participle. **Ir** is used to denote motion or change of condition.

Estoy estudiando.	*I am studying.*
Estábamos trabajando.	*We were working.*
Va corriendo.	{ *He is running.* *He goes on the run.*
Se fué poniendo pálida.	*She was turning pale.*

NOTES: 1. The progressive forms are used to express an act or state as in progress at the time to which the speaker refers. They are used less often and are more emphatic in Spanish than in English. 2. **Estar** is not used with the present participle of **estar, haber,** and **ir** to form the progressive tenses.

141. *Position of Object Pronouns (3).* Personal pronoun objects follow a present participle and are attached to it so that the verb and object or objects form one word. The participle then requires the accent mark.

mirándome   looking at me

NOTE: In compound progressive tenses the pronoun object frequently precedes the auxiliary verb: **me estaba mirando,** *he was looking at me.*

142. **Creer,** *to believe, think.*

PARTICIPLES	**creyendo, creído**
PRES. INDIC. } **IMPERF. INDIC.**	Regular
PRETERITE	**creí, creíste, creyó, creímos, creísteis, creyeron**
FUTURE } **CONDITIONAL**	Regular
COMMAND FORMS	**crea usted** **crean ustedes**

NOTE: **Leer** is conjugated like **creer.**

143. **Querer,** *to wish, want.*

PARTICIPLES	Regular
PRES. INDIC.	**quiero, quieres, quiere, queremos, queréis, quieren**
IMPERF. INDIC.	Regular
PRETERITE	**quise, quisiste, quiso, quisimos, quisisteis, quisieron**
FUTURE } **CONDITIONAL**	See § 96

EXERCISES

correr *to run*   **listo, –a** *ready*
creer *to believe, think*   **pálido, –a** *pale*
esperar *to hope, expect*   **que** rel. pron. *which*
el estado *state*   **usar** *to use*
la historia *history, story*

A. 1. Esta mañana Juan y yo nos levantamos a las seis. **2.** Nos desayunamos a las siete y salimos. **3.** Esperábamos encontrar a Carlos y a su hermana a las ocho y media. **4.** Pensábamos ir a varias tiendas y después al teatro. **5.** Como era temprano no fuimos a la casa de Carlos. **6.** Fuimos a la oficina de su primo en el banco. **7.** El primo de Carlos ya estaba trabajando. **8.** Nos dijo que Carlos estaba durmiendo todavía. — **9.** Mi tío vino a verme anoche. **10.** Yo estaba estudiando mis lecciones. **11.** Mi tío me dijo que había comprado un caballo. **12.** El caballo no era para él. **13.** Le pregunté si era para mi tía. **14.** Me contestó que si estudio mucho me lo dará a mí. — **15.** Ese libro que Pedro está leyendo no es suyo. **16.** Es mío, pero yo lo leí ayer. **17.** Es la historia de una guerra en Cuba. **18.** Fué escrita por un amigo mío. **19.** Si usted quiere leer el libro, se lo daré mañana. **20.** Pedro lo acabará pronto.

B. 1. ¿A qué hora se levantaron usted y Juan? **2.** ¿A qué hora se desayunaron? **3.** ¿A qué hora se desayunó usted esta mañana? **4.** ¿A quién esperaban encontrar ustedes? **5.** ¿A dónde pensaban ir? **6.** ¿A dónde fueron ustedes? **7.** ¿Qué hacía el primo de Carlos? **8.** ¿Qué hacía Carlos? **9.** ¿Quién vino a verle a usted anoche? **10.** ¿Qué estaba haciendo usted? **11.** ¿Qué le dijo su tío? **12.** ¿Qué le preguntó usted? **13.** ¿Qué le contestó su tío? **14.** ¿De quién es el libro que está leyendo Pedro? **15.** ¿Por quién fué escrito el libro? **16.** ¿Cuándo lo acabará Pedro?

C. *I. Give the present and past participles of the following verbs:*

abrir   empezar   haber   saber   ver
contar   escribir   poner   tener   volver

II. Translate: **1.** She fed him. **2.** They are going. **3.** That is not good. **4.** He will come. **5.** The house doesn't face the

street. 6. Did they come? 7. We lay down here. 8. We didn't
come. 9. We were going. 10. When would she come?

D. 1. Do you know where the servant is? 2. I think that she
is in Henry's room. 3. She told me that she was going to clean
it. 4. She must be cleaning it now. 5. It is necessary to have
it ready before Monday. 6. Henry will come early on [1] that day.
7. He is traveling now in New York state.[2] 8. He will leave New
York City [2] on Monday at five o'clock in [3] the morning. — 9. Do
you want this pencil? 10. No, I want that one which is on the
table. 11. But I prefer a pen. 12. This one is new and very
good. 13. It isn't mine, but you can use it. 14. Thank you. I
wish to write a letter to Mary. — 15. Where are my uncle and
my cousin (*f*.)? 16. I don't know, but I think that they are
resting. 17. You know well that they have traveled a great deal.
18. After arriving here yesterday they visited several buildings
in the city. 19. It is true;, they must be very tired. 20. And
they want to go to the theater tonight.

LECTURA

En una discusión que Rubén Darío [4] tuvo en un café de París
su contrincante [5] se enfadó y le dió una bofetada.[6] Los amigos
impidieron [7] mayores [8] consecuencias.[9]

Darío, queriendo castigar a su agresor [10] por medio de [11] la ley,[12]
consultó [13] a un abogado.[14] Éste le dijo que no se podía hacer
nada.

Al día siguiente Darío se encontró con el autor de la afrenta.[15]
Se acercó [16] a él muy serio,[17] le saludó [18] y le dijo:

— He consultado a mi abogado sobre la bofetada que usted
me dió. Me ha dicho que no puedo hacer nada. Ahí [19] la tiene
usted.

Y poniendo [20] la acción a la palabra [21] se la devolvió [22] corregida [23]
y aumentada.[24]

---

[1] *Omit.*   [2] *state (city) of New York.*   [3] *of.*   [4] Rubén Darío (1867–1916),
famous Nicaraguan poet.   [5] *opponent.*   [6] *slap in the face.*   [7] *prevented.*
[8] *greater.*   [9] *consequences.*   [10] *aggressor.*   [11] **por medio de,** *by means of.*
[12] *law.*   [13] *consulted.*   [14] *lawyer.*   [15] *affront.*   [16] *approached.*   [17] *seriously.*
[18] *greeted.*   [19] *There.*   [20] *suiting.*   [21] *word.*   [22] *returned.*   [23] *revised.*
[24] *enlarged.*

LESSON XXIX

144. *Imperative Mood.*

a)   SINGULAR   PLURAL

   I. **Comprar:** compra (tú)   comprad (vosotrós, –as)   *(you) buy*
  II. **Aprender:** aprende (tú)   aprended (vosotros, –as) *(you) learn*
III. **Vivir:**   vive (tú)   vivid (vosotros, –as)   *(you) live*

b) The imperative mood is used only in affirmative commands.

> **Niño, estudia la lección.** *Child, study the lesson.*

145. *Subjunctive Mood. Present Tense.*

a)

I. **Comprar**	II. **Aprender**	III. **Vivir**
compre	aprenda	viva
compres	aprendas	vivas
compre	aprenda	viva
compremos	aprendamos	vivamos
compréis	aprendáis	viváis
compren	aprendan	vivan

b) The present subjunctive (1) may be used to express a direct command or wish (see § 98); or (2) it may be used in subordinate clauses.

> **No compre usted eso.** *Don't buy that.*

146. *Numerals (3).*

veintiséis	*twenty-six*	cincuenta	*fifty*
veintisiete	*twenty-seven*	sesenta	*sixty*
veintiocho	*twenty-eight*	setenta	*seventy*
veintinueve	*twenty-nine*	ochenta	*eighty*
treinta	*thirty*	noventa	*ninety*
treinta y uno (–a)	*thirty-one*	cien (to)	*one (a)* **hundred**
cuarenta	*forty*		

NOTE: **Cien** is used directly before the noun.

147. *Present Indicative of* **conocer,** *to know.*

conozco	conocemos
conoces	conocéis
conoce	conocen

148. *Meaning of* **saber** *and* **conocer.**

a) **Saber** means *to know, know how, can* (= know how) (see § 133).

> ¿ **Sabe usted la lección?**   *Do you know the lesson?*
> ¿ **Sabe el niño escribir?**   *Does the child know how to write?*

b) **Conocer** means *to know* (= be acquainted with), *meet* (= become acquainted with).

> ¿ **Conoce usted al señor Ortiz?**   *Do you know Mr. Ortiz?*

149. **Salir,** *to go* (or *come*) *out, rise* (the sun); **salir** (**de**), *to leave a place.*

PARTICIPLES	Regular
PRESENT INDIC.	**salgo, sales, sale, salimos, salís, salen**
IMPERF. INDIC. PRETERITE	} Regular
FUTURE CONDITIONAL	} See § 132
IMPERATIVE	**sal salid**
PRES. SUBJ.	**salga, salgas, salga, salgamos, salgáis, salgan**

150. *Idioms.*

> **Salió a la calle.**   *He went out* (*into*) *the street.*
> **El sol sale a las seis.**   *The sun rises at six o'clock.*

EXERCISES

aunque *although*
la **bicicleta** *bicycle*
cincuenta *fifty*
conocer *to know* (be acquainted with), *meet* (become acquainted with)
cuarenta *forty*
el **invierno** *winter*
noventa *ninety*
la **página** *page*
la **plumafuente** *fountain pen*

sesenta *sixty*
setenta *seventy*
siempre *always*
la **universidad** *university*
veintiséis (veinte y seis) *twenty-six*
veintisiete (veinte y siete) *twenty-seven*
veintinueve (veinte y nueve) *twenty-nine*

A. 1. Juan ¿ ha escrito usted el ejercicio ?   2. He estudiado la lección pero no he escrito el ejercicio todavía.   3. No tengo pluma

5

y no quiero escribirlo con lápiz. 4. Si quiere, use esta plumafuente. 5. No use ésa porque no tiene tinta. 6. Gracias. Voy a escribirlo ahora. 7. Creo que no tendré tiempo esta noche. — 8. Me gustaría leer un buen libro esta noche. 9. Aquí tengo uno que le gustará. 10. Es la historia de este estado. 11. Tiene ciento setenta y ocho páginas. 12. Usted podrá leerlo en cinco o seis horas. 13. Gracias. Empezaré a leerlo ahora. 14. Me acostaré después de leerlo. — 15. Juan me dice que mañana se levantará a las ocho. 16. Yo me levantaré antes de las siete. 17. ¿ Se levanta usted siempre tan temprano? 18. Sí, me levanto cuando el sol sale. 19. Y mañana saldrá a las seis y media. 20. Estaré listo para ir a la ciudad a las siete y cuarto.

B. 1. ¿ Ha estudiado usted la lección? 2. ¿ Qué ha escrito usted? 3. ¿ Por qué no ha escrito usted el ejercicio? 4. ¿ Con qué no quiere escribirlo? 5. ¿ Por qué no puede usar una plumafuente? 6. ¿ Cuándo va a escribir el ejercicio? 7. ¿ Cuándo no tendrá tiempo? 8. ¿ Qué le gustaría a usted leer? 9. ¿ Cuántas páginas tiene el libro? 10. ¿ En cuántas horas podrá leerlo? 11. ¿ Cuándo empezará a leerlo? 12. ¿ Cuándo se acostará usted? 13. ¿ A qué hora se levantará Juan mañana? 14. ¿ A qué hora se levantará usted? 15. ¿ Cuándo se levanta usted? 16. ¿ A qué hora salió el sol hoy? 17. ¿ A qué hora saldrá mañana? 18. ¿ Cuándo estará usted listo?

C. *I. Translate, and then repeat, using the object pronoun instead of the noun:* 1. He is studying his lesson. 2. We are drinking coffee. 3. He is teaching me English. 4. He was selling the books. 5. She is cleaning the room.

II. Translate: (a) *in four different ways:* 1. Drink the milk. 2. Come in here. 3. Read this letter. 4. Run to the house; (b) *in two different ways:* 5. Don't work now. 6. Don't leave that on the table. 7. Don't sell the house. 8. Don't open the window.

D. 1. I wrote to my uncle yesterday. 2. I told him that I want thirty-five dollars. 3. I have seen a bicycle that I wish to buy. 4. It costs forty-four dollars and ninety-nine cents. 5. I think that my uncle will give me the money. 6. Where did you

Posada española.

see the bicycle? 7. I saw it in Mr. García's store. 8. You know that they sell good things there. — 9. Do you know who that young lady is? 10. Yes, I met her last night in Mrs. Brown's house. 11. She is going to spend the winter in this city. 12. She expected to study in the University. 13. But she told me that she intends to work in an office. 14. I think that she will be able to work and study too. — 15. What are you going to do today? 16. I am going to write to my friend Emily. 17. She has been ill for a week. 18. Although she is well now she will not be able to go out for several days. 19. The physician told her that she will be able to go out next week. 20. She thought that she could visit us today.

LECTURA

— ¡ Perico ! [1]

— ¿ Qué manda [2] usted ?

— Oye ¿ cuánto te debo ? [3]   ¿ Diez comidas y seis almuerzos ? [4]

---

[1] *Pete.*   [2] *order (wish).*   [3] *owe.*   [4] *luncheons.*

— No, señor, no son más que [1] cuatro almuerzos y ocho comidas.

— ¡ Ah! Entonces, tráeme un cubierto [2] de tres pesetas.[3] Creí que te debía más.

— ¿ Me va usted a pagar ?

— No, digo,[4] sí; pero otro día. Me van a colocar.[5]

— ¡ Ah! ¿ Sí ? . . . ¿ Dónde ?

— Creo que en San Bernardino.

— ¿ De [6] pobre ? [7] . . .

— No, hombre, de director de la escuela. Si quieres entonces una plaza [8] en el asilo [9] . . .

— No, señor, muchas gracias. Lo que quiero es que me pague [10] usted pronto.

— Por eso no tengas cuidado.[11] Anda,[12] tráeme la comida y no se te vaya a olvidar de [13] apuntarla [14] en mi cuenta.[15]

CARLOS FRONTAURA, Las tiendas.

LESSON XXX

151. *Forms of the Verb to Express a Direct Command or Wish.*

a) **Comprar**

AFFIRMATIVE

Singular

compra (tú) compre usted	buy
(que) compre él	let him buy
(que) compre ella	let her buy

Plural

compremos	let us buy
comprad (vosotros, –as) compren ustedes	buy
(que) compren ellos (–as)	let them buy

[1] **no son más que**, *it is only.* [2] *(course) dinner.* [3] *peseta,* ½ of a Spanish dollar. [4] *I say (I mean).* [5] *place (give a job).* [6] *As a.* [7] *(poor) inmate.* [8] *position.* [9] *asylum.* [10] *pay.* [11] **no tengas cuidado,** *don't worry.* [12] *Go ahead.* [13] **no se te vaya a olvidar de,** *don't forget.* [14] *note (put) it down.* [15] *account.*

NEGATIVE

Singular

	no compres (tú) ⎫	
	no compre usted ⎭	*do not buy*
(que)	no compre él	*let him not buy*
(que)	no compre ella	*let her not buy*

Plural

	no compremos	*let us not buy*
	no compréis (vosotros, –as) ⎫	
	no compren ustedes ⎭	*do not buy*
(que)	no compren ellos (–as)	*let them not buy*

b) All regular verbs of the first conjugation are thus inflected. Regular verbs of the second and third conjugations use similarly the forms of **aprender** and **vivir** given in §§ 144 and 145.

NOTE: In the third person the **que** may sometimes be omitted. Without **que** the command is more direct.

c) The Spanish present subjunctive used in direct commands is generally to be expressed in English by *let* and the infinitive if the subject is not in the second person (see above).

Que hable él.   *Let him speak.*   **Descansemos.**   *Let us rest.*

NOTES: 1. If *let* means *allow* or *permit*, it is to be translated by **dejar** or **permitir**: **Déjeme usted entrar**, *Let me go in;* **Permita usted que Juan hable**, *Permit John to speak, Let John speak.*
2. The final –d of the plural imperative is lost before the object pronoun os, *you, yourselves:* **levantaos** (for **levantad-os**), *get up.* Exception, **idos** from **irse**, *to go away.*
3. The final –s of the first person plural of the present subjunctive is omitted before the object pronoun nos, *us, ourselves:* **levantémonos** (for **levantemos-nos**), *let us get up.*

152. *Position of Object Pronouns (4).* Review § 99. If the verb is introduced by **que**, a personal pronoun object precedes the verb.

Que lo haga él.	*Let him do it.*
Que las compre ella.	*Let her buy them.*
Que lo escriban ellos.	*Let them write it.*

EXERCISES

dejar *to let, allow*	**el número** *number*
después *afterwards*	**permitir** *to permit, let*
irse *to go away*	**sentarse (ie)** *to seat oneself,*
el momento *moment*	*be seated, sit, sit down*

A. 1. Juan, corre a tu casa. 2. Pregúntale a tu padre si tiene dinero. 3. No, espera un momento. 4. He encontrado algo que había perdido. 5. Es un billete de cinco dólares. 6. Lo tenía en este bolsillo. 7. Con él podré comprar muchas cosas. 8. No compre nada en esa tienda. — 9. Si usted está cansado puede sentarse aquí. 10. Gracias, me sentaré un momento. 11. Pero no estoy cansado aunque trabajé mucho hoy. 12. No trabaje tanto mañana. 13. No, mañana tengo que ir a la oficina de don Juan. 14. Trabajaré cinco horas y después iré al teatro. — 15. Juan y su padre estaban en un cuarto. 16. Era el cuarto de Juan. 17. El padre de Juan le dijo: 18. « El año pasado no estudiaste mucho. 19. Estudia más este invierno. 20. Si estudias mucho te compraré una bicicleta. »

B. 1. ¿ A dónde ha de correr Juan ? 2. ¿ Qué ha de preguntarle a su padre ? 3. ¿ Qué ha encontrado usted ? 4. ¿ De cuánto es el billete ? 5. ¿ Dónde tenía el billete ? 6. ¿ Qué podrá comprar con él ? 7. ¿ Está usted cansado (–a) ? 8. ¿ Qué puede hacer si está cansado (–a) ? 9. ¿ A dónde tiene que ir mañana ? 10. ¿ Cuántas horas trabajará ? 11. ¿ A dónde irá después ? 12. ¿ Dónde estaban Juan y su padre ? 13. ¿ De quién era el cuarto ? 14. ¿ Qué le dijo su padre a Juan ? 15. ¿ Qué le comprará si estudia mucho ?

C. *I. Translate, and then repeat with the verb in the plural:* (*With* **tú** *as the subject*) 1. Answer the letter. 2. Speak to your friends. 3. Open your eyes. — (*With* **usted** *as the subject*) 4. Teach me Spanish. 5. Eat the salad. 6. Leave the book here.

II. Translate, and then repeat in the negative: 1. Go into that room. 2. Sell the building. 3. Cut the tree. 4. Use this book. 5. Read the history of the war.

D. 1. We are studying the thirtieth [1] lesson today. 2. Have you written the exercise ? 3. On going out leave the papers on

[1] = *lesson thirty.*

the table. 4. Philip, do you know how to count from thirty to one hundred ? 5. Open your books on page seventy-eight. 6. You will find the numbers on it. 7. Study them again for tomorrow. 8. And study also the thirty-first [1] lesson. — 9. Do you know that Mr. Castro wishes to sell his house ? 10. I didn't know (it), no one had told me.[2] 11. But if he wishes to sell it, let him sell it. 12. The house is his, not ours. 13. But who is going to buy that house ? 14. It is old, and Mr. Castro wants [too] much for it. — 15. Although it is early, I shall get up now. 16. I like to get up when the sun rises. 17. No, don't get up so early. 18. The others will not get up now. 19. If they do not wish to get up let them not get up. 20. Let them rest one hour longer (= more).

LECTURA

— ¿ Tiene usted una gramática [3] francesa ?

— Sí, señor. Aquí la tiene usted.

— Diga usted ¿ esto es para aprender francés ?

— Creo que sí.[4]

— Es que [5] me la han encargado [6] del pueblo. Es para el herrador,[7] porque le ha caído [8] la lotería [9] y ha estado en Francia . . . Y ahora quiere aprender, y me ha encargado que le compre [10] este librote.[11] También le ha dado gana [12] de aprender a [13] la mujer [14] del alcalde,[15] y aprenderán los dos a un tiempo [16] . . . ¿ Cuánto vale ?

— Para usted, veinte reales.[17]

— Pero, hombre, si [13] me han dicho que nueva vale diez y seis.

— Sí, pero con las nuevas no se [18] aprende tan pronto.

— ¡ Ah ! ya [19] entiendo,[20] como no están usadas [21] . . .

— Es claro, por eso vale cuatro reales más.

CARLOS FRONTAURA, Las tiendas.

[1] = *lesson thirty-one.*   [2] = *me (of) it.*   [3] *grammar.*   [4] **Creo que sí,** *I think so.*   [5] **Es que,** *The fact is that.*   [6] *asked me (to get it).*   [7] *blacksmith.*   [8] *fallen (to the lot of).*   [9] *lottery;* **le ha caído la lotería,** *has won a prize in the lottery.*   [10] *to buy for him.*   [11] *(big or worthless) book.*   [12] *desire;* **le ha dado la gana,** *has taken a fancy.*   [13] Omit.   [14] *wife.*   [15] *mayor.*   [16] **a un tiempo,** *at the same time* or *together.*   [17] *real,* $\frac{1}{20}$ *of a Spanish dollar.*   [18] *one.*   [19] *now.*   [20] *understand.*   [21] *'broken in.'*

REVIEW LESSON C

I. *A.* Use the definite article with the following nouns:

agua	jueves	martes	postres
carne -	lunes	miércoles	restaurant
día	luz	noche	sol
gente	mano	plumafuente	viernes
hacha			

B. Supply the possessive adjectives, and demonstrative adjectives and pronouns corresponding to those in parentheses:

1. (*My, this, his, that one*) —— hermana escribió —— carta y —— primo escribió ——. 2. (*His, his, that*) —— tío ha vendido —— caballos y ha comprado —— casa. 3. (*This, mine, that one, his*) —— bicicleta es —— y —— es ——. 4. (*That, yours, this one, mine*) —— sombrero es ——, —— es ——. 5. (*This, his, those, mine*) —— muchacho ha perdido —— libros; —— son ——.

II. *A.* Give the present and past participles of the following verbs:

abrir	hacer	pedir	servir
dormir	ir	poner	venir
escribir	leer	salir	volver

B. Give the first and third persons singular of the present indicative of **acostarse, conocer, decir;** the third persons, singular and plural, of the preterite of **poder, servir, venir;** the first persons, singular and plural, of the future of **hacer, irse, poner.**

C. Give the first persons, singular and plural, of the present subjunctive of the following verbs:

abrir	gustar	mirar	salir
cortar	lavar	partir	visitar
entrar	limpiar	preguntar	usar

III. *A.* Complete the following sentences by supplying the proper negative pronoun or adverb (**nada, nadie, ni, ninguno, nunca, tampoco**):

1. No comió ——. 2. No encontré a ——. 3. Ni come —— bebe. 4. No ha dicho ——. 5. No engaña a ——. 6. No costó ——. 7. No descansa ——. 8. No hemos viajado ——. 9. No sabía ——. 10. No miraste a ——. 11. Él no vino ——. 12. Ella tiene una plumafuente y yo no tengo ——.

B. Change the following sentences to the passive voice:

1. Juan cierra la puerta. 2. La criada sirvió la comida. 3. Mi prima escribió este libro. 4. El padre de María ha comprado esta casa. 5. El muchacho cortará aquel árbol. 6. Mi tío vendió los caballos. 7. El criado abre las ventanas. 8. La muchacha halló la carta.

IV. *A.* Translate, and then repeat in the negative:

1. Cut that tree. 2. Clean this room. 3. Look at the boy. 4. Run now. 5. Use this pencil. 6. Buy the cheese. 7. Leave the hat here. 8. Read this letter.

B. Translate, and then repeat, changing the subject and verb to the plural of the same person:

1. He said good morning to me. 2. I have just seen her. 3. She opened her eyes. 4. You became pale. 5. Do you wish to go ? 6. He will not go out now. 7. She wants to come. 8. I shall go away next month.

V. Translate:

1. He has a good appetite. 2. I ordered meat and potatoes. 3. I don't like that fruit. 4. At what time do you go to bed ? 5. I got up at seven o'clock. 6. Did you lose your hat ? 7. My hands are cold. 8. They put on their hats and went away. 9. Usually I come at eight o'clock. 10. He will arrive next week. 11. There weren't many people. 12. I have been here for two days. 13. She wrote to me last week. 14. He must be there now. 15. We began to study. 16. I intend to do it now. 17. Mondays, Wednesdays, and Fridays. 18. What did he say ? 19. The doors open at five o'clock. 20. It is known that he is poor. 21. Do you know your lessons ? 22. She became ill. 23. Don't do that. 24. What will he do ? 25. Will he be able to come ?

LESSON XXXI

153. *Radical-changing Verbs* (2).

a) Imperative mood:

Cerrar:	cierra	cerrad	*close*
Contar:	cuenta	contad	*count*
Perder:	pierde	perded	*lose*
Volver:	vuelve	volved	*return*
Preferir:	prefiere	preferid	*prefer*
Dormir:	duerme	dormid	*sleep*
Pedir:	pide	pedid	*ask (for)*

b) Present subjunctive:

Cerrar: cierre, cierres, cierre, cerremos, cerréis, cierren

Contar: cuente, cuentes, cuente, contemos, contéis, cuenten

Perder: pierda, pierdas, pierda, perdamos, perdáis, pierdan

Volver: vuelva, vuelvas, vuelva, volvamos, volváis, vuelvan

Preferir: prefiera, prefieras, prefiera, prefiramos, prefiráis, prefieran

Dormir: duerma, duermas, duerma, durmamos, durmáis, duerman

Pedir: pida, pidas, pida, pidamos, pidáis, pidan

NOTES: 1. In the imperative and in the present subjunctive, as in the present indicative, the radical vowel e changes to ie or i, and the radical vowel o changes to ue, when the root is stressed.

2. In the third conjugation (but not in the first or second), the

128

radical vowel **e** changes to **i**, and the radical vowel **o** changes to **u**, in the first and second persons plural of the present subjunctive.

154. *Subjunctive in Substantive Clauses (1).* The present subjunctive may be used to express a direct command (§§ 145*b*, 151). It is also used to express an indirect command or wish, after **mandar,** *to command, order;* **pedir,** *to ask;* **querer,** *to wish, want;* **preferir,** *to prefer;* **aconsejar,** *to advise;* **dejar,** *to let, allow;* **prohibir,** *to forbid,* and the like.

> **Él manda que yo cierre la puerta.**
> *He orders me to close (that I shall close) the door.*
>
> **Quiero que tú seas feliz.**
> *I wish you to be (that you may be) happy.*
>
> **Preferimos que él la escriba.**
> *We prefer that he write (that he should write) it.*
>
> **Prohibo que tú entres en aquella casa.**
> *I forbid your entering (that you should enter) that house.*

NOTES: 1. In these sentences the Spanish subjunctive is expressed in English by: (1) the simple subjunctive (as in *that he write*); (2) *shall, should,* or *may* and the infinitive; (3) the infinitive alone; (4) the present participle (or gerund).

2. **Decir, escribir,** and the like, may be used as verbs of command: **Me escribe que vuelva a casa,** *He writes me to return home.*

155. *Infinitive for the Subjunctive.* If the principal and the subordinate verbs of a sentence have the same subject, the infinitive is used in Spanish instead of the subjunctive.

> **Quiero ser feliz.** *I wish to be happy.*
> **Preferimos escribirla.** *We prefer to write it.*

NOTE: The infinitive is often used in English even when the principal and the subordinate verbs have different subjects (see § 154). In Spanish the infinitive may be thus used only after a few verbs, such as **mandar, dejar,** and the like, chiefly when the logical subject of an affirmative subordinate verb is an unstressed personal pronoun: **Me mandó venir,** *He ordered me to come;* **No le dejamos entrar,** *We do* (or *did*) *not let him come in.*

EXERCISES

aconsejar *to advise*	**mandar** *to command, order*
alto, -a *loud*	**la mañana:** por la —, *in the*
la **clase** *class, classroom*	*morning*
enfadarse *to get angry*	el **padre:** pl. *fathers* or *parents*
entonces *then*	**por** *through*
feliz *happy*	**prestar** *to lend*
Francia *France*	**prohibir** *to forbid*
luego *soon, then*	la **voz** *voice*

A. 1. Emilia le ha escrito una carta a su hermano. 2. Le dice que está estudiando el español. 3. Ella quiere que Juan lo estudie también. 4. Le aconseja que lo estudie mucho. 5. Cree que él y ella podrán ir a Méjico. 6. Si pueden, irán este año. 7. El año pasado fueron a Francia. 8. Sus padres quieren que viajen mucho. — 9. No me gusta leer en la [1] clase. 10. El maestro me manda abrir el libro. 11. Me dice que lo abra en la página sesenta y cuatro. 12. Luego me pide que lea en voz alta. 13. Es la historia de una niña que no es feliz. 14. Yo no puedo leer en voz alta. 15. El maestro se enfada y me dice que cierre el libro. 16. Yo lo cierro y me siento. — 17. Esta mañana le pregunté a la criada: 18. « ¿ Ha limpiado usted el cuarto de Felipe ? » 19. Me contestó que no había tenido tiempo. 20. Pero yo sabía que había estado leyendo un libro. 21. Me dijo que limpiaría el cuarto después de almorzar. 22. Entonces yo me enfadé y le dije: 23. « No, quiero que lo limpie ahora. 24. Y no vuelva a hacer eso. »

B. 1. ¿ A quién ha escrito Emilia ? 2. ¿ Qué le dice en la carta ? 3. ¿ Qué quiere ella que él estudie ? 4. ¿ Qué le aconseja ? 5. ¿ Qué cree ella ? 6. ¿ Cuándo irán a Méjico ? 7. ¿ A dónde fueron el año pasado ? 8. ¿ Qué quiere su padre ? 9. ¿ Qué le manda abrir el maestro ? 10. ¿ Qué le pide luego ? 11. ¿ De qué es la historia ? 12. ¿ Qué dice el maestro ? 13. ¿ Qué le preguntó a la criada esta mañana ? 14. ¿ Qué contestó la criada ? 15. ¿ Qué había estado leyendo la criada ? 16. ¿ Cuándo dijo que limpiaría el cuarto ? 17. ¿ Qué dijo luego la criada ? 18. ¿ Qué le dijo usted entonces ?

[1] Omit.

C. *I. Read, changing the subject of the subordinate verb to **usted**:*
1. Quiero correr a casa. 2. Carlos prefiere contarlo. 3. Le aconsejo estudiar más. 4. Prefiero comprar otra plumafuente. 5. Queremos abrir la puerta. 6. Le prohibo levantarse.

II. Translate with **usted** *as the subject:* 1. Close the door. 2. Do not close the window. 3. Count the books. 4. Do not count them. 5. Return now. 6. Do not return there. 7. Sleep here. 8. Do not sleep now. 9. Ask for it. 10. Do not ask for so much money.

D. 1. The boy became pale. 2. His mother told him last night: 3. "Count the money that you have given me. 4. I gave you a two-dollar bill.[1] 5. The book and the paper cost a dollar and [2] ten cents. 6. How much money is there here? 7. When you go to the store I always tell you: 8. 'Count the money that they give you, and do not lose it.'" — 9. Ask John for your bicycle. 10. He has had it for a week. 11. You lent it to him last Thursday. 12. I forbid you to lend it again. 13. If you are not careful you are going to lose it. 14. You know that it cost me forty dollars. 15. And I shall not be able to buy another this year. 16. If John wants a bicycle let him buy it. — 17. Do you want me to close this window? 18. No, don't close that one now. 19. I prefer that you close the other. 20. The light of the sun enters through it. 21. The light of the sun doesn't allow me to sleep in the morning. 22. Don't sleep so much, my friend. 23. If you don't get up early, you can not work long.[3]

LECTURA

Una vez [4] que [5] Mark Twain estaba en una iglesia,[6] el sermon que predicó [7] el ministro [8] encantó [9] a todos menos al gran humorista.[10]

Como el ministro prefería el elogio [11] de Mark Twain al de [12] toda la concurrencia,[13] se acercó a él y le preguntó:

— ¿ Y qué dice usted de mi sermón, mi querido amigo ?

---

[1] *bill of two dollars.* [2] *Omit.* [3] *much.* [4] *time;* **una vez,** *once.* [5] *when.*
[5] *church.* [7] *preached.* [8] *minister.* [9] *delighted.* [10] *humorist.* [11] *praise.*
[12] **al de,** *to that of.* [13] *gathering.*

— Muy bueno. Pero tengo en mi casa un libro que lo contiene [1] todo, desde la primera hasta [2] la última palabra.

— ¡ No puede ser ! — protestó [3] el ministro indignado.[4]

— ¡ Ya lo creo que [5] puede ser ! Si quiere convencerse [6] venga [7] conmigo [8] y se lo mostraré.[9]

Fueron los dos a la biblioteca [10] de Mark Twain, tomó éste un libro y se lo entregó [11] al ministro.

Era el diccionario [12] de la lengua inglesa.

LESSON XXXII

156. *Some Irregular Imperatives.*

Decir:	di	decid	say (*tell*)
Estar:	está	estad	be
Haber:	he	habed	have
Hacer:	haz	haced	do (*make*)
Ir:	ve	id	go
Poner:	pon	poned	put (*place*)
Salir:	sal	salid	go (*come*) out
Ser:	sé	sed	be
Tener:	ten	tened	have
Venir:	ven	venid	come

157. *Stem of the Present Subjunctive.*

a) The present subjunctive has, as a rule, the same stem as that of the first person singular of the present indicative.

	PRES. INDICATIVE *1st person*	PRES. SUBJUNCTIVE
Conocer:	conozco	conozc–a, –as, –a, –amos –áis, –an
Decir:	digo	dig–a, –as, –a, –amos, –áis, –an
Hacer:	hago	hag–a, –as, –a, –amos, –áis, –an
Poner:	pongo	pong–a, –as, –a, –amos, –áis, –an

[1] *contains.* [2] *to.* [3] *protested.* [4] *indignantly.* [5] **Ya lo creo (que),** *Of course, certainly.* [6] *be convinced.* [7] *come.* [8] *with me.* [9] *will show.* [10] *library.* [11] *handed.* [12] *dictionary.*

Salir:	salgc	salg–a, –as, –a, –amos, –áis, –an
Tener:	tengo	teng–a, –as, –a, –amos, –áis, –an
Venir:	vengo	veng–a, –as, –a, –amos, –áis, –an
Ver:	veo	ve–a, –as, –a, –amos, –áis, –an

b) The exceptions to this general rule are the six verbs whose present indicative, first person singular, does not end in **–o.**

	PRES. INDICATIVE	PRES. SUBJUNCTIVE
	1st person	
Dar:	doy	d–é, –es, –é, –emos, –eis, –en
Estar:	estoy	est–é, –és, –é, –emos, –éis, –én
Ir:	voy	vay–a, –as, –a, –amos, –áis, –an
Ser:	soy	se–a, –as, –a, –amos, –áis, –an
Haber:	he	hay–a, –as, –a, –amos, –áis, –an
Saber:	sé	sep–a, –as, –a, –amos, –áis, –an

c) **Poder** (**ue**) and **querer** (**ie**) are inflected in the present subjunctive like radical-changing verbs of the second conjugation.

158. *Subjunctive in Substantive Clauses* (2).

a) The subjunctive is required after expressions of feeling or emotion, such as **temer,** *to fear;* **esperar,** *to hope;* **alegrarse** (**de**), *to be glad* (*of*); **sentir** (**ie**), *to regret, be sorry;* **ser lástima,** *to be a pity, be too bad,* and the like.

Tememos que él no venga hoy.	*We fear that he will not come today.*
Siento que usted esté enfermo.	*I am sorry that you are ill.*
Es lástima que Juan no estudie más.	*It is a pity that John does not study more.*

NOTES: 1. The infinitive is used if the two verbs have the same subject (see § 155): **Tememos no llegar a tiempo,** *We fear we shall not arrive in time;* **Siento estar enfermo,** *I am sorry that I am ill.*

2. A preposition is usually retained before a substantive clause in Spanish, but omitted in English: **Me alegro de eso,** *I am glad of that;* **Me alegro de que usted no lo crea,** *I am glad that you do not believe it.*

b) The subjunctive is required after expressions of *doubting* or
denying such as **dudar,** *to doubt*, and **negar (ie),** *to deny*.

Dudo que sea feliz.	*I doubt that (whether) he is* (or *will be) happy.*
Niega que sea verdad.	*He denies that it is true.*

159. *Use of the Subjunctive with Certain Negative Expressions.*
Expressions of *believing* or *saying*, such as **creer,** *to believe;*
decir, *to say;* **estar seguro (de),** *to be sure (of)*, and the
like, usually take the indicative; but when they are negative
or interrogative they may express doubt or denial, in which
case they take the subjunctive.

Creo que es feliz.	*I believe that he is happy.*
But: **No creo que sea feliz.**	*I do not believe that he is happy.*
¿ Cree usted que sea feliz ?	*Do you believe that he is happy?* (The speaker implies that he is in doubt.)

NOTES: 1. **No dudo, no niego,** and the like, may take the indicative to stress a fact: **No dudo que es feliz,** *I do not doubt that he
is happy;* **No niega que es verdad,** *He does not deny that it is true.*
2. The Spanish present subjunctive may express either present or
future time, and it is sometimes best translated into English by the
present or future indicative.

EXERCISES

alegrarse (de) *to be glad (of)*	**negar (ie)** *to deny*
bastante *enough*	**por** *for*
conmigo *with me*	**quedar**(se) *to remain*
dudar *to doubt*	**seguro, –a** *sure*
fácilmente *easily*	**sentir (ie)** *to regret, be sorry*
jugar (ue) *to play*	**temer** *to fear*
la lástima *pity;* **ser —,** *to be a pity, be too bad*	**el tiempo: a —,** *in time*
	viejo, –a *old*

A. 1. Mis padres viven en el campo. 2. Yo tengo que venir
a la escuela en la ciudad. 3. ¿ Conoce usted a mi tío Carlos ?
4. Vivo con él en aquella casa blanca. 5. Él es muy viejo y se
enfada fácilmente. 6. No quiere que yo me siente en su silla.
7. Me ha prohibido que ponga el sombrero en la mesa. 8. No le
gusta que yo duerma por la mañana. 9. Quiere que me levante
temprano siempre. — 10. Me alegro de que ustedes vengan a

visitar la clase. 11. No podemos quedarnos mucho tiempo.
12. Mire usted, aquella muchacha está muy pálida. 13. ¿ Cree
usted que esté enferma ? 14. No, no creo que esté enferma. 15. El
maestro le ha pedido que lea en voz alta. 16. Se pone pálida
siempre que tiene que leer. 17. Dudo que le guste leer en voz
alta. — 18. Don Carlos ha prohibido a sus niños que salgan de
la casa. 19. No quiere que salgan a la calle. 20. Teme que se
pierdan. 21. Ellos quieren jugar conmigo. 22. No podemos
jugar en el jardín. 23. Es pequeño y no podemos correr mucho.
24. Es lástima que don Carlos no esté aquí. 25. ¿ Cree usted
que se enfadará si los niños salen por un momento ?

B. 1. ¿ Dónde viven sus padres ? 2. ¿ A dónde tiene usted
que ir ? 3. ¿ Dónde vive usted ? 4. ¿ Quién se enfada fácilmente ?
5. ¿ Qué no quiere el tío ? 6. ¿ Qué ha prohibido ? 7. ¿ Qué no
le gusta ? 8. ¿ De qué se alegra usted ? 9. ¿ Quién está pálida ?
10. ¿ Qué le ha pedido el maestro a la muchacha ? 11. ¿ Cuándo
se pone pálida ? 12. ¿ Qué ha prohibido don Carlos a sus niños ?
13. ¿ A dónde no quiere que salgan ? 14. ¿ Qué teme don Carlos ?
15. ¿ Qué quieren los niños ? 16. ¿ Dónde no pueden jugar ?
17. ¿ Por qué no pueden correr mucho ? 18. ¿ Le gusta a usted
correr ?

C. *I. Translate with both* **tú** *and* **usted** *as subjects:* 1. Tell the
truth. 2. Do it now. 3. Put that on the table. 4. Go to the
store. 5. Come out of that room. 6. Be good. 7. Come early.

II. Translate: 1. I want to put it here. 2. He wants me to
put it here. 3. It is a pity that he does not know that. 4. I
am sorry that I can not go. 5. He is sorry that I can not do it.
6. He prefers to do it. 7. I prefer him to do it. 8. She hopes to
come. 9. I hope she will come. 10. He is not sure that she will
buy it.

D. 1. Tell the servant to go to the city. 2. I want him to buy
meat, eggs, and coffee. 3. I doubt if (= that) he has money for
all that. 4. If he hasn't enough let him go to the bank. 5. But
I don't believe that he can go now. 6. He has to clean the rooms.
7. There is no time for that today. 8. Tell him to do it in the
morning. — 9. They tell me that John has returned from France.
10. Yes, I am glad that he is here. 11. I want Mary to meet him.

12. I don't believe that he can come to visit us today. 13. But I don't doubt that he will come tomorrow. 14. Do you know if Philip returned also? 15. I believe that he will return next month. 16. His family hopes that he will come soon. — 17. Henry says that his mother is not happy. 18. She is poor and is sick. 19. Although she works she can not earn much. 20. I am sorry that she is not happy. 21. Advise her not to work hard. 22. And tell Henry to give her more money. 23. I am sure that he will do so (= it). 24. He is a good boy, and loves his mother dearly (= much).

LECTURA

— ¿ Quiere usted dar dos platos de sopa a estos niños?

— Sí, buena mujer.

— Mamá, pan.

— Sí, hijita,[1] sí, ya [2] te van a dar una sopa muy rica.

— Pan, pan, mamá.

— Calla,[3] niño, aquí se come y se calla.

— Yo quiero más.

— Niño, por Dios,[4] más no hay.

— Yo también quiero más.

— Pero niño, ahora no se [5] puede comer mas.

— Diga usted, buena mujer ¿ y usted no come? . . .

— No tengo hambre.[6]

— Ni dinero ¿ eh? . . .

— Tampoco.[7] Yo necesito [8] que coman mis hijos más que comer yo misma.[9]

— ¡ Pobre mujer! . . . También a usted le voy a dar de comer.

— No, a mí no, a mis hijos. Los inocentes [10] no saben todavía tener resignación.[11] . . . Yo, sí.[12]

— A ellos también les daré más. Siéntese usted, que [13] usted y sus hijos van a comer carne y pan, y arroz [14] con leche.

— Dios pague a usted esta caridad [15] tan grande.

CARLOS FRONTAURA, *Las tiendas.*

---

[1] *my dear (daughter).*   [2] *at once.*   [3] *Hush.*   [4] *please.*   [5] *you.*   [6] **No tengo hambre,** *I am not hungry.*   [7] *No* (= *not that, either*).   [8] *need.*   [9] *myself.* [10] *darlings* (innocent ones).   [11] *resignation;* **tener resignación,** *to be re-signed.*   [12] **Yo sí,** *I do.*   [13] *for.*   [14] *rice;* **arroz con leche,** *rice pudding.* [15] *act of charity.*

LESSON XXXIII

160. *Subjunctive in Substantive Clauses (3).*

a) The subjunctive is required after such impersonal expressions as **es preciso,** *it is necessary;* **importa,** *it is important;* **conviene,** *it is proper (suitable, well);* **es posible,** *it is possible,* and the like.

> **Es preciso que él diga la verdad.**
> *It is necessary for him to (that he should) tell the truth.*

> **Importa que vengan hoy.**
> *It is important for them to (that they should) come today.*

> **No es posible que yo lo haga.**
> *It is not possible for me to do it.*

b) However, after most of these expressions the infinitive is used, as in English, if it does not have a definite subject, and it may be used if, in Spanish, its logical subject is an unstressed personal pronoun object of the principal verb.

Importa venir hoy.	*It is important to come today.*
Les importa venir hoy.	*It is important for them to come today.*
No es posible hacerlo.	*It is not possible to do it.*
No me es posible hacerlo.	*It is not possible for me to do it.*

161. *Imperfect (or Past) Subjunctive.*

a) Spanish has two imperfect tenses of the subjunctive mood. These tenses are formed by adding the following endings to the stem of the preterite indicative, third person:

I.
    1. –ase, –ases, –ase, –ásemos, –aseis, –asen
    2. –ara, –aras, –ara, –áramos, –arais, –aran

II.   1. –iese, –ieses, –iese, –iésemos, –ieseis, –iesen
III. 2. –iera, –ieras, –iera, –iéramos, –ierais, –ieran

Comprar

PRETERITE
3rd pers. pl.

compr–aron
    1. compr–ase, –ases, –ase, –ásemos, –aseis, –asen
    2. compr–ara, –aras, –ara, –áramos, –arais, –aran

Aprender

aprend-ieron $\left\{\begin{array}{l} \text{1. aprend–iese, –ieses, –iese, –iésemos, –ieseis, –iesen} \\ \text{2. aprend–iera, –ieras, –iera, –iéramos, –ierais, –ieran} \end{array}\right.$

Vivir

viv-ieron $\left\{\begin{array}{l} \text{1. viv–iese, –ieses, –iese, –iésemos, –ieseis, –iesen} \\ \text{2. viv–iera, –ieras, –iera, –iéramos, –ierais, –ieran} \end{array}\right.$

b) A simple way to form the imperfect subjunctive which will apply in all cases, even in all irregular verbs, is to drop the final syllable (**–ron**) of the third person plural preterite and add **–se** (**–ses**, *etc.*) or **–ra** (**–ras**, *etc.*):

dar:	**dieron**	**diese (diera),** *etc.*
decir:	**dijeron**	**dijese,** *etc.*
ir:	**fueron**	**fuese,** *etc.*
pedir:	**pidieron**	**pidiese,** *etc.*
tener:	**tuvieron**	**tuviese,** *etc.*

NOTE: In subordinate clauses either form may be used, but the form in **–ra** is more common in Spanish America.

162. *Use of the Imperfect Subjunctive.*

a) If the principal verb of a sentence is past or conditional, the subordinate subjunctive verb is usually in the imperfect tense.

> **Yo quería que usted fuera feliz.**
> *I wished you to be (that you might be) happy.*

> **Temíamos que él no viniera hoy.**
> *We feared that he would not come today.*

> **Negó que fuese verdad.**
> *He denied that it was true.*

> **No sería posible que Pablo lo hiciera.**
> *It would not be possible for Paul to do it.*

But (see § 155):

Yo quería ser feliz.	*I wished to be happy.*
No sería posible hacerlo.	*It would not be possible to do it.*

b) The present perfect or the imperfect subjunctive is used after the present tense if the time of the subordinate verb is logically past.

Siento que usted haya estado   *I am sorry that you have been*
   enfermo.   *ill.*
Dudo que fuese feliz.   *I doubt that he was happy.*

NOTE: The present perfect and the pluperfect subjunctive are formed with the present and the imperfect subjunctive of **haber** and the past participle: **haya comprado (aprendido, vivido),** etc., (*that I may*) *have bought* (*learned, lived*), etc.; **hubiese (hubiera) comprado (aprendido, vivido),** etc., (*that I might*) *have bought* (*learned, lived*), etc.

EXERCISES

alquilar *to rent*
la **comedia** *comedy*
comprender *to understand*
convenir (conjugated like **venir**)
   to be proper, be suitable, be well
esperar *to wait* (*for*)

importar *to be important*
marcharse *to go* (*away*)
posible *possible*
preciso, -a *necessary*
seguida: en —, *immediately*
solo, -a *alone*

A. 1. Mi hermano y su esposa piensan ir a España. 2. Estarán allí dos o tres años. 3. Usted sabe que tienen una casa muy grande. 4. Conviene que la alquilen o la vendan. 5. Yo le aconsejé a mi hermano que la vendiese. 6. Le costó bastante dinero. 7. Hay aquí una familia que quiere comprarla. 8. Mi hermano irá conmigo mañana a visitarla. — 9. María me dijo ayer que le era preciso salir. 10. Me pidió que me quedara en su casa con el niño. 11. Quería que jugara con él. 12. No me fué posible hacerlo. 13. Se enfadó porque no pude venir. 14. Le dijo a Emilia que yo no quise venir. 15. No es posible que haya dicho eso. 16. Sí, no sabe que yo tuve que trabajar. — 17. Yo quería que mis padres viesen una buena comedia. 18. Pero no nos es posible ir al teatro esta noche. 19. Es preciso que nos quedemos en casa. 20. Pedro nos escribió que vendría con su hermana. 21. Yo le había dicho que vinieran a visitarnos. 22. ¿ Cree usted que vengan temprano? 23. Sí, importa mucho que vengan temprano. 24. Es preciso que vuelvan al campo esta noche.

B. 1. ¿ Ha estado usted en España? 2. ¿ Quiénes piensan ir a España? 3. ¿ Cuántos años estarán allí? 4. ¿ Qué tienen ellos? 5. ¿ Qué le aconsejó usted a su hermano? 6. ¿ Quién quiere comprar la casa? 7. ¿ A dónde irán ustedes? 8. ¿ Qué le dijo

María ayer? 9. ¿Qué le pidió? 10. ¿Qué quería María? 11. ¿Por qué se enfadó María? 12. ¿Qué le dijo María a Emilia? 13. ¿Qué no sabe María? 14. ¿Qué quería usted? 15. ¿Irá usted al teatro esta noche? 16. ¿Qué escribió Pedro? 17. ¿Qué le había dicho usted? 18. ¿A dónde es preciso que vuelvan?

C. *I. Give the imperfect subjunctive, either form, of the following verbs:*

dar	haber	ir	querer
decir	hacer	poner	ser

II. Translate, and then repeat, changing the main verb to the imperfect or the preterite: 1. Is she glad that I am coming? 2. He forbids that we do it. 3. I hope she is happy. 4. It is important for us to buy that. 5. It is proper for you to do it. 6. I am not sure that he has one.

D. 1. Are you sure [1] that John has arrived? 2. Yes, he had written to me that he would come soon. 3. But I doubted that he would come today. 4. It is a pity that his parents have not come. 5. I hoped that they would come also. 6. It is not possible for them to travel much. 7. They are old, and they prefer to stay at home. — 8. Ask Charles if he will lend me his bicycle. 9. My mother wishes me to go to the bank. 10. I am afraid that Charles is not at home now. 11. I don't believe that he has returned from (the) school yet. 12. Are you sure of that? 13. I am not sure, but he always returns with me. 14. I returned alone today although I waited for him. — 15. John and his cousin came to our house last night. 16. On seeing them we understood that they were tired. 17. They told us that they had just arrived from the country. 18. We asked them to sit down. 19. Although they were tired they did not wish to sit down. 20. They told us that they wanted to go immediately.

LECTURA

Los incas [2] opinaban [3] que en la paz [4] y en la guerra los superiores [5] deben [6] superar [7] a los inferiores [8] en todo lo que tienen que aprender para su oficio.[9]

---

[1] Supply *de.* [2] Members of the ruling Peruvian tribe before the conquest of Peru. [3] *thought.* [4] *peace.* [5] *superiors.* [6] *should.* [7] *excel.* [8] *inferiors.* [9] *calling.*

Atahualpa y Pizarro.

Cuando Atahualpa [1] era prisionero [2] de los españoles pidió a uno de los soldados [3] que lo guardaban que le escribiese en la uña [4] del dedo pulgar [5] el nombre [6] de Dios. Luego pidió a otro soldado que leyese lo que el primero había escrito.

Cuando más tarde [7] entró Pizarro [8] a verle, Atahualpa le pidió que también leyese lo que tenía en la uña. Como Pizarro no sabía leer no pudo hacerlo. Desde entonces Atahualpa menospreció [9] a Pizarro y se cree que esto aceleró [10] la muerte [11] del Inca.

[1] Atahualpa (1502–1533), 'the last of the Incas.'   [2] *prisoner.*   [3] *soldiers.*
[4] *nail.*   [5] *thumb:* **dedo pulgar,** *thumb.*   [6] *name.*   [7] *late;* **más tarde,**
later.   [8] Francisco Pizarro (1471–1541), discoverer and conqueror of Peru.
[9] *despised.*   [10] *hastened.*   [11] *death.*

LESSON XXXIV

163. *Subjunctive in Adjective Clauses.* The subjunctive is used in adjective clauses (introduced by a relative pronoun):

a) After a negative.

> **No encontré a nadie que hablase español.**
> *I did not find any one who spoke Spanish.*

NOTE: A clause that modifies a noun or pronoun is called an adjectival clause.

b) If the relative pronoun has an indefinite antecedent.

> **Yo buscaba un hombre que hablase español.**
> *I was looking for a man* (= any man) *who spoke Spanish.*

But: **Yo conocía a un hombre que hablaba español.**
> *I knew a man* (= some definite man) *who spoke Spanish.*

> **Déme un libro que no cueste mucho.**
> *Give me a book* (= any book) *that will not cost much.*

But: **Le dí un libro que no costó mucho.**
> *I gave him a book* (= a definite book) *that did not cost much.*

c) In clauses containing *whoever, whatever, however.*

> **Quienquiera que sea.** *Whoever he may be.*
> **Sea lo que sea.** *Whatever it may be.*
> **Por bueno que sea.** *However good it may be.*

164. **Ver,** *to see.*

PRES. PART.	Regular
PAST PART.	visto
PRES. INDIC.	veo, ves, ve, vemos, veis, ven
IMPERFECT	veía, veías, veía, veíamos, veíais, veían
PRETERITE	ví, viste, vió, vimos, visteis, vieron
FUTURE	
CONDITIONAL	Regular
IMPERATIVE	
PRES. SUBJ.	See § 157
IMPERF. SUBJ.	viese, vieses, etc.
	viera, vieras, etc.

165. Traer, *to bring.*

PRES. PART.	trayendo
PAST PART.	traído
PRES. INDIC.	traigo, traes, trae, traemos, traéis, traen
IMPERFECT	Regular
PRETERITE	traje, trajiste, trajo, trajimos, trajisteis, trajeron
FUTURE	
CONDITIONAL	} Regular
IMPERATIVE	
PRES. SUBJ.	traiga, traigas, traiga, traigamos, traigáis, traigan
IMPERF. SUBJ.	{ trajese, trajeses, etc. { trajera, trajeras, etc.

EXERCISES

buscar *to look for*	**pagar** *to pay*
interesante *interesting*	**prometer** *to promise*
lejos *far*	**quienquiera** (pl. **quienes-**
mayor *greater, greatest;* **calle**	**quiera**) *whoever*
Mayor *Main Street*	**traer** *to bring*
menudo: a —, *often*	**la vez** *time;* **una** —, *once*
moderno, -a *modern*	

A. 1. Ayer encontramos a nuestra amiga Isabel. 2. Hacía mucho tiempo que no la veíamos. 3. Ella acababa de salir de una tienda. 4. Le preguntamos si quería ir al teatro. 5. Nos dijo que primero tenía que comprar un sombrero. 6. En la tienda no había ninguno que le gustara. 7. Fuimos con ella a otra tienda. 8. Allí Isabel compró uno que no le costó mucho. — 9. Mis primos acaban de marcharse. 10. Cuando vivían en aquella casa los veíamos todos los días. 11. Ahora los vemos una vez al mes. 12. Vienen a vernos cuando mi tío los trae. 13. Dicen que no pueden venir a menudo. 14. Digan lo que digan, no vienen porque no quieren. 15. Su casa no está lejos de aquí. 16. Y los dos tienen bicicletas. — 17. Pedro quería que le trajera varios libros. 18. Esta mañana me dijo: « Vaya primero al banco. 19. Vaya después a una librería donde se vendan libros españoles. 20. Tráigame cinco o seis libros que sean interesantes. 21. Tráigame una historia de España. » 22. Fuí a la librería que está en la calle Mayor. 23. Traigo estos cinco libros españoles. 24. ¿ Cree usted que le gusten a Pedro ?

B. 1. ¿ A quién encontraron ustedes ayer ? 2. ¿ De dónde acababa de salir ella ? 3. ¿ Qué le preguntaron ustedes ? 4. ¿ Qué dijo Isabel ? 5. ¿ Qué no había en la tienda ? 6. ¿ A dónde fueron ustedes con ella ? 7. ¿ Quiénes acaban de marcharse ? 8. ¿ Cuándo los veían ustedes ? 9. ¿ Cuándo los ven ahora ? 10. ¿ Quién los trae ? 11. ¿ Qué dicen ellos ? 12. ¿ Por qué no vienen ? 13. ¿ Dónde está su casa ? 14. ¿ Qué tienen ellos ? 15. ¿ Qué quería Pedro ? 16. ¿ Qué dijo Pedro esta mañana ? 17. ¿ Cuántos libros quería Pedro ? 18. ¿ A dónde fué usted ?

C. *I. Repeat, changing the main verb to the present indicative and correspondingly the verb in the subordinate clause:* 1. Yo prefería una casa que fuera grande. 2. ¿ Se alegró usted de que él viniese ? 3. Ella esperaba que yo fuese a su casa. 4. Era lástima que él no lo comprendiese. 5. Temíamos que no se quedaran. 6. Dudábamos que él pudiera venir.

II. Translate: 1. I want you to see it. 2. I advise you not to bring it. 3. I do not see any one who knows me. 4. Tell him to bring the money. 5. Is it true that he brought it ? 6. It is important that he should see it. 7. It is necessary for us to bring it. 8. He regrets that I have been ill.

D. 1. John's parents wanted to rent a house. 2. They had sold the house that they had in the country. 3. It was necessary for them to find another at once. 4. They wanted one that would not be far from our house. 5. Doña María preferred one that might be modern. 6. But don Carlos did not want one that would cost much. 7. He said that it was not possible for him to pay much. 8. They found one that had ten rooms. — 9. Have you seen the comedy in the Cosmos Theater ?[1] 10. No, I have not gone to the theater for a month. 11. They have told me that the comedy is very interesting. 12. But I don't wish to go alone. 13. However good the comedy may be, I think that I shall stay at home. 14. I have been waiting for my cousin an hour. 15. He promised to come at seven o'clock. 16. If he does not come soon I shall get angry with him. — 17. Are you acquainted with a boy

[1] *Theater Cosmos.*

who knows Spanish? 18. Yes, I know one who has studied it a great deal. 19. He is a very talkative and inquisitive boy. 20. He is a friend of Miss García. 21. Whoever he may be, I should like to know him. 22. Bring him to my house tonight. 23. I have not understood this lesson. 24. It is important that you understand it before writing the exercises.

LECTURA

— ¿ Tendrá usted por casualidad[1] copas[2] iguales[3] a ésta?

— ¿ Qué le ha pasado[4] a usted, buena moza?[5]

— Estaba poniendo las copas en el aparador[6] y se me ha caído[7] una . . . Eso le pasa a cualquiera.

— No hay cosa más fácil.

— Y la señorita[8] me ha dicho que compre otra y que me la descontará[9] del salario.

— Hay casas donde obligan[10] a eso a las criadas . . .

— Bien,[11] cuando se rompe[12] todos los días[13] algo, pero ya ve usted que yo en un mes que llevo[14] en la casa no he roto[12] más que dos floreros,[15] seis vasos,[16] una sopera,[17] unos platos[18] que no valían[19] nada y la copa. Me parece que no es ninguna exageración.

— No, no es mucho romper.[12] Pues aquí tiene usted una copa igual.

Carlos Frontaura, Las tiendas.

LESSON XXXV

166. *Subjunctive in Adverbial Clauses.* The subjunctive is used in adverbial clauses:

a) After the temporal conjunctions **cuando,** *when;* **antes que,** *before;* **hasta que,** *until;* **luego que,** *as soon as;* **mientras**

---

[1] *chance.* [2] *goblets.* [3] *similar;* **iguales a,** *like.* [4] *happened.* [5] *girl.* [6] *sideboard.* [7] **se me ha caído,** *I dropped.* [8] *mistress.* [9] *discount, take off.* [10] *they oblige.* [11] *All right.* [12] **romper,** *to break;* past part., **roto.** [13] **todos los días,** *every day.* [14] *I have been.* [15] *flower vases.* [16] *(drinking) glasses.* [17] *soup tureen.* [18] *dishes.* [19] *were worth.*

(**que**), *as long as, while,* and the like, if future time is implied.

Cuando venga a verme le recibiré cordialmente.
When he comes to see me I shall receive him cordially.

No lo venda usted antes que yo lo vea.
Do not sell it before I see it.

Dijo que esperaría hasta que llegara el tren.
He said that he would wait until the train arrived (or *should arrive*).

NOTES: 1. A clause that modifies a verb is called an adverbial clause.
2. If future time is not implied, the indicative is used: **Cuando viene a verme siempre le recibo cordialmente,** *When he comes to see me I always receive him cordially;* **Cuando vino a verme le recibí cordialmente,** *When he came to see me I received him cordially.*

b) After **para que,** *in order that;* **de modo (manera) que,** *so as, so that;* **con tal que** or **siempre que,** *provided that:* **a menos que,** *unless;* **aunque,** *although, even if;* **dado que,** *granted that,* and the like, if the subordinate verb does not state something as an accomplished fact.

Le dí papel, pluma y tinta para que escribiese la carta.
I gave him paper, pen, and ink in order that he should (or *might*) *write the letter.*

Me escribió que compraría la casa con tal que no costase mucho.
He wrote me that he would buy the house provided (that) it did not cost much.

No aprenderé esta lección aunque estudie toda la noche.
I shall not learn this lesson even if I study all night.

NOTE: After **aunque, de modo que,** and the like, the indicative is used to state something as an accomplished fact: **No aprendí la lección aunque estudié toda la noche,** *I did not learn the lesson although I studied all night.*

167. *Conditional Clauses.*

a) The imperfect subjunctive is used in a conditional clause (or *if*-clause) to imply that the statement is either contrary to fact in the present or doubtful in the future.

Si yo tuviese (or tuviera) dinero lo compraría.
If I had money, I should buy it. (This implies that I have no money.)

Si yo tuviese (or tuviera) dinero mañana, lo compraría.
If I should have money tomorrow, I should buy it. (This implies that it is possible that I shall not have money tomorrow.)

b) In the conclusion of such a sentence the conditional tense or, less often, the imperfect subjunctive in **-ra** is used, but not the imperfect subjunctive in **-se**.

Si yo tuviese (or tuviera) dinero, lo compraría (or comprara).
If I had money, I should buy it.

EXERCISES

acompañar *to accompany*
allá *there*
antes que *before*
el **arte** *art*
el **camino** *road, way*
cerrar *to shut*
la **condición** *condition*
construir *to construct, build*
cordialmente *cordially*
dado que *granted that*
hasta que *until*
la **manera** *manner;* **de — que** *so as, so that*
menos *less, least;* **a — que** *unless*

mientras (que) *as long as, while*
el **modo** *manner;* **de — que** *so as, so that*
necesitar *to need*
el **oro** *gold*
para que *in order that*
poco adv. *little*
recibir *to receive*
el **reloj** *clock, watch*
siempre que *whenever, provided that*
el **sitio** *place*
tal *such, such a;* **con — que** *provided that*
el **tren** *train*

A. 1. Mi amigo Pedro Morales trabaja en un banco. **2.** Aunque trabaja mucho gana muy poco. **3.** Gane lo que gane, necesita una casa. **4.** El y su esposa buscan una ahora. **5.** Quieren una casa moderna que sea pequeña. **6.** No les es posible pagar mucho. **7.** Creo que si vieran ésta la alquilarían. **8.** Hace un año que fué construida. — **9.** Ayer recibí una carta de nuestra prima Emilia. **10.** Nos dice que no podrá volver a la ciudad este mes. **11.** Mientras esté enferma tendrá que quedarse en el campo. **12.** Quiere que vayamos a verla. **13.** Si yo pudiera, iría a pasar algunos días con ella. **14.** Pero su casa está muy lejos. **15.** Yo he ido allá y no creo que esté lejos. 16. Siempre que no esté lejos mis padres me permitirán ir. — 17. Acabo de leer un libro muy interesante. 18. Es la historia del arte moderno. 19. La he comprado para que la leas. 20. Y deseo que la leas pronto. 21. Léela antes que María vuelva de Nueva York. 22. Es posible que ella vuelva el miércoles próximo. 23. Luego que la leas dásela a María. 24. Creo que ella puede usarla en una de sus clases.

B. 1. ¿Dónde trabaja Pedro Morales? 2. ¿Cuánto gana Pedro? 3. ¿Qué necesita Pedro? 4. ¿Qué buscan él y su esposa? 5. ¿Qué quieren? 6. ¿Cuánto pueden pagar? 7. ¿Qué recibió usted ayer? 8. ¿Qué dice Emilia? 9. ¿Dónde tendrá que quedarse? 10. ¿Qué quiere Emilia? 11. ¿Dónde está la casa de Emilia? 12. ¿Qué acaba de leer usted? 13. ¿Para qué ha comprado el libro? 14. ¿Qué desea usted? 15. ¿De dónde volverá María? 16. ¿Cuándo es posible que ella vuelva?

C. *Translate:* 1. Granted that he has money, he will buy it. 2. I shall give him money so that he may buy it. 3. Whoever says that does not know the truth. 4. I see him on Main Street frequently. 5. It is proper that we should write to him. 6. He can do that easily. 7. He denies that he knows it. 8. He is sorry that she has not come. 9. I met him here once. 10. Bring it before he comes.

D. 1. Henry wants me to sell him my bicycle. 2. I told him that I would sell it to him. 3. But I don't want to sell it unless I can buy another. 4. I asked him twelve dollars for it. 5. Although it is old, it is in very good condition. 6. He promised me to pay [for] it at once. 7. He may (= it is possible that he will) come to buy it soon. 8. When he brings me the money I shall give it to him. — 9. I shall not go unless you accompany me. 10. Do you wish to remain in this place? 11. No, I wish to return to my house at once. 12. But I doubt if it is possible for me to do so (it). 13. If I could go out I would go away immediately. 14. But the doors and windows are shut. 15. And I don't know the way to (= of) the city. 16. I don't know it either. — 17. Do you think your aunt will give you the money today? 18. She promised it to me three weeks ago. 19. She told me that she would give it to me today or tomorrow. 20. Provided she gives it to me, it doesn't matter whether it is today or tomorrow.

21. I am going to buy a gold watch. 22. I shall buy it even if she forbids me.[1] 23. I don't think that she will forbid you.[1] 24. But she doesn't want you to buy one that may cost much.

LECTURA

En un libro titulado [2] *Historietas* [3] *para todos* he hallado varias anécdotas interesantes. Voy a copiar tres o cuatro. Luego [4] las aprenderé y las recitaré [5] en la clase.

El médico ha dicho que Emilia necesita tomar aceite [6] de hígado [7] de bacalao.[8] Ella no quiere tomarlo, pero su madre la convence ofreciéndole un centavo por cada [9] cucharada.[10]

Emilia tiene una hucha [11] y siempre pone en ella los centavos que le da su madre.

Cuando se termina [12] la botella [13] del aceite rompen la hucha. Cuentan los centavos y hallan que el total sube [14] a más de cinco pesetas.

Emilia está muy contenta. Ha visto en la tienda varias cosas que desea comprar, pero le pregunta a su mamá:

— ¿Qué vas a comprarme con ese dinero?

— Otra botella de aceite de hígado de bacalao.

LESSON XXXVI

(In this lesson and in those that follow there is a review of rules of grammar given in preceding lessons, with the more important exceptions to the rules and certain less common constructions.)

168. *Definite Article (2).*

a)

	MASCULINE	FEMININE	NEUTER
Sing.	**el**	**la (el)**	**lo**
Pl.	**los**	**las**	

[1] *to me (you) it.* [2] *entitled.* [3] *Short Stories.* [4] *Later.* [5] *shall recite.* [6] *oil.* [7] *liver.* [8] *cod.* [9] *each.* [10] *spoonful.* [11] *money box.* [12] *is finished.* [13] *bottle.* [14] *amounts.*

b) The feminine **el** is used only immediately before a noun beginning with stressed a– or ha– (§ 105).

    el alma   *the soul*   **el hambre**   *the hunger*

c) Neuter **lo** is used with neuter adjectives that have the force of abstract nouns (§ 107); with (1) neuter pronouns, with (2) adverbs, and in (3) certain idiomatic expressions.

    (1) **lo mismo**   *the same*
         lo cual   *which*

    (2) **por lo menos**   *at least*
         lo más aprisa posible   *as fast as possible*

    (3) **Sabemos lo buena que es.**   *We know how good she is.*

169. *Use of the Article (3)*. The definite article is required:

a) With an adjective of nationality used to denote a language, except after **hablar** or **en** (§ 94*b*); with a noun used in a general sense to denote all of the thing or kind it names (§ 92*a*); with a proper noun modified by a title or descriptive adjective, except in direct address (§ 92*b*); instead of a possessive adjective, when speaking of parts of the body or articles of clothing, etc. (§ 111); with expressions of time modified by **próximo, pasado,** and the like (§ 119).

    He estudiado el francés.   *I have studied French.*
    No habla español.   *She does not speak Spanish.*
    Le gustan los caballos.   *He likes horses.*
    El señor Morales está aquí.   *Mr. Morales is here.*
    Perdió el sombrero.   *He lost his hat.*
    Vino el lunes pasado.   *He came last Monday.*

b) With some names of countries. These include all geographic names modified by an adjective, such as **los Estados Unidos** (also only **Estados Unidos**), and others, including the following:

    el Brasil   *Brazil*   **el Japón**   *Japan*
    el Canadá   *Canada*   **el Perú**   *Peru*
    el Ecuador   *Ecuador*

NOTE: Names of cities, as a rule, do not take the article, but to this rule, **la Habana,** *Havana,* and a few others are exceptions.

c) To modify an infinitive or a subject clause.

> **El hablar demasiado es un vicio.**
> *To talk tco much is a vice.*

> **Me enfada el que usted no quiera hacerlo.**
> *It angers me that you are not willing to do it.*

d) To express measure.

> **diez centavos la docena**   *ten cents a dozen*
> **a peso el metro**   *(at) a dollar a meter*

e) Before a noun used in apposition with a personal pronoun.

> **Nosotros los muchachos jugamos en la calle.**
> *We boys play in the street.*

> **Ustedes las muchachas prefieren quedarse en casa.**
> *You girls prefer to stay at home.*

170. *Changes in Spelling.*

a) According to the Spanish system of orthography, it is sometimes necessary to change the spelling of the stem of an inflected word, to show that the pronunciation does not change.

The sound of **k** occurs in: **ca, que, qui, co, cu**
The sound of hard **g** occurs in: **ga, gue, gui, go, gu**
The sound of **gw** occurs in: **gua, güe, güi, guo**
The sound of **h** (Spanish **j**) occurs in: **ja, ge (je), gi (ji), jo, ju**
The sound of **th** (Spanish **z**) occurs in: **za, ce, ci, zo, zu**

b) Study the changes in spelling that occur in the inflection of certain verbs (§ 244).

c) The preterite of **buscar, llegar, empezar.**

Buscar: busqué, buscaste, buscó, buscamos, buscasteis, buscaron
Llegar: llegué, llegaste, llegó, llegamos, llegasteis, llegaron
Empezar: empecé, empezaste, empezó, empezamos, empezasteis, empezaron

d) The present subjunctive of these verbs is:

> **busque, busques, busque, busquemos, busquéis, busquen**
> **llegue, llegues, llegue, lleguemos, lleguéis, lleguen**
> **empiece, empieces, empiece, empecemos, empecéis, empiecen**

NOTE: **Empezar** is also radical-changing.

EXERCISES

el **alma** f. *soul*
aprisa *fast;* **lo más — posible**
   as fast as possible
bello, –a *beautiful*
el **Brasil** *Brazil*
el **Canadá** *Canada*
cual *which;* **lo —,** *which*
la **cuenta** *account, bill*
demasiado adv. *too much*
la **docena** *dozen*
el **Ecuador** *Ecuador*
enfadar *to make angry*
la **estación** *station*
los **Estados Unidos** *United States*
la **Habana** *Havana*
el **hambre** f. *hunger;* **tener —,**
   to be hungry
la **iglesia** *church*

el **Japón** *Japan*
más *most*
menos: por lo —, *at least*
el **metal** *metal*
el **metro** *meter*
mismo, –a *same*
morir (ue) *to die*
la **paz** *peace*
el **Perú** *Peru*
el **peso** *dollar*
la **plata** *silver*
precioso, –a *precious*
que: lo —, *what*
rezar *to pray*
siguiente *following*
sufrir *to suffer*
útil *useful*
el **vicio** *vice*

A. 1. Acabo de recibir una carta del señor Castro. 2. Saldrá de la Habana el lunes próximo. 3. Su carta está escrita en inglés. 4. Me dice que sabe hablar inglés bien. 5. Pero no ha estudiado el francés. 6. Y cuando llegue de la Habana irá al Canadá. 7. Todavía no ha viajado por los Estados Unidos. 8. Es posible que yo le acompañe. — 9. Ayer cuando llegué a casa no ví a Enrique. 10. Le busqué en varios sitios pero no le encontré. 11. Entonces pregunté a María si le había visto. 12. Me dijo que Enrique estaba con la criada. 13. María le había dicho a ella: « Almuerce temprano. 14. Vaya a la tienda y pague esta cuenta. 15. Lleve al niño pero tenga mucho cuidado. 16. No quiero que el niño juegue en la calle. » — 17. Nuestra tía tiene una hermosa casa en el campo. 18. La semana pasada nos escribió que fuéramos allá. 19. Hoy salimos de nuestra casa temprano y fuimos a varias tiendas. 20. Llegamos a la estación antes que saliese el tren. 21. En el camino mi hermana había perdido el sombrero. 22. Yo le dije que en el campo lo necesitaba. 23. Yo no ·sabía lo cansada que ella estaba. 24. Aunque estaba cansada volvió al sitio donde había dejado el sombrero.

B. 1. ¿ Qué acaba de recibir usted ? 2. ¿ Cuándo saldrá de la Habana el señor Castro ? 3. ¿ En qué está escrita su carta ? 4. ¿ Qué le dice él ? 5. ¿ Qué no ha estudiado ? 6. ¿ A dónde irá ? 7. ¿ A quién no vió usted ayer ? 8. ¿ Dónde le buscó usted ? 9. ¿ Qué le preguntó a María ? 10. ¿ Con quién estaba Enrique ? 11. ¿ Qué le había dicho María a la criada ? 12. ¿ Qué tiene su tía en el campo ? 13. ¿ Qué escribió la semana pasada ? 14. ¿ De dónde salieron ustedes temprano ? 15. ¿ A dónde fueron ? 16. ¿ Cuándo llegaron a la estación ? 17. ¿ Qué había perdido su hermana ? 18. ¿ Qué le dijo usted a su hermana ?

C. *I. Give the preterite of* **almorzar, negar;** *the present subjunctive of* **jugar, pagar.**

II. Translate: 1. We shall do the same. 2. Write as fast as possible. 3. Study at least two hours. 4. We know how ill they are. 5. Horses are useful. 6. The child did not wash his face. 7. We English prefer peace. 8. They received us cordially. 9. I began to work. 10. Let us look for our father.

D. 1. What did Mary say to you when she was here ? 2. She said that she would buy the watch provided it was (of) gold. 3. I think that she will buy it even if her mother forbids her.[1] 4. She will have to pay at least fifty dollars. 5. She prefers gold to silver. 6. She says that gold is a precious metal. 7. She says also that she likes precious metals. 8. She always prefers what is beautiful to what is useful. — 9. The poor gentleman is in [a] bad condition. 10. We found him on the road resting. 11. He has not eaten anything for two days. 12. Hunger has made him suffer a great deal. 13. Go to the store as fast as possible. 14. Buy bread, meat, and eggs. 15. Do you know how much eggs cost ? 16. They cost thirty-five cents a dozen; that is what I paid yesterday. — 17. The paper was on the table. 18. I read the following on it: 19. "This morning I went to church. 20. I prayed

---

[1] *to her it.*

for the soul of my grandfather. 21. He always preferred peace
to war. 22. But he died in a war in Peru." 23. "Who has written this?" I asked. 24. "Don't you see that it is an exercise?"
John said.

LECTURA

Al leer la historieta que sigue [1] no pude menos de [2] reírme [3]
porque me recordó [4] un incidente en la escuela la semana pasada.

Perico llega de la escuela llorando.[5] Su mamá le acaricia [6] y
le pregunta:

— Pero hijo mío ¿ qué tienes? ¿ Por qué lloras?

El muchacho sigue [1] llorando y no contesta.

— ¿ Es que hiciste algo malo? Dime.

El muchacho llora más, pero al fin [7] contesta:

— Juan colocó un alfiler [8] en la silla del profesor para que se
pinchara [9] al sentarse. Yo, para que no se pinchara, quité [10] la
silla y el profesor cayó [11] al suelo.[12]

Perico llora un poco más y luego dice:

— Y el profesor me pegó [13] una bofetada.

— Bueno, hijo, no importa.

— Pero mamá, luego al salir de la escuela Juan me pegó otras
dos bofetadas para que no me metiera [14] en lo que no me importa.[15]

LESSON XXXVII

171. *Gender of Nouns (3).* The rule that nouns ending in –o are
usually masculine and those ending in –a are usually feminine has the following exceptions:

a) The name of a male being is masculine, even if the noun ends
in –a.

el cura *the priest* **el artista** *the artist,* m.

[1] **seguir,** *to follow* or *keep on.* [2] **no pude menos de,** *I couldn't help.*
[3] *laughing.* [4] *reminded (of).* [5] *weeping.* [6] *caresses.* [7] **al fin,** *finally.*
[8] *pin.* [9] *would be pricked.* [10] *took away.* [11] *fell.* [12] *floor, ground.* [13] *gave.*
[14] *interfere.* [15] *concern.*

b) **La mano,** *hand,* is feminine, and **el día,** *day,* is masculine.

> **Me corté la mano.**   *I cut my hand.*
> **Buenos días, amigo mío.**   *Good morning, my friend.*

c) **El mapa,** *map,* and some words of Greek origin ending in
 –ma or **–ta,** like **el poema,** *poem,* and **el planeta,** *planet,*
 are masculine.

> **¿ Tiene usted un mapa del Ecuador ?**
> *Have you a map of Ecuador?*

NOTE: Other nouns are **el clima,** *climate;* **el idioma,** *language;*
el diploma, *diploma;* **el programa,** *program;* **el telegrama,**
telegram; **el tema,** *theme, written exercise;* **el cometa,** *comet* (but
la cometa, *kite*), etc.

172. *Plural of Nouns* (2). A noun ending in a vowel adds **–s,**
and a noun ending in a consonant adds **–es,** to form the
plural. Exceptions to this rule are:

a) A noun that ends in a stressed vowel or diphthong adds **–es**
to form the plural.

> **rubí** *ruby*   **rubíes** *rubies*
> **rey** *king*   **reyes** *kings*

NOTE: But **mamá,** *mamma,* **papá,** *papa,* and all nouns ending in
stressed **–e,** add only **–s: papá, papás; café, cafés; pie,** *foot,*
pies, *feet.*

b) Nouns ending in unstressed **–es** or **–is** have the same form
in the plural as in the singular.

> **lunes** *Monday, Mondays*   **crisis** *crisis, crises*

c) Family names generally remain unchanged in the plural.

> **Martínez, los Martínez**   **García, los García**

173. *Nouns in Adjective Phrases.* An English noun used as an
adjective is generally expressed in Spanish by a noun preceded by **de** or **para.**

> **un reloj de oro** *a gold watch*   **una taza para café** *a coffee cup*
> NOTE: **Una taza de café** is *a cup of coffee.*

174. *Verbs in* –**cer** *and* –**cir**.

a) When a consonant precedes, **c** changes to **z** in the present indicative and present subjunctive whenever the verb ending begins with **o** or **a**.

Vencer, *to conquer, overcome*

PRES. INDIC.   venzo, vences, vence, vencemos, vencéis, vencen
PRES. SUBJ.   venza, venzas, venza, venzamos, venzáis, venzan

Zurcir, *to darn*

PRES. INDIC.   zurzo, zurces, zurce, zurcimos, zurcís, zurcen
PRES. SUBJ.   zurza, zurzas, zurza, zurzamos, zurzáis, zurzan

b) When a vowel precedes **cer** or **cir, z** is inserted before the **c** in the present indicative and present subjunctive whenever the verb ending begins with **o** or **a**.

Conocer, *to know*

PRES. INDIC.   conozco, conoces, conoce, conocemos, conocéis, conocen
PRES. SUBJ.   conozca, conozcas, conozca, conozcamos, conozcáis, conozcan

Lucir, *to shine*

PRES. INDIC.   luzco, luces, luce, lucimos, lucís, lucen
PRES. SUBJ.   luzca, luzcas, luzca, luzcamos, luzcáis, luzcan

EXERCISES

el **artista,** la **artista** *artist*	el **pie** *foot*
el **clima** *climate*	el **planeta** *planet*
el **cometa** *comet;* la **cometa** *kite*	el **poema** *poem*
la **crisis** *crisis*	el **programa** *program*
el **cura** *(parish) priest*	el **rey** *king*
el **diploma** *diploma*	el **rubí** *ruby*
gastar *to spend*	**tanto, –a** *so much (many)*
el **idioma** *language*	la **taza** *cup*
lucir *to shine*	el **telegrama** *telegram*
la **mamá** *mama, mother*	el **tema** *theme, written exercise*
el **mapa** *map*	**vencer** *to conquer, overcome*
el **papá** *papa, father*	**zurcir** *to darn*

A. 1. María, mamá dejó esto aquí para que usted lo zurciera. 2. Creo que papá lo necesita mañana. 3. Pero no es preciso que lo zurza ahora. 4. Zúrzalo antes que él vuelva. 5. Ahora tengo hambre y quiero que me dé algo. 6. Tráigame, por lo menos, una taza de café. 7. Tráigamela lo más aprisa posible. 8. Las tazas para café están en aquella mesa. — 9. La semana pasada mi primo fué al campo. 10. Fué a buscar un caballo que mi tío le había prometido. 11. Al pie de un árbol encontró dos muchachos. 12. Estos muchachos estaban durmiendo. 13. Uno de ellos tenía las manos muy frías. 14. Cuando abrieron los ojos vieron a mi primo. 15. Éste les dijo que se levantaran y le acompañaran. 16. Los muchachos tenían un mapa pero habían perdido el camino. — 17. Ayer recibí una carta de mi hermano Felipe. 18. En ella Felipe me dice lo siguiente: 19. « Siento que ustedes le den tanto dinero a Carlos. 20. Ha gastado mucho y no ha comprado nada bueno. 21. Creo que prefiere lo bello a lo útil. 22. El mes pasado compró dos lápices de oro. 23. Le costaron quince pesos y no los ha pagado todavía. 24. Me enfada el que no pague esa cuenta. »

B. 1. ¿ Para qué dejó algo la mamá ? 2. ¿ Quién lo necesitaba ? 3. ¿ Cuándo había de zurcirlo María ? 4. ¿ Tiene usted hambre ahora ? 5. ¿ Quiere usted una taza de café ? 6. ¿ A dónde fué su primo la semana pasada ? 7. ¿ Quién le había prometido un caballo ? 8. ¿ Dónde encontró dos muchachos ? 9. ¿ Qué tenía uno de los muchachos ? 10. ¿ A quién vieron cuando abrieron los ojos ? 11. ¿ Qué les dijo su primo ? 12. ¿ Qué tenían los muchachos ? 13. ¿ Qué recibió usted ayer ? 14. ¿ Qué dice Felipe en la carta ? 15. ¿ Qué ha comprado Carlos ? 16. ¿ Qué prefiere Carlos ? 17. ¿ Qué compró el mes pasado ? 18. ¿ Qué le enfada a Felipe ?

C. *I. Supply the proper form of the definite article before the following nouns, both in the singular and the plural:*

agua	flor	luz	papa
árbol	gente	madre	paz
billete	hacha	mano	plumafuente
café	hombre	martes	reloj
calle	jardín	mes	sol
carne	lápiz	metal	tren
ciudad	lección	mujer	vez
clase	lunes	noche	voz

II. Translate: 1. Has he a diploma ? 2. Do you like the program ? 3. I have not written the theme yet. 4. We saw the comet last night. 5. There have been many crises. 6. Let him conquer that vice. 7. Let us buy him a kite. 8. I don't want it to shine so much. 9. This costs a dollar a meter. 10. When did he die ?

D. 1. Have you read this poem ? 2. No, it is written in French, and I don't understand that language well. 3. It was written by a friend of mine. 4. It is the story of two kings of France. 5. Do you want me to tell it to you ? 6. One liked metals, and had much gold and silver. 7. The other liked rubies a great deal. 8. Don't tell me any more; I have read it in Spanish. — 9. I have just received a telegram from the González. 10. They want us to go and visit them. 11. They wish to meet (= know) you. 12. And I want you to know them. 13. One of the brothers, John, is an artist. 14. The other is the priest in (= of) that church. 15. John came (= arrived) from Brazil last Monday. 16. He says he doesn't like the climate. — 17. How many languages have you studied ? 18. I have studied German and French. 19. I am studying Spanish now. 20. I wish to travel through Ecuador and Peru. 21. You know that that language is spoken there. 22. Have you lessons every day ? 23. No, I spend (= pass) Saturdays and Sundays in the country. 24. I return Mondays and I meet my teacher in the station.

LECTURA

Un señor de aspecto muy distinguido entra en un restaurant, se sienta y después de mirar la lista [1] pide un plato de sopa. El mozo se la sirve. Después de un momento llama al mozo y le dice:

— Mozo, yo no puedo comer esta sopa.

El mozo se sorprende. Le da la lista y el señor pide otra clase [2] de sopa. El mozo se la sirve. Después de un momento el señor vuelve a decir:

— Mozo, yo no puedo comer esta sopa.

El mozo, muy sorprendido, no comprende lo que ocurre.[3] No

---

[1] *menu.* [2] *kind.* [3] *is happening.*

¡ No me han puesto cuchara!

le dice nada al señor y llama al administrador.[1]   Éste [2] se acerca
muy respetuosamente [3] y pregunta:

— ¿ Qué es lo que tiene [4] esa sopa ?   Todos los parroquianos [5]
la han encontrado muy rica.

— Oh, yo no digo que no sea [6] rica — contestó el señor — pero
yo no puedo comerla porque no me han puesto [7] cuchara.[8]

LESSON XXXVIII

175. *Omission of the Definite Article.*   The definite article is omitted
in Spanish, though required in English:

a) Usually before a noun in apposition.

Santiago, capital de Chile   *Santiago, the capital of Chile*

[1] *manager.*   [2] *The latter.*   [3] *respectfully.*   [4] **Qué es lo que tiene,**
What is the matter with.   [5] *customer.*   [6] *it is not.*   [7] *set (given).*   [8] *(a) spoon.*
6*

b) Before a numeral modifying a title.

Carlos Quinto	*Charles the Fifth*
Alfonso Doce	*Alfonso the Twelfth*

176. *Omission of the Indefinite Article* (2). The indefinite article is regularly omitted:

a) Before an unqualified noun in the predicate (see § 64a).

Su hermano es médico.	*Her brother is a physician.*

b) Before a noun in apposition.

Lima, ciudad del Perú	*Lima, a city in Peru*

c) Before **cierto,** *a certain;* **otro,** *another;* **ciento,** *one* (*a*) *hundred;* **mil,** *a* (*one*) *thousand;* and after **tal,** *such a.*

Cierto amigo mío me lo dió.	*A certain friend of mine gave it to me.*
Tengo otro hermano.	*I have another brother.*
Él tiene mil libros.	*He has a thousand books.*
No he visto tal cosa.	*I have not seen such a thing.*

d) In many idioms, such as:

Nunca lleva chaleco.	*He never wears a waistcoat* (*vest*).
No dice palabra.	*He never says a word.*
¡ Qué lástima!	*What a pity!*

177. *Possessive Adjectives* (3). Review §§ 48, 49, 134.

178. *Comparison of Adjectives* (1). Most Spanish adjectives form their comparative of superiority by prefixing **más,** *more,* to the positive, and their superlative by prefixing the definite article or a possessive adjective to the comparative. In the superlative the adjective stands in the same relative position as in the positive construction, and the article is not repeated after the noun.

Este hombre es rico.	*This man is rich.*
Este hombre es más rico que aquél.	*This man is richer than that one.*

| **Ellos son los hombres más ricos del mundo.** | *They are the richest men in the world.* |
| **Juan es mi más íntimo amigo.** | *John is my most intimate friend.* |

NOTE: When there is no real comparison, *most* may be expressed by **muy**, or the suffix **–ísimo**: **Es muy útil** or **Es utilísimo**, *It is most useful*.

179. *Verbs in* –**ger**, –**gir**, –**guir**, –**quir**.

a) All verbs in –**ger** or –**gir**, regular or not, change **g** to **j** before **o** or **a** of the endings in the present indicative and present subjunctive.

Coger, *to catch, gather*

PRES. INDIC.   **cojo, coges, coge, cogemos, cogéis, cogen**
PRES. SUBJ.   **coja, cojas, coja, cojamos, cojáis, cojan**

Dirigir, *to direct, address*

PRES. INDIC.   **dirijo, diriges, dirige, dirigimos, dirigís, dirigen**
PRES. SUBJ.   **dirija, dirijas, dirija, dirijamos, dirijáis, dirijan**

b) In the present indicative and present subjunctive, verbs in –**guir** omit their unpronounced **u**, which is not needed to indicate a 'hard' **g** before **o** or **a**.

Distinguir, *to distinguish*

PRES. INDIC.   **distingo, distingues, distingue, distinguimos, distinguís, distinguen**
PRES. SUBJ.   **distinga, distingas, distinga, distingamos, distingáis, distingan**

c) Verbs in –**quir** change **qu** to **c** before **o** or **a** of the endings of the present indicative and present subjunctive, as **qu** (denoting the **k** sound) is written in Spanish only before **e** or **i**.

Delinquir, *to be delinquent*

PRES. INDIC.   **delinco, delinques, delinque, delinquimos, delinquís, delinquen**
PRES. SUBJ.   **delinca, delincas, delinca, delincamos, delincáis, delincan**

EXERCISES

bonito, –a *pretty*
la capital *capital (city)*
cierto, –a *certain*
coger *to catch, gather*
el chaleco *waistcoat, vest*
la dalia *dahlia*
delinquir *to be delinquent*
dirigir *to direct, address*
distinguir *to distinguish*
Europa *Europe*
el guante *glove*
el hotel *hotel*
Inglaterra *England*
íntimo, –a *intimate*

Jorge *George*
llevar *to carry, wear*
mandar *to send*
mil *thousand, one (a) thousand*
el mundo *world*
la palabra *word*
parecer *to appear, seem*
la parte *part*
presentar *to present, introduce*
qué *what a*
quinto, –a *fifth*
la rosa *rose*
sexto, –a *sixth*

A. 1. ¿Qué tiene usted en la mano? 2. Es otra carta y un telegrama de mi primo Juan. 3. Acaba de llegar a Nueva York. 4. Vuelve de Europa con cierto amigo suyo. 5. Ha viajado mucho con este amigo. 6. Fueron recibidos cordialmente en muchas partes. 7. Dice que fueron presentados a Jorge Sexto. 8. Jorge Sexto es rey de Inglaterra. — 9. ¡Qué lástima que los niños no puedan ir al jardín! 10. Papá les ha prohibido entrar en él. 11. No quiere que jueguen allí. 12. Dice que mamá tiene flores muy bonitas. 13. No quiere que los niños las cojan. 14. A mí me gustan mucho las rosas. 15. Son más bonitas que las dalias. 16. Mamá tiene muchas rosas y dalias. — 17. Me dicen que aquel artista es muy pobre. 18. Sí, creo que gasta mucho y gana poco. 19. Su hermano es más rico que él. 20. Pero el artista parece más feliz. 21. Si fuera rico no sería feliz. 22. No comprendo por qué usted dice eso. 23. Si no fuera pobre trabajaría menos. 24. El trabajo le hace feliz.

B. 1. ¿De quién son la carta y el telegrama? 2. ¿A dónde acaba de llegar Juan? 3. ¿De dónde vuelve? 4. ¿Con quién ha viajado? 5. ¿Cómo fueron recibidos? 6. ¿A quién fueron presentados? 7. ¿A dónde no pueden ir los niños? 8. ¿Qué les ha prohibido su papá? 9. ¿Quién tiene flores muy bonitas? 10. ¿Le gustan a usted las rosas? 11. ¿Quién tiene muchas rosas? 12. ¿Quién es muy pobre? 13. ¿Gana mucho o poco el artista ? 14. ¿ Quién es más rico que él ? 15. ¿ Quién parece más feliz ? 16. ¿ Qué no comprende usted ? 17. ¿ Trabajaría el artista más si fuera rico ? 18. ¿ Qué le hace feliz ?

C. *Translate:* 1. Address the letter to him. 2. Don't gather those flowers. 3. Have you a map of France ? 4. Who was Alfonso the Twelfth ? 5. His brother is not a teacher. 6. Have you another pencil ? 7. I have a hundred and [1] twenty dollars. 8. He didn't say such a thing. 9. These are our diplomas. 10. Are these his rubies ? 11. Let him distinguish the good from the bad. 12. I don't want this to shine so much. 13. Let them overcome that vice. 14. Did the boy wash his feet ? 15. She brought me a cup of coffee.

D. 1. Have you received a [1] letter from your father ? 2. Yes, he is in Toledo, a city in Spain. 3. He hopes to spend two months there. 4. It is necessary for him to return soon. 5. His cousin, the priest, is very ill. 6. He wants us to write to him immediately. 7. It would be well to send him a telegram. 8. Address it to the hotel where he lives. — 9. That boy does not wear a hat in winter. 10. He does not wear a vest or gloves either. 11. I don't know if you are acquainted with him. 12. He is the son of an intimate friend of mine. 13. His father, Peter Vargas, is a physician. 14. I don't think you know Peter either. 15. Peter does not live here now. 16. He lives in Quito, the capital of Ecuador. — 17. For what are the axes that you bought ? 18. They are to cut several trees. 19. My uncle wishes to build two houses. 20. There are nine or ten trees that are very tall. 21. They are the tallest that I have seen here. 22. The trees would be taller than the houses. 23. My uncle wants them to be cut today. 24. They will begin to build the houses next week.

LECTURA

Pedro invita a Fernando a [1] ir al teatro.

— Acepto — contesta Fernando. — Pero primero tendrás que comer conmigo.

— Con mucho gusto.[2]

---

[1] Omit. [2] *pleasure.*

Al pagar le dice Fernando al mozo:

— Mozo, aquí tiene las veintidós pesetas de la comida. Como yo le respeto a usted, no le daré una propina,[1] pues considero que la propina degrada [2] tanto [3] al que la da como [3] al que la recibe. O mejor, le daré sólo un real para que medite [4] sobre la humillación de la propina.

Los dos jóvenes [5] van al teatro. Al salir, Fernando se empeña en [6] pagar a la mujer del guardarropa [7] y le da cinco pesetas.

— Mira, Fernando — dice Pedro — no te comprendo. Has dado al mozo sólo un real y a esta mujer cinco pesetas. ¿Y tus principios? [8]

— Necio. ¿No te has fijado en [9] el sobretodo [10] que esa mujer me dió?

LESSON XXXIX

180. *Apocopation of Adjectives* (2).

a) **Bueno,** *good;* **malo,** *bad;* **uno,** *one, an* or *a;* **alguno,** *some;* **ninguno,** *no, none:* **primero,** *first;* and **tercero,** *third,* lose the final –o of the masculine singular when they precede their noun.

un buen hombre *a good man*   **el primer libro** *the first book*

b) **Grande,** *great;* **santo,** *saint;* and **ciento,** *one (a) hundred,* generally lose the final syllable before the word they modify.

una gran ciudad	*a great city*
San Pablo	*Saint Paul*
cien pesos	*one hundred dollars*
But: **ciento dos pesos**	*one hundred and two dollars*

Note: **Santa** does not lose the final syllable: **Santa Isabel,** *Saint Elizabeth.*

[1] *tip.*   [2] *is degrading.*   [3] **tanto ... como,** *both ... and.*   [4] *you may meditate.*   [5] *young men.*   [6] *insists on.*   [7] *coatroom.*   [8] *principles.*   [9] **No te has fijado en,** *Didn't you notice.*   [10] *overcoat.*

181. *Position of Adjectives* (2). To the rule that Spanish descriptive adjectives usually follow their noun, there are these exceptions:

a) A descriptive adjective usually precedes its noun if it does not distinguish one object from another but merely names a quality characteristic of the object. It is then often used in a figurative sense. Compare:

la casa blanca	*the white house*
la blanca nieve	*the white snow*
una voz ronca	*a raucous voice*
el ronco trueno	*the raucous thunder*

b) A few adjectives have one meaning before, and another after, their noun.

un gran hombre	*a great man*
un hombre grande	*a big man*
una pobre mujer	*a poor woman*
una mujer pobre	*a poor (poverty-stricken) woman*
mi caro amigo	*my dear friend*
un caballo caro	*a dear (expensive) horse*
varios papeles	*several papers*
papeles varios	*miscellaneous papers*

182. *Agreement of Adjectives* (2). To the rule that an adjective agrees in number with its noun, there are the following apparent exceptions:

a) If an adjective modifies several singular nouns, the plural form of the adjective is used (see § 42).

El árbol y el edificio son altos.   *The tree and the building are tall.*
La leche y el café están fríos.   *The milk and the coffee are cold.*

b) Sometimes a plural noun is modified by several singular adjectives. This occurs when each adjective modifies only one of the individuals denoted by the noun.

Las lecciones primera y segunda.   *The first and second lessons.*

NOTE: For other rules for adjectives, see: Inflection, §§ 38, 39, 93; Position, § 40; Agreement, § 42.

183. *Change in Diphthongal Verb Endings* –ió *and* –ie–.

a) Verbs of the second and third conjugations, regular or not, whose stem ends in a vowel, change the **i** of the diphthongal endings –**ió** and –**ie**– to **y**, as unaccented **i** can not stand between vowels in Spanish (see §§ 142, 217, and 246).

Creer: cre–yendo (for cre–iendo); cre–yó (for cre–ió); cre–yeron (for cre–ieron); cre–yese (for cre–iese), etc.; cre–yera (for cre–iera), etc.; cre–yere (for cre–iere), etc.

b) The **i** of the endings –**ió** and –**ie**– disappears after certain irregular preterite stems ending in **j**.

Traer: trajo, trajeron, trajese, etc. (see § 165).

EXERCISES

algo *somewhat*	**ronco, –a** *raucous*
deber *should, ought*	**san** = **santo**
gran (**de**) *big, large*	**santo, –a** *holy, saint*
histórico, –a *historical*	**segundo, –a** *second*
llover (**ue**) *to rain*	el **trueno** (*peal of*) *thunder*
la **nieve** *snow*	**varios, –as** *several, miscella-*
Pablo *Paul*	*neous*

A. 1. Isabel fué a las tiendas ayer con su tía. 2. Era la primera vez que iba a la ciudad. 3. Le dimos algún dinero para que trajera varias cosas. 4. En una tienda vió un lápiz y una pluma de oro muy bonitos. 5. Creyendo que me gustarían los compró. 6. Costaron ocho pesos cuarenta y nueve centavos. 7. Yo los llevo siempre en el chaleco. 8. No los uso mucho porque no quiero perderlos. — 9. Pedro es un buen muchacho, pero es algo haragán. 10. Hace un mes que llegó del Ecuador. 11. El primer día que estuvo aquí durmió diez horas. 12. Me parece que no debe dormir tanto. 13. Éste es el primer invierno que pasa aquí. 14. Ayer se levantó a las diez de [1] la mañana. 15. Cuando vió la blanca nieve en la calle dijo: 16. « Yo no había visto nunca tal cosa. » — 17. Le dije al muchacho que trajese rosas para María. 18. Las ha puesto en la mesa con las dalias que yo traje. 19. Debemos dárselas a María antes que salga de aquí. 20. Ella parte para San Juan el lunes próximo. 21. ¿ Sabe usted dónde está

---

[1] *in.*

San Juan? 22. Sí, San Juan, capital de Puerto Rico, es una ciudad histórica. 23. Es una gran ciudad, pero no tiene muchos hoteles grandes. 24. María estará allí varios meses estudiando el español.

B. 1. ¿A dónde fué Isabel? 2. ¿Para qué le dieron dinero? 3. ¿Qué vió en una tienda? 4. ¿Por qué los compró? 5. ¿Cuánto costaron? 6. ¿Dónde los lleva usted siempre? 7. ¿Por qué no los usa mucho? 8. ¿Quién es un buen muchacho? 9. ¿Cuánto tiempo hace que llegó del Ecuador? 10. ¿Cuántas horas durmió el primer día? 11. ¿A qué hora se levantó ayer? 12. ¿Qué dijo cuando vió la blanca nieve? 13. ¿Qué le dijo usted al muchacho? 14. ¿Dónde ha puesto las rosas? 15. ¿A quién debemos dárselas? 16. ¿Para dónde parte ella el lunes próximo? 17. ¿Qué es San Juan? 18. ¿Cuánto tiempo estará María allí?

C. *I. Read, placing the proper form of the article before each noun:*

clima	diploma	mapa	papá	tema
cometa	idioma	papa	planeta	rubí

II. Translate, and then repeat, changing the form of the principal verb to the imperfect or the preterite, and correspondingly the subordinate verb: 1. I want him to believe me. 2. They hope we will believe them. 3. We ask them to bring it. 4. She writes us to bring them. 5. I doubt if she believes him.

D. 1. Who is that tall man? 2. I think that he is an intimate friend of Charles. 3. What a pity that Charles has not come! 4. It seems that the poor man has no friend here. 5. I addressed him in the French and Spanish languages. 6. He looked at me, but he didn't say a word. 7. Have you not introduced him to any one? 8. Yes, I have introduced him to several persons. — 9. A certain friend of ours came to see me last night. 10. I had not seen him for a long time. 11. "Have you some money?" he asked me. 12. Before I could reply he said to me: 13. "I need one hundred dollars at once." 14. "What [1] do you want so much money for?" I asked him. 15. Then, with a raucous voice, he said to me: 16. "I have to send it to my poor brother." — 17. Don't you want me to gather some flowers? 18. No, we

---

[1] *For what . . .*

gathered some yesterday and we still have them. 19. If it does not rain tomorrow we can gather more. 20. But I think that it is going to rain soon. 21. It is the third day that it has been raining, isn't it ? 22. Yes, it is a bad day for going out to the garden. 23. I don't like to go out when it rains. 24. I don't like it either because I am not well.

LECTURA

Eugenio María de Hostos,[1] el gran pensador [2] puertorriqueño,[3] tenía muy mala letra.[4] Sólo él podía descifrar [5] lo que escribía y algunas veces con dificultad.[6]

Cuando era Director de la Escuela Normal [7] de Santo Domingo se formó [8] allí una sociedad [9] protectora [10] de los animales.[11] Para cooperar [12] en la buena obra, Hostos escribió un artículo [13] sobre los animales amigos del [14] hombre.

En el artículo, al hacer el elogio del burro [15] escribió la frase [16]: « el pacienzudo [17] asno ». [15] El cajista,[18] no pudiendo leer bien el adjetivo,[19] puso: « el pescuezudo [20] asno ». Hostos corrigió la prueba [21] y escribió al margen [22]: « pacienzudo ». El cajista volvió a poner: « pescuezudo ». Entonces Hostos, habiendo perdido la paciencia, escribió: « más pescuezudo es el cajista ».

LESSON XL

184. *Comparison of Adjectives* (2). The following adjectives are compared irregularly:

bueno, mejor, el mejor, *good, better, best*
malo, peor, el peor, *bad, worse, worst*

grande, $\begin{cases} \text{más grande, el más grande, } large, larger, the\ largest \\ \text{mayor, el mayor, } large, larger \text{ or } older, the\ largest \text{ or } oldest \end{cases}$

[1] (1839–1903). [2] *thinker.* [3] *Puerto Rican* [4] *hand(writing).* [5] *decipher, make out.* [6] *difficulty.* [7] *Normal.* [8] *was formed.* [9] *society.* [10] *protective.* [11] *animals.* [12] *co-operate.* [13] *article.* [14] **amigo de,** *friendly to.* [15] **asno** (or **burro**), *donkey.* [16] *phrase.* [17] *exceedingly patient.* [18] *compositor* (in printing). [19] *adjective.* [20] *thick-necked.* [21] *proof.* [22] *margin.*

Eugenio María de Hostos.

pequeño, $\begin{cases} \text{más pequeño, el más pequeño, } small, smaller, the \\ \quad smallest \\ \text{menor, el menor, } small, smaller \text{ or } younger, the smallest \\ \quad \text{or } youngest \end{cases}$

mucho, más, *much, more* or *most*
poco, menos, *little (few), less (fewer),* or *least (fewest)*

NOTES: 1. **Mayor** means *larger* and **menor,** *smaller* in quantitative expressions such as **en mayor (menor) cantidad,** *in larger (smaller) quantity.*
2. When applied to persons, **mayor** means *older,* and **menor,** *younger.*
3. *Most,* used with a noun or pronoun, is generally expressed by **la mayor parte (de): la mayor parte de mis libros,** *most of my books.*

185. *Comparison of Adverbs.*

a) Spanish adverbs are compared like Spanish adjectives.

aprisa, más aprisa, (lo) más aprisa, *fast, faster, (the) fastest*

NOTE: The article is used with a superlative adverb only when the adverb is followed by **posible** or a like expression: **Pablo es quien estudia más,** *Paul is the one who studies most;* **Llegué lo más pronto posible,** *I came as soon as possible.*

b) The following adverbs are compared irregularly:

bien, mejor, (lo) mejor, *well, better, (the) best*
mal, peor, (lo) peor, *badly, worse, (the) worst*
mucho, más, (lo) más, *much (a great deal), more, (the) most*
poco, menos, (lo) menos, *little, less, (the) least*

c) Correlative *the . . . the,* followed by comparatives, is usually expressed in Spanish by **cuanto . . . (tanto). Tanto** is often omitted.

> **Cuanto más gana, (tanto) más gasta.**
> *The more he earns, the more he spends.*

> **Cuanto menos tiene, menos quiere.**
> *The less he has, the less he wants.*

NOTE: *The . . . the* may also be expressed by **mientras . . . —,** with which **tanto** is never used: **Mientras más gana, más gasta,** *The more he earns, the more he spends.*

186. *Than.*

a) *Than* is usually expressed by **que**.

> **Juan es más alto que María.** *John is taller than Mary.*

b) Before a numeral, *more than* and *less than* are expressed by **más de** and **menos de**.

> **Hemos gastado más de cien pesos.**   *We have spent more than one hundred dollars.*
>
> **Ella tiene menos de diez libros.**   *She has less than ten books.*

c) Before a clause (containing a verb), *than* is usually **de lo que**; but *than* is **del que** (or **de la que, de los que, de las que**) when the noun object of the principal verb is understood after **del** (or **de la, de los, de las**).

> **Él sabe más de lo que usted cree.**
> *He knows more than (what) you think.*
>
> **Tenemos más libros de los que teníamos.**
> *We have more books than (the books which) we used to have.*

187. *Verbs in* –**iar** *and* –**uar.** A certain number of verbs in –**iar** and –**uar** take a written accent on the **i** or **u** of the three persons of the singular and the third person plural of their present tenses (indicative, subjunctive, imperative). See § 247.

> **Enviar,** *to send*
>
> **envío, envías, envía, (enviamos, enviáis), envían**
> **envíe, envíes, envíe, (enviemos, enviéis), envíen**
> **envía**
>
> **Continuar,** *to continue*
>
> **continúo, continúas, continúa, (continuamos, continuáis), continúan**
> **continúe, continúes, continúe, (continuemos, continuéis), continúen**
> **continúa**

EXERCISES

ahorrar *to save*
asustar *to frighten*
la **cantidad** *quantity*
continuar *to continue*

cuanto: — ... **tanto** *the ... the*
enviar *to send*
excelente *excellent*

llamar *to call;* —se *to be named;*
se llama *his name is*
mal *badly*
más: — de *more than*
mayor *larger, largest; older,
oldest;* la — parte *most*
mejor *better, best*
menor *smaller, smallest; younger,
youngest*
menos *less (fewer), least (fewest);*
— de *less than*
mientras: — ... *the ... the*
mucho, -a *much;* adv. *much, a
great deal*

o *or*
oír *to hear;* p.p. oído
olvidar (se) (de) *to forget*
el país *country* (nation)
peor *worse, worst*
poco, -a *little (few);* adv. *little*
posible *possible;* lo más pronto
—, *as soon as possible*
pues *for, since*
que conj. *than;* del (de lo, de
la, etc.) —, *than*
tal vez *perhaps*

A. 1. Mi hermana no salió ayer porque llovía. 2. Tenía que ir a visitar a María Ortiz. 3. Dice que María es su mejor amiga. 4. Hoy llueve más y quiere salir. 5. Creo que saldrá aunque continúe lloviendo. 6. Me parece que debe quedarse en casa. 7. ¿No me dijo usted que los truenos la asustan? 8. Sí, es verdad, pero no hemos oído ninguno. — 9. El primo de Felipe trabaja mucho. 10. Parece que cuanto más tiene tanto más quiere. 11. No, no es eso, pues tiene menos que antes. 12. Tiene menos de lo que tenía el año pasado. 13. Creo que gasta la mayor parte de su dinero. 14. Comprará muchas cosas que no necesita. 15. O tal vez lo envía a sus padres. 16. Es un buen muchacho y nunca se olvida de ellos. — 17. El programa que tenemos hoy es excelente. 18. Sí, por eso ha venido mucha gente. 19. ¿Conoce usted a aquellos cinco muchachos? 20. Los tres más grandes son hijos de don Carlos. 21. Se llaman Enrique, Pablo y Felipe. 22. El mayor de los tres es Enrique. 23. Pablo es más grande que Enrique. 24. Felipe es el menor pero no es muy pequeño.

B. 1. ¿Por qué no salió su hermana ayer? 2. ¿A quién tenía que visitar? 3. ¿Qué dice de María? 4. ¿Qué quiere hacer hoy? 5. ¿Qué debe hacer? 6. ¿Qué no hemos oído? 7. ¿Quién trabaja mucho? 8. ¿Cuánto dinero gasta? 9. ¿Qué compra? 10. ¿A quién envía su dinero tal vez? 11. ¿De quiénes no se olvida nunca? 12. ¿Cómo es el programa? 13. ¿Qué ha venido? 14. ¿A quién conoce usted? 15. ¿Cuántos hijos tiene

don Carlos? 16. ¿Cómo se llama el mayor? 17. ¿Cómo se
llama el menor? 18. ¿Cómo se llama usted?

C. *Translate:* 1. He reads well. 2. She reads better. 3. He
is the smallest boy here. 4. I have received more letters than he
has written. 5. Send it to me. 6. Let us send it now. 7. Let
him continue working. 8. I distinguish this from that. 9. It is
one of the best. 10. These gloves cost more than those. 11. I
have less than fifteen dollars. 12. He wants more than twenty
dollars. 13. Continue reading. 14. Most men are lazy. 15. I
like this climate better.

D. 1. Are you sure that your friends will come today? 2. Yes,
they wish to be here before Father returns. 3. I think that they
will try to come as soon as possible. 4. John sent us a telegram
yesterday. 5. He wants us to wait for him at the station. 6. But
it is already four and they have not arrived yet. 7. I am going
to ask if there is another train. 8. It is possible that they have
not left very early. — 9. I was speaking with John and I told
him the[1] following: 10. "You work less than I, don't you?
11. But you always have more money than I." 12. He answered
me: "It is because you spend much. 13. The more you earn
the more you spend. 14. Don't you think that you should save
money?" 15. He advised me to save as much as possible. 16. I
am going to put more than thirty dollars in the bank next week.
— 17. Have you read what my cousin says here? 18. "The
city that we are going to visit is very historic. 19. It is one
of the largest in the country. 20. But I don't think that it is
the largest. 21. Before the war it had many beautiful buildings.
22. Now it has less than it had then. 23. But soon it will have
more than it has now. 24. They are constructing several very
large (ones)."

LECTURA

El compañero de la señora habíase[2] quedado callado.

Ella miró el reloj y exclamó:

— ¡ Faltan[3] cinco minutos nada más![4]

— ¿ Eh? — dijo él como[5] asustado, saliendo del estado de reflexión en que se hallaba.

[1] lo.   [2] se había.   [3] *There remain* (= *We have*).   [4] nada más, *only*.   [5] *as if*.

— Que [1] faltan cinco minutos nada más.

Sonrió [2] el viajero.

— ¡ Bah ! — dijo. — No hay prisa.[3]

— ¿ Cómo que [4] no hay prisa ?

— En llegando [5] a tiempo . . .

— ¡ Es que [6] ya se han marchado todos los viajeros a los vagones ! [7]

— Bueno [8]; déjeles usted que se vayan.

— No, no; me parece que me voy sin tomar el café.

— ¡ Si [1] ya lo traen !

— Pero, hombre . . .

— ¿ Ve usted ? Ya está aquí el café. ¡ Buena cara [9] tiene !

— Pero . . .

— Voy a servirle a usted; no hay prisa.

La campana [10] de la estación dió el aviso.[11]

— ¡ Vámonos ! — gritó la señora. — ¡ Que [1] se va a ir el tren !

EUSEBIO BLASCO, *Una señora comprometida.*[12]

[1] Omit.   [2] *smiled.*   [3] *hurry.*   [4] **Cómo que,** *What do you mean.*   [5] **En llegando,** *Provided we arrive.*   [6] **Es que,** *The fact is that* (= *But*).   [7] *cars.*   [8] *All right.*   [9] *appearance.*   [10] *bell.*   [11] *signal.*   [12] *in a predicament.*

REVIEW LESSON D

I. *A.* Use the definite article with the plural of the following words:

condición	lunes	reloj	tren
crisis	paz	rey	vez
estación	pie	rubí	viernes

B. Supply the definite and indefinite articles, and the possessive adjectives, as indicated in the parentheses, and add the adjective endings:

1. (*a, a*) —— lápiz y —— pluma bonit—. 2. (*the, the*) —— agua y —— leche fresc—. 3. (*the, the*) —— carne y —— ensalada frí—. 4. (*my*) —— libros ingles— y español—. 5. (*the, the*) —— lunes y —— martes pasad—. 6. (*the, the*) —— pescado y —— carne fresc—. 7. (*our, their*) —— manos y —— pies. 8. (*the, the*) —— cara y —— mano blanc—. 9. (*the, the*) —— teatro y —— iglesia hermos—. 10. (*our, their*) —— guantes y —— sombreros.

II. *A.* Give the forms of the present subjunctive of the following verbs in the persons indicated:

SINGULAR

1. decir, estar, vencer, traer.
2. dar, hacer, saber, ver.
3. conocer, haber, llover, venir.

PLURAL

1. ir, llegar, poner, rezar.
2. buscar, empezar, salir, ser.
3. enviar, morir, sentir, tener.

B. Give the forms of the imperfect subjunctive (**–se or –ra**) of the following verbs in the persons indicated:

SINGULAR

1. dar, hacer, saber, ver.
2. conocer, traer, vencer, venir.
3. decir, estar, haber, llover.

PLURAL

1. enviar, morir, sentir, tener.
2. ir, llegar, poner, rezar.
3. buscar, empezar, salir, ver.

III. *A*. Supply the proper form (indicative or subjunctive) of the verb in parentheses:

1. (costar) No me dió ningún libro que —— mucho. 2. (pedir) Le presté el dinero que me ——. 3. (traer) Compraremos lo que ——. 4. (ser) Estudiaremos un idioma que no —— difícil. 5. (ser) Me envió por un camino que —— muy largo. 6. (enseñar) Busco un hombre que —— el español. 7. (costar) No le dé un reloj que —— mucho. 8. (parecer) Visitamos una iglesia que nos —— interesante. 9. (hablar) No conoce a nadie que —— español. 10. (ser) Quiero un libro que —— moderno.

B. Supply the proper form of the verb in parentheses:

1. (quedarse) Cuando llueve yo —— —— en casa; cuando llovía —— —— en casa; cuando llueva —— —— en casa. 2. (comprar) Me da dinero para que —— el reloj; me dió dinero para que —— el reloj. 3. (costar) Compraré la casa con tal que no —— mucho; compraría la casa con tal que no —— mucho. 4. (prometer) No lo hizo aunque lo ——; no lo hará aunque lo ——. 5. (conocer) Si yo —— a ese hombre le hablaría.

C. Supply the equivalent for *than:*

1. Soy más alto —— ella. 2. Tenemos más —— quinientos dólares. 3. Tengo más —— usted me dió. 4. Hoy ha llovido más —— ayer. 5. Felipe trabaja más —— usted. 6. Me dió menos —— treinta dólares. 7. Tengo más hambre —— usted cree. 8. Han traído más huevos —— usted pidió. 9. Ha comprado más pescado —— necesitamos. 10. Hay más lodo —— había ayer. 11. El libro tiene más páginas —— creíamos. 12. Le he dado más sopa —— puede comer.

IV. *A*. Translate, and then repeat, changing the subject of the subordinate verb to **usted** or **ustedes:**

1. I prefer to wait. 2. Mary is glad to be here. 3. John regrets that he is going away. 4. We are afraid to lose it. 5. I wish to send him a bicycle. 6. We prefer to bring it. 7. The girl is afraid to come in. 8. He wishes to buy the watch.

B. Translate, and then repeat, changing the main verb to the present indicative:

1. I wrote to him to come. 2. He forbade me to go. 3. I didn't believe that he had come. 4. I didn't deny that he had done it. 5. I was glad he was here. 6. He wanted me to see it. 7. I was afraid she would not come. 8. He advised me to remain here.

V. Translate:

1. He gave me a five-dollar bill. 2. How much does it cost? 3. Ask your father for some money. 4. Let him close the door. 5. Where are his parents? 6. Do you know that boy? 7. He wants to go away. 8. Are you sorry I am ill? 9. We hope to see you soon. 10. Tell him to come here. 11. He intends to build a house. 12. He likès to go to the theater. 13. We see him every day. 14. It rains frequently in this country. 15. Is your house far from here? 16. He will not come unless I am here. 17. I doubt if he can go. 18. We saw him two days ago. 19. He put on his hat. 20. Eggs cost forty-two cents a dozen. 21. I want a cup of coffee. 22. Your hands are cold. 23. Has he a gold watch? 24. My uncle is a physician. 25. What a pity! He can't come. 26. He is the richest man in the country. 27. Send him a telegram. 28. We saw him several times. 29. How many hours did you sleep? 30. He doesn't save much money.

LESSON XLI

188. *Personal Pronouns.* The Spanish personal pronouns used as the subject or object of verbs are:

SINGULAR

Subject		Direct Object		Indirect Object	
yo	*I*	**me**	*me*	**me**	*to me*
tú	*you (thou)*	**te**	*you (thee)*	**te**	*to you (to thee)*
él (m.)	*he, it*	**le** or **lo**	*him, it*		*to him*
ella (f.)	*she, it*	**la**	*her, it*	**le** {	*to her* (**la,** *to her*)
ello (n.)	*it*	**lo**	*it*		*to it*

PLURAL

nosotros, −as	*we*	**nos**	*us*	**nos**	*to us*
vosotros, −as	*you (ye)*	**os**	*you*	**os**	*to you*
ellos, −as	*they*	**los** (m.) } **las** (f.)	*them*	**les**	*to them* (**las,** *lo them,* f.)

NOTES: 1. **Ello** is rarely used as the subject of a verb, except in the expression **ello es que . . .,** *the fact is that . . .*

2. English *it,* as subject, is usually not expressed at all in Spanish: **llueve,** *it rains (is raining).*

3. As direct object, *it* is **lo** (m.) or **la** (f.) when it refers to a definite thing, and **lo** (n.) when it refers to a statement or idea: **lo hallé,** *I found it* (**el libro**); **la tiene,** *she has it* (**la pluma**); **no lo creemos,** *we do not believe it.*

178

4. The feminine dative forms **la**, *to her*, and **las**, *to them*, are sometimes used, but their use is not sanctioned by the Spanish Academy. See also §§ 46, 51, 75, 76, 80, 84, 110, 141, 152.

189. Usted, ustedes.

SINGULAR

Subject		*Direct object*		*Indirect Object*	
usted	*you*	**le** or **lo** (m.) **la** (f.) } *you*		**le** **le (la)** } *to you*	

PLURAL

ustedes	*you*	**los** (m.) **las** (f.) } *you*		**les** **les (las)** } *to you*	

NOTE: **Usted** and **ustedes** are of the second person in meaning, but they require the verb in the third person.

190. *The Pronoun* se.

a) **Se** means *himself, herself, oneself, itself, yourself, themselves, yourselves* (see § 110).

Él se engaña.	*He deceives himself.*
Ella se sentó.	*She seated herself.*
Ellos se engañaban.	*They deceived themselves.*

b) **Se,** with a singular verb, sometimes has the force of English *one, people,* etc., used as indefinite pronouns.

Se dice.	*One says (It is said).*
Se cree que es verdad.	*People believe (It is believed) that it is true.*

c) Some intransitive verbs may be used as reflexives, with change of meaning.

ir	*to go*	**dormir**	*to sleep*
irse	*to go away*	**dormirse**	*to fall asleep*

191. *Verbs ending in* –uir. These verbs add **y** to the pronounced **u** of the stem in the present tenses (indicative, subjunctive, and imperative) except where the flectional ending begins with **i**. Besides, the unaccented **i** between vowels is changed to **y** (see §§ 183 and 260).

Construir, *to build, construct*

PARTICIPLES	construyendo, construido
PRES. INDIC.	construy–o, construy–es, construy–e, construy–imos, constru–ís, construy–en
PRES. SUBJ.	construy–a, construy–as, construy–a, construy–amos, construy–áis, construy–an
IMPERATIVE	construy–e constru–id
FUTURE	construir–é, etc.
CONDITIONAL	construir–ía, etc.
PRETERITE	constru–í, constru–iste, constru–yó, constru–irnos, constru–isteis, constru–yeron
IMPERF. SUBJ.	{ constru–yese, constru–yeses, etc. { constru–yera, constru–yeras, etc.

EXERCISES

la clase *kind*	sin *without*
dormirse *to fall asleep*	todo, –a *every;* todos (–as) los
doscientos, –as *two hundred*	(las) días (semanas) *every*
ello *it*	*day* (*week*)
mudarse *to move* (*away*)	el trabajo *work*
ocupado, –a *busy*	

A. 1. Emilia vino a visitarnos la semana pasada. 2. Le pidió ochenta dólares a mi padre. 3. Le dijo que necesitaba este dinero en seguida. 4. Quiere comprar una mesa y varias sillas. 5. Mi padre le dijo que se lo daría. 6. Pero Emilia se fué sin el dinero. 7. Yo creo que Emilia se olvidó de él. 8. Papá quiere que vuelva, pero ella prefiere que se lo envíe. — 9. Es verdad que yo gano poco en la tienda. 10. Mi hermano gana más en la oficina. 11. Pero yo tengo más dinero que él. 12. Tengo más de doscientos dólares en el banco. 13. Todas las semanas ahorro algo. 14. Algunas semanas ahorro más que otras. 15. Mi hermano tiene una hija en la escuela. 16. Me parece que él le envía lo más posible. — 17. La librería de don Enrique es excelente. 18. Juan y yo acabamos de venir de ella. 19. No tiene mucho libros ingleses y franceses. 20. Pero tiene buena cantidad de libros españoles. 21. Se dice que es la mejor de la ciudad. 22. Pero si creen que es la mejor del estado se engañan. 23. Hay tres o cuatro que son más grandes. 24. Éstas tienen mayor cantidad de libros de todas clases.

B. 1. ¿Quién vino a visitarnos la semana pasada? 2. ¿Qué le pidió a su padre? 3. ¿Qué le dijo a su padre? 4. ¿Qué quiere comprar? 5. ¿Qué le dijo su padre? 6. ¿De qué se olvidó Emilia? 7. ¿Quién gana poco en la tienda? 8. ¿Quién gana más que usted? 9. ¿Quién tiene más dinero? 10. ¿Cuánto dinero tiene usted en el banco? 11. ¿Cuánto ahorra usted todos los meses? 12. ¿Qué tiene su hermano? 13. ¿Quién tiene una librería? 14. ¿Qué clases de libros tiene? 15. ¿Qué se dice de la librería? 16. ¿Cuántas librerías hay en el estado que son más grandes?

C. *I. Translate each sentence four times, using (1)* **tú,** *(2)* **usted,** *(3)* **vosotros, -as,** *and (4)* **ustedes,** *or the proper object pronouns:*
1. You (*m.*) are tired. 2. You (*f.*) are ill. 3. He saw you (*m.*) yesterday. 4. I saw you (*f.*) this morning. 5. We told you the truth. 6. You brought them. 7. You fell asleep. 8. Did you go away?

II. Translate: 1. It is true. 2. It is raining. 3. I don't believe it. 4. I doubt it. 5. Spanish is spoken here. 6. We went to bed at ten o'clock. 7. We got up at seven o'clock. 8. I have it here. 9. I gave it to her. 10. She gave it to me. 11. Her name is Mary. 12. That is worse.

D. 1. Do you know who is building that house? 2. I don't know although I have asked several times. 3. Perhaps it is for Mr. Lope. 4. I have seen him there every day. 5. It is said that he is very rich now. 6. When he came to this country he was very poor. 7. He has worked hard, and he has made (= earned) much money. 8. He has saved most of his money. — 9. Charles has not written to us for a long time. 10. It is true, I have written two or three letters to him. 11. But he has not answered any. 12. He must be busy with his work. 13. Do you know if he continues living in the same house? 14. Yes, for if he had moved he would have told [1] me. 15. When I was there he studied a great deal. 16. He told me that the more he studied the less he knew. — 17. Have you seen little Elizabeth? 18. Isn't she doña María's daughter? 19. Yes, we hope that she has not gone away. 20. We saw her here a moment ago. 21. She was reading

[1] Supply *it.*

Domingo Faustino Sarmiento.

a very large book. 22. She told us that it was a very interesting history. 23. But she fell asleep in the chair. 24. She may have [1] gone to bed.

LECTURA

Dos anécdotas de Sarmiento [2]

Cuando Sarmiento era Presidente [3] de la Argentina, un empleado [4] muy joven presentó su renuncia [5] de escribiente [6] en una de las oficinas públicas [7] porque no estaba de acuerdo [8] con la marcha [9] del Gobierno.

El Presidente le llamó a su oficina y le dijo con mucha seriedad [10] y cortesía [11]: « Señor, me veo obligado a aceptar [12] su renuncia, pero supongo [13] que usted me permitirá seguir gobernando. » [14]

---

[1] *It is possible that she has . . .* [2] Domingo Faustino Sarmiento (1811–1888). [3] *president.* [4] *employee.* [5] *resignation.* [6] *clerk.* [7] *public.* [8] *accord;* **de acuerdo,** *in agreement.* [9] *course.* [10] *seriousness;* **con seriedad,** *seriously.* [11] *courtesy;* **con cortesía,** *courteously.* [12] *accept.* [13] *I suppose.* [14] *governing.*

Era tan general la creencia [1] en la locura [2] de Sarmiento que él mismo contaba [3] esto a sus amigos:

Visitaba un día el manicomio [4] de Buenos Aires y al llegar a un patio [5] se suscitó [6] mucha agitación [7] entre los locos [8] que estaban allí. Después de muchas consultas [9] uno, el cual parecía haber sido delegado [10] por los otros, se acercó a él con los brazos [11] abiertos y exclamó: «¡ Al fin, señor Sarmiento, entre nosotros! »

LESSON XLII

192. *Position of Object Pronouns* (5). Spanish object pronouns usually precede their verb; but an object pronoun follows its verb and is attached to it when the verb is an infinitive, a present participle or an affirmative imperative (or subjunctive used imperatively). See §§ 76, 84, 99, 102*b*, 141, 152.

NOTE: If the sentence or clause begins with the verb, the object pronoun may follow, but this rarely occurs in colloquial Spanish: — **Pláceme** — dice el juez, "*It pleases me*," *says the judge.*

193. *Position of* se. Reflexive se, whether direct or indirect object, always precedes another object pronoun.

Se me figura.   *It seems to me.*

NOTE: See also § 84*b*.

194. *Prepositional Forms of the Personal Pronouns* (2).

a) When personal pronouns are governed by a preposition, the following forms are used:

SINGULAR		PLURAL	
mí	*me*	**nosotros, –as**	*us*
ti	*you (thee)*	**vosotros, –as**	*you*
él (m.)	*him, it*		
ella (f.)	*her, it*	**ellos, –as**	*them*
ello (n.)	*it*		

[1] *belief.* [2] *madness.* [3] *related.* [4] *insane asylum.* [5] *courtyard.* [6] *was stirred up.* [7] *agitation, excitement.* [8] *madmen.* [9] *consultations.* [10] *delegated.* [11] *arms.*

b) **Usted(–es),** *you,* and **sí,** *himself, herself,* etc., are also used with prepositions.

Esto es para usted.	*This is for you.*
Habla de sí.	*He talks about himself.*

NOTE: *With me* is **conmigo;** *with you* (*thee*) is **contigo;** and *with himself, herself,* etc., is **consigo.** See also §§ 85, 86.

195. *Emphatic Reflexive.* If English *myself, yourself,* etc., are emphatic, they are to be expressed in Spanish by the reflexive pronoun in the prepositional form, modified by **mismo (–a, –os, –as).**

Me engaño a mí mismo (–a).	*I deceive myself.*
Ella se burla de sí misma.	*She makes fun of herself.*

196. *Reciprocal Construction.* In the plural a reflexive verb may become reciprocal. Usually no distinction of form is made in Spanish between reflexive and reciprocal verbs; thus, **nos engañamos** may mean *we deceive ourselves,* or *we deceive each other* or *one another.* But a reciprocal verb may be made explicit by the use of **el uno al (del) otro, unos a (de) otros,** etc.

Se engañan el uno al otro.	*They deceive each other.*
Se burlan unas de otras.	*They make fun of one another.*

197. *Verbs in* –**ducir.**

a) In the present indicative and the present subjunctive, verbs ending in –**ducir** are conjugated like the inceptive verbs (see § 174*b).*

Traducir, *to translate*

PRES. INDIC.	**traduzco, traduces, traduce, traducimos, traducís, traducen**
PRES. SUBJ.	**traduzca, traduzcas, traduzca, traduzcamos, traduzcáis, traduzcan**

b) In the preterite, and tenses formed from it, these verbs have a stem in –**j**– after which the –**i**– of a diphthongal ending is lost (see **traer,** § 165).

PRETERITE traduje, tradujiste, tradujo, tradujimos, tradujisteis, tradujeron

IMPERF. SUBJ. { tradujese, tradujeses, etc.
{ tradujera, tradujeras, etc.

NOTE: See also § 282.

EXERCISES

amable *amiable, kind*
burlarse de *to make fun of, mock*
la caja *box*
el cine (cinematógrafo) *moving pictures, "movies"*
consigo *with himself (herself, yourself, themselves, yourselves)*
contento, -a *content, glad, happy*
contigo *with you (thee)*
contrario, -a *contrary;* por el —, *on the contrary*
el chico (coll.) *boy, young fellow*
desde *from, since*
dulce *sweet;* los dulces *candy*
figurarse *to seem, appear*
la frase *sentence*
el gusto *pleasure;* tener —, *to be pleased*
José *Joseph*

el juez *judge*
mismo, -a *self*
nos *each other, one another*
olvidar: se me olvidó *I forgot*
la película *film, picture*
la persona *person*
placer *to please*
por *because of;* — eso *that's why*
que (with mismo) *as*
recordar (ue) *to recall, remember*
reírse (de) *to laugh (at)*
la reunión *meeting*
se *each other, one another*
sí *himself, herself, yourself, themselves, yourselves*
suceder *to happen*
supe *I learned*
el teléfono *telephone*
traducir *to translate*
triste *sad*

A. 1. María dice que no quiere ir al teatro contigo. 2. Me parece que es por algo que sucedió una noche. 3. El martes de la semana pasada fuimos al cine. 4. La película que vimos era algo triste y ella se puso a llorar. 5. Yo, por el contrario, me reí varias veces. 6. Cuando salimos del teatro nos burlamos la una de la otra. 7. Es posible que se haya enfadado conmigo. 8. No sé, pero estoy segura de que prefiere quedarse en casa. — 9. Aquel chico le trajo una caja de dulces a mi madre. 10. Ella no estaba en casa y él dejó los dulces. 11. Se le olvidó decir que eran para mamá. 12. Se los dió a la criada sin decir nada. 13. A mí se me figuró que eran para mí. 14. Yo había comido algunos cuando mamá volvió a casa. 15. José, como se llama el muchacho, volvió con ella. 16. Entonces supe que los dulces eran para ella y no para mí. — 17. El primo de Carlos vive en Lima, capital del Perú. 18. La semana pasada Carlos recibió una carta de él. 19. Carlos comprende la mayor parte de su carta. 20. Pero hay dos frases que no comprende. 21. Quiere que usted se las traduzca. 22. Ésta es una de las frases: « Dícese que no hay tal. » 23. Eso es lo mismo que: « Se dice que no hay tal cosa. » 24. No recuerdo la otra frase ahora.

B. 1. ¿ Qué dice María ? 2. ¿ A dónde fueron ustedes la semana pasada ? 3. ¿ Cómo era la película ? 4. ¿ Qué hizo usted ? 5. ¿ Qué hicieron cuando salieron del teatro ? 6. ¿ Qué prefiere ella ? 7. ¿ Qué trajo aquel chico ? 8. ¿ Quién no estaba en casa ? 9. ¿ A quién le dió los dulces ? 10. ¿ Qué se le figuró a usted ? 11. ¿ Cómo se llama el muchacho ? 12. ¿ Le gustan a usted los dulces ? 13. ¿ Dónde vive el primo de Carlos ? 14. ¿ Qué recibió Carlos ? 15. ¿ Qué no comprende Carlos ? 16. ¿ Qué quiere él ?

C. *Translate:* 1. Give it to Henry. 2. Give it to him. 3. Do not give it to Henry. 4. Do not give it to him. 5. Give it to *me*. 6. Do not give it to *me*. 7. Tell *me* the truth. 8. Bring me a pen. 9. I shall bring it to you at once. 10. He likes it. 11. She does not like it. 12. I wish to do so (it). 13. Come with me. 14. I can't go with you. 15. Have you a letter for me ? 16. Charles makes fun of himself. 17. They deceive each other. 18. They make fun of each other. 19. I don't like it. 20. He deceives himself.

D. 1. Have you been in one of these meetings before ? 2. No, my friend (*f.*), this is the first time that I have come. 3. That's why I don't see any one whom I know here. 4. If it is so, I shall be very pleased to introduce you to several persons. 5. Just [1] a moment, I see there two girls whom I know. 6. When they lived here we used to visit one another very frequently. 7. Four years ago they moved to another town. 8. We had not seen one another since then. — 9. Peter wishes to go to the country with us. 10. He is less busy than he was last month. 11. If he wishes to go, he will have to get up at four o'clock. 12. He says that he will be ready whenever we wish. 13. It is not difficult for him to get up at that hour. 14. He always gets up early when he goes to the office. 15. He goes to sleep earlier than any one here

[1] Omit.

every night. 16. We are glad that he can go, for we have a great deal to do. — 17. Was it not Philip to whom you were speaking now? 18. Yes, he telephoned from his house. 19. Why didn't you tell him not to talk so much about himself? 20. Allow me to tell you that you are mistaken.[1] 21. The truth is that he was speaking about you and not about himself. 22. He was saying that he has never met any one so kind. 23. He is very glad that he has spent a few days here. 24. He wants you to promise to go and visit him.

LECTURA

A las diez de la noche la casa de doña Teresa se hallaba llena [2] de gente, con gran satisfacción de la señora y de don Hilario. Los bailes [3] se sucedían sin interrupción en medio de [4] la alegría [5] general. Todo era animación, entusiasmo y cordialidad. De buena gana [6] se hubieran abrazado [7] unos a otros para colmo [8] de dicha [9] tan suprema.

La fiesta [10] no podía haber empezado mejor. No faltaban ya jóvenes para las niñas, ni niñas para los jóvenes. Lo que comenzaba a faltar era espacio y aire para tanta gente.

Don Hilario creyó al fin llegada la hora de abandonar [11] la puerta, porque no era cosa [12] de llevarse [13] allí de plantón [14] toda la noche para esperar a unos pocos rezagados.[15] Pero apenas se hubo sentado con un platillo [16] de helado [17] en la mano, cuando se le acercó doña Teresa y le dijo a media voz [18]:

— Ya sería bueno, Hilario, que no llegase más gente.

ROMÁN VIAL, Un convidado convida a ciento.

[1] *You deceive yourself.* [2] *full.* [3] *dances.* [4] **en medio de,** *in the midst of.* [5] *gaiety.* [6] **De buena gana,** *Willingly.* [7] *embraced.* [8] *crown;* **para colmo de,** *to crown.* [9] *happiness.* [10] *entertainment.* [11] *leave unattended.* [12] *a question.* [13] *spending.* [14] *sentry.* [15] *late comers.* [16] *small dish.* [17] *ice cream.* [18] **a media voz,** *in a low voice.*

LESSON XLIII

198. *Possessive Pronouns.*

a)   **SINGULAR**

el mío (la mía, lo mío, los míos, las mías), *mine*

el tuyo (la tuya, lo tuyo, los tuyos, las tuyas), *yours* (*thine*)

el suyo (la suya, lo suyo, los suyos, las suyas), *his, hers, its, yours*

PLURAL

el nuestro (la nuestra, lo nuestro, los nuestros, las nuestras), *ours*

el vuestro (la vuestra, lo vuestro, los vuestros, las vuestras), *yours*

el suyo (la suya, lo suyo, los suyos, las suyas), *theirs, yours*

b) The possessive pronouns require the definite article in Spanish though not in English.

Prefiero la casa de usted a la mía.	*I prefer your house to mine.*
La de usted es más grande que la mía.	*Yours is larger than mine.*

c) But the definite article is used with a possessive, in the predicate, only in a question beginning with *which*, or in answer to such a question.

    ¿ Qué libro es el de usted ? — Éste es el mío.
    Which book is yours? — This one is mine.

    ¿ Cuál de las plumas es la mía ? — Ésta es la de usted.
    Which pen is mine? — This is yours.

But: **¿ De quién es este libro ? — Es mío.**
    Whose book is this? — It is mine.

199. El de él, de ella, etc. The definite article may be used with **de él, de ella,** etc., instead of **suyo,** etc., to make the meaning clear or emphatic (see § 87).

    Tengo el libro de él; no tengo el de ella.
    I have his book; I haven't hers.

    Prefiere la casa de usted a la de ellos.
    He prefers your house to theirs.

200. *Demonstratives.* Study §§ 58, 59, 135. *That of, the one of* etc., are usually expressed by **el (la, lo, los, las) de.**

La pluma de acero y la de oro.	*The steel pen and the gold one* (lit. 'The pen of steel and that of gold').
Lo de ayer.	*The affair of yesterday.*

201. *Interrogative Pronouns.*

quién (–es)	*who (whom)*
de quién (–es)	*whose*
qué	*what (which)*
cuál (–es)	*which*
cuánto (–a, –os, –as)	*how much (many)*

NOTES: 1. All except **quién (–es)** may be used as pronominal adjectives.
2. In questions, *which*, used as an attributive (or adherent) adjective, is **qué**: **¿Qué libro quiere usted?** *Which book do you want?*
3. In exclamations, *what (a)* or *how* is **qué**: **¡Qué bonita niña!** *What a pretty child!* **¡Qué pálida estás!** *How pale you are!*

202. **Dar** *and* **ir.**

Dar. Review §§ 108, 109, 157*b*. Study §§ 217, 218, 267.

Da la una.	*It is striking one.*
Dan las dos.	*It is striking two.*
dar con	*to meet, find, come upon*
dar un paseo	*to take a walk*

Ir. Review §§ 103, 104, 138*c*, 156, 157*b*. Study §§ 217, 218, 265.

ir a caballo	*to ride, be riding on horseback*
ir a pie	*to go on foot, walk*
ir en automóvil	*to ride, drive*
¿Cómo le va? (coll.)	*How are you?*

EXERCISES

el **acero** *steel*
el **automóvil** *automobile*
el **club** *club*
cuál (–es) interrog. *which*
la **chica** (coll.) *girl*

dar: — **con** *to meet, find, come upon;* — **un paseo** *take a walk;* **da la una** (**dan las dos**) *it is striking one (two)*
el (la, etc.**) de** *that of, the one of,* etc.

enfadado, –a *angry*
funcionar *to work, run* (as an engine)
ir: — a caballo *to ride, be riding on horseback;* — a pie *go on foot, walk*
llamar: — por teléfono *to telephone*
la máquina *engine*
el mío, la mía, etc. *mine*
negro, –a *black*

el nuestro, la nuestra, etc. *ours*
el paseo *walk;* dar un —, *to take a walk*
la playa *beach*
¿ qué? *which?*
raro, –a *rare, strange*
el regalo *gift, present*
el suyo, la suya, etc. *his, hers, its, yours, theirs*
el tuyo, la tuya, etc. *yours (thine)*
el vuestro, la vuestra, etc. *yours*

A. 1. ¿ De quién es aquella casa blanca? 2. Es la casa a donde se mudaron José y su familia. 3. José dice que la casa es de él. 4. Pero a mí se me figura que es de su padre. 5. El padre de José es el juez a quien conocimos ayer. 6. Me parece que es una persona muy amable. 7. Su casa es más grande que la mía. 8. Sí, pero la de usted es más moderna. — 9. Cuando dieron las siete salimos a dar un paseo. 10. Dimos en la calle con Felipe y su esposa. 11. Nos dijeron que iban al restaurant. 12. Pensaban ir al cine después de comer. 13. Lo raro es que iban a pie. 14. Su casa está muy lejos del teatro. 15. Siempre van al teatro en automóvil. 16. Creo que la máquina de su automóvil no funciona. — 17. ¿ Por qué está su amiga Juana tan triste? 18. Se me figura que es porque su prima está enfadada con ella. 19. Juana tenía que escribir un tema para mañana. 20. No había podido encontrar su plumafuente. 21. Su prima le prestó la suya. 22. Ahora Juana ha perdido también la de su prima. 23. La plumafuente de su prima es un regalo de su abuelo. 24. Por eso su prima no quería perderla.

B. 1. ¿ A dónde se mudaron José y su familia? 2. ¿ Qué dice José? 3. ¿ Qué se le figura a usted? 4. ¿ Quién es el padre de José? 5. ¿ Cuál de las casas es más grande? 6. ¿ Cuál es más moderna? 7. ¿ Cuándo salieron ustedes a dar un paseo? 8. ¿ Con quiénes dieron ustedes? 9. ¿ Qué dijeron ellos? 10. ¿ A dónde pensaban ir después? 11. ¿ Dónde está su casa? 12. ¿ A dónde van siempre en automóvil? 13. ¿ Qué no funciona? 14. ¿ Quién está triste? 15. ¿ Quién está enfadada? 16. ¿ Quién tenía que escribir un tema? 17. ¿ Qué no había podido encontrar? 18. ¿ Quién le prestó la suya?

C. *Translate:* 1. Did you give him yours (*f.*)? 2. We have ours (*m. sing.*). 3. Where is theirs (*f.*)? 4. This money is mine. 5. He has my pen, and I have his. 6. I have my books, not hers. 7. What a pretty girl! 8. How pale she is! 9. How much money have you? 10. We found them here. 11. Who gave him that? 12. They make fun of each other (*f.*). 13. He doesn't want me to give it (*f.*) to her. 14. I want to go with you. 15. He doesn't speak of himself. 16. It has struck one. 17. Whose pencil is this? 18. Which book do you want? 19. His house is larger than ours. 20. Our house is prettier than theirs.

D. 1. Which of the watches that we saw are you going to buy? 2. I shall have to buy the one of silver for myself. 3. I can use it when I go to the beach. 4. I don't wish to take the watch that my father bought me. 5. I shall buy the gold one (= one of gold) for my cousin. 6. He never forgets to bring me something. 7. Last night he brought me a box of candy. 8. It seems to me that you are laughing at me. — 9. Who telephoned a moment ago? 10. It was a girl (whom) I met at a meeting of our club. 11. She called me from the house of a friend whom she is visiting. 12. Her friend's name is Juana García. 13. She told me that they are going to the moving pictures. 14. They are going to see a French film and Juana does not understand French well. 15. She wants me to go with them so that I may translate for them [1] what they do not understand. 16. Don't you want to go with us? — 17. Look, from here we can see the horses. 18. Which of those two is yours? 19. The white one is mine, the black is my brother's. 20. The three large ones which are under the tree are my father's. 21. We can ride on horseback from here if you wish. 22. When we reach (= arrive at) Carlos' house we can go by (= **en**) automobile. 23. The road is better from there. 24. Do you believe that we shall arrive tonight?

LECTURA

Doña Teresa, naturalmente, se disgustaba [2] más [3] a medida que [4] veía llegar convidados, porque en la sala estaban [5] que ya

---

[1] Use indirect object. [2] *became displeased.* [3] *more and more.* [4] **a medida que,** *as.* [5] Supply *so crowded.*

7*

no podían darse vuelta.[1]   Alarmada,[2] salió al fin y le dijo a don Hilario:

— Por lo visto [3] no has dejado perro ni gato [4] a quienes [5] no has convidado.

— ¿ Yo, mujer ? [6]

— Sí, tú, porque no he sido yo quien los ha ido a buscar.

— Ni siquiera [7] los conozco, hija [6]; en mi vida [8] los he visto.

— Razón de más [9] para que no los admitieras.[10]

— Pero cómo, si me son presentados en toda regla.[11]

— En toda regla se les despide [12]; se les dice que dispensen,[13] que no hay lugar,[14] en fin,[15] cualquier cosa . . . ¡ Yo había de estar [16] en tu lugar ! . . . Palabras no faltan . . .

— ¡ Lo que es a ella [17] le sobran ! [18] — murmuró don Hilario mientras doña Teresa se volvía a la sala.

Román Vial, Un convidado convida a ciento.

LESSON XLIV

203. *Relative Pronouns.*

> que, *who (whom), which, that*
> el cual (la cual, lo cual, los cuales, las cuales) ⎫ *who (whom),*
> el que (la que, lo que, los que, las que)   ⎬   *which*
> quien (–es), *who (whom)*   ⎭
> cuanto (–a, –os, –as), *all who, all that*
> cuyo (–a, –os, –as), *whose*

204. *Uses of the Relative Pronouns.*

  (a) **Que,** the most common of the Spanish relative pronouns, is invariable.   It is used as subject or object of a verb, and it

---

    turn; **darse vuelta,** *turn around.*   [2] *Alarmed.*   [3] **Por lo visto,** *Apparently.*   [4] *cat;* **perro ni gato,** *Tom, Dick, and Harry.*   [5] *whom.*   [6] *my dear.*   [7] **Ni siquiera . . .,** *I don't even . . .*   [8] **en mi vida,** *never.*   [9] *See* **demás.**   [10] *admit.*   [11] *rule;* **en toda regla,** *properly.*   [12] *dismiss;* **se les despide,** *they are sent away.*   [13] *to excuse (us).*   [14] *room, place.*   [15] **en fin,** *in short.*   [16] **¡ Yo había de estar . . .!** *I should be . . .*   [17] **Lo que es a ella,** *In her case.*   [18] *they exceed* (= *she has too much to say*).

may refer to persons or things. After a preposition, *whom* is **quien(-es)**.

> **El alumno que partió hoy.**
> *The student* (m.) *who (that) left today.*

> **La alumna que ví esta mañana.**
> *The student* (f.) *whom (that) I saw this morning.*

> **Los alumnos de quienes hablábamos.**
> *The students of whom we were speaking.*

NOTE: The preposition **a** is not used with **que**.

b) The pronouns **el cual** (**la cual**, etc.), **el que** (**la que**, etc.), or **quien(-es)**, may be used to avoid ambiguity. **El cual** and **el que** indicate the gender and number of the antecedent. **Quien** makes clear that the antecedent is a person and indicates the number.

He escrito al hijo de doña Francisca, el cual estudia para médico.
> *I have written to Doña Francisca's son who is studying to be a physician.*

Ayer ví al dueño de la casa, quien está en la ciudad.
> *Yesterday I saw the owner of the house who is in town.*

c) *He who, she who, the one who*, etc., are expressed by **el que, la que**, etc., or by **quien(-es)**.

> **El que desea mucho siempre es pobre.**
> *He who desires much is always poor.*

> **Estos muchachos son los que usted buscaba.**
> *These boys are the ones that you were looking for.*

> **Quien calla, otorga.** *He who is silent gives consent.*

> **No tengo a quien dirigirme.**
> *I haven't any one to whom to apply.*

d) Neuter *that which* or *what* (= *that which*), referring to a statement or idea, is **lo que**, and neuter *which* is commonly **lo cual**.

¿ Sabe usted lo que quiere? *Do you know what he wants?*

Prometió estudiar más, lo cual agradó mucho a su padre.
> *He promised to study more, which greatly pleased his father.*

c) A Spanish relative pronoun can not be omitted, nor can it precede its preposition, as in English. Compare *the man we were talking about* with **el hombre de quien hablábamos.**

205. **Poner.** Review §§ 122, 123, 125c, 156, 157, 161. Study §§ 217, 218, 269. **Tener.** Review §§ 26, 41, 47, 53, 70, 78, 96, 111c, 156, 157, 161. Study §§ 217, 218, 262. **Venir.** Review §§ 113, 138c, 156, 157, 161. Study §§ 217, 218, 268.

206. *Idioms.*

> **poner la mesa,** *to set the table*
>
> > **Pon la mesa, María.** *Set the table, Mary.*
>
> **ponerse,** *to set* (the sun)
>
> > **El sol se pone a las siete.** *The sun sets at seven o'clock.*
>
> **tener calor (frío, hambre (f.), miedo, prisa, sed (f.), sueño),** *to be warm (cold, hungry, afraid, in a hurry, thirsty, sleepy)*
>
> > | | |
> > |---|---|
> > | **Tengo calor.** | *I am warm.* |
> > | **Tenía hambre.** | *He was hungry.* |
> > | **Tendremos mucha sed.** | *We shall be very thirsty.* |
> > | **¿ Cuántos años tiene ?** | *How old is he?* |
> > | **Tiene diez años.** | *He is ten years old.* |
>
> **venir bien,** *to fit, be becoming*
>
> > **Ese sombrero te viene bien.** *That hat is becoming to you.*

EXERCISES

agradar *to please*

ahí *there*

el (la) alumno (–a) *student*

azul *blue*

el calor *warmth;* **tener —,** *to be warm*

casi *almost*

cerca de *near*

el color *color*

cual: el (la, etc.**) —,** *who (whom), which*

cuanto, –a *all who, all that*

cuyo, –a *whose*

deber *to owe*

después: poco —, *a short time (soon) afterwards*

dirigirse (a) *to go (to), apply*

el dueño *owner*

Francisca *Frances*

fuera *outside*

gastar *to use up, wear out*

gritar *to shout*

el jefe *boss*

el miedo *fear;* **tener —,** *to be afraid*

mucho *greatly*

otorgar *to grant, give assent*

el **parque** *park*
  poner: — **la mesa** *to set the table;* **ponerse** *set* (the sun)
la **prisa** *hurry;* **tener** —, *to be in a hurry*
  proyectar *to show*
  pues *well*
  que *who (whom), which, that;* **el (la,** etc.**)** —, *who (whom), which, that; he (she,* etc.*) who,*

  the one who, etc.; **lo** —, *that which, what*
  quien (**-es**) *who, whom*
la **sed** *thirst;* **tener** —, *to be thirsty*
el **sueño** *sleep;* **tener** —, *to be sleepy*
el **vaso** *(drinking) glass*
  venir: — **bien** *to fit, be becoming*
  verde *green*
el **zapato** *shoe*

A. 1. Dígale a la criada que ponga la mesa en seguida. 2. Yo tengo hambre y quiero comer cuando venga mi padre. 3. Han dado las seis y llegará pronto. 4. Viene todos los días en el tren de las seis y cuarto. 5. Voy a la estación a buscarle en el automóvil. 6. Por la mañana le gusta ir a la estación a pie. 7. Pero por la noche viene cansado y prefiere que le encontremos. 8. Esta noche vamos al cine después de comer. 9. Proyectan una película que él quiere ver. — 10. Les he dado cuanto dinero tenía. 11. Éste es para pagar lo que usted debe en la tienda. 12. El que le dí al chico es para él y su hermana. 13. Quiero que él compre un sombrero. 14. No me gusta el que lleva ahora. 15. Es muy pequeño y no le viene bien. 16. Tiene que comprar un par de zapatos también. 17. Los que tiene están muy gastados. — 18. Me sentaré aquí fuera porque tengo mucho calor. 19. Casi siempre usted dice que tiene frío. 20. Ahora tengo calor porque acabo de dar un paseo por el parque. 21. Allí ví a nuestro amigo Jorge, el cual iba en automóvil. 22. Me parece que el automóvil en que iba no era el suyo. 23. Era nuevo, grande y de color azul. 24. El suyo es viejo, pequeño y de color verde. 25. Cuando Jorge venga a vernos nos dirá de quien es.

B. 1. ¿ Quién pone la mesa ? 2. ¿ Cuándo quiere usted comer ? 3. ¿ En qué tren viene el padre ? 4. ¿ A qué va usted a la estación ? 5. ¿ Cómo viene el padre por la noche ? 6. ¿ Cuándo irán ustedes al cine ? 7. ¿ Qué les ha dado usted ? 8. ¿ Para quién es el dinero que le dió al chico ? 9. ¿ Qué debe comprar el chico ? 10. ¿ Por qué no le viene bien el sombrero ? 11. ¿ Qué otra cosa tiene que comprar el muchacho ? 12. ¿ Cómo están los que tiene ? 13. ¿ Dónde quiere usted sentarse ? 14. ¿ Tiene usted

calor o frío ? 15. ¿ Cuándo dió usted un paseo ? 16. ¿ En qué
iba Jorge ? 17. ¿ Cómo es su automóvil ? 18. ¿ Qué nos dirá
Jorge ?

C. *Translate:* 1. The lady who arrived yesterday. 2. The lady
to whom I was speaking. 3. The young lady whom I saw this
morning. 4. The man that brought the book. 5. The book of
which we were speaking. 6. The house he sold. 7. The house
in which he lives. 8. I have written to Mr. Herrera's daughter
who is in New York. 9. I have written also to Mr. Martinez'
son who is in Havana. 10. This boy is the one who bought the
bicycle. 11. What do you want ? 12. Tell me what you want.
13. I believe you don't know what you want. 14. What did he
buy ? 15. He is working harder, which pleases me.

D. 1. We have not seen Philip for several days. 2. Is Philip
the man who sent you that present ? 3. No, he is the man whose
automobile I bought last week. 4. He lives with his sister in that
white house. 5. They tell me that he never returns home early.
6. Almost always he returns after the sun has set. 7. He says
that he who works little does not earn much. 8. I have to go to
his house tonight to give him two hundred dollars. — 9. Do you
know who that tall man is ? 10. Do you mean the one who is
near the door ? 11. Yes, he looks at me a great deal, which does
not please me. 12. It seems strange to me that you do not know
him. 13. He is the one who brought my brother's automobile.
14. He is a friend of George, who introduced him to me yesterday.
15. I was in a hurry then, and I could not talk a great deal with
him. 16. But he has just told me that he will come to see me
tomorrow. — 17. Do you know what happened in the office today ?
18. Well, at eleven o'clock a man whom I didn't know came in.
19. He told me: "I must see my brother, who works here."
20. Without asking him what his name was, I told him that he
was not there. 21. He told me that he was very thirsty, and I
gave him three glasses of water. 22. Then he asked me to allow
him to sit down and wait for his brother. 23. He was sleepy and
soon afterwards he went to sleep on the chair. 24. At twelve
o'clock my boss came back to the office. 25. He saw the man
sleeping on the chair, and shouted: "What is my brother doing
there ?"

LECTURA

Ha llegado la media noche [1] y siguen apareciendo [2] convidados. Don Hilario ya no se atreve a [3] rechazar [4] a nadie, por más que [5] su esposa le dirige cada mirada que le hace temblar.[6] El pobre señor se ha convencido de que no tiene carácter.[7]

Por fin [8] se le acerca doña Teresa y le dice:

— ¡ Hasta [9] cuándo Hilario !

— Eso es lo mismo que digo yo: ¡ hasta cuándo !

— Pero no haces nada de tu parte. Todo se vuelve [10]: ¡ adelante ! [11]

— ¿ Y qué quieres que haga ?

— Plantarte [12] en tus trece ! [13]

— ¡ Qué trece ! si ya van [14] más de cien !

— Yo no veo más remedio [15] que cerrar la puerta.

— La golpean,[16] hija, y entonces tenemos el trabajo [17] de abrirla.

— Pero ¿ qué hacemos, hombre ? ¿ No se te ocurre nada ?

ROMÁN VIAL, *Un convidado convida a ciento.*

LESSON XLV

207. *Indefinite Pronouns and Pronominal Adjectives.*

a)

alguien	$\begin{cases} \text{some one, somebody} \\ \text{any one, anybody} \end{cases}$

alguno (–a, –os, –as), *some, any, a few*

alguna cosa
algo $\Big\}$ *something, anything*

uno (–a, –os, –as), *one, some*

cada (adj., invar.), *each, every*

cada uno (–a), *each one*

---

[1] media noche (medianoche), *midnight.* [2] *appearing (coming).* [3] atreverse a, *to dare (to).* [4] *refuse (to admit).* [5] por más que, *although.* [6] *tremble.* [7] no tiene carácter, *he is not firm.* [8] *Finally.* [9] *Until.* [10] Todo se vuelve, *It all turns to* (= *All you say is*). [11] *come in.* [12] *Stand (firm).* [13] trece, *thirteen;* plantarse (estarse) en sus trece, *to stand firm, stick to it.* [14] *have gone in.* [15] *remedy.* [16] *knock (on).* [17] *trouble.*

ambos (–as) ⎫
los (las) dos ⎬ *both*

los (las) demás, *the rest*

cualquiera (cualesquiera), *any (one) at all, whatever*

nadie, *no one, nobody*

ninguno (–a, –os, –as), *none, no*

ninguna cosa ⎫
cosa alguna ⎬ *nothing*
nada⁻ ⎭

mucho (–a, –os, –as), *much, many*

poco (–a, –os, –as), *little, few*

todo (–a, –os, –as), *all, every;* n., *everything*

mismo (–a, –os, –as), *same, self*

otro (–a, –os, –as), *other, another*

tanto (–a, –os, –as), *as*

tal, *such, such a*

quienquiera (quienesquiera), *whoever*

Más vale algo que nada.	*Something is better than nothing.*
Todo hombre debe cumplir con su deber.	*Every man should do his duty.*
Todos los muchachos jugaban a la pelota.	*All the boys were playing ball.*
Va al teatro todas las noches (cada noche).	*He goes to the theater every (each) night.*
Cada dos horas sale un tren.	*A train leaves every two hours.*
Nos quiere a los dos.	*He likes us both.*
Murió el mismo día.	*He died the same day.*
Él mismo me lo dijo.	*He told me so himself.*
Quisiéramos otros dos.	*We should like two others.*
Hay tantos hombres como mujeres.	*There are as many men as women.*
Nunca pasé tal noche.	*I never passed such a night.*

b) An unemphatic *some* or *any* is usually not expressed in Spanish.

¿ Quiere usted uvas ?	*Do you want some grapes?*
¿ Tiene usted peras ? — No tengo.	*Have you any pears? — I haven't any.*

c) A *little* (denoting quantity) is **un poco de.**

¿ Puede usted prestarme un poco de dinero ?
Can you lend me a little money?

d) **Cualquiera** (**cualesquiera**) may lose the final –a when it precedes the noun it modifies.

Cualquier hombre es bueno para eso.   *Any man is good (enough) for that.*

But: **Para eso cualquiera es bueno.**   *For that any one (at all) is good.*

e) Review § 115.

208. **Decir.** Review §§ 125*c*, 128, 138*c*, 156, 157, 161. Study §§ 217, 218, 271. **Hacer.** Review §§ 116, 136, 156, 157, 161. Study §§ 217, 218, 270.

es decir	*that is to say*
querer decir	*to mean*
se dice	*it is said*

hacer calor (frío, viento, sol), *to be warm (cold, windy, sunny)*

Hace calor.	*It is warm.*
Hace mucho frío.	*It is very cold.*
Hace buen (mal) tiempo.	*The weather is fine (bad).*

EXERCISES

algo *anything*

alguien *some one, somebody; any one, anybody*

alguno, –a *some, any, a few*

ambos, –as *both*

cada *each, every;* — **uno** (–a) *each one*

castigar *to punish*

cosa: — **alguna** *nothing;* **alguna —,** *something;* **ninguna —,** *nothing*

cualquiera (**cualesquiera**) *any (one) at all, whatever*

cumplir *to fulfil*

el **deber** *duty*

demás *rest, others*

dos: los (las) —, *both*

el **lago** *lake*

llamar *to knock*

llorar *to cry, weep*

el **neumático** *tire*

el **pato** *duck*

la **pelota** *ball*

la **pera** *pear*

la **ropa** *clothes*

tanto, –a *as*

el **tiempo** *weather*

todo, –a *all, every;* n. *everything*

uno, –a *one, some*

la **uva** *grape*

valer *to be worth;* **más vale** *it is better*

el **viento** *wind;* **hace** (**hacía,** etc.) **—,** *it is* (*was,* etc.) *windy*

la **yerba** *grass*

A. 1. Todos los niños me dijeron que querían dar un paseo. 2. Como hacía buen tiempo fuimos al parque. 3. Hacía sol y ya

los árboles y la yerba estaban verdes. 4. Cada uno de los niños
llevaba algo consigo. 5. Unos llevaban dulces y otros uvas y
peras. 6. Nos sentamos cerca del lago para dar de comer a los
patos. 7. Poco después no teníamos ni dulces ni frutas. 8. Algunos de los niños tenían hambre y tuvimos que volver a casa. —
9. Me parece que alguien llama a la puerta. 10. Creo que es
el mismo muchacho que estuvo aquí ayer. 11. Hace tres días
que le ví en la calle con otro muchacho. 12. Los dos estaban cansados y tenían hambre y frío. 13. Yo les dí un poco de dinero
para que comieran algo. 14. Querían ropa y zapatos pero no les
dí nada de eso. 15. Les dije que viniesen hoy a verle a usted.
16. Pues démosles cuanta ropa y cuantos zapatos no necesitemos.
— 17. Se dice que aquel señor es muy rico. 18. No hay nadie
en esta ciudad más rico que él. 19. Nadie sabe cuanto dinero
tiene. 20. Pero no dudo que él tiene tanto como cualquiera otro.
21. Aunque es tan rico gasta muy poco. 22. El otro día un pobre
le pidió unos centavos. 23. Hacía frío y el pobre tenía hambre.
24. Pero el señor no le dió nada al pobre.

B. 1. ¿ Qué dijeron los niños ? 2. ¿ A dónde fueron ustedes ?
3. ¿ Qué tiempo hacía ? 4. ¿ Qué llevaban los niños ? 5. ¿ Dónde
se sentaron ustedes ? 6. ¿ Cuándo volvieron a casa ? 7. ¿ Quién
llama a la puerta ? 8. ¿ Dónde le vió usted ? 9. ¿ Con quién
estaba usted ? 10. ¿ Qué les dió usted ? 11. ¿ Qué querían ellos ?
12. ¿ Qué les dijo usted ? 13. ¿ Qué se dice de aquel señor ?
14. ¿ Quién es más rico que él ? 15. ¿ Cuánto dinero tiene ?
16. ¿ Cuánto gasta ? 17. ¿ Qué le pidió un pobre el otro día ?
18. ¿ Qué le dió el señor ?

C. *Translate:* 1. Both men ran to the house. 2. I haven't
any of the books. 3. I have never seen such a thing. 4. He has
almost two hundred dollars. 5. The maid set the table. 6. Any
one can do that. 7. Some one told me so (it). 8. No one gave
it to me. 9. Have you any friends here ? 10. He doesn't know
any one here. 11. Have you any money today ? 12. All men
ought to work. 13. I believe anything he says. 14. He saw us
both. 15. He arrived the same day.

D. 1. Who is the owner of that blue automobile ? 2. Mr. Ortiz,
whose sister you know well, is the owner. 3. I told you that he
owes me some money. 4. Now he wants to sell me the auto-

La cocinera no es mal parecida.

mobile. 5. It is the same automobile that his sister had last year. 6. She told me that the engine runs well. 7. One of the tires is much [1] worn. 8. The others seem to be in good condition. — 9. Who is crying and shouting so much in that room? 10. It is little Elizabeth, John's sister. 11. She is very angry with John and she wants us to punish him. 12. The latter told her that he was going to use her bicycle. 13. She didn't say anything, and he went to the park on her bicycle. 14. She doesn't know that he who is silent gives consent. 15. I don't understand what that means. 16. Study the lesson well and you will understand the sentence. — 17. It is warm today but Charles says that he is cold. 18. He has been outside for two hours. 19. Yes, he is waiting for Philip, one of his older brother's friends. 20. Each time that Philip comes to the house he brings him candy. 21. This pleases Charles [very] much. 22. But it seems to me that Philip will not come today. 23. He went to visit his uncle who lives far from here. 24. It will not be possible for him to return until next Monday.

LECTURA

Mando a la agencia de sirvientes [2] para que, sin considerar el salario, me proporcionen [3] la mejor de las cocineras.[4] Me la pro-

---

[1] *nery.*   [2] *servants.*   [3] *supply (with).*   [4] *cooks.*

meten, se guardan [1] el importe [2] de la comisión, y yo me quedo esperando a la cocinera.

Al día siguiente, en efecto, llega la mujer, joven todavía, no mal parecida,[3] con un moño [4] muy empingorotado [5] y con la cara bien revocada de [6] polvo [7] de arroz, de harina [8] o cosa por el estilo.[9]

— ¿ Es usted cocinera ? — le pregunto después de contestar a su reverente [10] y coquetón [11] saludo.[12]

— Para servirle.

— Justamente [13] la necesito para eso.

— ¿ Hay niños en la casa ?

— Sí, algunos, pero son grandecitos.[14] No tenga usted cuidado por eso.

— Al contrario, los grandecitos son los atrevidos.[15]

— Vamos,[16] tranquilícese,[17] que no son niños, sino hombres hechos y derechos.[18]

ROMÁN VIAL, Las cocineras.

LESSON XLVI

209. *Cardinal Numerals (4).*

a)

1	un(o), -a	9	nueve
2	dos	10	diez
3	tres	11	once
4	cuatro	12	doce
5	cinco	13	trece
6	seis	14	catorce
7	siete	15	quince
8	ocho	16	diez y seis

[1] *keep (for themselves).* [2] *amount.* [3] **mal parecida,** *bad looking.* [4] *chignon, topknot.* [5] *high.* [6] **revocada de,** *plastered with.* [7] *powder.* [8] *flour.* [9] *style;* **cosa por el estilo,** *something of the sort.* [10] *respectful.* [11] *coquettish.* [12] *greeting.* [13] *Just.* [14] *already grown up.* [15] *bold (ones).* [16] *Come.* [17] *be calm.* [18] **hechos y derechos,** *in every respect.*

17	diez y siete	60	sesenta
18	diez y ocho	70	setenta
19	diez y nueve	80	ochenta
20	veinte	90	noventa
21	veintiun(o), –a	100	cien(to)
22	veintidós	200	doscientos, –as
23	veintitrés	300	trescientos, –as
24	veinticuatro	400	cuatrocientos, –as
25	veinticinco	500	quinientos, –as
26	veintiséis	600	seiscientos, –as
27	veintisiete	700	setecientos, –as
28	veintiocho	800	ochocientos, –as
29	veintinueve	900	novecientos, –as
30	treinta	1000	mil
31	treinta y un(o), –a	2000	dos mil
40	cuarenta	1,000,000	un millón
50	cincuenta	2,000,000	dos millones

NOTES: 1. Sixteen, seventeen, etc., are also written **dieciséis,
diecisiete,** etc.

2. Twenty-one, twenty-two, etc., are also written **veinte y uno,
veinte y dos,** etc., but not pronounced thus. **Veintiún** requires
the accent mark.

b) For the apocopation of **uno** and **ciento,** see § 180. Note
also the use of **un** and **una** in such expressions as **veintiún días,** *twenty-one days,* **veintiuna semanas,** *twenty-one
weeks.*

c) For the omission of **un** before **cien(to)** and **mil,** see § 176c.
But note **veintiún mil,** 21,000, etc.

d) **Millón** is a masculine noun; its plural is **millones.** It requires the preposition **de** before the word it multiplies: **un
millón de pesos,** *a million dollars.*

e) In compound numbers, **y,** *and,* is placed before the last
numeral, provided the numeral that immediately precedes
is less than 100. Thus, **ciento noventa y cinco,** *195;* but
doscientos cinco, *205.*

f) Counting by hundreds is not carried above nine hundred in
Spanish; beginning with ten hundred, **mil** is used: **mil
novecientos cuarenta y uno,** *1941.*

210. *Ordinal Numerals.*

a)

1st	primer (o), −a, −os, −as	6th	sexto, −a, −os, −as
2nd	segundo, −a, −os, −as	7th	séptimo, −a, −os, −as
3rd	tercer (o), −a, −os, −as	8th	octavo, −a, −os, −as
4th	cuarto, −a, −os, −as	9th	noveno, −a, −os, −as
5th	quinto, −a, −os, −as	10th	décimo, −a, −os, −as

b) The Spanish ordinals above **décimo** are little used. Their place is usually taken by the cardinals.

> **Luis quince.**   *Louis the Fifteenth.*
> **El capítulo cincuenta.**   *The fiftieth chapter.*

NOTES: 1. The ordinals may be abbreviated as follows: 1º (1ᵉʳ), 1ª, 1ᵃᵐ, 1ᵃˢ, etc.

2. For the apocopation of **primero** and **tercero**, see § 180*a*.

211. *Fractions.*

a)

$\frac{1}{2}$	medio, −a; la mitad
$\frac{1}{3}$	un tercio; la tercera parte
$\frac{3}{4}$	tres cuartos
$\frac{1}{5}$	un quinto; la quinta parte

$\frac{1}{11}$ to $\frac{1}{99}$. Fractional numerals are commonly formed by adding −avo to the cardinal after dropping a final vowel, except the −e of −siete and −nueve: $\frac{1}{11}$, un onzavo; $\frac{2}{12}$, dos dozavos; $\frac{5}{20}$, cinco veintavos, etc.; but $\frac{1}{17}$, un diecisieteavo.

b) *Half (a half, one half, half a)* as substantive is expressed by **la mitad**; as adjective, by **medio** (−a).

> **La mitad de mis bienes.**   *One half of my goods.*
> **Trabajó medio día.**   *He worked half a day.*

212. *Arithmetical Signs.*

+	más or y	×	(multiplicado) **por**
−	menos	:	dividido por
=	es (igual a), son (iguales a)		

$2 + 3 = 5$	dos más (or y) tres son cinco
$5 − 3 = 2$	cinco menos tres son (or es igual a) **dos**
$3 × 3 = 9$	tres (multiplicado) por tres son nueve
$9 : 3 = 3$	nueve dividido por tres son tres

213. **Poder.** Review §§ 137, 138c, 161. Study §§ 217, 218, 274.
Saber. Review §§ 133, 148a, 157b, 161. Study §§ 217,
218, 272.

no poder más, *to be played out, be exhausted*

No puedo más. *I am exhausted.*

no poder menos de, *to be necessary:* (pres.) *can not but, can not
help;* (past) *could not help*

No pudo menos de hacerlo. *He could not help doing so.*

saber a, *to taste of* (*like*)

El agua sabe a leche. *The water tastes of milk.*
¿ Quién sabe ? *Who knows? Perhaps.*

EXERCISES

ahogarse *to drown*
bajo, -a *low*
la biblioteca *library*
los bienes *goods, property*
caer (se) *to fall*
el capítulo *chapter*
coger *to pick*
la comida *food*
cuarto, -a *fourth*
el daño *harm;* hacerse —, *to
harm or hurt oneself*
décimo, -a *tenth*
dividir *to divide*
el estudio *study*
el gasto *expense*
igual *equal*
Luis *Louis*
más *plus*
menos *minus*
el millón *million*
la mitad *half*
multiplicar *to multiply*
nadar *to swim*
novecientos, -as *nine hundred*

noveno, -a *ninth*
octavo, -a *eighth*
pesar *to weigh*
el piso *floor*
poder: no — más *to be played
out, be exhausted;* no — menos
de *be necessary;* (pres.) *can
not but, can not help;* (past)
could not help
la rama *branch*
saber: — a *to taste of* (*like*);
¿ quién sabe ? *who knows?
perhaps*
séptimo, -a *seventh*
setecientos, -as *seven hundred*
el sótano *basement, cellar*
subir (tr.) *to bring or take up;*
(intr.) *go, come, get up*
el tercio *third*
terminar *to finish*
el verano *summer*
el viaje *trip;* hacer un —, *to take
a trip*
el volumen *volume*

A. 1. Juan y yo pensamos hacer un viaje largo el verano que
viene. 2. Juan termina sus estudios el quince de junio y yo el

dieciocho. 3. Saldremos el veinte del mismo mes y volveremos el primero de septiembre. 4. Juan quiere que vayamos en su automóvil porque es más grande. 5. El mío es más nuevo pero es más pequeño. 6. Juan necesita comprar dos o tres neumáticos. 7. Dos costarán veinte y cinco pesos y tres treinta y seis. 8. Ya le he dicho a Juan que yo pagaré la mitad de los gastos. — 9. Nos mudamos a nuestra casa nueva la semana pasada. 10. Es una casa de tres pisos y diez y seis cuartos. 11. Le costó a papá veintiún mil quinientos pesos. 12. En el sótano papá tiene unas treinta cajas de libros. 13. Quiere que se los suba a la biblioteca en el segundo piso. 14. Hoy he trabajado más de seis horas haciendo eso. 15. He subido setecientos ochenta y seis libros. 16. Ahora voy a descansar porque no puedo más. — 17. Cuando Juan se cayó no pudimos menos de reírnos. 18. Quería una pera más grande que la que yo le había dado. 19. La pera estaba en una rama baja. 20. Era posible cogerla sin subirse al árbol. 21. Juan se subió en una silla que estaba allí. 22. La silla era vieja y Juan pesa mucho. 23. Si no hubiese sido por la yerba se hubiera hecho daño. 24. Él se rió con los demás, se levantó y cogió la pera.

B. 1. ¿ Quiénes piensan hacer un viaje ? 2. ¿ Cuándo termina Juan sus estudios ? 3. ¿ Cuándo saldrán ustedes ? 4. ¿ Qué quiere Juan ? 5. ¿ Cuál de los automóviles es más pequeño ? 6. ¿ Qué necesita comprar Juan ? 7. ¿ Cuánto cuesta un neumático ? 8. ¿ Cuándo se mudaron ustedes a su casa nueva ? 9. ¿ Cuántos cuartos tiene la casa ? 10. ¿ Cuánto costó la casa ? 11. ¿ Qué hay en el sótano ? 12. ¿ Dónde está la biblioteca ? 13. ¿ Cuántos libros ha subido ? 14. ¿ Quién se cayó ? 15. ¿ Qué quería Juan ? 16. ¿ Dónde estaba la pera ? 17. ¿ A dónde se subió Juan ? 18. ¿ Qué hizo Juan después de levantarse ?

C. *Read or write in Spanish:* 21; 32; 43; 54; 65; 76; 87; 98; 123; 234; 345; 456; 567; 678; 789; 1240; 2357; 5962; 15,749; 100,154; 1.000,000; 2.100,150; el año 1492; el año 1808; el año 1892; el año 1917; el año 1920; el año 1940; la página 35; la lección 46; el capítulo 175; Carlos V; Luis 14; el volumen 8; $\frac{1}{2}$; $\frac{2}{3}$; $\frac{1}{4}$; $\frac{2}{5}$; $\frac{5}{8}$; $\frac{9}{10}$; $\frac{1}{50}$; $\frac{5}{75}$; $3 + 5 = 8$; $8 - 2 = 6$; $3 \times 15 = 45$; $48 : 16 = 3$.

D. 1. The boys say that they will not work tomorrow. 2. Some wish to go to the country, and others prefer to play ball. 3. They are angry because they do not pay them so much in the store. 4. They say that the food that they give them is not good. 5. It is true that the coffee tastes like water with milk. 6. But it is better that they should not do such a thing now. 7. It is necessary that each one should do his duty. 8. If they do not work much they will receive less money. — 9. Do you know why Henry is crying ? 10. Yes, his father told ¹ me a moment ago. 11. Henry used to like to go to the lake to feed the ducks. 12. His father had forbidden him to go because he does not know how to swim. 13. This morning Henry went to the lake and fell into it. 14. If he had not called several times he would have drowned. 15. His father has punished him by ² forbidding him to go out today and tomorrow. — 16. Where do you intend to spend the summer ? 17. I like to spend it here because the sun rises early and sets late. 18. Some one has told me that it is very warm. 19. No, it is not so warm as in other places. 20. In winter it is very cold and I don't like it. 21. That is why I prefer to go to Florida then. 22. I always meet some of my friends there. 23. But I don't know if I shall be able to go next winter.

LECTURA

Pasa un día, pasan dos, tres, y seguimos comiendo como de ³ milagro.⁴

Al fin veo llegar una cocinera que no tiene malas trazas ⁵ y que probablemente voy a aceptar, si es que ella me acepta a mí, que es lo más difícil.⁶

— Me han dicho que aquí necesitan cocinera.

— No la han engañado. ¿ Quiere usted servir ? ⁷

— Cómo no ⁸ ; a eso venía.

— ¿ Es usted limpia ? ⁹

— Por eso no le dé cuidado, porque estoy acostumbrada a servir en casas extranjeras, y si gusta le puedo traer recomendación ¹⁰ de *mis* ¹¹ *Meri.*¹²

---

¹ Supply *it.*   ² Omit.   ³ *by a.*   ⁴ *miracle.*   ⁵ *appearance.*   ⁶ *difficult.*
⁷ *work* (as a servant).   ⁸ **Cómo no,** *Of course.*   ⁹ *neat.*   ¹⁰ *reference.*
¹¹ *Miss.*   ¹² *Mary.*

— ¿ Quién es *mis Meri?*

— *Mis Meri* es una señora inglesa.

— Es decir que usted por lo menos sabrá hacer los bisteques.[1]

— Yo toda clase [2] de postres.

— ¡ Qué bueno! . . . Pero en eso se gasta mucho.

— No, patrón [3]; yo no soy desperdiciadora [4] como otras, y *mis Meri* me acostumbró a ser muy arreglada.[5]

ROMÁN VIAL, Las cocineras.

LESSON XLVII

214. *Use of* **ojalá** (**que**) *with the Subjunctive.*

¡Ojalá (que) viva mil años !
Oh that he may (or *I hope he will) live a thousand years!*

¡Ojalá (que) viviese (viviera) mil años !
Oh that he might (or *I wish he would) live a thousand years!*

¡Ojalá (que) yo pudiera hacerlo ! *I wish I could do it!*

NOTE: **Que** is often omitted after **ojalá.**

215. *Softened Statements.*

a) Yo quisiera vender la casa.
I should like (or *I should be glad) to sell the house.*

Yo quisiera que usted la comprase (comprara).
I wish you would buy it.

Usted debiera hacer las reparaciones.
You ought to (or *should) make the repairs.*

NOTE: These are milder expressions, and therefore more commonly used than the following: **Quiero vender la casa,** *I want to sell the house;* **Quiero que usted la compre,** *I wish you to buy it;* **Usted debe hacer las reparaciones,** *You must make the repairs.*

b) The conditional is also thus used.

Me gustaría mucho hacerlo.   *I should like very much to do so.*
Ella preferiría pasearse en coche.   *She would prefer to go driving.*

---

[1] *beefsteaks.*   [2] *all kinds.*   [3] *boss.*   [4] *wasteful.*   [5] *careful, moderate.*

216. '*Will*' *and* '*should.*' *Will* (= *am, art, is*, etc., *willing*) is expressed by **quiero, quieres,** etc. (see § 102*b*); *should* (= *ought to*) is expressed by **debiera, debieras,** etc.

   ¿ **Quiere usted venderla ?**   *Will you sell it?*
   ¿ **Debiera (or debería) yo hacerlo ?**   *Should I do it?*

217. *Future (or Hypothetical) Subjunctive.* This tense may be formed for all verbs by adding the following endings to the stem of the preterite indicative, third person:

<table>
<tr><th colspan="2">I</th><th colspan="2">II AND III</th></tr>
<tr><td>−are</td><td>−áremos</td><td>−iere</td><td>−iéremos</td></tr>
<tr><td>−ares</td><td>−areis</td><td>−ieres</td><td>−iereis</td></tr>
<tr><td>−are</td><td>−aren</td><td>−iere</td><td>−ieren</td></tr>
</table>

<table>
<tr><th>PRETERITE</th><th>FUTURE SUBJUNCTIVE</th></tr>
<tr><td>*3rd pers. pl.*</td><td></td></tr>
<tr><td>**Comprar:** compraron</td><td>compr−are, −ares, −are, −áremos, −areis, −aren</td></tr>
<tr><td>**Pedir:** pidieron</td><td>pid−iere, −ieres, −iere, −iéremos, −iereis, −ieren</td></tr>
<tr><td>**Estar:** estuvieron</td><td>estuv−iere, −ieres, −iere, −iéremos, −iereis, −ieren</td></tr>
</table>

NOTE: This tense has in all cases the same stem as the imperfect subjunctive. See §§ 161*b*, 165, 183, 191, 197*b* for verbs which are irregular in the imperfect subjunctive.

218. *Use of the Future Subjunctive.* The future subjunctive denotes a condition or hypothesis. In the spoken Spanish of today it is rarely used except in proverbs, legal expressions, etc. Its place is regularly taken by the present subjunctive, or by the present indicative if used with **si.**

Donde fueres haz como vieres.
   Wherever you go, do as you see. (Cf. 'When in Rome, do as the Romans do.')

Si algún accionista pidiere (or pide) que la reunión se difiera, decidirá la mayoría.
   If any shareholder asks that the meeting be postponed, the majority shall decide.

219. *Dative of Separation.* In Spanish, verbs meaning *to take from*, *ask of*, and the like, take the dative of the person.

Pido un favor a mi padre.   *I ask a favor of my father.*
Lo compró al señor García.   *He bought it of Mr. García.*

NOTE: We say also: **Le pido un favor,** *I ask a favor of him;* **Se lo compró,** *He bought it from him.*

220. Salir. Review §§ 132, 149, 156, 157.

IMPERF. SUBJ.	$\begin{cases} \text{\textbf{saliera, salieras,} etc.} \\ \text{\textbf{saliese, salieses,} etc.} \end{cases}$
FUT. SUBJ.	**saliere, salieres,** etc.

221. Querer. Review §§ 96, 143.

PRES. SUBJ.   **quiera, quieras, quiera, queramos, queráis, quieran**

IMPERF. SUBJ. $\begin{cases} \text{\textbf{quisiese, quisieses,} etc.} \\ \text{\textbf{quisiera, quisieras,} etc.} \end{cases}$

FUT. SUBJ.   **quisiere, quisieres,** etc.

querer decir, *to mean*

     ¿ Qué quiere decir eso?   *What does that mean?*

EXERCISES

el (la) accionista *shareholder*
bajarse *to get down*
el coche *carriage, coach, car;* **ir (pasearse) en —,** *to drive*
la compañía *company*
el correo *mail*
el cuaderno *notebook*
decidir *to decide*
la deuda *debt*
diferir (ie) *to postpone*
el empleo *position, job*
entre *among, between*
explotar *to work, develop* (a mine)
el favor *favor*
Lope de Vega: Lope Félix de

Vega Carpio, Spanish dramatist, 1562–1635
la mayoría *majority*
la mina *mine*
la noticia *news (item):* **las noticias** *news*
la obra *work*
ojalá *would that, I wish he (she, etc.) would, I hope*
pasearse *to walk, drive* or *ride for pleasure, stroll*
el peligro *danger*
reducir *to reduce*
la reparación *repair*
seco, –a *dry*
la tesis *thesis*

A. 1. Luis piensa hacer un viaje el verano próximo. 2. Cuando termine sus estudios vendrá a visitarnos. 3. Es posible que pase dos o tres semanas con nosotros. 4. De aquí saldrá para el Canadá la segunda semana de julio. 5. Me ha escrito que quiere que yo le acompañe. 6. Si puedo me gustaría mucho hacerlo. 7. ¡ Ojalá que mi padre me lo permita ! 8. Yo he ahorrado bastante y me parece que tengo unos setecientos dólares. — 9. Esos niños no debieran subirse a ese árbol. 10. Algunas de las ramas están muy secas. 11. Podrían caerse de una de ellas y hacerse daño. 12. Si el árbol fuera más bajo no habría tanto peligro. 13. ¿ Quiere usted decirles que se bajen en seguida ? 14. Pueden jugar en el sótano si quieren. 15. No, es mejor que vayan al lago a nadar. 16. Hace buen tiempo y todos saben nadar bien. — 17. Mi madre está triste porque acaba de recibir una mala noticia. 18. Mi tío le ha escrito que no continuarán explotando la mina. 19. La compañía ha gastado más de un millón de pesos. 20. Dice que los bienes serán divididos entre los accionistas. 21. Los gastos y las deudas serán divididos también. 22. Si la compañía quisiere podrá continuarse el trabajo. 23. Pero él no cree que sea posible hacerlo. 24. Esto quiere decir que mi hermano perderá su empleo.

B. 1. ¿ Quién piensa hacer un viaje ? 2. ¿ Cuándo vendrá a visitarnos ? 3. ¿ Cuánto tiempo ha de pasar con nosotros ? 4. ¿ Para dónde saldrá de aquí ? 5. ¿ Qué le gustaría a usted hacer ? 6. ¿ Cuánto dinero tiene usted ? 7. ¿ A dónde se han subido los niños ? 8. ¿ Cómo están algunas de las ramas ? 9. ¿ De dónde podrían caerse los niños ? 10. ¿ Dónde pueden jugar ? 11. ¿ Qué es mejor que hagan ? 12. ¿ Qué saben hacer todos ? 13. ¿ Por qué está triste su madre ? 14. ¿ Qué le ha escrito su tío ? 15. ¿ Cuánto ha gastado la compañía ? 16. ¿ Entre quiénes serán divididos los bienes ? 17. ¿ Qué podrá continuarse si la mayoría lo quisiere ? 18. ¿ Quién perderá su empleo ?

C. *Translate:* 1. I should like to know what he is doing. 2. What does that mean ? 3. We are studying the eighth chapter. 4. They are laughing at you. 5. He could not help doing it. 6. This apple tastes like a pear. 7. I gave him half of my bread. 8. I don't want you to take that. 9. Did you like the food ? 10. Who knows where he is ? 11. He says that he is exhausted. 12. Multiply two hundred and fifty-four by twenty-seven. 13. Of whom did you buy the bicycle ? 14. Whom did he ask for the book ? 15. He shouldn't do that. 16. Have you decided to do it ?

D. 1. My dear friend: I am writing to you to ask you a favor.
2. I have to write a seventy-five-hundred-word thesis.[1] 3. I have
not been able to find in our library a book that I need. 4. It is
the sixth volume of the works of Lope de Vega. 5. I know that
your father has it. 6. Ask him if he can lend it to me for a week.
7. As it weighs so much it will cost a great deal to send it by mail.
8. I can go and get[2] it next Saturday. — 9. Buy the books and
notebooks of that poor man. 10. He wants fifty cents for each
book and five cents for each notebook. 11. He has fifteen books
and ten notebooks. 12. Fifteen times fifty are seven hundred
and fifty. 13. That is to say, seven dollars and a half for the
books. 14. The ten notebooks at five cents each are fifty cents.
15. I should have to pay eight dollars for the books and the notebooks. 16. I should prefer to give him two dollars, and not to
buy anything of him. — 17. Will you buy a new automobile?
18. I should like a new one, but I haven't much money. 19. I
need one soon to take a long trip with my brother. 20. Why don't
you buy John's? 21. It is not so new; it needs repairs, and the
engine does not run well. 22. He bought it two years ago and he
has used it a great deal. 23. That's why he wishes to sell it for
little money. 24. But you should not buy it unless he reduces
the price.

LECTURA

Como iba[3] diciendo, era un jueves.

Silvestre se levantó a las ocho de la mañana.

Y se levantó a esa hora por tres razones.

Primera, porque tenía que ir a la oficina.

Segunda, porque quiso.

Y tercera, porque se levantó.

¡Ah! Todavía una razón poderosa.[4] Se levantó porque se
había acostado. Eso es.

Antes de comenzar la historia de aquel día, es preciso decir
para mejor inteligencia[5] del que lea, que además de[6] su suerte[7]
perra,[8] Silvestre tiene ocurrencias[9] del demonio.[10]

[1] *a thesis of seventy-five hundred words.* [2] *to get* (**buscar**) *it.* [3] *I was.*
[4] *powerful.* [5] *understanding.* [6] **además de,** *besides.* [7] *luck.* [8] *unfortu-*
nate. [9] *ideas, occurrences.* [10] *devil.*

¿ Qué ocurre, señorito ?

Por ejemplo,[1] la de meter [2] el reloj en una bota.[3]

Figúrese [4] usted si venderán por ahí [5] relojeras [6] baratas.[7]

Pues no señor, no sirve eso [8]; el reloj de Silvestre duerme siempre en una bota.

El día en que comienzan estos renglones,[9] mi amigo fué a tomar su reloj . . . ¡ Sí, sí! busque usted el reloj. No había tal cosa.

— ¡ Muchacha ! — grita Silvestre. — ¡ Muchacha !

— ¿ Qué ocurre, señorito ? [10]

— ¿ Y mi reloj ?

— ¿ Qué reloj ?

— ¡ El mío, mujer, el mío !

— ¡ Qué sé yo ! ¡ Yo no entiendo de [11] relojes !

Eusebio Blasco, *Un día de prueba.*[12]

[1] *example.*   [2] *putting.*   [3] *boot.*   [4] *Just imagine.*   [5] *anywhere.*   [6] *watch-cases.*   [7] *cheap.*   [8] **no sirve eso,** *that is not good.*   [9] *lines.*   [10] *master.* [11] **Yo no entiendo de,** *I know nothing about.*   [12] *trial;* **de prueba,** *trying.*

LESSON XLVIII

222. *Adverbs.*

a) **Aquí, acá,** *here, hither;* **ahí,** *there* (near the person addressed, or not very remote); **allí, allá,** *there, thither* (more remote). **Aquí** and **allí** denote a more specific and limited place than do **acá** and **allá**.

Venga acá.	*Come here.*
Siéntese aquí.	*Sit down right here.*

b) **Mucho,** *much, a great deal;* **muy,** *very.*

Ha estudiado mucho.	*He has studied much (a great deal).*
Está muy enferma.	*She is very ill.*

Notes: 1. **Muy,** not **mucho,** is used before a past participle not occurring in a perfect tense: **Le estaré muy agradecido,** *I shall be much obliged to him.*

2. *Very,* when standing alone, is **mucho,** as **muy** can never stand alone: **¿ Es interesante el libro ? — Sí, mucho.** *Is the book interesting? — Yes, very.*

c) Both **si,** *if,* and **sí,** *yes,* may be used as intensive adverbs.

¡ Si no lo creo !	*Indeed I don't believe it!*
¡ Si partió esta mañana !	*Why, he left this morning!*
Ahora sí lo creo.	*Now I do believe it.*
Eso sí que es bueno.	*That is indeed good.*

d) **Ya,** *already, now, in due time, indeed;* **ya no,** *no longer, no more.*

Ya acabé.	*I have already finished.*
Ya entendemos.	*Now we understand.*
Ya volverá.	*He will return in due time.*
¡ Ya lo creo !	*I should say so!*
Ya no tengo dinero.	*I have no more money.*

e) In Spanish, adverbs may be formed from many descriptive adjectives by adding **–mente** to the feminine singular of the adjective, as **correctamente** (from **correcto**), *correctly;* **fácilmente** (from **fácil**), *easily,* etc.

Él habla distintamente. *He speaks distinctly.*

Note: When several adverbs in –mente modify the same word, –mente is omitted from all but the last: **Hable usted clara y distintamente,** *Speak clearly and distinctly.*

223. *Agreement of Subject and Verb.* A verb agrees with its subject in number and person.

yo soy	*I am*
tú eres	*you are*
usted y Juan son	*you and John are*

Note: When the subjects are of different persons, the verb is in the first person plural if any of the subjects is of the first person; and it is in the second person plural if the subjects are of the second and third persons: **tú y yo somos,** *you and I are;* **él y yo somos,** *he and I are;* **tú y él sois,** *you and he are.*

224. Caer, *to fall, fit.* Review §§ 125*d*, 138*d*, 183*a*.

PRES. INDIC.	**caigo, caes, cae, caemos, caéis, caen**
PRES. SUBJ.	**caiga, caigas, caiga, caigamos, caigáis, caigan**
IMPERAT.	**cae** **caed**
FUTURE CONDITIONAL	} Regular
PRETERITE	**caí, caíste, cayó, caímos, caísteis, cayeron**
IMPERF. SUBJ.	{ **cayese, cayeses,** etc. { **cayera, cayeras,** etc.
FUTURE SUBJ.	**cayere, cayeres,** etc.

Ese sombrero te cae bien.	*That hat fits you well.*
Ya caigo.	*Now I understand.*
Se me cayó.	*I dropped it.*

Note: This verb is frequently used as a reflexive: **El niño se cayó,** *The child fell.*

225. Oír, *to hear.* Review §§ 125*d*, 138*d*, 183*a*.

PRES. INDIC.	**oigo, oyes, oye, oímos, oís, oyen**
PRES. SUBJ.	**oiga, oigas, oiga, oigamos, oigáis, oigan**
IMPERAT.	**oye** **oíd**
FUTURE CONDITIONAL	} Regular
PRETERITE	**oí, oíste, oyó, oímos, oísteis, oyeron**
IMPERF. SUBJ.	{ **oyese, oyeses,** etc. { **oyera, oyeras,** etc.
FUTURE SUBJ.	**oyere, oyeres,** etc.

oír decir, *to hear (it said)*

    He oído decir que vendrá. *I have heard that he will come.*

oír hablar, *to hear (spoken of)*

    ¿ Ha oído usted hablar de él ? *Have you heard of him?*

    ¡ Oye ! ¡ Oiga ! *Listen! Hear! I declare! The idea!*

EXERCISES

acá *here*
agradecido, –a *grateful, obliged*
ayudar *to aid, help*
la **beca** *scholarship*
caer *to fall, fit;* **ya caigo** *now I understand;* **se me cayó** *I dropped it*
el **camión** *truck*
claro, –a *clear*
coger *to take*
cómodo, –a *comfortable*
la **conferencia** *lecture*
distintamente *distinctly*
entender (ie) *to understand*

la **habitación** *room*
hasta *until, as far as*
instar *to urge*
misteriosamente *mysteriously*
muy *much*
oír *to hear;* — **decir** *to hear (it said);* — **hablar** *to hear (spoken of);* **¡ oye ! ¡ oiga !** *listen! hear! I declare! the idea!*
el **paquete** *package, parcel*
sobre *about*
la **tarde** *afternoon, evening*
ya *now, in due time;* — **no** *no longer, no more*

A. 1. Ví a Carlos esta mañana y me pidió un favor. 2. Quiere que le llame por teléfono esta noche a las ocho. 3. Le pregunté si no podía decirme por qué quería que hiciese eso. 4. Me dijo misteriosamente que tenía que darme una noticia. 5. Aunque le insté mucho no me dijo otra cosa. 6. ¡ Ya caigo ! ¿ No ha oído usted decir que le han otorgado una beca ? 7. Ha escrito una tesis excelente sobre el idioma español. 8. Y es posible que haga un viaje a España el verano próximo. — 9. Ya han hecho las reparaciones en el camino. 10. Vamos a pasearnos esta tarde en el automóvil. 11. La máquina está en buena condición y funciona bien. 12. Podemos ir hasta la casa de nuestro abuelo en el campo. 13. Hace algún tiempo que no le vemos y él no está bien. 14. ¿ Llegaremos allá antes de las seis ? 15. ¡ Ya lo creo ! Él no vive muy lejos de aquí. 16. Salgamos luego que Juan vuelva de la iglesia. — 17. Los accionistas de la compañía tuvieron una reunión ayer. 18. Decidieron continuar explotando la mina. 19. Para eso necesitan cuatro o cinco hombres más. 20. Acabo de escribirle a nuestro primo que venga acá. 21. Cuando venga le daremos un empleo. 22. Él ha trabajado mucho en una mina de plata. 23. Si quiere podrá vivir con nosotros. 24. Aquí tendrá una habitación muy cómoda.

B. 1. ¿ A quién vió usted esta mañana? 2. ¿ Qué quiere él? 3. ¿ Qué le preguntó usted? 4. ¿ Qué le dijo él? 5. ¿ Qué le han otorgado? 6. ¿ Sobre qué ha escrito una tesis? 7. ¿ Cuándo es posible que haga un viaje? 8. ¿ Dónde han hecho las reparaciones? 9. ¿ En qué vamos a pasearnos? 10. ¿ Cómo está la máquina? 11. ¿ Hasta dónde podemos ir? 12. ¿ Dónde vive el abuelo? 13. ¿ Quiénes tuvieron una reunión ayer? 14. ¿ Qué decidieron? 15. ¿ Qué necesitan para eso? 16. ¿ A quién acaba usted de escribirle? 17. ¿ A quién le darán un empleo? 18. ¿ Dónde ha trabajado él? 19. ¿ Qué tendrá aquí?

C. *Translate:* 1. What have you there? 2. We are grateful to you. 3. Is that good? — Yes, very. 4. Indeed it is true. 5. Now I do see him. 6. I have already written it. 7. He does not live here now. 8. We can do it easily. 9. I don't want you to fall. 10. Did he fall from the chair? 11. Did you hear what he said? 12. Have you heard of him? 13. Have you a notebook? 14. You must pay that debt. 15. There is no danger. 16. I hope he will come soon! 17. Have you read this work? 18. Has he a position? 19. Let us stroll in the park. 20. They decided not to come.

D. 1. I hope they will postpone the meeting until Monday. 2. I should like to take a friend of mine who is not here now. 3. Indeed it is not possible! Don't you know that Mr. Castro arrived yesterday? 4. We saw him at the hotel a moment ago and he received us very cordially. 5. He is the one who is going to speak about the works of Lope de Vega. 6. He has studied them a great deal, and he has translated several into English. 7. I am sure that his lecture will be very interesting. 8. Don't you think that your friend can return immediately? — 9. When I came in, the child had gotten up on a chair. 10. I imagine that it was not easy for him because he is small yet. 11. He wanted to take some candy that was on the table. 12. I told him to get down before his mother should come. 13. As he did not want to do so, I gave him a pear. 14. He got down then, but he went

out of the room running and he fell. 15. He did not hurt himself,
but he began to cry. 16. Soon afterwards his mother came, and
both went out to take a walk. — 17. Please take these packages
to the post office. 18. I declare! Don't you see all that I have
here? 19. That is true! Why, you need a truck for all that.
20. I have had to buy many things for the family. 21. But I
have no more money, and I could not buy a hat for myself. 22. I
don't like the one that I have because it doesn't fit me well. 23. I
see our friend Philip Vega over there. 24. Let us ask him to help
us with all this.

LECTURA

Sucede que un hombre honrado,[1] trabajando con constancia,[2]
llega a [3] reunir [4] doce mil duros,[5] con arreglo a [6] los cuales gasta
con más lucimiento [7] que cualquiera de sus conciudadanos [8] mi-
llonarios,[9] y los doce mil duros se convierten [10] a los ojos del mundo
en doce millones que abren al dueño un crédito extraordinario.

Esto era lo que sucedía en casa del señor de Aguaseca, que así
se llamaba el jefe de la familia.

Vivía en compañía de su esposa y su hijo; gastaba con arreglo
a [6] un capital de trescientos mil reales que a fuerzas de [11] afanes [12]
había podido reunir, y pasaba por uno de los primeros capitalistas
de la villa.[13]

Decían algunos murmuradores [14] que en aquella época en que
la afición [15] a las minas despertó en todos los españoles, Aguaseca
supo darse tal maña [16] en comprar y vender acciones,[17] que había
logrado [18] hacerse millonario; por todo lo cual las gentes de la
ciudad dieron en [19] llamarle *don Pedro el accionista*, y por *el accionista* se le conocía en todas partes.

Eusebio Blasco, *Cuatrocientos veinte reales.*

---

[1] *honest.*   [2] *steadiness.*   [3] *succeeds in.*   [4] *getting together.*   [5] *dollars*
(Spain).   [6] *in accordance with.*   [7] *freedom.*   [8] *fellow citizens.*   [9] *million-*
aire.   [10] *are converted.*   [11] *by dint of.*   [12] *toil.*   [13] *town.*   [14] *gossipers.*
[15] *fondness, liking.*   [16] *cunning;* **darse tal maña,** *manage so well.*   [17] *shares.*
[18] *succeeded in.*   [19] *persisted in.*

LESSON XLIX

226. *The Prepositions* **por** *and* **para.**

a) *For* is expressed by **por** or **para.** If *for* means *for the sake of, on account of* or *in exchange for*, it is expressed by **por;** if it denotes purpose or destination, it is expressed by **para.**

Yo daría la vida por ella.	*I would give my life for her.*
Le castigó por haber dicho una mentira.	*He punished him for having told a lie.*
Pagamos doscientos pesos por el caballo.	*We paid two hundred dollars for the horse.*
Le envié por el médico.	*I sent him for the physician.*
Tengo un paquete para usted.	*I have a package for you.*
Mañana parto para la Habana.	*I leave for Havana tomorrow.*

b) **Por** also means *through, by, per.*

El ladrón entró por la ventana.	*The thief entered through the window.*
Me cogió por la mano.	*He caught me by the hand.*
Me pagan cinco mil pesos por año.	*They pay me five thousand dollars a (per) year.*
Ganamos seis por ciento por año.	*We earn six per cent per annum.*

c) Before an infinitive, *to*, meaning *for the sake of, in exchange for*, is **por,** and meaning *in order to* is **para.**

Luchando por entrar.	*Fighting to enter.*
Lo hizo para engañarme.	*He did it to deceive me.*

227. *Conjunctions.*

a) **Y** or **e** before initial **i–** or **hi–** (not before **hie–**), *and.* **O** or **u** before initial **o–** or **ho–**, *or.*

padre y madre	*father and mother*	**cinco o seis**	*five or six*
padre e hijo	*father and son*	**siete u ocho**	*seven or eight*

NOTE: But we say **nieve y hielo,** *snow and ice.*

b) **Pero, mas, sino,** *but.* **Pero** and **mas** are synonymous, but **pero** is the more common. **Sino** is used after a negative statement that is offset by an affirmative statement.

> **Él lo dice, pero (mas) yo no lo creo.**
> *He says so, but I do not believe it.*

> **No voy a Nueva York sino a Wáshington.**
> *I am not going to New York but to Washington.*

c) **Donde** (interrogatively, **dónde**), *where,* is often made more explicit by prefixing **a, en,** or **de.**

La casa en donde vive.	*The house in which he lives.*
¿ A dónde va usted ?	*Where are you going?*
¿ De dónde viene él ?	*Where does he come from?*

228. *Word Order.*

a) When a verb precedes both its subject and a noun object or predicate adjective, the subject is placed before the object or predicate adjective if the subject is the shorter, but if it is longer it follows.

¿ Compró la casa su señor padre ?	*Did your father buy the house?*
¿ Compró su padre todas estas casas ?	*Did your father buy all these houses?*
¿ Es fácil la lección de castellano ?	*Is the Spanish lesson easy?*
¿ Es la lección fácil o difícil ?	*Is the lesson easy or difficult?*

b) In a subordinate clause, the subject often follows the verb if there is no noun object.

> **Esperaremos hasta que llegue el tren.**
> *We shall wait until the train arrives.*

229. Traer, *to bring.* Review §§ 125*d*, 138*d*, 165, 183*b*.

IMPERF. SUBJ.	{ trajese, trajeses, etc.
	trajera, trajeras, etc.
FUTURE SUBJ.	trajere, trajeres, etc.

230. Ver, *to see.* Review §§ 98*c*, 125*c*, 157*a*, 164.

IMPERF. SUBJ.	{ viese, vieses, etc.
	viera, vieras, etc.
FUTURE SUBJ.	viere, vieres, etc.

A ver, *Let's see.*

tener que ver con, *to have to do with*

  ¿ Qué tengo yo que ver con eso ?   *What have I to do with that?*

EXERCISES

el **aeroplano** *aeroplane*
  andar *to walk*
la **cama** *bed*
la **cárcel** *jail*
la **costumbre** *custom, manner*
  despertar (ie) *to awake, wake up*
  difícil *difficult*
  e *and*
el **efecto** *effect, object*
el **hielo** *ice*
el **ladrón** *thief*
  luchar *to struggle*
  llevar *to take;* refl. *take or carry*
  away
  mas *but*
la **mentira** *lie*
  necesario, -a *necessary*
el **negocio** *business*
  perderse *to become or get lost*
el **periódico** *newspaper*

la **policía** *police*
  por *per, to, for the sake of, on*
  account of, in exchange for
  profundamente *profoundly,*
  soundly
  querer a (with pers. obj.) *to*
  love, be fond of
  sacar *to take out*
  servir: no sirve para nada *it is*
  good for nothing
  sino *but*
el **sofá** *sofa*
  sorprender *to surprise*
la **tarde: por la —,** *in the afternoon*
  (*evening*)
  u *or*
el **vecino** *neighbor*
  ver: a —, *let's see;* **tener que**
  — con *to have to do with*
la **vida** *life*

A. 1. He oído decir que Felipe ha gastado mucho dinero este mes. 2. Ha comprado un camión y un aeroplano. 3. El camión es para su negocio y el aeroplano es para sí mismo. 4. Pagó setecientos u ochocientos dólares por el camión. 5. Quién sabe cuánto ha pagado por el aeroplano. 6. No debiera gastar dinero en cosas que no necesita la compañía. 7. El camión es necesario porque el que tenían ya no servía para nada. 8. Pero él no puede viajar mucho y no necesita el aeroplano.—9. ¡Qué cómodos estaban los dos muchachos en el sofá! 10. Cuando los vimos dormían profundamente. 11. Estarían muy cansados, pues habían andado casi todo el día. 12. Se habían perdido y no llegaron a casa hasta las seis. 13. Pero era preciso despertarlos para que se acostasen en su cama. 14. Los cogimos por la mano y los llevamos a su habitación. 15. Nos dijeron que se habían caído varias veces y se habían hecho daño. 16. Temían ser castigados por no haber vuelto a casa temprano. — 17. A ver ¿ qué noticias trae el periódico hoy ? 18. En la primera página hay noticias de la guerra. 19. Aquí en la segunda página hay una noticia interesante. 20. Un ladrón entró anoche en la casa de un vecino nuestro. 21. Había cogido varios efectos de plata cuando alguien le oyó. 22. Una de las mujeres en la casa llamó a la policía por teléfono. 23. Un hombre sorprendió al ladrón y luchó con él. 24. La policía llegó pronto y se llevó al ladrón a la cárcel.

B. 1. ¿ Qué ha oído usted decir ? 2. ¿ Qué ha comprado Felipe ? 3. ¿ Para quién es el aeroplano ? 4. ¿ Cuánto pagó por el camión ? 5. ¿ Por qué es necesario el camión ? 6. ¿ Por qué no necesita Felipe el aeroplano ? 7. ¿ Dónde estaban los dos muchachos ? 8. ¿ Por qué estaban muy cansados ? 9. ¿ Cuándo llegaron a casa ? 10. ¿ Por qué era preciso despertarlos ? 11. ¿ A dónde los llevaron ustedes ? 12. ¿ Por qué temían ser castigados ? 13. ¿ Qué hay en la primera página del periódico ? 14. ¿ Dónde hay una noticia interesante ? 15. ¿ En dónde entró el ladrón ? 16. ¿ Qué había cogido el ladrón ? 17. ¿ Quién llamó a la policía ? 18. ¿ Quién luchó con el ladrón ?

C. *Translate:* 1. I have a letter for you. 2. He entered through the door. 3. They went out through the window. 4. We pay him three dollars a day. 5. Father and son, both were ill. 6. It is not high, but low. 7. Where did they come from ? 8. Is the book interesting ? 9. He did it for her. 10. She paid twelve dollars for the hat. 11. Bring me the notebook. 12. We are grateful to him. 13. He wants me to bring the package. 14. Where did he fall ? 15. He told me to bring the ball. 16. We have nothing to do with that. 17. I urged him, but he didn't bring it. 18. He speaks clearly. 19. Don't urge him so much. 20. He told me a lie.

D. 1. Where is the silver pencil that your father gave you ? 2. I was in the street, and they called me from the house. 3. They wanted me to come and see my uncle Peter. 4. He had never come to visit us. 5. I had heard of him, but I didn't know him. 6. When they told me that he had just arrived I ran to the house. 7. I had the pencil in this pocket and I dropped it. 8. I have

Que me vengan a afeitar.

looked for it, but I have not been able to find it. — 9. Do you know where the boy who was here has gone ? 10. He told me that he was going to the library to take a book out. 11. But I think that he was not going there, but to his cousin's room. 12. I saw him pass by there a moment ago. 13. He brought a package for his cousin this morning. 14. The package is not here, and I think that he has taken it away. 15. Those two boys are very fond of each other. 16. I am sure that either of them would give his life for the other. — 17. Henry, come here and tell me where you came from now. 18. I came from a lecture that Mr. Castro gave. 19. It was a lecture about the life and customs in (**de**) France. 20. Mr. Castro spoke distinctly in French, and I understood him well. 21. I wish to hear that language as much as possible before the first of July. 22. They have given me a scholarship at the University, and I hope to travel in France. 23. I spoke with Mr. Castro, and he promised to help me. 24. I am going to see him tomorrow afternoon in his room at the hotel.

8*

LECTURA

Tomé chocolate, me levanté, me lavé, medio me vestí, leí los
periódicos, escribí dos cartas, almorcé, acabé de vestirme, fuí a
casa de Antonio, disputé [1] sobre geología,[2] comí, dí un paseo, fuí
al café, tomé un sorbete,[3] entré en casa de la Baronesa,[4] me dió
te,[5] vine acá, me senté al balcón [6] al fresco [7] y ahora voy a acos-
tarme.

Ya dijo Iriarte [8]:

> Levántome a las mil,[9] como quien soy.
> Me lavo. Que me vengan a afeitar.[10]
> Traigan el chocolate, y a peinar.[11]
> Un libro ... Ya leí ... Basta [12] por hoy.
>
> Si me buscan, que digan que no estoy [13] ...
> Polvo ... Venga [14] el vestido [15] verdemar [16] ...
> ¿ Si [17] estará ya la Misa [18] en el altar ?
> ¿ Han puesto [19] la berlina ? [20] ... Pues me voy.
>
> Hice ya tres visitas: a comer ...
> Traigan barajas [21]: ya jugué. Perdí.
> Pongan [22] el tiro.[23] Al campo y a correr ...
>
> Ya doña Eulalia esperará por mí ...
> Dió la una. A cenar [24] y a recoger.[25]
> ¿ Y es esto racional ? [26] ... Dicen que sí.

PEDRO A. DE ALARCÓN, *Diario de un madrileño.*[27]

LESSON L

231. *Augmentatives and Diminutives.* There are many augmentative and diminutive suffixes in Spanish, which occur commonly in colloquial language. The foreigner should use them

[1] *argued.* [2] *geology.* [3] *sherbet.* [4] *Baroness.* [5] *tea.* [6] *balcony.* [7] *in
the open.* [8] Tomás de Iriarte, Spanish fabulist (1750–1791). [9] **a las mil,**
very late. [10] *to shave.* [11] *comb (my) hair.* [12] *(It is) enough.* [13] *I am not
at home.* [14] *Let me have.* [15] *suit.* [16] *sea-green.* [17] *I wonder if.* [18] *Mass;*
la Misa en el altar, *Mass has begun.* [19] **poner,** *to harness, hitch.* [20] *landau.*
[21] *cards.* [22] **poner,** *to harness, hitch.* [23] *(team of) horses.* [24] *have supper.*
[25] *retire.* [26] *rational.* [27] *Madrilenian (inhabitant of Madrid).*

with the greatest caution. It is generally safe to use –ito
(–cito, –ecito), but it is best to avoid the other suffixes
until one has become familiar with their use. The suffixes
are attached to the stem of a word after it has dropped a
final unstressed vowel. A few of the more common suffixes
are given below.

232. *Augmentative Suffixes.* The suffixes –ón (–ona) and –azo
(–a) denote largeness, with or without grotesqueness. Feminine nouns usually become masculine upon adding the suffix
–ón, unless sex is indicated.

Aquel hombrón es alemán.	*That big man is German.*
Aquella mujeraza es su hermana.	*That large woman is his sister.*
Tráigame usted un cucharón.	*Bring me a large spoon.*

233. *Diminutive Suffixes.*

a) The suffix –ito, –a (–cito, –a; –ecito, –a) denotes smallness, and may also express affection or pity; –illo, –a
(–cillo, –a; –ecillo, –a) denotes smallness, and may also
express indifference or ridicule; –uelo, –a (–zuelo, –a;
–ezuelo, –a) denotes smallness, and may also express ridicule
or scorn.

¿Cómo está su hijita, señora?	*How is your (dear) little daugh-ter, madam?*
Mi hermanito se llama Jua-nito.	*My little brother's name is Johnny.*
Tenemos una casita de campo.	*We have a cottage in the country.*
En la jaula hay varios paja-rillos.	*In the cage there are several tiny birds.*
No fué más que un descui-dillo.	*It was only a little slip.*

b) The longer forms (–cito, –cillo, –zuelo, etc.) are used only
with words of more than one syllable ending in –n or –r.

En la casita de su muñequita hay tres silloncitos.
In her doll's little house there are three little armchairs.

Ese jovencito es un autorcillo de poca importancia.
That youth is a petty author of little importance.

c) The still longer forms (–ecito, –ecillo, –ezuelo, etc.) are used with monosyllables, with words ending in –e, and with those that have the radical diphthong ie or ue.

¡ Qué bella florecita !	*What a beautiful little flower!*
Venció a varios reyezuelos.	*He conquered several petty kings.*
¡ Madrecita mía !	*My dear little mother!*
La pobrecita está muy enferma.	*The poor little girl is very ill.*
Cada pueblecito tiene su plazuela.	*Every small town has its little public square.*

d) All the diminutives are most commonly used with nouns; but they are also used with adjectives, participles, and adverbs to denote smallness of quality or degree.

Estamos un poquillo cansaditos.	*We are just a little tired.*
Ya estamos cerquita.	*Now we are quite near.*
Ahorita llegamos.	*We shall arrive very soon.*

234. Andar, *to go, walk.*

PARTICIPLES	⎫
PRES. INDIC.	⎪
IMPERATIVE	⎬ Regular
FUTURE	⎪
CONDITIONAL	⎪
IMPERF. INDIC.	⎭
PRETERITE	anduve, anduviste, anduvo, anduvimos, anduvisteis, anduvieron
IMPERF. SUBJ.	anduviese, anduvieses, etc. anduviera, anduvieras, etc.
FUTURE SUBJ.	anduviere, anduvieres, etc.

¿ Cómo anda el negocio ?	*How is business going?*
Mi reloj no anda.	*My watch does not go.*

235. Caber, *to be contained, fit.*

PARTICIPLES	Regular
PRES. INDIC.	quepo, cabes, cabe, cabemos, cabéis, caben
PRES. SUBJ.	quepa, quepas, quepa, quepamos, quepáis, quepan
IMPERATIVE	cabe cabed
FUTURE	cabré, cabrás, cabrá, cabremos, cabréis, cabrán

CONDITIONAL	cabría, cabrías, cabría, cabríamos, cabríais, cabrían
IMPERF. INDIC.	Regular
PRETERITE	cupe, cupiste, cupo, cupimos, cupisteis, cupieron
IMPERF. SUBJ.	cupiese, cupieses, etc. cupiera, cupieras, etc.
FUTURE SUBJ.	cupiere, cupieres, etc.

No cabemos aquí.	*There is no room for us here.*
¿ Cuántas personas caben en este cuarto ?	*How many persons does this room hold?*

236. Valer, *to be worth.*

PARTICIPLES	Regular
PRES. INDIC.	valgo, vales, vale, valemos, valéis, valen
PRES. SUBJ.	valga, valgas, valga, valgamos, valgáis, valgan
IMPERATIVE	val or vale valed
FUTURE	valdré, valdrás, valdrá, valdremos, valdréis, valdrán
CONDITIONAL	valdría, valdrías, valdría, valdríamos, valdríais, valdrían
IMPERF. INDIC. PRETERITE IMPERF. SUBJ. FUTURE SUBJ.	Regular

Eso no vale la pena.	*That is not worth while.*
¿ Cuánto vale eso ?	*How much is that worth?*
Más vale tarde que nunca.	*Better late than never.*

EXERCISES

la acción *share*
acostado, -a *lying down*
alemán, -ana *German*
andar *to go*
asustado, -a *frightened*
el autor *author*
el bosque *forest*
cerca *near*
costoso, -a *costly, expensive*

la cuchara *spoon*
cumplir: *to complete;* — años *reach one's birthday*
demasiado *too*
el descuido *neglect, slip*
devolver (ue) *to return, give back*
envolver (ue) *to wrap*
la importancia *importance*
la jaula *cage*

el (la) joven *young man (woman)*
el lado *side*
la muñeca *doll*
¡ oh ! *O! oh!*
el pájaro *bird*
pegar *to hit, strike*
la pena *difficulty, trouble;* no vale
la —, *it is not worth while*

perfectamente *perfectly*
la plaza *public square*
preocupado, –a *worried*
público, –a *public*
el pueblo *town*
regañar *to scold*
el sillón *armchair*
tarde *late*

A. 1. María quiere mucho a su hermanito Juan. 2. Juanito no tiene más que cuatro años. 3. Casi toditos los días María le trae un regalito. 4. La semana pasada le trajo un pajarillo. 5. Pagó por él lo menos siete u ocho dólares. 6. Ayer Juanito abrió la puerta de la jaula y el pajarillo se escapó. 7. No valió la pena comprar tal cosa. 8. Dudo que María vuelva a traerle un regalo tan costoso. — 9. Don Enrique y su hijo se habían perdido en el bosque. 10. Después de andar mucho salieron a un camino esta tarde. 11. Padre e hijo estaban cansados y tenían mucha hambre. 12. Pero anduvieron hasta que llegaron a un pueblecillo. 13. En una plazuela vieron un aeroplano. 14. Este aeroplano es de un vecino nuestro. 15. Como caben más de dos personas en él nuestro vecino los llevó cerquita de su casa. 16. ¡ Qué contenta estaba la familia cuando los vió llegar ! — 17. Acabamos de venir de la oficina de Pedro. 18. Habíamos salido a dar un paseo por el parque. 19. Pensábamos andar luego hasta la biblioteca pública. 20. Pero no fuimos a la biblioteca sino a la oficina. 21. Anduvimos desde el parque y llegamos algo tarde. 22. Pero Pedro estaba todavía en su oficina trabajando. 23. Él está muy preocupado porque su negocio no anda bien. 24. Nos dijo que las acciones de su compañía no valen mucho.

B. 1. ¿ A quién quiere María mucho ? 2. ¿ Cuántos años tiene Juanito ? 3. ¿ Qué le trae María casi toditos los días ? 4. ¿ Qué le trajo la semana pasada ? 5. ¿ Cuánto pagó por él ? 6. ¿ Qué hizo Juanito ayer ? 7. ¿ Quiénes se habían perdido en el bosque ? 8. ¿ Cuándo salieron al camino ? 9. ¿ Hasta dónde anduvieron ? 10. ¿ Qué vieron en una plazuela ? 11. ¿ De quién es el aeroplano ? 12. ¿ De dónde acaban de venir ustedes ? 13. ¿ A dónde habían salido a dar un paseo ? 14. ¿ A dónde pensaban ir luego ? 15. ¿ A dónde fueron ? 16. ¿ Desde dónde anduvieron ? 17. ¿ Qué hacía Pedro en su oficina ? 18. ¿ Por qué está preocupado Pedro ? 19. ¿ Cuánto valen las acciones de su compañía ?

C. *Translate, using the augmentatives or diminutives of the words in italics:* 1. You surprised me. 2. *Young-friend*, how are you ? 3. There is room for three persons here. 4. *Johnny* was crying. 5. It is not worth while to do that. 6. Look at those *tiny-flowers*. 7. Isn't that difficult ? 8. There is a *little-house very-near* here. 9. He left for Cuba yesterday. 10. She has a *little-horse*. 11. That is the custom. 12. I have never told you a lie. 13. Any man would seem a *big-man* here. 14. Gold is worth more than silver. 15. This *armchair* is very comfortable.

D. 1. Have you a little box in which I may put this ? 2. It is a watch that I bought yesterday in the store of a friend of mine. 3. I wish to send it to my little brother when he is ten years old. 4. It cost me eight dollars, but it is worth much more. 5. It seems to me that it goes perfectly, and it is very pretty. 6. This little box is good only to make a small package. 7. The watch fits in it, but it is well to wrap it in paper. 8. Your little brother will be very glad when he receives it. — 9. The little boy went into the small house of little Elizabeth when no one was there. 10. He carried away the little dolls, two or three small chairs, and a small armchair. 11. The police went to his house and found him lying on a sofa. 12. He was sleeping soundly and they had to wake him. 13. When he saw the police at his side, he got up frightened. 14. Did they take the young thief to (the) jail ? 15. No, because he was too young for that. 16. But they scolded him and told him to return what he had taken. — 17. We should take the ice and these other things out of here. 18. There is no room for them with all that we have to carry. 19. Don't you think that we can wrap the ice in this newspaper ? 20. No, let us leave the ice, and let us wrap the rest in the newspaper. 21. Oh, look ! Read what it says here. 22. A man was struggling with the police. 23. They wanted to take him to (the) jail because he had struck his little daughter. 24. Then came a large woman with a large spoon and they could not take the man away.

LECTURA

La patrona¹ de la casa iba y venía por un lado y por otro, dando órdenes² a los criados para que tuvieran las cosas arregladitas³; porque a la patrona, que con perdón de ustedes,⁴ se llamaba Zoa, le gustaban las cosas muy arregladitas.

— Vamos, vamos, — decía dirigiéndose a la cocinera — que no se pase el punto⁵ del arroz; y esas patatas que estén bien doraditas,⁶ bien doraditas. ¡ A ver, rellenar⁷ bien esos calabacines! ⁸

— ¡ Hombre! ⁹ ¿ Hay ¹⁰ calabacines? ¡ Me alegro! — decía un caballero¹¹ asomándose¹² a la puerta de la cocina.¹³

— ¡ Hola, don Andrés! Sí, señor, hoy tiene usted calabacines rellenos; porque yo no me olvido de que le gustan a usted.

— Gracias, gracias. ¿ Y cómo andamos de novedades,¹⁴ doña Zoa? ¿ No han venido hoy mujeres?

— Sí, señor; hoy tiene usted dos huéspedas¹⁵ nuevas, muy reguapas.¹⁶

— ¡ Bueno! ¡ bueno! ¡ Eso me gusta! Póngamelas usted cerquita¹⁷ en la mesa. ¿ Y quiénes son, quiénes son?

— Yo no sé, han venido con dos caballeros.

— Eso ya no me gusta.

Eusebio Blasco, *Los huéspedes.*

¹ *landlady.* ² *orders.* ³ *in shipshape order.* ⁴ **con perdón de ustedes,** *begging your pardon.* ⁵ **se pase el punto,** *be overdone.* ⁶ *(golden) browned.* ⁷ *stuff.* ⁸ *(small) pumpkins.* ⁹ *Oh, boy!* ¹⁰ *Have we.* ¹¹ *gentleman.* ¹² *appearing.* ¹³ *kitchen.* ¹⁴ *news;* **cómo andamos de novedades,** *what's new.* ¹⁵ *(lady) guests.* ¹⁶ *very pretty.* ¹⁷ *quite near.*

REVIEW LESSON E

I. Continue:

1. Los dulces son para mí, los dulces son para ti, etc. 2. Yo me burlo de mí mismo (-a), tú te burlas de ti mismo (-a), etc. 3. Yo tengo el mío, tú tienes el tuyo, etc. 4. Yo quiero las mías, tú quieres las tuyas, etc.

II. *A.* In the following sentences, supply the proper equivalent for the relative pronoun in parentheses:

1. (*that*) El trabajo —— hace. 2. (*that*) La frase —— traduje. 3. (*whom*) El chico a —— llamamos. 4. (*that*) Los zapatos —— me compró. 5. (*that*) La pelota —— encontró. 6. (*which*) La pera —— está en la mesa. 7. (*that*) La pluma —— yo tengo. 8. (*that*) El capítulo —— he leído. 9. (*whom*) El accionista a —— las vendimos. 10. (*that*) El peligro —— corre. 11. (*whom*) El muchacho a —— debo eso. 12. (*who*) La muchacha —— trajo el libro. 13. (*who*) El niño —— se cayó. 14. (*who*) El criado —— me despertó. 15. (*whom*) El hombre a —— oí decir eso.

B. In the following sentences, supply one of the indefinite pronouns and adjectives in parentheses, and then translate into English: (algo, alguien, algunos, cada uno, cualquiera, mismos, mucho, nada, nadie, ningunos, poco)

1. Tengo —— para usted. 2. —— lo ha hecho. 3. Él tiene —— dinero, pero ella tiene ——. 4. —— de los muchachos le han ayudado. 5. —— de ellos tienen que hacerlo. 6. No nos ha dicho ——. 7. —— puede subir. 8. Nosotros —— los llevamos.

III. *A.* Using all the subject pronouns, give:

1. The present indicative of **querer** with **le** as the object. 2. The preterite of **dormirse**. 3. The third persons, singular and plural, of the present indicative, preterite, and present subjunctive of **construir**.

B. Give:

1. The first persons, singular and plural, of the present indicative and present subjunctive of **oír, poner, saber**. 2. The first and third persons of the singular of the preterite indicative and future subjunctive of **andar, dar, poder, traducir**. 3. The third persons, singular and plural, of the future and conditional of **querer, salir, tener, venir**.

IV. *A.* In the following sentences, supply **para** or **por,** and then translate into English:

1. Los zapatos son —— María. 2. Dejamos eso —— el verano que viene. 3. La tesis fué escrita —— mi hermana. 4. El paquete es —— mi primo. 5. Huyó —— miedo a la policía. 6. El pájaro salió —— la puertecita. 7. No lo hizo —— descuido. 8. No viene —— estar enfermo. 9. Lo haremos —— él. 10. ¿ Cuánto pagó usted —— eso ?

B. 1. Count in Spanish by twos from 11 to 29, and from 12 to 30; by threes from 29 to 50, and from 30 to 51; by fours from 51 to 75; by fives from 75 to 100. 2. Give both the cardinal and ordinal numbers by twos from 1 (1st) to 9 (9th), and from 2 (2nd) to 10 (10th). 3. Read or write in Spanish: 123, 987, 345, 654, 567, 321, 789, 876, 901, 1098, 1876, 2765, 3654.

C. In the following sentences, give in the diminutive form the equivalent of the words in parentheses, and then translate into English:

1. (*box*) La —— es de acero. 2. (*present*) Le haremos un ——. 3. (*duck*) Mira esos ——. 4. (*branch*) Tráeme una ——. 5. (*carriage*) Quiero ese ——. 6. (*job*) No me gusta el ——. 7. (*package*) Haz un ——. 8. (*bed*) La —— es para el niño. 9. (*forest*) El —— no está lejos. 10. (*bird*) El —— no está en la jaula. 11. (*square*) Lo ví en la ——. 12. (*armchair*) Le compré un ——.

V. *A.* Translate:

1. We see him every day. 2. Did he forget to do it ? 3. Is it true ? 4. What is his name ? 5. He went to the movies with me. 6. Joseph and Frances love each other. 7. Why are you so sad ? 8. The child began to cry. 9. No one had struck her. 10. How are you, young fellow ? 11. Write that sentence again. 12. His brother is a judge. 13. He translated the letter. 14. Let us take a walk. 15. We went to the park on foot. 16. This engine runs well. 17. What is the color of her automobile ? 18. Whom did you see at the club ? 19. That pleases me. 20. Are you warm ? 21. The boss was shouting. 22. Set the table now. 23. Are you in a hurry ? 24. I am sleepy. 25. Give all you have.

B. Translate:

1. The water of that lake looks green. 2. I like pears. 3. We have to buy new clothes. 4. We have finished the twelfth chapter. 5. I gave the boy half of the pear. 6. We took a trip there last summer. 7. The

boy is in the basement playing. 8. This water tastes like coffee. 9. He has less money than I. 10. Do you know how to swim ? 11. Is it very cold here in the winter ? 12. I hope he will grant me that ! 13. I wish he would give it back to me ! 14. You should not punish the child. 15. Will you help me ? 16. Ask the boy for the ball. 17. He fell from the tree and hurt himself. 18. Come here, my friend. 19. The truck passed this way. 20. I can hear him distinctly. 21. I know it well. 22. He no longer lives here. 23. Indeed he is here ! 24. It is not a bed but a sofa. 25. I'll give him seven or eight dollars.

THE VERB

237. The Spanish verb system, being derived from that of Latin, shows flexional endings characteristic of mood, tense, person, and number:

habl–ar	to speak	habl–amos	we speak
habl–ando	speaking	habl–aba	I (he) was speaking,
habl–o	I speak		used to speak

The perfect tenses are compounded by adding to the auxiliary verb **haber,** to have, the invariable past participle of the main verb:

he hablado *I have spoken*   **había hablado** *I (he) had spoken*

238. The Spanish verb may be divided into five leading classes: (1) the regular verb, (2) the radical-changing verb, (3) the verb with inceptive endings, (4) the –**uir** verb, (5) the irregular verb.

239. The future of the indicative and the conditional of all verbs are based upon their infinitive form. This may suffer some modification in the case of irregular verbs:

$$\text{hablar, } \textit{to speak} \begin{cases} \textbf{hablar–é, } \textit{I shall speak} \\ \textbf{hablar–ía, } \textit{I should speak} \end{cases}$$

$$\text{decir, } \textit{to say} \begin{cases} \textbf{dir–án, } \textit{they will say} \\ \textbf{dir–ían, } \textit{they would say} \end{cases}$$

NOTE: The endings of the future of the indicative and the conditional are derived from the present and the imperfect, respectively, of the indicative of **haber,** *to have* (omitting **h–** or **hab–**).

240. *Verb Stems.*

 a) For regular verbs the stem may be found by cutting off the ending –**o** of the first person singular of the present indicative, or the ending –**ar,** –**er,** –**ir** of the infinitive:

234

habl-o	*I speak*	**habl-ar**	*to speak*
aprend-o	*I learn*	**aprend-er**	*to learn*
escrib-o	*I write*	**escrib-ir**	*to write*

In regular verbs this stem is the basis of all forms except those of the future of the indicative and of the conditional.

b) In the case of radical-changing and irregular verbs the stem of the third singular (or plural) of the preterite indicative is the same as that of the two imperfect (or past) subjunctives and of the future (or hypothetical) subjunctive:

Pedir, *to ask:* **pid-ió (pid-ieron),** *he asked (they asked);* Impf. Subj., **pid-iese,** etc., **pid-iera,** etc.; Fut. Subj., **pid-iere,** etc.

Saber, *to know;* **sup-o (sup-ieron),** *he knew (they knew);* Impf. Subj., **sup-iese,** etc., **sup-iera,** etc.; Fut. Subj., **sup-iere,** etc.

241. *The Regular Verb.* There are three regular conjugations in Spanish characterized by the vowels of their infinitive endings, namely, **-ar** for the first conjugation, **-er** for the second, and **-ir** for the third. But, as a matter of fact, the endings of the second and third conjugations are the same except in the infinitive (and the infinitive stem of the future and conditional indicative), in the first and second persons plural of the present indicative, and in the second person plural of the imperative.

Paradigms

I	II	III

INFINITIVE MOOD

PRESENT	PRESENT	PRESENT
Habl-ar, *to speak*	Aprend-er, *to learn*	Viv-ir, *to live*

PARTICIPLES

PRESENT (GERUND)	PRESENT (GERUND)	PRESENT (GERUND)
habl-ando, *speaking*	aprend-iendo, *learning*	viv-iendo, *living*

PAST	PAST	PAST
habl-ado, *spoken*	aprend-ido, *learned*	viv-ido, *lived*

INDICATIVE MOOD

PRESENT	**PRESENT**	**PRESENT**
I speak, do speak, am speaking, etc.	*I learn, do learn, am learning, etc.*	*I live, do live, am living, etc.*
habl–o	aprend–o	viv–o
habl–as	aprend–es	viv–es
habl–a	aprend–e	viv–e
habl–amos	aprend–emos	viv–imos
habl–áis	aprend–éis	viv–ís
habl–an	aprend–en	viv–en

IMPERFECT	**IMPERFECT** [1]	**IMPERFECT** [1]
I spoke, was speaking, used to speak, etc.	*I learned, was learning, used to learn, etc.*	*I lived, was living, used to live, etc.*
habl–aba	aprend–ía	viv–ía
habl–abas	aprend–ías	viv–ías
habl–aba	aprend–ía	viv–ía
habl–ábamos	aprend–íamos	viv–íamos
habl–abais	aprend–íais	viv–íais
habl–aban	aprend–ían	viv–ían

PRETERITE	**PRETERITE**	**PRETERITE**
I spoke, did speak, etc.	*I learned, did learn, etc.*	*I lived, did live, etc.*
habl–é	aprend–í	viv–í
habl–aste	aprend–iste	viv–iste
habl–ó	aprend–ió	viv–ió
habl–amos	aprend–imos	viv–imos
habl–asteis	aprend–isteis	viv–isteis
habl–aron	aprend–ieron	viv–ieron

[1] In the imperfect indicative of the second and third conjugations and also in the conditional of all three conjugations the accent remains on the same vowel throughout all the forms and is always written.

FUTURE	FUTURE	FUTURE
I shall speak, etc.	*I shall learn, etc.*	*I shall live, etc.*
hablar-é	aprender-é	vivir-é
hablar-ás	aprender-ás	vivir-ás
hablar-á	aprender-á	vivir-á
hablar-emos	aprender-emos	vivir-emos
hablar-éis	aprender-éis	vivir-éis
hablar-án	aprender-án	vivir-án

CONDITIONAL	CONDITIONAL	CONDITIONAL
I should speak, etc.	*I should learn, etc.*	*I should live, etc.*
hablar-ía	aprender-ía	vivir-ía
hablar-ías	aprender-ías	vivir-ías
hablar-ía	aprender-ía	vivir-ía
hablar-íamos	aprender-íamos	vivir-íamos
hablar-íais	aprender-íais	vivir-íais
hablar-ían	aprender-ían	vivir-ían

IMPERATIVE MOOD

	speak	learn	live
Sing. 2	habl-a	aprend-e	viv-e
Pl. 2	habl-ad	aprend-ed	viv-id

SUBJUNCTIVE MOOD

PRESENT	PRESENT	PRESENT
(that I may) speak,	*(that I may) learn,*	*(that I may) live,*
(let me) speak, etc.	*(let me) learn, etc.*	*(let me) live, etc.*
habl-e	aprend-a	viv-a
habl-es	aprend-as	viv-as
habl-e	aprend-a	viv-a
habl-emos	aprend-amos	viv-amos
habl-éis	aprend-áis	viv-áis
habl-en	aprend-an	viv-an

−se IMPERFECT	−se IMPERFECT	−se IMPERFECT
that (or *if*) *I might speak, etc.*	*that* (or *if*) *I might learn, etc.*	*that* (or *if*) *I might live, etc.*
habl−ase	aprend−iese	viv−iese
habl−ases	aprend−ieses	viv−ieses
habl−ase	aprend−iese	viv−iese
habl−ásemos	aprend−iésemos	viv−iésemos
habl−aseis	aprend−ieseis	viv−ieseis
habl−asen	aprend−iesen	viv−iesen

−ra IMPERFECT	−ra IMPERFECT	−ra IMPERFECT
I should speak, that (or *if*) *I might speak, etc.*	*I should learn, that* (or *if*) *I might learn, etc.*	*I should live, that* (or *if*) *I might live, etc.*
habl−ara	aprend−iera	viv−iera
habl−aras	aprend−ieras	viv−ieras
habl−ara	aprend−iera	viv−iera
habl−áramos	aprend−iéramos	viv−iéramos
habl−arais	aprend−ierais	viv−ierais
habl−aran	aprend−ieran	viv−ieran

FUTURE (or HYPOTHETICAL)	FUTURE (or HYPOTHETICAL)	FUTURE (or HYPOTHETICAL)
that I may (or *shall*) *speak, etc.*	*that I may* (or *shall*) *learn, etc.*	*that I may* (or *shall*) *live, etc.*
habl−are	aprend−iere	viv−iere
habl−ares	aprend−ieres	viv−ieres
habl−are	aprend−iere	viv−iere
habl−áremos	aprend−iéremos	viv−iéremos
habl−areis	aprend−iereis	viv−iereis
habl−aren	aprend−ieren	viv−ieren

Perfect tenses of **hablar**

INFINITIVE	PARTICIPLE (GERUND)
to have spoken	*having spoken*
haber hablado	habiendo hablado

INDICATIVE

PRESENT PERFECT

I have spoken, etc.
he hablado
has hablado, etc.

PRETERITE PERFECT

I had spoken, etc.
hube hablado
hubiste hablado, etc.

PLUPERFECT

I had spoken, etc.
había hablado, etc.

FUTURE PERFECT

I shall have spoken, etc.
habré hablado, etc.

CONDITIONAL PERFECT

I should have spoken, etc.
habría hablado, etc.

SUBJUNCTIVE

PRESENT PERFECT

*that I may have
spoken, etc.*
haya hablado, etc.

−ra PLUPERFECT

*I should have spoken, that I
might have spoken, etc.*
hubiera hablado, etc.

−se PLUPERFECT

*that I might have
spoken, etc.*
hubiese hablado, etc.

**FUTURE (or HYPO-
THETICAL) PERFECT**

*that I may (or shall) have
spoken, etc.*
hubiere hablado, etc.

NOTES: 1. The following tables of moods and tenses give (1) the English names and (2) the Spanish names, to which preference is given in this book, and (3) the names given in the *Gramática de la lengua castellana* (Madrid, 1913) published by the Royal Spanish Academy:

	1	2	3
	INFINITIVE	INFINITIVO	INFINITIVO
hablar:	present	presente	presente
haber hablado:	perfect	perfecto	pretérito
	PARTICIPLES	PARTICIPIOS	———
hablando:	present	presente	gerundio
hablado:	past	pasado	participio (pasivo)

	1	2	3
	INDICATIVE	INDICATIVO	INDICATIVO
hablo:	present	presente	presente
hablaba:	imperfect	imperfecto	pretérito imperfecto
hablé:	preterite	pretérito	pretérito perfecto
hablaré:	future	futuro	futuro imperfecto
hablaría:	conditional	condicional	pretérito imperfecto (de subjuntivo)
he hablado:	present perfect	presente perfecto	pretérito perfecto
había hablado:	pluperfect	pluscuamperfecto	pretérito pluscuamperfecto
hube hablado:	preterite perfect	pretérito perfecto	pretérito perfecto
habré hablado:	future perfect	futuro perfecto	futuro perfecto
habría hablado:	conditional perfect	condicional perfecto	pretérito pluscuamperfecto (de subjuntivo)
habla:	IMPERATIVE	IMPERATIVO	IMPERATIVO
	SUBJUNCTIVE	SUBJUNTIVO	SUBJUNTIVO
hable:	present	presente	presente
hablase / **hablara**	imperfect	imperfecto	pretérito imperfecto
hablare:	future	futuro	futuro imperfecto
haya hablado:	present perfect	presente perfecto	pretérito perfecto
hubiese / **hubiera** **hablado:**	pluperfect	pluscuamperfecto	pretérito pluscuamperfecto
hubiere hablado:	future perfect	futuro perfecto	futuro perfecto

In the nomenclature of the Spanish Academy the three tenses **hablé, he hablado,** and **hube hablado** have the same name: *pretérito perfecto de indicativo.* Likewise **hablase, hablara,** and **hablaría** are called the *pretérito imperfecto de subjunctivo;* and **hubiese hablado, hubiera hablado,** and **habría hablado** are called the *pretérito pluscuamperfecto de subjuntivo.* Confusion of names may be avoided in part, as follows: **hablé,** *pretérito perfecto simple;* **he hablado,** *pretérito perfecto compuesto* (with **he, has,** etc.).

2. The tense names recommended in the *Report of the Joint Committee on Grammatical Nomenclature* (University of Chicago Press, 1913), which differ from those to which preference is given in this book, are **hablaba,** *past descriptive;* **hablé,** *past absolute;* **hablaría,** *past future;* **había hablado,** *past perfect;* **hube hablado,** *2nd past perfect;* **habría hablado,** *past future perfect;* **hablase** or **hablara,** *past subjunctive.*

242. *Compound Progressive Tenses.* The present participle of a principal verb may be combined with the auxiliary **estar** (never **ser**) to form a progressive construction.

estamos hablando *we are speaking*

Certain verbs of motion or rest such as **ir**, *to go*, **quedar**, *to remain*, may appear instead of **estar** in this construction.

243. *Changes in Spelling.* It is a regular tendency of Spanish verbs to preserve throughout their conjugation the consonantal *sound* at the end of the stem (found ordinarily by cutting off the infinitive ending –**ar**, –**er**, –**ir**). Hence, before certain vowels of the flexional suffix a change in spelling of the end of the stem is necessitated. This is so not only for regular verbs but for many others also.

244. Before flexional –**e** these changes occur:

   a) Verbs in –**c**–**ar** change **c** to **qu** to keep the **k** sound ("hard" **c** sound):

Buscar, *to seek*

PRET. INDIC. *1st Sing.*	busqué

PRES. SUBJ.   busque, busques, busque, busquemos, busquéis, busquen

   b) Verbs in –**g**–**ar** add to the **g** an unpronounced **u** to keep the "hard" **g** sound:

Pagar, *to pay*

PRET. INDIC. *1st Sing.*	pagué

PRES. SUBJ.   pague, pagues, pague, paguemos, paguéis, paguen

   c) Verbs in –**gu**–**ar** take a diaeresis over the **u** to show that this **u** of the stem has always a pronounced value:

Averiguar, *to ascertain*

PRET. INDIC. *1st Sing.*	averigüé

PRES. SUBJ.   averigüe, averigües, averigüe, averigüemos, averigüéis, averigüen *d*) Verbs in –**z**–**ar** change **z** to **c,** without involving any difference in sound:

Cazar, *to hunt*

PRET. INDIC. ⎱
  1st Sing. ⎰ cacé

PRES. SUBJ. cace, caces, cace, cacemos, cacéis, cacen

NOTE: It is to be noted that only seven forms of the verb inflexion are concerned in the four cases just mentioned.

245. Before flexional **o** or **a** the following changes occur:

a) Verbs in –**c**–**er** and –**c**–**ir** preceded by a consonant change **c** to **z:**

Vencer, *to conquer*

PRES. INDIC., *1st Sing.* venzo   PRES. SUBJ. venza, etc.

Zurcir, *to darn*

PRES. INDIC., *1st Sing.* zurzo   PRES. SUBJ. zurza, etc.

NOTE: Most verbs in –**cer** or –**cir** preceded by a vowel belong to the class with inceptive endings. See § 259.

b) All verbs in –**g**–**er** or –**g**–**ir,** regular or not, change **g** to **j:**

Coger, *to catch, gather*

PRES. INDIC., *1st Sing.* cojo   PRES. SUBJ. coja, etc.

Elegir, *to choose*

PRES. INDIC., *1st Sing.* elijo   PRES. SUBJ. elija, etc.

c) Verbs in –**qu**–**ir** change **qu** to **c,** as **qu** (denoting the **k** sound) is written in Spanish only before **e** or **i:**

Delinquir, *to be delinquent*

PRES. INDIC., *1st Sing.* delinco   PRES. SUBJ. delinca, etc.

d) Verbs in –**gu**–**ir** omit their unpronounced **u,** which is not needed to indicate a "hard" **g** before **o** or **a:**

Distinguir, *to distinguish*

PRES. INDIC., *1st Sing.* distingo   PRES. SUBJ. distinga, etc.

NOTE: It is to be noted that only seven forms of the verb inflexion are concerned in the four cases above.

246. Diphthongal endings –ió and –ie–:

 a) Verbs of the second and third conjugations (regular or not),
 whose stem ends in a vowel, change the **i** of the diphthongal
 endings –ió and –ie– to **y**, as unaccented **i** cannot stand between vowels in Spanish:

> **Cre–er**, *to believe:* cre–yendo (*for* cre–iendo), cre–yó (*for* cre–ió),
> cre–yeron (*for* cre–ieron), cre–yese (*for* cre–iese), etc., cre–yera
> (*for* cre–iera), etc., cre–yere (*for* cre–iere), etc.
>
> **Conclu–ir**, *to conclude:* conclu–yendo, conclu–yó, conclu–yeron,
> etc.

 b) The **i** of the endings –ió and –ie– disappears after all verb
 stems ending in **ll** or **ñ** and after certain irregular preterite
 stems ending in **j**:

> **Bull–ir**, *to boil:* bullendo, bulló, bulleron, bullese, etc., etc.
> **Gruñ–ir**, *to grunt:* gruñ–endo, gruñ–ó, gruñ–eron, etc., etc.
> **Tra–er**, *to bring:* traj–o, traj–eron, traj–ese, etc., etc.

247. *Verbs in* –iar *and* –uar. A certain number of verbs in –iar
 and –uar (to be learned by practice) take a written accent
 on the **i** or **u** of the three persons of the singular and the
 third person plural of their present tenses (indicative, subjunctive, imperative):

> **Criar**, *to bring up:*   crío, crías, cría, crían
> críe, críes, críe, críen
> cría
>
> **Continuar**, *to continue:* continúo, continúas, continúa, continúan
> continúe, continúes, continúe, continúen
> continúa

Among the commonest verbs with this peculiarity are:

aliar, *to ally*	**espiar**, *to spy*
ataviar, *to adorn*	**expiar**, *to expiate*
confiar, *to confide*	**fiar**, *to trust*
contrariar, *to oppose, vex*	**guiar**, *to guide*
desafiar, *to challenge*	**inventariar**, *to take an inventory of*
desconfiar, *to distrust*	**liar**, *to bind*
desvariar, *to rave*	**porfiar**, *to persist*
desviar, *to divert*	**resfriar**, *to chill*
enviar, *to send*	**telegrafiar**, *to telegraph*

vaciar, *to empty*	**graduar,** *to graduate*
variar, *to vary*	**habituar,** *to habituate*
acentuar, *to accentuate*	**insinuar,** *to insinuate*
atenuar, *to attenuate*	**perpetuar,** *to perpetuate*
conceptuar, *to conceive*	**puntuar,** *to punctuate*
efectuar, *to effectuate*	**situar,** *to situate*
exceptuar, *to except*	**valuar,** *to appraise*

NOTE: A considerable number of verbs do not take this accent: cf. **afiliar,** *to affiliate,* **afilio; anunciar,** *to announce,* **anuncio; apremiar,** *to press,* **apremio; cambiar,** *to change,* **cambio; diferenciar,** *to differentiate,* **diferencio; encomiar,** *to extol,* **encomio; estudiar,** *to study,* **estudio; iniciar,** *to initiate,* **inicio; lidiar,** *to fight,* **lidio; premiar,** *to reward,* **premio; presenciar,** *to witness,* **presencio; principiar,** *to begin,* **principio;** etc.

248. *Radical-changing Verbs.* Under certain conditions some verbs change their radical (root) vowels **e** to **ie** or **i** and **o** to **ue** or **u.** The conditions are such as to make three classes thus represented:

I. If accented $\begin{cases} \text{the radical vowel } \mathbf{e} \text{ becomes } \mathbf{ie}. \\ \text{the radical vowel } \mathbf{o} \text{ becomes } \mathbf{ue}. \end{cases}$

II. If accented $\begin{cases} \text{the radical vowel } \mathbf{e} \text{ becomes } \mathbf{ie}. \\ \text{the radical vowel } \mathbf{o} \text{ becomes } \mathbf{ue}. \end{cases}$

If unaccented $\begin{cases} \text{the radical vowel } \mathbf{e} \text{ becomes } \mathbf{i} \\ \text{the radical vowel } \mathbf{o} \text{ becomes } \mathbf{u} \end{cases}$ $\begin{cases} \text{before a follow-} \\ \text{ing } \mathbf{-a-}, \mathbf{-ie-}, \\ \text{or } \mathbf{-i\acute{o}} \text{ of the} \\ \text{flexional end-} \\ \text{ing.} \end{cases}$

III. If accented the radical vowel **e** becomes **i.**

If unaccented the radical vowel **e** becomes **i** before a following **-a-, -ie-,** or **-ió** of the flexional ending.

249. *Class I.* This comprises only first and second conjugation verbs. The change of accented **e** to **ie** and accented **o** to **ue** can occur in only nine forms, viz., all the singular and the third plural of the present indicative and present subjunctive and the second singular of the imperative; all other forms show the original **e** or **o.** The endings are regular. These verbs illustrate the class:

1. **Cerrar,** *to close*

PARTICIPLES	cerrando cerrado			
PRES. INDIC.	cierro cierras cierra	cierran	*But:* cerramos cerráis
PRES. SUBJ.	cierre cierres cierre	cierren	*But:* cerremos cerréis
IMPERAT.	cierra		*But:*	cerrad

IMPF. INDIC.	cerraba, etc.	FUT. INDIC.	cerraré, etc.
PRET. INDIC.	cerré, etc.	COND. INDIC.	cerraría, etc.
IMPF. SUBJ.	cerrase, etc. / cerrara, etc.	FUT. or HYP. SUBJ.	cerrare, etc.

2. **Entender,** *to understand*

PARTICIPLES entendiendo entendido
PRES. INDIC. entiendo entiendes entiende
                        entienden *But:* entendemos entendéis
PRES. SUBJ. entienda entiendas entienda
                        entiendan *But:* entendamos entendáis
IMPERAT.   entiende   *But:*   entended

All other forms with the radical vowel **e** are perfectly regular as of the second conjugation.

3. **Contar,** *to count*

PARTICIPLES	contando contado			
PRES. INDIC.	cuento cuentas cuenta	cuentan	*But:* contamos contáis
PRES. SUBJ.	cuente cuentes cuente	cuenten	*But:* contemos contéis
IMPERAT.	cuenta		*But:*	contad

IMPF. INDIC.	contaba, etc.	FUT. INDIC.	contaré, etc.
PRET. INDIC.	conté, etc.	COND. INDIC.	contaría, etc.
IMPF. SUBJ.	contase, etc. / contara, etc.	FUT. or HYP. SUBJ.	contare, etc.

4. **Volver,** *to return*

PARTICIPLES volviendo vuelto
PRES. INDIC. vuelvo vuelves vuelve vuelven *But:* volvemos volvéis
PRES. SUBJ. vuelva vuelvas vuelva vuelvan *But:* volvamos volváis
IMPERAT.   vuelve   *But:*   volved

All other forms with the radical vowel **o** are perfectly regular as of the second conjugation.

NOTE: The past participle of this verb and of other verbs in –olver is irregular. So devolver, *to give back,* devuelto; envolver, *to wrap up*, **envuelto**; **revolver**, *to stir*, **revuelto**; **solver**, *to loosen*, **suelto**; **absolver**, *to absolve*, **absuelto**; **disolver**, *to dissolve*, **disuelto**; **resolver**, *to resolve*, **resuelto**; etc. Most radical-changing verbs of this class have regular participles; thus **mover**, *to move;* **muevo**, *I move*, etc.; **movido**.

250. The changes in spelling of the end of the stem, already listed for regular verbs, occur here also; cf. §§ 243–245.

a) Before **e, c** becomes **qu:**

    Revolcar, *to wallow:*   PRET. INDIC., *1st Sing.* revolqué
                             PRES. SUBJ. revuelque, etc.

b) Before **e, g** becomes **gu:**

    Negar, *to deny:*   PRET. INDIC., *1st Sing.* negué
                         PRES. SUBJ. niegue, etc.

c) Before **e, z** becomes **c:**

    Empezar, *to begin:*   PRET. INDIC., *1st Sing.* empecé
                           PRES. SUBJ. empiece, etc.

d) Before **o** or **a, c** becomes **z:**

    Torcer, *to twist:*   PRES. INDIC., *1st Sing.* tuerzo
                        PRES. SUBJ. tuerza, etc.

e) After **g, ue** from **o** takes a diaeresis:

    Degollar, *to behead:*   PRES. INDIC. degüello degüellas, etc.
                            PRES. SUBJ. degüelle, etc.
                            IMPERAT. degüella

251. When initial, the stressed **e** and **o** of radical-changing verbs become **ye** and **hue** respectively, as Spanish does not write **ie** and **ue** at the beginning of words:

  1. **Errar**, *to err:*   PRES. INDIC. yerro yerras, etc.
                    PRES. SUBJ. yerre, etc.
                    IMPERAT. yerra

  2. **Oler**, *to smell:*   PRES. INDIC. huelo hueles, etc.
                    PRES. SUBJ. huela, etc.
                    IMPERAT. huele

NOTE: In derivatives the change of **o** to **hue** occurs also; thus desosar, *to remove the bones from*, deshueso, etc.; desovar, *to spawn*, deshuevan, etc. (cf. hueso, *bone*, and huevo, *egg*).

252. Being based on second conjugation (–er) verbs, some derivatives of the third (–ir) conjugation have their stem-stressed forms treated as of this first radical-changing class. These are concernir, *to concern*,[1] and discernir, *to discern* (cf. the simple verb cerner, *to sift*, cierno, etc.), adquirir, *to acquire*, and inquirir, *to inquire* (cf. the simple verb querer, *to wish*, quiero, etc.). Adquirir and inquirir have i in the unstressed stem everywhere.

1. Discernir, *to discern*

PRES. INDIC.	discierno	disciernes	discierne	
			disciernen *But:*	discernimos discernís
PRES. SUBJ.	discierna	disciernas	discierna	
			disciernan *But:*	discernamos discernáis
IMPERAT.		discierne	*But:*	discernid

2. Adquirir, *to acquire*

PRES. INDIC.	adquiero	adquieres	adquiere	
			adquieren *But:*	adquirimos adquirís
PRES. SUBJ.	adquiera	adquieras	adquiera	
			adquieran *But:*	adquiramos adquiráis
IMPERAT.		adquiere	*But:*	adquirid

253. **Jugar,** *to play*, had originally an o stem (cf. Latin *jocari*). The stem-stressed forms show ue, the others have u:

PRES. INDIC.	juego	juegas	juega	juegan	*But:* jugamos	jugáis
PRES. SUBJ.	juegue	juegues	juegue	jueguen	*But:* juguemos	juguéis
IMPERAT.		juega			*But:*	jugad

254. *Class II.* This includes only verbs of the third conjugation with the radical vowel e or o. As in Class I, the e becomes ie and the o becomes ue when accented. Unaccented, the e becomes i and the o becomes u before an immediately following –a–, –ie–, or –ió of the flexional suffix; otherwise the unaccented e and o remain.

---

[1] **Concernir** has only third person forms in the finite tenses.

1. **Sentir**, *to feel*

PARTICIPLES	sint–iendo	sentido			
PRES. INDIC.	siento	sientes	siente		
			sienten	*But:* sentimos	sentís
PRES. SUBJ.	sienta	sientas	sienta		
	sint–amos	sint–áis	sientan		
IMPERAT.			siente	*But:*	sentid
IMPF. INDIC.	sentía, etc. (*reg.*)				
PRET. INDIC.	sentí	sentiste	sint–ió	sentimos sentisteis sint–ieron	
-se IMPF. SUBJ.	sint–iese sint–ieses sint–iese sint–iésemos sint–ieseis				
			sint–iesen		
-ra IMPF. SUBJ.	sint–iera, etc.				
FUT. or HYP. SUBJ.	} sint–iere, etc.				

2. **Dormir**, *to sleep*

PARTICIPLES	durm–iendo		dormido		
PRES. INDIC.	duermo	duermes	duerme		
			duermen	*But:* dormimos	dormís
PRES. SUBJ.	duerma	duermas	duerma		
	durm–amos	durm–áis	duerman		
IMPERAT.		duerme		*But:*	dormid
IMPF. INDIC.	dormía, etc. (*reg.*)				
PRET. INDIC.	dormí	dormiste	durm–ió		
	dormimos	dormisteis	durm–ieron		
-se IMPF. SUBJ.	durm–iese [1]	durm–ieses	durm–iese	durm–iésemos	
		durm–ieseis	durm–iesen		
-ra IMPF. SUBJ.	durm–iera, etc.				
FUT. or HYP. SUBJ.	} durm–iere, etc.				

NOTE: The only simple o verbs in Class II are **dormir** and **morir**, *to die;* in the past participle **morir** has only the irregular form **muerto.** In perfect tenses this, if intransitive, means *died:* **el hombre ha muerto,** *the man has died;* if transitive with a *personal* object, it means *killed:* **han muerto al hombre,** *they have killed the man.* But in the perfect tenses of the reflexive verb **matado,** past participle of **matar,** *to kill,* must be used: **el hombre se ha matado,** *the man has killed himself.* With the verb *to be,* and equivalent verbs, **muerto (–a, –os, –as)** naturally means *dead:* **la mujer está muerta,** *the woman is dead.*

[1] As to the stem of the imperfect and future forms of the subjunctive of radical-changing verbs, see § 240*b*.

255. *Class III.* As in Class II, so here only third conjugation
verbs are concerned, and, furthermore, only those with the
radical vowel **e**. This changes in precisely the same cases
as in Class II, except that here the **e** becomes **i** both
under the accent and when unaccented and followed by –a–, –ie–,
or –ió. The original **e** maintains itself here in the cases in
which it persists in Class II.

Pedir, *to ask*

PARTICIPLES	pid–iendo		pedido		
PRES. INDIC.	pido	pides	pide		
			piden	*But:* pedimos	pedís
PRES. SUBJ.	pida	pidas	pida		
	pidamos	pidáis	pidan		
IMPERAT.		pide		*But:*	pedid
IMPF. INDIC.	pedía, etc. (*reg.*)				
PRET. INDIC.	pedí	pediste	pid–ió	pedimos	pedisteis
			pid–ieron		
–se **IMPF. SUBJ.**	pid–iese	pid–ieses	pid–iese	pid–iésemos	pid–ieseis
			pid–iesen		
–ra **IMPF. SUBJ.**	pid–iera, etc.				
FUT. or HYP. SUBJ.	pid–iere, etc.				

256. Changes in spelling of the end of the stem occur here in
accordance with the rules previously stated (§ 245):

 a) **g** (**i**, **e**) becomes **j** before **o** or **a**:

> **Corregir,** *to correct:* PRES. INDIC., *1st Sing.* corrijo
> PRES. SUBJ. corrija, etc.

 b) **gu** (**i**, **e**) drops the **u** before **o** or **a**:

> **Seguir,** *to follow:* PRES. INDIC., *1st Sing.* sigo
> PRES. SUBJ. siga, etc.

 c) After **ñ**, –ie– and –ió lose their **i**:

> **Ceñir,** *to gird:* PRES. PART. ciñ–endo
> PRET. INDIC., *3rd Sing.* ciñ–ó, *3rd Pl.* ciñ–eron
> –se IMPF. SUBJ. ciñ–ese, etc.
> –ra IMPF. SUBJ. ciñ–era, etc.
> FUT. or HYP. SUBJ. ciñ–ere, etc.

257. Verbs in –e**í**r are of Class III. In them the **i** of the stem ending and that of the –**ie**– and –**ió** in the flexional endings following coalesce:

> Re**í**r, *to laugh:* riendo (*for* ri–iendo); rió (*for* ri–ió); rieron (*for* ri–ieron); riese (*for* ri–iese), etc.; riera (*for* ri–iera), etc.; riere (*for* ri–iere), etc.

258. The verb **erguir**, *to erect*, may be conjugated as of either Class II or Class III with due attention to changes in spelling of the stem ending; thus **yergo** (cf. § 251, 1) or **irgo, yergues** or **irgues,** etc.

> NOTE: Class I contains many verbs of the –ar and –er conjugations. Class II contains all verbs in –entir, –erir, and –ertir, as well as **hervir**, *to boil*, and its derivative **rehervir**, *to boil again*. Class III contains all verbs in –ebir, –edir, –egir, –eguir, –e**í**r, –emir, –enchir, –endir, –e**ñ**ir, –estir, and –etir, as well as **servir**, *to serve*, and its derivative **deservir**, *to do a disservice*.

259. *Verbs with Inceptive Endings.* Verbs in –cer and –cir, having a vowel before these infinitive endings, insert a **z** before the **c** in their present indicative and present subjunctive wherever the verb ending begins with **o** or **a.** All the other forms are perfectly regular, and the –**zc**– or inceptive forms are only seven in number, viz., the first person singular of the present indicative and all six forms of the present subjunctive. There is no obvious inceptive *meaning* in the verbs of this class. While certain of them are related to Latin inceptive verbs (cf. Spanish **conocer** and Latin *cognoscere*), others have no such connections.

1. Conocer, *to know*

PARTICIPLES   conociendo   conocido

PRES. INDIC., } conozco (All other forms reg.)
1st Sing.

PRES. SUBJ. conozca conozcas conozca conozcamos conozcáis conozcan

The rest of the verb regular as of the second conjugation.

2. Lucir, *to shine*

PARTICIPLES   luciendo   lucido

PRES. INDIC.,
1st Sing. } luzco (All other forms reg.)

PRES. SUBJ. luzca luzcas luzca luzcamos luzcáis luzcan

The rest of the verb regular as of the third conjugation.

NOTE: The c is simply changed to z in mecer, *to rock*, and its derivative remecer, *to rock again*, which are regular verbs, and in cocer, *to boil*, and its derivatives recocer, *to boil again*, and escocer, *to smart*, which are radical-changing verbs of the first class. Hence the forms mezo; meza, etc.; cuezo; cueza, etc. The irregular verbs hacer, *to do, make*, and decir, *to say*, with their derivatives, have no inceptive endings, but irregular verbs in –ucir (conducir, etc.) have them (conduzco, etc.).

260. *The* –uir *Verb.* This class comprises only verbs with a pronounced u (huir, argüir, etc., but not seguir and the like). In their present forms (indicative, subjunctive, and imperative) they add y to the u of the stem (hu–yo, etc.), except where the flexional ending begins with i. All the other forms are regular. In accordance with the rule stated previously (cf. § 246a) an unaccented i between vowels will be written y in the third person of the preterite indicative, in all the forms of the two imperfects and the future of the subjunctive, and in the present participle (gerund):

Huir, *to flee*

PARTICIPLES	hu–yendo	huido			
PRES. INDIC.	huy–o	huy–es	huy–e		
			huy–en	*But:* huimos	huis
PRES. SUBJ.	huy–a	huy–as	huy–a		
	huy–amos	huy–áis	huy–an		
IMPERAT.		huy–e		*But:*	huid
FUT. INDIC.	huiré, etc. (*reg.*)				
COND. INDIC.	huiría, etc. (*reg.*)				
IMPF. INDIC.	huía, etc. (*reg.*)				
PRET. INDIC.	huí	huiste	hu–yó	huimos	huisteis	hu–yeron
–se IMPF. SUBJ.	hu–yese	hu–yeses, etc.			
–ra IMPF. SUBJ.	hu–yera	hu–yeras, etc			
FUT. or HYP. SUBJ.	hu–yere	hu–yeres, etc			

NOTE: Verbs in –güir retain the diaeresis only before a written i: argüir, *to argue*, argüido, argüimos, argüía, argüi, etc.; but arguyendo, arguyo, arguyes, arguya, etc.

Irregular Verbs

261. **Haber,** *to have*

PARTICIPLES
hab–iendo hab–ido

PRES. INDIC.

| he | has | ha | hemos | hab–éis | han |

PRES. SUBJ.

| hay–a | hay–as | hay–a | hay–amos | hay–áis | hay–an |

IMPERAT.

| (he) | | | | hab–ed | |

FUT. INDIC.

| habr–é | habr–ás | habr–á | habr–emos | habr–éis | habr–án |

COND. INDIC.

| habr–ía | habr–ías | habr–ía | habr–íamos | habr–íais | habr–ían |

IMPF. INDIC.

| hab–ía | hab–ías | hab–ía | hab–íamos, etc. (*reg.*) | | |

PRET. INDIC.

| hub–e | hub–iste | hub–o | hub–imos | hub–isteis | hub–ieron |

–se IMPF. SUBJ.

hub–iese hub–ieses hub–iese hub–iésemos, etc.

–ra IMPF. SUBJ.

hub–iera hub–ieras, etc.

FUT. or HYP. SUBJ.

hub–iere hub–ieres, etc.

NOTE: The indicative future and conditional have a contract infinitive basis. It is not absolutely certain that he is a part of haber; it occurs most often with the adverb aquí, *here;* he aquí, *behold.* Haber is also the impersonal verb (*there*) *to be,* and as such it employs only the third singular of its finite forms. In the impersonal use the third singular present indicative (and only this one form) appends the otherwise obsolete adverb y, *here, there:* hay, *there is* (*are*).

Note that haber has in the first and third singular of the preterite indicative so-called "strong" forms, i.e., forms stressing the stem and not the flexional ending. This is a marked characteristic also of the irregular verbs **tener, estar, andar, querer, poder, caber, saber, hacer, venir, poner, traer, decir,** and the derivatives in –ducir (**aducir, conducir, deducir,** etc.).

262.   **Tener,** *to have, hold*

PARTICIPLES
ten–iendo   ten–ido

PRES. INDIC.

| teng–o | tien–es | tien–e | ten–emos | ten–éis | tien–en |

PRES. SUBJ.

| teng–a | teng–as | teng–a | teng–amos | teng–áis | teng–an |

IMPERAT.

| ten | | | | ten–ed | |

FUT. INDIC.

| tendr–é | tendr–ás | tendr–á | tendr–emos | tendr–éis | tendr–án |

COND. INDIC.

| tendr–ía | tendr–ías | tendr–ía | tendr–íamos | tendr–íais | tendr–ían |

IMPF. INDIC.

| ten–ía | ten–ías (*reg.*) |

PRET. INDIC.

| tuv–e | tuv–iste | tuv–o | tuv–imos | tuv–isteis | tuv–ieron |

–se IMPF. SUBJ.

| tuv–iese | tuv–ieses | tuv–iese | tuv–iésemos, etc. |

–ra IMPF. SUBJ.

| tuv–iera | tuv–ieras, etc. |

FUT. or HYP. SUBJ.

| tuv–iere | tuv–ieres, etc. |

NOTE: The indicative future and conditional have a contract infinitive basis with a phonetically developed **d: tendr–;** for the same phenomenon, cf. also **venir, poner, salir,** and **valer.** Certain present forms show radical-changing peculiarities. Like **venir, poner, valer, salir, hacer,** and **decir, tener** has no flexional ending in the imperative singular.

263.   **Ser,** *to be*

PARTICIPLES	s–iendo	s–ido				
PRES. INDIC.	soy	eres	es	somos	sois	son
PRES. SUBJ.	se–a	se–as	se–a	se–amos	se–áis	se–an

	IMPERAT.		sé			sed		
	FUT. INDIC.	ser–é	ser–ás	ser–á	ser–emos	ser–éis	ser–án
	COND. INDIC.	ser–ía	ser–ías	ser–ía	ser–íamos	ser–íais	ser–ían
	IMPF. INDIC.	era	eras	era	éramos	erais	eran
	PRET. INDIC.	fu–í	fu–iste	fu–é	fu–imos	fu–isteis	fu–eron
–se	IMPF. SUBJ.	fu–ese	fu–eses	fu–ese	fu–ésemos, etc.
–ra	IMPF. SUBJ.	fu–era	fu–eras, etc.
FUT. or HYP. SUBJ. }		fu–ere	fu–eres, etc.

264.   Estar, *to be*

	PARTICIPLES	est–ando	est–ado				
	PRES. INDIC.	est–oy	est–ás	est–á	est–amos est–áis est–án
	PRES. SUBJ.	est–é	est–és	est–é	est–emos est–éis est–én
	IMPERAT.		est–á		est–ad
	FUT. INDIC.	estar–é	estar–ás	estar–á estar–emos, etc. (*reg.*)
	COND. INDIC.	estar–ía	estar–ías, etc. (*reg.*)
	IMPF. INDIC.	est–aba	est–abas	est–aba est–ábamos, etc. (*reg.*)
	PRET. INDIC.	estuv–e	estuv–iste estuv–o estuv–imos estuv–isteis estuv–ieron
–se	IMPF. SUBJ.	estuv–iese estuv–ieses estuv–iese estuv–iésemos, etc.
–ra	IMPF. SUBJ.	estuv–iera estuv–ieras, etc.
FUT. or HYP. SUBJ. }		estuv–iere estuv–ieres, etc.

NOTE: This is the Latin *stare*, whose sense has weakened from *stand* to *be*. It is regular, as of the first conjugation, in its present tenses and in the future, conditional, and imperfect of the indicative except for the y added in **estoy**. This y is found also in **soy** from **ser**, **voy** from **ir**, and **doy** from **dar**. Note the frequency of the written accent in the present tenses.

265.   Ir, *to go*

	PARTICIPLES	yendo	ido				
	PRES. INDIC.	voy	vas	va	vamos	vais	van
	PRES. SUBJ.	vay–a	vay–as	vay–a	vay–amos	vay–áis	vay–an
	IMPERAT.		ve		(vamos)	id
	FUT. INDIC.	ir–é	ir–ás, etc. (*reg.*)
	COND. INDIC.	ir–ía	ir–ías, etc. (*reg.*)
	IMPF. INDIC.	iba	ibas	iba	íbamos	ibais	iban
	PRET. INDIC.	fu–í	fu–iste, etc. (*as for* ser)
–se	IMPF. SUBJ.	fu–ese	fu–eses, etc. (*as for* ser)

-ra IMPF. SUBJ.	fu–era	fu–eras, etc. (*as for* **ser**)
FUT. or HYP. SUBJ. }	fu–ere	fu–eres, etc. (*as for* **ser**)

NOTE: This verb is very irregular; its forms are related to those of three different Latin verbs, *ire, vadere,* and *esse.* It is obvious that it borrows from **ser** the forms of its preterite indicative and its two imperfects and future of the subjunctive. The grammars usually register for it a first plural of the imperative, **vamos,** *let us go* (also used as an interjection, *come now,* etc.), which is strictly speaking an older form of the first plural of the present subjunctive. **Vayamos** is restricted to the purely subjunctive use in clauses that are clearly subordinate; **vamos** occurs only in clauses that are independent or apparently so.

266. **Andar,** *to go, walk*

PARTICIPLES	and–ando	and–ado
PRES. INDIC.	and–o	and–as, etc. (*reg.*)
PRES. SUBJ.	and–e	and–es, etc. (*reg.*)
IMPERAT.		anda, etc. (*reg.*)
FUT. INDIC.	andar–é	andar–ás, etc. (*reg.*)
COND. INDIC.	andar–ía	andar–ías, etc. (*reg.*)
IMPF. INDIC.	and–aba	and–abas, etc. (*reg.*)
PRET. INDIC.	anduv–e anduv–iste anduv–o anduv–imos anduv–isteis anduv–ieron	
-se IMPF. SUBJ.	anduv–iese	anduv–ieses, etc.
-ra IMPF. SUBJ.	anduv–iera	anduv–ieras, etc.
FUT. or HYP. SUBJ. }	anduv–iere	anduv–ieres, etc.

NOTE: This verb is perfectly regular as of the first conjugation in its infinitive, participles, present tenses, and future, conditional, and imperfect of the indicative. With the stem **anduv–** it is of the second or third regular conjugation in the preterite indicative and the three subjunctive tenses that follow it.

267. **Dar,** *to give, strike*

PARTICIPLES	d–ando	d–ado		
PRES. INDIC.	d–oy	d–as	d–a	d–amos, etc.
PRES. SUBJ.	d–é	d–es	d–é	d–emos, etc.
IMPERAT.		d–a		d–ad
FUT. INDIC.	dar–é	dar–ás, etc. (*reg.*)		
COND. INDIC.	dar–ía	dar–ías, etc. (*reg.*)		

9*

IMPF. INDIC.	d–aba	d–abas, etc. (*reg.*)				
PRET. INDIC.	d–í	d–iste	d–ió	d–imos	d–isteis	d–ieron
-se IMPF. SUBJ.	d–iese	d–ieses	d–iese	d–iésemos, etc.		
-ra IMPF. SUBJ.	d–iera	d–ieras, etc.				
FUT. or HYP. SUBJ.	d–iere	d–ieres, etc.				

NOTE: With the stem d–, this verb is regular as of the first conjugation (save for the y of doy) in its infinitive, participles, present tenses, and future, conditional, and imperfect of the indicative; and it is regular as of the second or third conjugation in the preterite indicative and the three subjunctive tenses that follow it.

268.   **Venir,** *to come*

PARTICIPLES	vin–iendo	ven–ido				
PRES. INDIC.	veng–o	vien–es	vien–e	ven–imos	ven–ís	vien–en
PRES. SUBJ.	veng–a	veng–as	veng–a	veng–amos	veng–áis	veng–an
IMPERAT.	ven				ven–id	
FUT. INDIC.	vendr–é	vendr–ás	vendr–á	vendr–emos	vendr–éis	vendr–án
COND. INDIC.	vendr–ía	vendr–ías, etc.				
IMPF. INDIC.	ven–ía	ven–ías, etc. (*reg.*)				
PRET. INDIC.	vin–e	vin–iste	vin–o	vin–imos	vin–isteis	vin–ieron
-se **IMPF. SUBJ.**	vin–iese	vin–ieses, etc.				
-ra **IMPF. SUBJ.**	vin–iera	vin–ieras, etc.				
FUT. or HYP. SUBJ.	vin–iere	vin–ieres, etc.				

NOTE: This is one of several irregular verbs which add g or ig to the verb stem in the first singular of the present indicative and in all six forms of the present subjunctive; the others are tener, poner, asir, salir, and valer, which add g, and caer, oír, and traer, which add –ig. In part venir is, like tener, of the radical-changing class.

269. **Poner,** *to put*

PARTICIPLES
pon–iendo puesto

PRES. INDIC.
| pong–o | pon–es | pon–e | pon–emos | pon–éis | pon–en |

PRES. SUBJ.
| pong–a | pong–as | pong–a | pong–amos | pong–áis | pong–an |

IMPERAT.
pon   pon–ed

FUT. INDIC.
| pondr–é | pondr–ás | pondr–á | pondr–emos | pondr–éis | pondr–án |

COND. INDIC.
pondr–ía pondr–ías, etc.

IMPF. INDIC.
pon–ía pon–ías, etc. (*reg.*)

PRET. INDIC.
| pus–e | pus–iste | pus–o | pus–imos | pus–isteis | pus–ieron |

-se IMPF. SUBJ.
pus–iese pus–ieses, etc.

–ra IMPF. SUBJ.
pus–iera pus–ieras, etc.

FUT. or HYP. SUBJ.
pus–iere pus–ieres, etc.

NOTE: The past participle, the preterite indicative, and the imperfects and future of the subjunctive have irregular formations.

270. **Hacer,** *to do, make*

PARTICIPLES
hac–iendo hecho

PRES. INDIC.
| hag–o | hac–es | hac–e | hac–emos | hac–éis | hac–en |

PRES. SUBJ.
| hag–a | hag–as | hag–a | hag–amos | hag–áis | hag–an |

IMPERAT.
haz   hac–ed

FUT. INDIC.
| har–é | har–ás | har–á | har–emos | har–éis | har–án |

COND. INDIC.
har–ía har–ías, etc.

IMPF. INDIC.
hac–ía hac–ías, etc. (*reg.*)

PRET. INDIC.

| hic–e | hic–iste | hiz–o | hic–imos | hic–isteis | hic–ieron |

–se IMPF. SUBJ.

hic–iese   hic–ieses, etc.

··ra IMPF. SUBJ.

hic–iera   hic–ieras, etc.

FUT. or HYP. SUBJ.

hic–iere   hic–ieres, etc.

NOTE: This verb, like **decir**, has many irregularities; notable are the formation of the past participle, the **–g–** in certain of the present forms, the contract infinitive basis, **har–**, of the future and conditional of the indicative, and the preterite stem **hic–, hiz–**.

271.   **Decir**, *to say*

PARTICIPLES	dic–iendo	dicho

PRES. INDIC.	dig–o	dic–es	dic–e	dec–imos	dec–ís	dic–en
PRES. SUBJ.	dig–a	dig–as	dig–a	dig–amos	dig–áis	dig–an
IMPERAT.		di			dec–id	
FUT. INDIC.	dir–é	dir–ás	dir–á	dir–emos	dir–éis	dir–án
COND. INDIC.	dir–ía	dir–ías, etc.				
IMPF. INDIC.	dec–ía	dec–ías, etc. (*reg.*)				
PRET. INDIC.	dij–e	dij–iste	dij–o	dij–imos	dij–isteis	dij–eron

–se IMPF. SUBJ.   dij–ese   dij–eses, etc.

–ra IMPF. SUBJ.   dij–era   dij–eras, etc.

FUT. or ⎫
HYP. SUBJ. ⎭ dij–ere   dij–eres, etc.

NOTE: Leading peculiarities are the irregular past participle, a **–g–** stem and radical-changing forms in the present tenses, the contract infinitive basis of the indicative future and conditional, and the preterite stem **dij–** with the loss of **i** in the diphthongal endings after it (**dijo, dijeron, dijese**, etc.).

272.   **Saber**, *to know*

PARTICIPLES	sab–iendo	sab–ido

PRES. INDIC.	sé	sab–es	sab–e	sab–emos	sab–éis	sab–en
PRES. SUBJ.	sep–a	sep–as	sep–a	sep–amos	sep–áis	sep–an
IMPERAT.		sab–e			sab–ed	
FUT. INDIC.	sabr–é	sabr–ás	sabr–á	sabr–emos	sabr–éis	sabr–án
COND. INDIC.	sabr–ía	sabr–ías, etc.				
IMPF. INDIC.	sab–ía	sab–ías, etc. (*reg.*)				

PRET. INDIC.	sup–e	sup–iste	sup–o	sup–imos	sup–isteis	sup–ieron
–se IMPF. SUBJ.	sup–iese	sup–ieses, etc.				
–ra IMPF. SUBJ.	sup–iera	sup–ieras, etc.				
FUT. or HYP. SUBJ.	sup–iere	sup–ieres, etc.				

273. Caber, *to be contained, fit*

PARTICIPLES
    cab–iendo   cab–ido

PRES. INDIC.
    quep–o   cab–es   cab–e   cab–emos   cab–éis   cab–en

PRES. SUBJ.
    quep–a   quep–as   quep–a   quep–amos   quep–áis   quep–an

IMPERAT.   cab–e   cab–ed

FUT. INDIC.
    cabr–é   cabr–ás   cabr–á   cabr–emos   cabr–éis   cabr–án

COND. INDIC.
    cabr–ía   cabr–ías, etc.

IMPF. INDIC.
    cab–ía   cab–ías, etc. (*reg.*)

PRET. INDIC.
    cup–e   cup–iste   cup–o   cup–imos   cup–isteis   cup–ieron

–se IMPF. SUBJ.
    cup–iese   cup–ieses, etc.

–ra IMPF. SUBJ.
    cup–iera   cup–ieras, etc.

FUT. or HYP. SUBJ.
    cup–iere   cup–ieres, etc.

NOTE: **Saber** and **caber** are exactly alike in their peculiarities, except that **saber** has a reduced form sé (instead of **sepo**) in the present indicative, first singular, where **caber** has **quepo**. The interchange of –p– and –b– in the present stem, the contract infinitive basis for the indicative future and conditional, and the irregular preterite stem, **sup–**, **cup–**, are to be noted.

274. Poder, *to be able*

PARTICIPLES
    pud–iendo   pod–ido

PRES. INDIC.
    pued–o   pued–es   pued–e   pod–emos   pod–éis   pued–en

PRES. SUBJ.
    pued–a   pued–as   pued–a pod–amos   pod–áis   pued–an

IMPERAT. (*None*)

FUT. INDIC.
    podr–é   podr–ás   podr–á podr–emos   podr–éis   podr–án

COND. INDIC.
    podr–ía   podr–ías, etc.

IMPF. INDIC.
    pod–ía   pod–ías, etc. (*reg.*)

PRET. INDIC.
    pud–e   pud–iste pud–o pud–imos   pud–isteis pud–ieron

–se IMPF. SUBJ.
    pud–iese   pud–ieses, etc.

–ra IMPF. SUBJ.
    pud–iera   pud–ieras, etc.

FUT. or HYP. SUBJ.
    pud–iere   pud–ieres, etc.

NOTE: **Poder** has certain features of the radical-changing verb and a contract stem in the future and conditional of the indicative. Its preterite stem is **pud–**. Its sense precludes its having a real imperative.

275.   **Querer,** *to wish, be fond of*

PARTICIPLES
    quer–iendo quer–ido

PRES. INDIC.
    quier–o   quier–es quier–e quer–emos quer–éis   quier–en

PRES. SUBJ.
    quier–a   quier–as quier–a quer–amos quer–áis   quier–an

IMPERAT.   quier–e   quer–ed

FUT. INDIC.
    querr–é   querr–ás querr–á querr–emos querr–éis   querr–án

COND. INDIC.
    querr–ía   querr–ías, etc.

IMPF. INDIC.
    quer–ía   quer–ías. etc. (*reg.*)

PRET. INDIC.
    quis–e   quis–iste quis–o   quis–imos   quis–isteis quis–ieron

–se IMPF. SUBJ.
    quis–iese   quis–ieses, etc.

-ra IMPF. SUBJ.

    quis–iera   quis–ieras, etc.

FUT. or HYP. SUBJ.

    quis–iere   quis–ieres, etc.

NOTE: **Querer** has features of the radical-changing verb, a contract infinitive in the future and conditional of the indicative, and a preterite stem **quis–**.

276. Asir, *to grasp*

PARTICIPLES	as–iendo	as–ido				
PRES. INDIC.	asg–o	as–es	as–e	as–imos	as–ís	as–en
PRES. SUBJ.	asg–a	asg–as	asg–a	asg–amos	asg–áis	asg–an

All the other forms are perfectly regular as of the third conjugation.

277. Valer, *to be worth*

PARTICIPLES

    val–iendo   val–ido

PRES. INDIC.

valg–o	val–es	val–e	val–emos	val–éis	val–en

PRES. SUBJ.

valg–a	valg–as	valg–a	valg–amos	valg–áis	valg–an

IMPERAT.   val *or* vale   val–ed

FUT. INDIC.

valdr–é	valdr–ás	valdr–á	valdr–emos	valdr–éis	valdr–án

COND. INDIC.

    valdr–ía   valdr–ías, etc.

IMPF. INDIC.

    val–ía   val–ías, etc. (*reg.*)

PRET. INDIC.   (*reg.*)

-se IMPF. SUBJ.   (*reg.*)

-ra IMPF. SUBJ.   (*reg.*)

FUT. or HYP. SUBJ.   (*reg.*)

278. Salir, *to go out, come out*

PARTICIPLES	sal–iendo	sal–ido				
PRES. INDIC.	salg–o	sal–es	sal–e	sal–imos	sal–ís	sal–en
PRES. SUBJ.	salg–a	salg–as	salg–a	salg–amos	salg–áis	salg–an
IMPERAT.		sal			sal–id	

The other forms follow the model of **valer**.

279. **Caer,** *to fall*

PARTICIPLES	ca–yendo	ca–ído				
PRES. INDIC.	caig–o	ca–es	ca–e	ca–emos	ca–éis	ca–en
PRES. SUBJ.	caig–a	caig–as	caig–a	caig–amos	caig–áis	caig–an
IMPERAT.		ca–e			ca–ed	
PRET. INDIC.	ca–í	ca–íste	ca–yó	ca–ímos	ca–ísteis	ca–yeron

The other forms are regular; the imperfect and future subjunctive show the change of unaccented i between vowels to y, as in **cayese, cayera, cayere,** etc.

NOTE: The noticeable peculiarity here, as in the case of the two verbs following, is the addition of –ig– to the present stem for the 1st singular of the present indicative and for all of the present subjunctive.

280. **Oír,** *to hear*

PARTICIPLES	o–yendo	o–ído				
PRES. INDIC.	oig–o	oy–es	oy–e	o–ímos	o–ís	oy–en
PRES. SUBJ.	oig–a	oig–as	oig–a	oig–amos	oig–áis	oig–an
IMPERAT.		oy–e			o–íd	
PRET. INDIC.	o–í	o–íste	o–yó	o–ímos	o–ísteis	o–yeron

The other forms are regular; the imperfect and future subjunctive show the change of unaccented i between vowels to y, as in **oyese, oyera, oyere,** etc.

NOTE: Note the three present stems: **oig–** before –o and –a; **oy–** before –e; and **o–** before –i.

281. **Traer,** *to bring*

PARTICIPLES					
tra–yendo	tra–ído				
PRES. INDIC.					
traig–o	tra–es	tra–e	tra–emos	tra–éis	tra–en
PRES. SUBJ.					
traig–a	traig–as	traig–a	traig–amos	traig–áis	traig–an
IMPERAT.	tra–e			tra–ed	
FUT. INDIC.	(*reg.*)				
COND. INDIC.	(*reg.*)				
IMPF. INDIC.	(*reg.*)				
PRET. INDIC.					
traj–e	traj–iste	traj–o	traj–imos	traj–isteis	traj–eron

-se IMPF. SUBJ.

traj–ese	traj–eses	traj–ese	traj–ésemos	traj–eseis	traj–esen

-ra IMPF. SUBJ.

traj–era	traj–eras	traj–era	traj–éramos	traj–erais	traj–eran

FUT. or HYP. SUBJ.

traj–ere	traj–eres	traj–ere	traj–éremos	traj–ereis	traj–eren

NOTE: **Traer** and verbs in **-ducir** have a preterite stem in –j–
after which the –i– of a diphthongal ending is lost.

282. Conducir, *to conduct*

PARTICIPLES	conduc–iendo	conduc–ido	
PRES. INDIC.	conduzc–o	conduc–es	conduc–e
	conduc–imos	conduc–ís	conduc–en
PRES. SUBJ.	conduzc–a	conduzc–as	conduzc–a
	conduzc–amos	conduzc–áis	conduzc–an
IMPERAT.		conduc–e	
		conduc–id	
FUT. INDIC.	(*reg.*)		
COND. INDIC.	(*reg.*)		
IMPF. INDIC.	(*reg.*)		
PRET. INDIC.	conduj–e	conduj–iste	conduj–o
	conduj–imos	conduj–isteis	conduj–eron
-se IMPF. SUBJ.	conduj–ese	conduj–eses	conduj–ese
	conduj–ésemos	conduj–eseis	conduj–esen
-ra IMPF. SUBJ.	conduj–era	conduj–eras	conduj–era
	conduj–éramos	conduj–erais	conduj–eran
FUT. or	conduj–ere	conduj–eres	conduj–ere
HYP. SUBJ.	conduj–éremos	conduj–ereis	conduj–eren

NOTE: Like **conducir** are conjugated the other derivatives in
-ducir: aducir, deducir, inducir, producir, reducir, seducir;
in the present tenses they show inceptive endings.

283. Ver, *to see*

PARTICIPLES	v–iendo	visto				
PRES. INDIC.	ve–o	v–es	v–e	v–emos	v–eis	v–en
PRES. SUBJ.	ve–a	ve–as	ve–a	ve–amos	ve–áis	ve–an
IMPERAT.		v–e			v–ed	
FUT. INDIC.	ver–é	ver–ás, etc.				
COND. INDIC.	ver–ía	ver–ías, etc.				
IMPF. INDIC.	ve–ía	ve–ías	ve–ía	ve–íamos	ve–íais	ve–ían
PRET. INDIC.	v–í	v–iste	v–ió	v–imos	v–isteis	v–ieron

-se IMPF. SUBJ.	v–iese	v–ieses, etc.
-ra IMPF. SUBJ.	v–iera	v–ieras, etc.
FUT. or HYP. SUBJ.	v–iere	v–ieres, etc.

NOTES: 1. The full stem **ve–** of the present is reduced to **v–** before –e, as in **v–er, v–es**, etc.; the preterite stem is **v–**.

2. The derivatives in –**ver**, e.g., **antever, prever**, are conjugated as above.

3. **Proveer**, *to provide*, has the full stem **prove–** throughout and is regular in its conjugation. It has, however, both **proveído** and **provisto** as the past participle.

284. *Irregular Past Participles.* Four verbs of the third conjugation: **abrir**, *to open;* **cubrir**, *to cover;* **escribir**, *to write;* and **imprimir**, *to print, impress*, have only irregular past participles; these are **abierto, cubierto, escrito,** and **impreso**. Otherwise these verbs are entirely regular. Two second conjugation verbs, **prender**, *to catch, arrest*, and **romper**, *to break, tear*, are perfectly regular throughout, but they have irregular past participles beside the regular ones; the irregular forms, **preso** and **roto,** are preferred for the perfect tenses and in the literal sense.

NOTE: Verbs etymologically related to **escribir** have similarly irregular past participles: **adscribir**, *to inscribe*, **adscrito; describir**, *to describe*, **descrito**, etc. They also have a less common form in –**pto: adscripto**, etc.

285. *Defective Verbs.* The verbs **placer**, *to please*, and **yacer**, *to lie*, are now used chiefly in the third person forms, **place, yace**, etc. Perhaps the commonest form of **placer** is the imperfect subjunctive **pluguiera**, employed especially in ¡ **pluguiera a Dios!** *would to God;* **yacer** figures in tombstone inscriptions, **aquí yace** (**yacen**), *here lies* (*lie*), and occasionally in other uses in higher style. The radical-changing verb **concernir**, *to concern*, occurs only in the forms of the third singular and plural of the various tenses. The radical-changing verb **soler**, *to be accustomed*, is used frequently only in the forms of the indicative present and imperfect, as follows:

| suelo | sueles | suele | solemos | soléis | suelen |
| solía | solías | solía | solíamos | solíais | solían |

286. *List of Verbs*

The following list embraces radical-changing, –uir, and irregular verbs. The verbs with inceptive endings (–cer or –cir preceded by a vowel) are not included: they simply follow the models given in § 259. In the case of derivatives, reference is made to the conjugation of the simple verbs, which they follow. Radical-changing verbs are indicated by (ie), (ue), or (i) placed after the verb. The numbers refer to paragraphs.

abnegar (ie) to renounce: 244*b*; 250*b*

abrir to open: *p.p. irr.* 284

absolver (ue) to absolve: *p.p. irr.* 249, 4

abstenerse to abstain: *irr.* 262

abstraer to abstract: *irr.* 281

abuñolar (ue) to make fritter-shaped: *also* **abuñuelar,** *reg.*

acertar (ie) to hit the mark

aclocarse (ue) to stretch out; brood: 244*a*; 250*a*

acordar (ue) to resolve, remind, tune; — **se (ue)** to remember

acostar (ue) to lay down; —**se (ue)** to lie down

acrecentar (ie) to increase

adestrar (ie) to guide: *also* **adiestrar,** *reg.*

adherir (ie) to adhere

adormir (ue) to make drowsy

adquirir (ie) to acquire: 252, 2

aducir to adduce: *irr.* 282; 259, note; 246*b*

advertir (ie) to observe, advise

afollar (ue) to blow with bellows

aforar (ue) to give a charter: **aforar** to gauge, *reg.*

agorar (ue) to divine, prognosticate: 250*e*

alebrarse (ie) to squat, cower

alentar (ie) to breathe; encourage

aliquebrar (ie) to break the wings

almorzar (ue) to breakfast: 244*d*; 250*c*

alongar (ue) to lengthen: 244*b*; 250*b*

amoblar (ue) to furnish: *also* **amueblar,** *reg.*

amolar (ue) to whet

amover (ue) to remove, dismiss

andar to go, walk: *irr.* 266

antedecir to foretell: *irr.* 271

anteponer to put before, prefer: *irr.* 269

antever to foresee: *irr.* 283

apacentar (ie) to graze

apercollar (ue) to collar, snatch

apernar (ie) to seize by the legs

aplacer to please: *irr.* 285

apostar (ue) to bet, post: **apostar** to post troops, *reg.*

apretar (ie) to squeeze, press

aprobar (ue) to approve

argüir to argue: 260

arrendar (ie) to rent, hire

arrepentirse (ie) to repent

ascender (ie) to ascend

asentar (ie) to seat, set down

asentir (ie) to assent, acquiesce

aserrar (ie) to saw

asir to seize, grasp: *irr.* 276

asolar (ue) to level to ground, raze

asoldar (ue) to hire

asonar (ue) to assonate, be in assonance

asosegar: *see* sosegar

atender (ie) to attend, mind

atenerse to abide, hold: *irr.* 262

atentar (ie) to try: atentar to attempt a crime, *reg.*

aterrar (ie) to fell: aterrar to terrify, *reg.*

atestar (ie) to cram, stuff: atestar to attest, *reg.*

atraer to attract: *irr.* 281; 246*b*

atravesar (ie) to cross

atribuir to attribute: 260

atronar (ue) to make a thundering din, stun

avenir to reconcile: *irr.* 268

aventar (ie) to fan, winnow

avergonzar (ue) to shame: 244*d*; 250*c, e*

azolar (ue) to shape with the adze

bendecir to bless: *irr.* 271; 246*b*

bruñir to burnish: 246*b*

bullir to boil: 246*b*

caber to be contained, find room: *irr.* 273

caer to fall: *irr.* 279

calentar (ie) to warm

cegar (ie) to blind: 244*b*; 250*b*

ceñir (i) to gird: 246*b*; 256*c*

cerner (ie) to sift; bud

cerrar (ie) to close

cimentar (ie) to found, establish

circuir to encircle: 260

clocar (ue) to cluck: 244*a*; 250*a*

cocer (ue) to boil, bake: 259, note

coextenderse (ie) to be coextensive

colar (ue) to strain, filter

colegir (i) to collect: 245*b*; 256*a*

colgar (ue) to hang up: 244*b*; 250*b*

comedirse (i) to behave

comenzar (ie) to commence: 244*d*; 250*c*

competir (i) to compete

complacer to please, content: *irr.* 285

componer to compose: *irr.* 269

comprobar (ue) to verify, confirm

concebir (i) to conceive

concernir (ie) to concern: 252, 1, footnote 1; 285

concertar (ie) to concert, regulate

concluir to conclude: 260; 246*a*

concordar (ue) to accord, agree

condescender (ie) to condescend

condolerse (ue) to condole

conducir to conduct: *irr.* 282; 259, note; 246*b*

conferir (ie) to confer

confesar (ie) to confess

confluir to join: 260

conmover (ue) to move, affect

conseguir (i) to obtain, attain: 245*d*; 256*b*

consentir (ie) to consent

consolar (ue) to console

consonar (ue) to be in consonance, rhyme

constituir to constitute: 260

constreñir (i) to compel, constrain: 246*b*; 256*c*

construir to construct: 260

contar (ue) to count, tell

contender (ie) to contend

contener to contain: *irr.* 262

contorcerse (ue) to be distorted, writhe: 245*a*

contradecir to contradict: *irr.* 271; 246*b*; 259, note

contraer to contract: *irr.* 281; 246*b*

contrahacer to counterfeit: *irr.*
270; 259, note

contraponer to oppose, compare:
irr. 269

contravenir to contravene: *irr.*
268

contribuir to contribute: 260

controvertir (ie) to controvert

convenir to agree, fit: *irr.* 268

convertir (ie) to convert

corregir (i) to correct: 245*b*; 256*a*

costar (ue) to cost

creer to believe: 246*a*

cubrir to cover: *p.p. irr.* 284

dar to give: *irr.* 267

decaer to decay: *irr.* 279

decentar (ie) to begin to use

decir to say: *irr.* 271; 259, note;
246*b*

deducir to deduce: *irr.* 282;
259, note; 246*b*

defender (ie) to defend

deferir (ie) to defer

degollar (ue) to behead, cut the
throat: 250*e*

demoler (ue) to demolish

demostrar (ue) to demonstrate

denegar (ie) to deny: 244*b*; 250*b*

denostar (ue) to insult

dentar (ie) to tooth, indent; to
teethe

deponer to depose, depone: *irr.*
269

derrengar (ie) to sprain the hip,
cripple: 244*b*; 250*b*

derretir (i) to melt

derrocar (ue) to pull down, demolish: 244*a*; 250*a*

derruir to cast down, destroy: 260

desacertar (ie) to blunder, err

desacordar (ue) to make discordant; —se (ue) to forget

desaferrar (ie) to loosen, unfurl

desalentar (ie) to put out of
breath; discourage

desamoblar (ue) to unfurnish, remove furniture: *also* **desamue-
blar**, *reg.*

desandar to retrace steps, undo:
irr. 266

desapretar (ie) to slacken, loosen

desaprobar (ue) to disapprove

desarrendarse (ie) to shake off
the bridle

desasentar (ie) to disagree, displease; —se (ie) to get up

desasir to let go, release hold:
irr. 276

desasosegar (ie) to disturb, dis-
quiet: 244*b*; 250*b*

desatender (ie) to disregard, neglect

desatentar (ie) to perturb, perplex

desavenir to discompose, disconcert: *irr.* 268

descender (ie) to descend

desceñir (i) to ungird: 246*b*; 256*c*

descolgar (ue) to unhang, take
down: 244*b*; 250*b*

descollar (ue) to stand forth, excel

descomedirse (i) to be disre-
spectful, behave badly

descomponer to disconcert, de-
compose: *irr.* 269

desconcertar (ie) to disconcert,
confound

desconsentir (ie) to dissent

desconsolar (ue) to make discon-
solate

descontar (ue) to discount

desconvenir to disagree, be unlike: *irr.* 268

descordar (ue) to remove cords

descornar (ue) to remove horns

descubrir to uncover, discover:
p.p. irr. 284

desdar to untwist: *irr.* 267

desdecir to gainsay: *irr.* 271;
246*b*

desdentar (ie) to remove teeth

desempedrar (ie) to unpave

desencerrar (ie) to release from
confinement

desencordar (ue) to remove
strings, loosen

desengrosar (ue) to make lean

desentenderse (ie) to disregard,
feign not to notice

desenterrar (ie) to disinter

desenvolver (ue) to unfold, un-
ravel: *p.p. irr.* 249, 4

deservir (i) to neglect duty, do a
disservice

desflocar (ue) to remove flocks
(*of wool*): 244*a*; 250*a*

desgobernar (ie) to derange the
government, misgovern

deshacer to undo, destroy: *irr.*
270; 259, note

deshelar (ie) to thaw

desherbar (ie) to pluck out herbs

desherrar to uniron, remove horse-
shoes

desleír (i) to dilute: 257

deslendrar (ie) to remove nits
(*from hair*)

desmajolar (ue) to uproot vines

desmedirse (i) to go beyond
bounds, be unreasonable

desmembrar (ie) to dismember

desmentir (ie) to belie

desnegar (ie) to retract denial:
244*b*; 250*b*

desnevar (ie) to melt away (*of
snow*)

desobstruir to remove obstruc-
tion: 260

desoír not to heed, feign not to
hear: *irr.* 280

desolar (ue) to make desolate

desoldar (ue) to unsolder

desollar (ue) to flay

desosar (ue) to remove bones:
251, note

desovar (ue) to spawn: 251, note

despedir (i) to dismiss; —se (i)
to take leave

despernar (ie) to remove legs,
cripple

despertar (ie) to awaken

despezar (ie) to arrange (stones)
at intervals, taper at the end:
244*d*; 250*c*

desplacer to displease: 285

desplegar (ie) to unfold, unfurl:
244*b*; 250*b*

despoblar (ue) to depopulate

desproveer to leave unprovided,
deprive of supplies: 283, note 3;
246*a*

desteñir (i) to discolor, fade: 246*b*;
256*c*

desterrar (ie) to exile

destituir to deprive, remove from
office: 260

destorcer (ue) to untwist: 245*a*;
250*d*

destrocar (ue) to return a bar-
tered object: 244*a*; 250*a*

destruir to destroy: 260

desventar (ie) to vent, let out air

desvergonzarse (ue) to be shame-
less *or* impudent: 244*d*; 250*c, e*

detener to detain: *irr.* 262

detraer to detract: *irr.* 281; 246*b*

devolver (ue) to give back: *p.p.
irr.* 249, 4

diferir (ie) to defer, delay, differ

digerir (ie) to digest

diluir to dilute: 260

discernir (ie) to discern: 252, 1

disconvenir: *see* desconvenir

discordar (ue) to disagree, be discordant

disentir (ie) to dissent

disminuir to diminish: 260

disolver (ue) to dissolve: *p.p. irr.* 249, 4

disonar (ue) to be in dissonance

dispertar: *see* despertar

displacer to displease: *irr.* 285

disponer to dispose: *irr.* 269

distender (ie) to distend

distraer to distract: *irr.* 281; 246b

distribuir to distribute: 260

divertir (ie) to divert

dolar (ue) to plane, smooth (*wood, etc.*)

doler (ue) to pain, grieve

dormir (ue) to sleep

educir to educe, bring out: *irr.* 282; 259, note; 246b

elegir (i) to elect: 245b; 256a

embestir (i) to invest, attack

emparentar (ie) to be related by marriage

empedrar (ie) to pave

empeller to urge, push: 246b

empezar (ie) to begin: 244d; 250c

emporcar (ue) to sully, befoul: 244a; 250a

encender (ie) to light, kindle

encentar (ie) to begin to use for first time

encerrar (ie) to shut up, confine

enclocar (ue) to cluck: 244a; 250a

encomendar (ie) to commend

encontrar (ue) to meet, find

encorar (ue) to cover with leather, renew the skin

encordar (ue) to string (*musical instruments*), lash

encovar (ue) to put into a cave *or* cellar, lock up

encubertar (ie) to cover over

endentar (ie) to mortise in

engorar (ue) to lay addled eggs: 250e

engreír (i) to elate, puff up: 257

engrosar (ue) to fatten, strengthen

enhestar (ie) to erect, set upright

enmelar (ie) to honey, sweeten

enmendar (ie) to amend, correct

enrodar (ue) to break on the wheel

ensangrentar (ie)·to cover with blood

entender (ie) to hear, understand

enterrar (ie) to inter

entortar (ue) to make crooked; to deprive of one eye

entredecir to interdict: *irr.* 271; 246b; 259, note

entremorir (ue) to pine away: *p.p. irr.* 254, note

entreoír to hear indistinctly: *irr.* 280

entrepernar (ie) to put the legs in between (*something else*)

entreponer to interpose: *irr.* 269

entretener to delay; entertain: *irr.* 262

entrever to see imperfectly, catch a glimpse of: *irr.* 283

envolver (ue) to involve, wrap up; complicate: *p.p. irr.* 249, 4

equivaler to equal, be equivalent: *irr.* 277

erguir (ie *or* i) to erect: 258; 245d

errar (ye–) to err, wander: 251, 1

escarmentar (ie) to give warning example, learn by experience escocer (ue) to smart: 259, note; 245a; 250d

escribir to write: *p.p. irr.* 284

esforzar (ue) to strengthen; —se (ue) to attempt: 244d; 250c

estar to be: *irr.* 264

estatuir to establish: 260

estregar (ie) to rub, scour, grind: 244b; 250b

estreñir (i) to bind, restrain: 246b

excluir to exclude: 260

expedir (i) to expedite, despatch

exponer to expose: *irr.* 269

extender (ie) to extend

extraer to extract: *irr.* 281; 246b

ferrar (ie) to put on iron points

fluir to flow: 260

follar (ue) to blow with bellows

forzar (ue) to force: 244d; 250c

fregar (ie) to rub, scour: 244b; 250b

freír (i) to fry: 257

gemir (i) to groan, moan

gobernar (ie) to govern

gruir to cry like cranes: 260

gruñir to grunt: 246b; 256c

haber to have: *irr.* 261

hacendar (ie) to transfer property

hacer to do, make: *irr.* 270; 259, note (*thus derivatives in* –facer)

heder (ie) to have a stench, stink

helar (ie) to freeze

henchir (i) to stuff, cram

hender (ie) to cleave, split

herbar (ie) to dress skins

herir (ie) to wound

herrar (ie) to shoe (*horses*), brand (*cattle*)

hervir (ie) to boil, bubble

holgar (ue) to rest, cease working: 244b; 250b

hollar (ue) to trample on, tread on

huir to flee: 260

imbuir to imbue: 260

impedir (i) to impede

imponer to impose: *irr.* 269

imprimir to print: *p.p. irr.* 284

improbar (ue) to disapprove, censure

incensar (ie) to perfume, incense

incluir to include: 260

indisponer to indispose, disincline: *irr.* 269

inducir to induce: *irr.* 282; 259, note; 246b

inferir (ie) to infer

infernar (ie) to damn, vex

influir to influence: 260

ingerir (ie) to graft, insert

inquirir (ie) to inquire: 252, 2

instituir to institute: 260

instruir to instruct: 260

interdecir to indict: *irr.* 271; 246b

interponer to interpose: *irr.* 269

intervenir to intervene: *irr.* 268

introducir to introduce: *irr.* 282; 259, note; 246b

invernar (ie) to winter

invertir (ie) to invert, spend, invest

investir (i) to invest, gird

ir to go: *irr.* 265

jugar (ue) to play: 253

leer to read: 246a

llover (ue) to rain

maldecir to curse; *irr.* 271; 246b

malherir (ie) to wound seriously

malsonar (ue) to make cacophony
maltraer to maltreat: *irr.* 281; 246*b*
manifestar (ie) to manifest
mantener to maintain: *irr.* 262
mecer to rock, lull, mix: 259, note
medir (i) to measure
melar (ie) to boil to honey, deposit honey (*of bees*)
mentar (ie) to mention
mentir (ie) to lie
merendar (ie) to lunch
moblar (ue) to furnish: *also* mueblar, *reg.*
moler (ue) to grind
morder (ue) to bite
morir (ue) to die: *p.p. irr.* 254, note
mostrar (ue) to show
mover (ue) to move

negar (ie) to deny: 244*b*; 250*b*
nevar (ie) to snow, *impers.*

obstruir to obstruct: 260
obtener to obtain: *irr.* 262
oír to hear: *irr.* 280
oler (hue–) to smell, have an odor: 251, 2
oponer to oppose: *irr.* 269

pedir (i) to ask
pensar (ie) to think, mean, believe
perder (ie) to lose, spoil, destroy
perniquebrar (ie) to break the legs
perseguir (i) to pursue, persecute: 245*d*; 256*b*
pervertir (ie) to pervert
placer to please: *irr.* 285
plañir to lament, bewail: 246*b*; 256*c*
plegar (ie) to fold: 244*b*; 250*b*

poblar (ue) to found, people, fill
poder to be able; can: *irr.* 274
poner to put: *irr.* 269
poseer to possess: 246*a*
posponer to place after, postpone: *irr.* 269
predecir to predict: *irr.* 271; 246*b*
predisponer to predispose: *irr.* 269
preferir (ie) to prefer
prender to arrest, catch: 284
preponer to put before, prefer: *irr.* 269
presentir (ie) to forebode, foresee
presuponer to presuppose: *irr.* 269
prevalerse to prevail: *irr.* 277
prevenir to forestall, prevent: *irr.* 268
prever to foresee: *irr.* 283
probar (ue) to prove, try, taste
producir to produce: *irr.* 282; 259, note; 246*b*
proferir (ie) to utter, pronounce
promover (ue) to promote
proponer to propose: *irr.* 269
proseguir (i) to pursue, prosecute: 245*d*; 256*b*
prostituir to prostitute: 260
proveer to provide: 246*a*; 283, note 3
provenir to proceed: *irr.* 268

quebrar (ie) to break
querer to wish, like: *irr.* 275

reapretar (ie) to squeeze again
rebendecir to bless again: *irr.* 271; 259, note; 246*b*
recaer to fall back, relapse: *irr.* 279
recalentar (ie) to heat again
recentar (ie) to leaven

recluir to shut up, seclude: 260

recocer (ue) to boil again: 259, note; 250*d*

recolar (ue) to strain again

recomendar (ie) to recommend

recomponer to recompose, mend: *irr.* 269

reconducir to renew lease *or* contract: *irr.* 282; 259, note; 246*b*

reconstruir to reconstruct: 260

recontar (ue) to recount

reconvenir to accuse, rebuke: *irr.* 268

recordar (ue) to remind

recostar (ue) to lean against, recline

redargüir to reargue: 260

reducir to reduce: *irr.* 282; 259, note; 246*b*

reelegir (i) to re-elect: 245*b*; 256*a*

referir (ie) to relate, refer

refluir to flow back: 260

reforzar (ue) to strengthen, fortify: 244*d*; 250*c*

refregar (ie) to rub over again: 244*b*; 250*b*

refreír to fry again: 257

regar (ie) to water: 244*b*; 250*b*

regir (i) to rule, direct: 245*b*; 256*a*

regoldar (ue) to belch, eruct: 250*e*

rehacer to make again, mend: *irr.* 270; 259, note

rehenchir (i) to fill again, restuff

reherir (ie) to wound again

reherrar (ie) to shoe (*horses*) again

rehervir (ie) to reboil

rehollar (ue) to trample under foot

rehuir to withdraw, deny: 260

reír to laugh: 257

remendar (ie) to repair, patch

rementir (ie) to lie again

remoler (ue) to grind again

remorder (ue) to bite repeatedly, cause remorse

remover (ue) to remove, alter

rendir (i) to subdue, render; —se (i) to surrender

renegar (ie) to deny, disown: 244*b*; 250*b*

renovar (ue) to renovate, renew

reñir (i) to quarrel, scold: 246*b*; 256*c*

repensar (ie) to think over again

repetir (i) to repeat, recite

replegar (ie) to refold, double again: 244*b*; 250*b*

repoblar (ue) to repopulate

reponer to put back, replace: *irr.* 269

reprobar (ue) to reject, condemn

reproducir to reproduce: *irr.* 282; 259, note; 246*b*

requebrar (ie) to court, make love

requerir (ie) to investigate, require, request

resalir to project, be prominent: *irr.* 278

resegar (ie) to reap again: 244*b*; 250*b*

resembrar (ie) to sow again

resentirse (ie) to begin to give way, resent

resolver (ue) to resolve: *p.p. irr.* 249, 4

resollar (ue) to respire

resonar (ue) to resound

resquebrar (ie) to crack, split, burst

restituir to restore, re-establish: 260

restregar (ie) to scrub: 244*b*; 250*b*

retemblar (ie) to shake, tremble much, brandish

retener to retain: *irr.* 262

retentar (ie) to threaten (with a relapse)

reteñir (i) to dye over again: 246*b*; 256*c*

retorcer (ue) to twist, contort: 245*a*; 250*d*

retostar (ue) to toast again, scorch well

retraer to retract: *irr.* 281; 246*b*

retribuir to make retribution, recompense: 260

retronar (ue) to thunder again

retrotraer to make retroactive: *irr.* 281; 246*b*

revenirse to be consumed gradually, sour, ferment: *irr.* 268

reventar (ie) to burst

rever to see again, review, revise: *irr.* 283

reverter (ie) to revert

revestir (i) to put on vestments

revolar (ue) to fly again

revolcarse (ue) to wallow: 244*a*; 250*a*

revolver (ue) to stir, revolve: *p.p. irr.* 249, 4

rodar (ue) to roll

rogar (ue) to entreat, ask: 244*b*; 250*b*; *derivatives* (abrogar, derogar) *reg.*

romper to break: *p.p. irr.* 284

saber to know: *irr.* 272

salir to go out, come out: *irr.* 278

salpimentar (ie) to season with pepper and salt

sarmentar (ie) to gather prunings of vine

satisfacer to satisfy: *irr.* 270; 259, note

segar (ie) to reap: 244*b*; 250*b*

seguir (i) to follow: 245*d*; 256*b*

sembrar (ie) to sow

sementar (ie) to sow

sentar (ie) to seat, set; suit

sentir (ie) to feel, regret

ser to be: *irr.* 263

serrar (ie) to saw

servir (i) to serve

sobre(e)ntenderse (ie) to be understood

sobreponer to put above, add: *irr.* 269

sobresalir to rise above, surpass: *irr.* 278

sobresembrar (ie) to sow over again

sobresolar (ue) to pave again, put on new sole

sobrevenir to happen, supervene: *irr.* 268

sobreverterse (ie) to overflow

sobrevestir (i) to put on an outer coat

sofreír (i) to fry slightly: 257

solar (ue) to floor, pave, sole

soldar (ue) to solder, mend

soler (ue) to be wont *or* accustomed: 285

soltar (ue) to untie, loosen

solver (ue) to loosen: *p.p. irr.* 249, 4

sonar (ue) to sound

sonreír (i) to smile: 257

sonrodarse (ue) to stick in the mud

soñar (ue) to dream

sorregar (ie) to change channels: 244*b*; 250*b*

sosegar (ie) to appease, rest: 244*b*; 250*b*

sostener to sustain: *irr.* 262

soterrar (ie) to put underground, bury

subarrendar (ie) to take a sub-lease, subrent

subentender (ie) to imply

subseguir (i) to be next in sequence: 245*d*; 256*b*

substituir: *see* **sustituir**

substraer: *see* **sustraer**

subtender (ie) to subtend

subvenir to aid, give a subvention: *irr.* 268

subvertir (ie) to subvert

sugerir (ie) to suggest

superponer to superimpose: *irr.* 269

supervenir to supervene: *irr.* 268

suponer to suppose: *irr.* 269

sustituir to substitute: 260

sustraer to subtract: *irr.* 281; 246*b*

tañer to ring, peal; touch: 246*b*

temblar (ie) to tremble

tender (ie) to stretch

tener to have, hold: *irr.* 262

tentar (ie) to feel, try

teñir (i) to tinge, dye, stain: 246*b*; 256*c*

torcer (ue) to twist, bend: 245*a*; 250*d*

tostar (ue) to toast

traducir to translate: *irr.* 282; 259, note; 246*b*

traer to bring: *irr.* 281; 246*b*

transcender: *see* **trascender**

transferir (ie) to transfer

transfregar: *see* **trasfregar**

transponer: *see* **trasponer**

trascender (ie) to transcend

trascolar (ue) to filter through

trascordarse (ue) to forget

trasegar (ie) to upset, decant: 244*b*; 250*b*

trasfregar (ie) to rub: 244*b*; 250*b*

trasoír to misunderstand, hear imperfectly: *irr.* 280

trasoñar (ue) to dream

trasponer to transpose, go beyond; —**se** to set (*of sun*): *irr.* 269

trastrocar (ue) to change about, invert order: 244*a*; 250*a*

trasverter (ie) to overflow

trasvolar (ue) to fly across *or* beyond

travesar (ie) to cross

trocar (ue) to exchange, barter: 244*a*; 250*a*

tronar (ue) to thunder

tropezar (ie) to stumble: 244*d*; 250*c*

valer to be worth: *irr.* 277

venir to come: *irr.* 268

ventar (ie) to blow

ver to see: *irr.* 283

verter (ie) to pour, shed

vestir (i) to dress, clothe

volar (ue) to fly, rise, blow up

volcar (ue) to overturn: 244*a*; 250*a*

volver (ue) to return, come back: *p.p. irr.* 249, 4

yacer to lie: *irr.* 285

yuxtaponer to put in juxtaposition: *irr.* 269

za(m)bullirse to dive: 246*b*

zaherir (ie) to reproach, censure

287.   *Reference List of Verbs*

taking a Direct Infinitive Object, or requiring a Preposition before a Subordinate Infinitive

If the principal verb is followed by a direct infinitive object without the interposition of a preposition, this fact is indicated by a dash (–) placed after the principal verb, thus: **querer –,** *to wish to.*

If a preposition is required before the subordinate infinitive, the preposition is given after the principal verb, thus: **empezar a,** *to begin to;* **tratar de,** *to try to.*

If the gerund may be used instead of a subordinate infinitive, this fact is indicated thus: **continuar a** *or ger.*

After many verbs in the list, the infinitive is used only when the principal and the subordinate verbs have the same subject. This is true of verbs of *affirming, denying, believing, doubting, knowing,* etc. (**afirmar, asegurar, confesar, creer, dudar, negar, reconocer, saber, sostener,** etc.), verbs of *willing* or *wishing* (**anhelar, desear, querer,** etc.), and verbs that express *feeling* or *emotion* (**alegrarse de, sentir, temer,** etc.).

The following list does not include verbs and expressions with which an infinitive is used only as subject of the sentence, such as **importar** (e.g., **me importa hacerlo**), **ocurrir** (e.g., **se me ocurre hacerlo**), **ser fácil, necesario,** etc. (e.g., **es fácil hacerlo**), **tocar** (e.g., **me toca hacerlo**), **valer más** (e.g., **vale más hacerlo**), etc. Nor is reference made to the use of an infinitive subject with such verbs as **convenir** (e.g., **me conviene hacerlo**), **gustar** (e.g., **me gusta hacerlo**), etc.

abandonar(se) a to give (oneself) up to

abstenerse de to refrain from

acabar de to finish, have just; **—por** to end by

acceder a to accede, agree to

acomodarse a to conform to

aconsejar –, to advise to

acordarse de to remember

acostumbrar –, to be used to; **—(se) a** to make (become) used to

acudir a to go, come, hasten to

acusar de to accuse of

adherir(se) a to stick to

afanarse por to exert oneself to

aficionarse a to become addicted to

afirmar –, to affirm, declare

afligirse de to lament

agraviarse de to be grieved at

ajustarse a to agree to

alcanzar a to reach, attain to

alegrarse de to be glad to

amenazar –, to threaten to; **—con** to threaten with

anhelar –, to long to

animar a to encourage to

aplicarse a to apply oneself to

aprender a to learn to

apresurar(se) a to hurry, hasten to

aprovecharse de to profit by

apurarse por to exert oneself to

arrepentirse de to repent of

arriesgar con to risk by

asegurar –, to assure, claim to

aspirar a to aspire to
asustarse de to be terrified at
atreverse a to dare to
autorizar a to authorize to
aventurarse a to venture to
avergonzarse de to be ashamed of
ayudar a to aid, help to

bastar con to be enough, suffice to

cansar(se) de to tire, make (grow) weary of
celebrar –, to be glad to
cesar de to cease to
comenzar a to begin, commence to
complacerse en to take pleasure in
comprometer(se) a to engage (oneself), agree to
condenar a to condemn to
condescender a to condescend to
conducir a to lead, conduct to
confesar –, to confess
confiar en to trust, hope to
conformarse a to conform, agree to
consagrar(se) a to devote (oneself) to
conseguir –, to succeed in
consentir en to consent to
consistir en to consist in
conspirar a to conspire to
consumirse en to be consumed in
contar con to count on
contentarse con to content oneself with; — de to be satisfied to
continuar a *or ger.* to continue (to)
contribuir a to contribute to
convenir(se) –, en, *or* a to agree to
convidar a to invite to

correr a to run to
creer –, to believe, think

dar a to give to; —se a to give oneself up to
deber –, should, ought to; -- de ought to (*supposition*)
decidir(se) – *or* a to decide, determine to
declarar –, to declare
dedicar(se) a to dedicate (oneself) to
dejar –, to let, allow, permit to; — de to leave off, cease to
deleitarse en to take delight in
desafiar a to challenge to
descender a to descend to
descuidar de to neglect to
desdeñar(se) – *or* de to disdain to
desear –, to desire to
desesperar(se) de to despair of
desistir de to desist from
destinar a to destine to
detenerse a to stop to
determinarse a to determine to
dignarse – *or* de to deign to
disculpar(se) de to excuse oneself for
dispensar de to excuse from
disponer(se) a to get ready, prepare to
disuadir de to dissuade from
divertirse en, con, *or ger.* to amuse oneself by *or* with
dudar –, to doubt; — en to hesitate to

echar(se) a to begin to
elegir –, to choose to
empeñarse en to insist on
empezar a to begin to
encargarse de to undertake to
enseñar a to teach to

entrar a to enter on, begin to

entretener(se) a *or ger.* to entertain oneself by *or* with

enviar a to send to

equivocarse en to be mistaken in

escuchar –, to listen to

esforzar(se) a, en, *or* **por** to attempt, endeavor to

esmerarse en to take pains in

esperar –, to hope to

estar para to be about to; **— por** to be inclined to

evitar –, to avoid

excitar a to excite to

excusar(se) de to excuse (oneself) from

exhortar a to exhort to

exponer(se) a to expose (oneself) to

fastidiar(se) de to weary, be weary of

fatigar(se) de to tire, be tired of

felicitar(se) de to congratulate (oneself) on

fijarse en to pay attention to

fingir –, to pretend to

forzar a to force to

gozar(se) de to enjoy; **—(se) en** *or ger.* to take pleasure in

guardarse de to guard against

haber de to have to

habituar(se) a to accustom one(self) to

hacer –, to make, have; **— por** to try to

hartarse de to be sated with

humillar(se) a to humiliate (oneself) to

imaginarse –, to imagine

impedir –, to prevent, hinder

impeler a to impel to

incitar a to incite to

inclinar a to induce to; **—se a** to be inclined to

incomodarse de to be annoyed at; **— por** to put oneself out to

indignarse de to be indignant at

inducir a to induce to

insistir en to insist on

inspirar a to inspire to

intentar –, to try, attempt

invitar a to invite to

ir a to go to

jactarse de to boast of

jurar –, to swear to

justificar(se) de to justify (oneself) for

librar de to free from

limitar(se) a to limit (oneself) to

lograr –, to succeed in

llegar a to come to, succeed in

mandar –, to command, have; **— a** to send to

matarse por to try hard to

meditar en to meditate upon

merecer –, to deserve to

meterse a to undertake to

mezclarse en to take part in

mirar –, to look at, watch

morirse por to be dying to

necesitar –, to need, want to

negar –, to deny; **—se a** to decline, refuse to

obligar(se) a to oblige (oneself) to

obstinarse en to persist in

ocupar(se) en to busy (oneself) with

odiar –, to hate to
ofrecer(se) –, to offer, promise to; —(se) a to offer to
oír –, to hear
olvidar –, to forget to; —(se) de to forget
oponerse a to be opposed to
ordenar –, to order to

pararse a to stop to
parecer –, to seem to
particularizarse en to specialize in
pasar a to proceed, pass to
pensar –, to intend to; — en to think of
permitir –, to permit to
perseverar en to persevere in
persistir en to persist in
persuadir(se) a to persuade (oneself) to
poder –, can, may, to be able to
poner a to put to; —se a to begin to
preciarse de to boast of
preferir –, to prefer to
preparar(se) a to prepare, make ready to
presumir –, to presume to
pretender –, to claim, try to
principiar a to begin to
privar(se) de to deprive, be deprived of
probar a to try to
proceder a to proceed to
procurar –, to try to
prohibir –, to forbid
prometer –, to promise to
proponer –, to propose, purpose to
provocar a to provoke to
pugnar por to strive, struggle to

quedar(se) a to remain to; — en to agree to; — por to remain to (be . . .)
quejarse de to complain of
querer –, to wish to

rabiar por to be crazy to
recelarse –, to fear
recomendar –, to recommend to
reconocer –, to acknowledge, confess to
recordar –, to remember
recrear(se) en *or ger.* to divert (oneself) by
reducir(se) a to bring (oneself) to
rehusar(se) – *or* a to refuse to
renunciar a to renounce
resignarse a to resign oneself, submit to
resistirse a to resist
resolver(se) a to resolve, decide to
reventar por to be bursting to

saber –, to know how, be able to, can
salir a to go (*or* come) out to
sentarse a to sit down to
sentir –, to regret, be sorry to
ser de to be
servirse –, to please, be so kind as to
sobresalir en to excel in
soler –, to be wont, used to
soltar a to start to
someter(se) a to submit (oneself) to
soñar con to dream of
sospechar de to suspect of
sostener –, to maintain, affirm
subir a to go up to
sugerir –, to suggest

tardar en to delay, be long in
temer –, to fear to
terminar en to end by

tornar a to return to; to . . . again
tratar de to try to

urgir a to urge to

vacilar en to hesitate to
valerse de to avail oneself of

venir a to come to; — de to come from, have just

ver –, to see
volar a to fly to
volver a to return to; to . . . again

VOCABULARY

Spanish–English

ABBREVIATIONS: *adj.* adjective; *adv.* adverb; *coll.* colloquial; *conj.* conjunction; *f.* feminine; *inf.* infinitive; *interrog.* interrogative; *m.* masculine; *n.* noun; *neut.* neuter; *part.* participle; *pl.* plural; *prep.* preposition; *pres.* present; *pron.* pronoun; *rel.* relative; *v.* verb.

The sign * indicates active vocabulary used in the lessons.

A

*a to, at; from
abandonar to abandon, leave unattended
*abierto *past part. of* abrir
abnegado, –a unselfish
el abogado lawyer
aborrecer to hate
abrazar to embrace
*abril *m.* April
*abrir to open
*el abuelo grandfather
*acá here
*acabar to finish; — de + *inf.* have just + *past part.*
acariciar to caress
*la acción action; share
*el (la) accionista shareholder
el aceite oil
acelerar to hasten
aceptar to accept
acercarse to approach
*el acero steel
*acompañar to accompany, go with
*aconsejar to advise
el acontecimiento event
*acostado, –a lying down
*acostarse (ue) to lie down, go to bed
el acuerdo accord; de —, in agreement
la adaptación adaptation
¡ adelante ! come in !

además (de) besides
adiós good-bye, greetings
el adjetivo adjective
el administrador manager
admitir to admit
*el aeroplano aeroplane
el afán toil
afeitar to shave
la afición fondness, liking
*la afrenta affront
agarrar to grasp
la agencia agency
la agitación agitation, excitement
agitar to agitate
*agosto *m.* August
agotar to exhaust
*agradar to please
*agradecido, –a grateful, obliged
el agresor aggressor
*el agua *f.* water
*ahí there (*near the person addressed*); por —, anywhere (*there*)
*ahogarse to drown, be drowned
*ahora now
*ahorrar to save (*money*)
el aire air
*al to the, on the; — + *inf.* on, upon, + *pres. part.*
el alambre wire
alarmar to alarm
el alcalde mayor
*alegrarse (de) to be glad (of)
la alegría gaiety
*alemán, –ana German

281

el **alfiler** pin
***algo** anything, something; somewhat
***alguien** any one, anybody, some one, somebody
***alguno** (**algún**), -a any, some, a few
*el **alma** *f.* soul
el **almirante** admiral
***almorzar** (ue) to breakfast (late), have (late) breakfast *or* lunch, to lunch, have luncheon
el **almuerzo** (late) breakfast, lunch
***alquilar** to rent
el **altar** altar
altivo, -a haughty
***alto**, -a high, tall; loud
*el **alumno**, la **alumna** student
***allá** there
***allí** there
***amable** amiable, kind
***amar** to love
***amarillo**, -a yellow
***ambos**, -as both
amenazar to threaten
*el **amigo**, la **amiga** friend; *adj.* **amigo**, -a **de** friendly to
el **amo** master
el **amor** love
el **anciano** old man
***andar** to go, walk; **anda** go ahead
Andrés Andrew
la **anécdota** anecdote
la **animación** animation
el **animal** animal
***anoche** last night
la **ansiedad** anxiety
el **antepasado** forefather
***antes** before, formerly; — **de** before; — **que** before
Antonio Anthony
*el **año** year; **tener . . . —s** to be . . . years old
el **aparador** sideboard
aparecer to appear
apenas hardly
*el **apetito** appetite
el **apoderado** attorney
el **apoyo** support
***aprender** to learn
***aprisa** fast

apuntar to note, make a note of
el **apunte** note
***aquel**, **–ella**, **–os**, **–as** that, those
***aquél**, **–élla**, **–os**, **–as** that one, those
***aquello** that (thing)
***aquí** here
*el **árbol** tree
argentino, -a Argentine
arreglado, -a careful, moderate; **arregladito** in shipshape order
arreglar to manage
el **arreglo** order; **con** — **a** in accordance with
el **arroz** rice; — **con leche** rice pudding
*el **arte** art
el **artículo** article
*el (la) **artista** artist
el **asilo** asylum
asomar(se) to appear, go, come
el **aspecto** aspect
el **asunto** subject
***asustado**, -a frightened
***asustar** to frighten
atender (ie) to attend (to)
atreverse (a) to dare
atrevido, -a bold, daring
aumentar to increase, enlarge
***aunque** although, though
*el **automóvil** automobile; **pasearse en** —, to drive
*el **autor** author
la **aventura** adventure
el **aviso** signal
el **ay** lament; ¡ **ay** ! ouch !
***ayer** yesterday
***ayudar** to aid, help
***azul** blue

B

el **bacalao** cod
el **baile** dance
***bajar(se)** to get down
***bajo**, -a low; *prep.* under
el **balcón** balcony
*el **banco** bank
la **baraja** (pack of) cards
barato, -a cheap
la **baronesa** baroness

*bastante enough
bastar to be enough
la batalla battle
*beber to drink
*la beca scholarship
*bello, -a beautiful
la berlina landau
*la biblioteca library
*la bicicleta bicycle
*bien well, all right
*los bienes goods, property
el biftec (bistec) beefsteak
*el billete bill
*blanco, -a white
blanquear to whiten
la bofetada slap in the face
*el bolsillo pocket
*bonito, -a pretty
*el bosque forest
la bota boot
la botella bottle
*el Brasil Brazil
el brazo arm
*bueno (buen), -a good, all right; estar —, to be well; sería —, it would be well
*burlarse de to make fun of, mock
el burro donkey
*buscar to look for, seek

C

el caballero gentleman
*el caballo horse; ir a —, to ride, be riding on horseback
el cabello hair
*cada each, every; — uno (-a) each one
*caer(se) to fall, fit; ya caigo now I understand; se me cayó I dropped it
*el café coffee
*la caja box
el cajista compositor (*in printing*)
el calabacín small *or* tender pumpkin
*el calor warmth; tener —, to be warm; hace (hacía, *etc.*) —, it is (was, *etc.*) warm
callarse to keep silent; calla hush

*la calle street
*la cama bed
*el camino road, way
*el camión truck
el campamento camp
la campana bell
*el campo country
*el Canadá Canada
*cansado, -a tired
cantar to sing
*la cantidad quantity
el capital capital (*money*)
*la capital capital (*city*)
*el capitalista capitalist
*el capítulo chapter
*la cara face
el carácter character, firmness
*la cárcel jail
el cardo thistle
la caridad charity
*Carlos Charles
*la carne meat, flesh
*caro, -a dear, expensive
*la carta letter
*la casa house, home; a —, (to) home; en —, at home
*casi almost
*castellano, -a Castilian, Spanish
*castigar to punish
la casualidad chance
*catorce fourteen
cenar to have supper
*el centavo cent
*cerca *adv.* near; — de *prep.* near; cerquita quite near
el cerdo pig
*cerrar (ie) to close, shut
cesar to cease; sin —, unceasingly
el Cid Lord (*see page 66*)
el cielo sky, heavens
*cien(to) one (a) hundred, cent(um); por —, per cent
*cierto, -a certain
el cigarro cigar
*cinco five
*cincuenta fifty
*el cine (cinematógrafo) moving pictures, "movies"
*la ciudad city
*claro, -a clear

*la clase class, classroom; kind
*el clima climate
*el club club
*la cocina kitchen
la cocinera cook
*el coche carriage, coach, car; ir
(pasearse) en —, to drive
*coger to catch, gather, pick,
take
la cólera wrath
el colmo crown; para — de to
crown (= *top off*)
colocar to place
Colón Columbus
*el color color
*la comedia comedy
comentar to comment
comenzar (ie) to begin
*comer to eat, dine
*el cometa comet; la cometa kite
*la comida meal, dinner, food
la comisión commission
*como as, as if, like; tanto ...
—, both ... and; cómo no of
course; *interrog.* cómo how
cómodamente comfortably
*cómodo, -a comfortable
el compañero companion
*la compañía company
*comprar to buy
*comprender to understand, re-
alize
comprometido, -a in a predicament
*común common; por lo —,
usually
*con with
el concierto concert
el conciudadano fellow citizen
la concurrencia gathering
*la condición condition
la conducta conduct
*la conferencia lecture
*conmigo with me
*conocer to know (*be acquainted
with*), meet (*become acquainted
with*)
la consecuencia consequence
considerar to consider
*consigo with himself (herself,
yourself, themselves, yourselves)

la constancia steadiness; con —,
steadily
*construir to construct, build
la consulta consultation
consultar to consult
*contar (ue) to count, relate
contener to contain
*contento, -a content, glad,
happy, pleased
*contestar to answer, reply
*contigo with you (thee)
el continente continent
*continuar to continue
contra against
*contrario, -a contrary; por el
—, on the contrary
el contrincante opponent
convencer to convince
*convenir to be proper, be suit-
able, be well
la conversación conversation
conversar to converse, talk
cooperar to co-operate
la copa goblet
copiar to copy
coquetón, -ona coquettish
la cordialidad cordiality
*cordialmente cordially
la cordillera (range of) mountains
corregir (i) to correct, devise
*el correo mail
*correr to run, ride
*cortar to cut
la corte court
la cortesía courtesy; con —, courteously
corto, -a short
*la cosa thing; question; alguna
—, anything; *after neg.* nothing; ninguna —, nothing
la costa coast
*costar (ue) to cost
*costoso, -a costly, expensive
*la costumbre custom, manner
el crédito credit
la creencia belief
*creer to believe, think; creo que
sí I think so; ya lo creo
(que) of course, certainly
*el criado, la criada servant
*la crisis crisis
cristiano, -a Christian

Cristóbal Christopher

*el cuaderno notebook

*cual which; el (la, lo) —, los (las) —es who (whom), which; cuál *interrog.* which

la cualidad quality

*cualquier(a) (*pl.* cualesquier(a)) any (one) at all, whatever

*cuando when; cuándo *interrog.* when

*cuanto, –a all who, all that; — ... tanto ..., the ... the ...; cuánto, –a *interrog.* how much (many)

*cuarenta forty

*cuarto, –a fourth; *n.* fourth, quarter; room

*cuatro four

el cubierto (course) dinner

*la cuchara spoon

la cucharada spoonful

*la cuenta account, bill

el cuento story

*el cuidado care; tener —, to be careful; no tengas —, don't worry

*cumplir to fulfill, complete; — años to reach one's birthday

*el cura (parish) priest

*cuyo, –a whose

Ch

*el chaleco waistcoat, vest

*el chico (*coll.*) boy, young fellow; la chica (*coll.*) girl

el chocolate chocolate

D

*dado que granted that

*la dalia dahlia

*el daño harm; hacerse —, to harm *or* hurt oneself

*dar to give; — a face; — con meet, find, come upon; — en persist in; — de comer feed, give something to eat; — los buenos días say good morning (day); — un paseo take a walk; da(n) la(s) una (dos) it is striking one (two)

*de of, from, about, by, in, as a

*debajo de under

*deber ought to, should; to owe

*el deber duty

*decidir to decide

*décimo, –a tenth

*decir to say, tell; es —, that is to say; querer —, mean; digo I mean; se dice (decía) it is (was) said

dedicar to devote

*el dedo finger

el defensor defender

degradar to degrade

*dejar to leave, let, allow

delante ahead

delegar to delegate

*delinquir to be delinquent

*demás (de más) other, another, others, rest, extra

*demasiado too, too much

democrático, –a democratic

el demonio devil

derecho, –a right, straight; hecho y —, in every respect

*desayunarse to breakfast, have (early) breakfast

*descansar to rest

descifrar to decipher, make out

desconocido, –a unknown

descontar (ue) to discount, take off

el descubrimiento discovery

descubrir to discover

*el descuido neglect, slip

*desde from, since

*desear to wish

desierto, –a deserted; *n.* desert

despedir (i) to dismiss, send away

desperdiciador, –ora wasteful

*despertar (ie) to awake, wake up

el despertar awakening

*después afterwards; poco —, a short time (soon) afterwards; — de (que) after

*la deuda debt

*devolver (ue) to return, give back

*el día day; todos los —s every day

el **diario** diary
el **diccionario** dictionary
***diciembre** m. December
dictar to dictate
la **dicha** happiness
***diecinueve (diez y nueve)** nineteen
***dieciocho (diez y ocho)** eighteen
***dieciséis (diez y seis)** sixteen
***diecisiete (diez y siete)** seventeen
el **diente** tooth
***diez** ten
diferente different
***diferir (ie)** to postpone
***difícil** difficult
la **dificultad** difficulty
*el **dinero** money
Dios God; **por —**, please
*el **diploma** diploma
el **director** director
***dirigir** to direct, address; *refl.* go, apply
discutir to discuss
disgustarse to be *or* become displeased
el **disparo** shot
dispensar to excuse
disputar to argue
***distinguir** to distinguish
***distintamente** distinctly
***dividir** to divide
***doce** twelve
*la **docena** dozen
*el **dólar** dollar
*el **domingo** Sunday
el **dominio** rule
***don (doña)** Mr. (Mrs.)
***donde** where; **dónde** *interrog.* where
dorado, -a golden; **doraditos, -as** (golden) browned
***dormir (ue)** to sleep; *refl.* fall asleep
***dos** two; **los (las) —,** both
***doscientos, -as** two hundred
***dudar** to doubt
*el **dueño** owner
***dulce** sweet; **los dulces** candy
durante during
el **duro** dollar (*Spain*)

E

*e and
*el **Ecuador** Ecuador
la **edad** age
*el **edificio** building
*el **efecto** effect, object
*el **ejemplo** example
*el **ejercicio** exercise
el **ejército** army
*el **(la,** *etc.***) the; — (la,** *etc.***) de** that of, the one of, *etc.*
*él he, him, it
el **elogio** praise
*ella she, her, it
*ello it
*ellos, -as they, them
el **embajador** ambassador
*Emilia Emily
empeñarse en to insist on
*empezar (ie) to begin
empingorotado, -a high, stuck up
el **empleado** employee
*el **empleo** position, job
la **empresa** undertaking
*en in, at, on, into, by
encantar to charm, delight
encargar to ask (*some one to do something*)
encima (de) on top of, over
*encontrar (ue) to find, meet; **—se con** meet
el **enemigo** enemy
*enero January
*enfadado, -a angry
*enfadar to make angry; *refl.* become angry
*enfermo, -a ill, sick
*engañar to deceive
*Enrique Henry
*la **ensalada** salad
*enseñar to teach
*entender (ie) to understand; **no entiendo de** I know nothing about
*entonces then
*entrar (en) to enter (into), go (*or* come) in
*entre among, between
entregar to hand
la **entrevista** interview

el **entusiasmo** enthusiasm
*enviar to send
*envolver (ue) to wrap
la época epoch, time
escoger to choose
el escribiente clerk
*escribir to write
*la escuela school
*ese, –a, esos, –as that, those
*ése, –a, ésos, –as that (one), those
el esfuerzo effort
*eso that
el espacio space, room
*España Spain
*español, –ola Spanish; n. Spaniard, Spanish woman
*esperar to expect, hope, wait (for)
*la esposa wife
la esquina corner
*la estación station
*el estado state; (los) Estados Unidos United States
*estar to be
*este, –a, estos, –as this, these
*éste, –a, éstos, –as this (one), these
el estilo style; por el —, of the sort
*esto this
*estudiar to study
*el estudio study
*Eulalia Eulalia
*Europa Europe
la exageración exaggeration
examinar to examine
la excavación excavation
*excelente excellent
exclamar to exclaim
la expedición expedition
*explotar to work, develop (a mine)
expresar to express
extenso, –a extensive
extranjero, –a foreign; n. foreigner
extraordinario, –a extraordinary
exuberante exuberant

F

*fácil easy
*fácilmente easily

10*

faltar to be lacking, fail (to come)
*la familia family
*el favor favor
*febrero m. February
*Felipe Philip
*feliz happy
Fernando Ferdinand
la fiebre fever
la fiesta festivity, entertainment
*figurarse to appear, imagine, seem
fijarse (en) to notice
el fin end; al (en, por) —, finally; en —, in short
*la flor flower
el florero flower vase
el fondo background
formar to form
la fortuna fortune
fracasar to fail
*francés, –esa French
*Francia France
*Francisca Frances
*la frase phrase, sentence
frecuentemente frequently
frente a in front of
*fresco, –a cool, fresh; al —, in the open
*el frío cold; tener —, to be cold; hace (hacía) —, it is (was) cold
frío, –a cold
*frito, –a fried
la(s) fruta(s) fruit
el fuego fire
*fuera outside
fuerte loud
la fuerza force, strength; a —(s) de by dint of
*funcionar to work, run (as an engine)

G

la gallina hen, chicken
la gana desire; de buena —, willingly; le ha dado la —, the fancy struck him (her), he (she) has taken a fancy
*ganar to earn, win
*gastar to spend, use up, wear out

*el **gasto** expense
el **gato** cat
general general
generoso, –a generous
*la(s) **gente(s)** people
la **geología** geology
gobernar to govern
el **gobierno** government
golpear to strike, knock
*gracias** thanks, thank you
la **gramática** grammar
*grande (gran)** big, large, great;
 grandecito, –a already (*or*
 somewhat) grown up
grave grave, serious
*gritar** to shout
el **grupo** group
*el **guante** glove
guardar to keep, watch
el **guardarropa** coatroom
*la **guerra** war
el **guerrero** warrior
guiar to guide, lead
*gustar** to please; **me gusta(n)**
 I like it (them); **nos gusta(n)**
 we like it (them)
*el **gusto** pleasure; **tener —,** to be
 pleased

H

*la **Habana** Havana
*haber** to have; **— de** be to;
 hay que + *inf.* one must, it is
 necessary; **hay . . . que** +
 inf. there is . . . + *inf.*; **¿ qué
 hay?** what is the matter ?
 hay (había, *etc.*) **luna (sol)**
 the moon (sun) is (was, *etc.*)
 shining; **hay (había,** *etc.*)
 lodo (neblina, polvo) it is
 (was, *etc.*) muddy (foggy,
 dusty)
*la **habitación** room
 *hablador, –ora** talkative
 *hablar** to speak
 *hacer** to do, make; **hace (hacía,**
 etc.) **calor (frío, sol, viento)**
 it is (was, *etc.*) warm (cold,
 sunny, windy); **— un viaje**
 take a trip; **—se daño** harm
 or hurt oneself

*el **hacha** *f.* ax
 *hallar** to find
*el **hambre** *f.* hunger; **tener —,** to
 be hungry
 *haragán, –ana** idle, lazy
la **harina** flour
 *hasta** until, as far as; **— que**
 until
la **hazaña** feat
el **helado** ice cream
*el **hermano** brother
 *hermoso, –a** beautiful, handsome
el **héroe** hero
el **herrador** blacksmith
*el **hielo** ice
el **hígado** liver
*la **hija** daughter; **—** (*or* **hijita**)
 my dear (daughter)
*el **hijo** son; **—s** children
 Hilario Hilary
el **hilo** thread, wire
 hispanoamericano, –a Spanish
 American
*la **historia** history, story
 *histórico, –a** historical
 historieta short story
la **hoja** leaf
*el **hombre** man; **¡ — !** man alive !
 well ! oh boy !
 honrado, –a honest
*la **hora** hour
*el **hotel** hotel
 *hoy** today
el **hueso** bone
el **huésped** guest
*el **huevo** egg
 huir to flee
la **humillación** humiliation
el **humorista** humorist

I

la **idea** idea
el **ideal** ideal
*el **idioma** language
*la **iglesia** church
 *igual** equal, similar
la **impaciencia** impatience
 impedir (i) to prevent
*la **importancia** importance
 importante important

*importar to be important, concern
el importe amount
imposible impossible
el incidente incident
la independencia independence
individualista individualist
el individuo individual
inferior inferior
el ingenio mind
Inglaterra England
*inglés, –esa English; n. Englishman, Englishwoman
inmortal immortal
inocente innocent; los —s the darlings (children)
*instar to urge
la inteligencia intelligence, understanding
el interés interest
*interesante interesting
interesar to interest
interrumpir to interrupt
la interrupción interruption
*íntimo, –a intimate
intrépido, –a intrepid, daring
el inventor inventor
*el invierno winter
invitar to invite
*ir to go; — a caballo ride, be riding on horseback; — a pie go on foot, walk; — en automóvil ride, drive; ¿cómo le va? how are you? refl. go away
*Isabel Elizabeth

J

*el Japón Japan
*el jardín flower garden
*la jaula cage
*el jefe boss, head, leader
*Jorge George
*José Joseph
*joven young; el (la) —, young man (woman)
*Juan John
*el jueves Thursday
*el juez judge
*jugar (ue) to play
*julio m. July

*junio m. June
justamente just, justly
la juventud youth

L

*la her, you, it
*el lado side; por un — y por otro this way and that
*el ladrón thief
*el lago lake
la lámina picture
*el lápiz pencil
*largo, –a long
*las them, you
*la lástima pity; es —, it is a pity, it is too bad
*lavar to wash
*le him, to him, her, to her, you, to you, it, to it
*la lección lesson
la lectura reading; libro de —, reader
*la leche milk; arroz con —, rice pudding
*leer to read
*lejos far
la lengua language
*les them, to them, you, to you
la letra handwriting
*levantarse to rise, get up
la ley law
la leyenda legend
liberal liberal
liberar to free
la libertad liberty, freedom
*la librería bookstore
*el libro book
el librote (big or worthless) book
*limpiar to clean
limpio, –a clean, neat
la lista list, menu
*listo, –a ready
la literatura literature
*lo it, him, you
loco, –a mad; n. madman
la locura insanity, madness
*el lodo mud; hay (había, etc.) —, it is (was, etc.) muddy
lograr to attain, succeed in
Londres London
*los them, you

la **lotería** lottery; **le ha caído la —**, he has won a prize in the lottery

el **lucimiento** splendor, freedom

***lucir** to shine

***luchar** to fight, struggle

***luego** soon, later, then; **— que** as soon as

el **lugar** place

***Luis** Louis

*la **luna** moon; **hay (había,** *etc.*) **—**, the moon is (was, *etc.*) shining

*el **lunes** Monday

*la **luz** light

Ll

***llamar** to call, knock; **— por teléfono** telephone; *refl.* be named; **se llama** his name is

***llegar** to arrive; **— a +** *inf.* succeed in

lleno, -a full

***llevar** to take, carry; wear; *refl.* take *or* carry away; spend

***llorar** to cry, weep

***llover (ue)** to rain

M

*la **madre** mother

madrileño, -a Madrilenian (*native of Madrid*)

*el **maestro** teacher

***mal** badly

***malo (mal), -a** bad; **estar —,** to be ill, sick

*la **mamá** mamma, mother

***mandar** to command, order, send

el **mando** command

*la **manera** manner, way; **de — que** so as, so that

el **manicomio** insane asylum

*la **mano** hand

el **manojo** bunch

la **maña** cunning; **darse —,** to manage

*la **mañana** morning; **por la —,** in the morning; *adv.* tomorrow

*el **mapa** map

*la **máquina** engine

el **mar** sea

la **maravilla** wonder

la **marcha** course

***marchar** to go; *refl.* go away

el (*or* la) **margen** margin

***María** Mary

*el **martes** Tuesday

***marzo** *m.* March

***mas** but

***más** more, most, plus; **— de** more than; **no ... — que** only; **por — que** although

material material

***mayo** *m.* May

***mayor** larger, largest; greater, greatest; older, oldest; **Calle Mayor** Main Street; **la — parte de** most of

el **mayordomo** butler

*la **mayoría** majority

***me** me, to me, myself

*el **médico** physician

la **medida** measure; **a — que** according as, as

***medio, -a** half; *n.* midst, means; **por — de** by means of

meditar to meditate

***Méjico** Mexico

***mejor** better, best

***menor** smaller, smallest; younger, youngest

***menos** less, least, fewer, fewest, minus, except; **a — que** unless; **— de** less than; **por lo —,** at least

menospreciar to underrate, despise

*la **mentira** lie

***menudo: a —,** often

merecer to deserve

*el **mes** month

*la **mesa** table

*el **metal** metal

meter to put; *refl.* get (into), interfere

*el **metro** meter

***mi(s)** my; **mí** me

*el **miedo** fear; **tener —,** to be afraid

***mientras (que)** as long as, while

*el **miércoles** Wednesday

***mil** thousand, a (one) thousand

el **milagro** miracle
militar military
*el **millón** million
el **millonario** millionaire
*la **mina** mine
el **ministro** minister
*el **minuto** minute
* **mío, -a** my, (of) mine; **el mío,
la mía,** *etc.* mine
la **mirada** glance, look
* **mirar** to look
la **misa** Mass
* **mismo, -a** same, self
* **misteriosamente** mysteriously
*la **mitad** half
* **moderno, -a** modern
*el **modo** manner, way; **de — que**
so as, so that
*el **momento** moment
el **moño** chignon, topknot
moral moral
* **morir (ue)** to die
mostrar (ue) to show
la **moza** girl
el **mozo** boy, waiter
*la **muchacha** girl
*el **muchacho** boy
* **mucho, -a** much (many), "a
lot of"; *adv.* much, a great
deal, very; **trabaja —,** he
works hard; **me agrada —,** it
pleases me greatly
* **mudarse** to move
la **muerte** death
*la **mujer** woman, wife; my dear
* **multiplicar** to multiply
*el **mundo** world
*la **muñeca** doll
el **murmurador** gossiper
murmurar to murmur, gossip
la **musa** muse
* **muy** very, much

N

nacer to be born
* **nada** nothing; **no . . . —,** not . . .
anything
* **nadar** to swim
* **nadie** no one, nobody; **no . . .
—,** not . . . any one
naturalmente naturally

la **nave** vessel
la **navegación** navigation
navegar to navigate, sail
*la **neblina** fog; **hay (había,** *etc.*)
—, it is (was, *etc.*) foggy
* **necesario, -a** necessary
* **necesitar** to need
el **necio** fool
* **negar (ie)** to deny
*el **negocio** business, affair; *pl.*
business affairs
* **negro, -a** black
*el **neumático** tire
* **ni** nor; **ni . . . ni** neither . . .
nor; **ni . . . tampoco** nor . . .
either
*la **nieve** snow
* **ninguno (ningún), -a** no,
none; **no . . . —,** not . . . any
*el **niño** small boy, child; **la niña**
small girl, child; **los niños**
children
* **no** no, not
noble noble
*la **noche** night; **esta —,** tonight;
media —, midnight
nombrar to name, appoint
el **nombre** name
normal normal
el **norte** north
* **nos** us, to us, ourselves, each
other, one another
* **nosotros, -as** we, us
*la **noticia** news (item); *pl.* news
* **novecientos, -as** nine hundred
la **novedad** new thing *or* event;
**¿ cómo andamos de nove-
dades ?** what's new ?
* **noveno, -a** ninth
* **noventa** ninety
* **noviembre** *m.* November
* **nuestro, -a** our, (of) ours; **el
nuestro, la nuestra,** *etc.* ours
* **nueve** nine
* **nuevo, -a** new
*el **número** number
* **nunca** never; **no . . . —,** not
. . . ever, never

O

* **o** or
obligar to oblige

*la obra work
obtener to obtain
el océano ocean
*octavo, –a eighth
*octubre *m.* October
*ocupado, –a busy
la ocurrencia occurrence, idea
ocurrir to occur, happen
*ochenta eighty
*ocho eight
*la oficina office
el oficio calling
ofrecer to offer
*¡ oh ! o ! oh !
*oír to hear; — decir hear (it said); — hablar hear (spoken of); ¡ oiga ! listen ! hear ! I declare ! the idea !
*ojalá would that, I wish he (she, *etc.*) would, I hope
*el ojo eye
*olvidar(se) (de) to forget; se me olvidó I forgot; no se te vaya a olvidar don't forget
*once eleven
opinar to think, be of the opinion
la oratoria oratory
*la orden order (*command*)
el original original
*el oro gold
*os you, to you, yourselves
osado, –a daring
*otorgar to grant, give assent
*otro, –a other, another

P

*Pablo Paul
la paciencia patience
pacienzudo, –a exceedingly patient
*el padre father; los padres parents
*pagar to pay
*la página page
*el país country (*nation*)
*el pájaro bird
*la palabra word
*pálido, –a pale
*el pan bread
*la papa (*Spanish America*) potato
*el papá papa, father

*el papel paper
*el paquete package, parcel
el par pair, couple
*para for; *before inf.* to, in order to; — que in order that
*el parque park
el parroquiano customer
*la parte part; a (en, por) todas —s everywhere
*pasado, –a past, last
*pasar to pass, spend (*time*); happen
*pasearse to walk, drive *or* ride for pleasure, stroll
*el paseo walk, promenade; dar un —, to take a walk
el paso crossing
*la patata (*Spain*) potato
el patio courtyard
*el pato duck
el patrón boss
la patrona landlady
la pausa pause
*la paz peace
*pedir (i) to ask for, order
*Pedro Peter
*pegar to hit, strike, give
peinar to comb the hair
*la película film, picture
*el peligro danger
*la pelota ball
*la pena trouble, difficulty; no vale la —, it is not worth the trouble
el pensador thinker
*pensar (ie) to think; *before inf.* intend
*peor worse, worst
*pequeño, –a little, small
*la pera pear
*perder (ie) to lose; *refl.* become *or* get lost
el perdón pardon; con — de ustedes begging your pardon
*perfectamente perfectly
Perico Pete
*el periódico newspaper
*permitir to permit, let
*pero but
perro, –a unfortunate; *n.* dog
*la persona person
el personaje character

*el **Perú** Peru
pesar to weigh
*el **pescado** fish (*after being caught*)
pescuezudo, -a thick-necked
la **peseta** peseta (⅕ *of a Spanish
dollar*)
*el **peso** dollar
el **piano** piano
*el **pie** foot; **ir a —,** to go on foot,
walk
pinchar to prick
*el **piso** floor
placer to please
*el **planeta** planet
plantarse to stand firm; **— en
sus trece** stand firm, stick to it
el **plantón** sentry
*la **plata** silver
el **platillo** small dish, saucer
el **plato** dish, plate
*la **playa** beach
*la **plaza** public square; position
*la **pluma** pen
*la **plumafuente (pluma fuente)**
fountain pen
****pobre** poor; *n.* poor inmate
****poco,** -a little; (*pl.*) few; **un —
de** a little; *adv.* **poco** little
****poder** to be able, can; **no —
más** be played out, be exhausted; **no — menos de** be
necessary; *pres.* can not but,
can not help; *past* could not
help
poderoso, -a powerful
*el **poema** poem
el **poeta** poet
*la **policía** police
*el **polvo** dust, powder; **hay —,**
it is dusty
****poner** to put, place, suit, harness, hitch; **— la mesa** set
the table; **—se** become, turn,
put on (*clothes*), set (*the sun*);
—se a begin
****por** for, by, through, to, per, for
the sake of, in exchange for,
because of; **— eso** that's why;
— qué *interrog.* why
****porque** because
el **porte** bearing
la **posada** inn

posible possible; **lo más aprisa
—,** as fast as possible; **lo más
pronto —,** as soon as possible
*los **postres** dessert
precioso, -a precious
preciso, -a necessary
el **predicador** preacher
predicar to preach
preferir (ie) to prefer
preguntar to ask (*questions*)
preguntón, -ona inquisitive
la **preocupación** worry
preocupado, -a worried
preparar to prepare
presentar to present, introduce
el **presidente** president
prestar to lend
primero, -a first
*el **primo,** la **prima** cousin
el **principio** principle
*la **prisa** hurry; **tener —,** to be in
a hurry
el **prisionero** prisoner
probablemente probably
*el **profesor** professor
profundamente profoundly,
soundly
*el **programa** program
prohibir to forbid
prometer to promise
pronto soon, quickly
la **propina** tip
propio, -a own
proporcionar to supply
el **propósito** end
protector, -ora protective
protestar to protest
la **proximidad** proximity, nearness
próximo, -a next
proyectar to show
la **prueba** trial, proof; **de —,** trying
público, -a public
el **pueblecito** village
*el **pueblo** town, people
*la **puerta** door
el **puerto** harbor
puertorriqueño, -a Puerto
Rican
pues for, since, well
el **pulgar** thumb; **dedo —,** thumb
el **púlpito** pulpit

*el **punto** point; **pasarse el —,** to be overdone
puntual punctual

Q

***que** conj.* that, for, than, as, when
***que** rel. pron.* that, who (whom), which; **el (la,** *etc.*) **—,** who (whom), which; he (she, *etc.*) who; **lo —,** what, which
*¿ **qué?** what ? ¿ **a (para, por) —?** why ? ¡ **— !** what, what a, how !
***quedar(se)** to remain
***querer** to wish, want; *with personal object* love, be fond of
***querido,** –a dear, beloved
*el **queso** cheese
***quien(es)** who (whom), the one (those) who; **quién(es)** *interrog.* who (whom); **de —,** whose
***quien(es)quiera** whoever
***quince** fifteen
***quinientos,** –as five hundred
***quinto,** –a fifth
quitar to take away

R

racional rational; *n. m.* (human) being
*la **rama** branch
raro, –a rare, strange
la **razón** reason
el **real** real ($\frac{1}{20}$ *of a Spanish dollar*)
***recibir** to receive
recitar to recite
recoger(se) to retire
la **recomendación** recommendation, reference
recordar (ue) to recall, remember, remind of
rechazar to reject, refuse (to admit)
rededor: al — de about, around
***reducir** to reduce
la **reflexión** meditation, reflection
el **refrán** proverb
*el **regalo** gift, present
***regañar** to scold

la **regla** rule; **en toda —,** properly
reguapo, –a very good-looking, pretty
***reírse (de)** to laugh (at)
*el **reloj** clock, watch
la **relojera** watchcase
rellenar to stuff
el **remedio** remedy; **no . . . más —, . . .** no other remedy
la **rendición** surrender
el **renglón** line
la **renuncia** resignation
renunciar to resign
*la **reparación** repair
el **representante** representative
representar to represent
la **resignación** resignation; **tener —,** to be resigned
resonar (ue) to resound
respetar to respect
respetuosamente respectfully
*el **restaurant(e)** restaurant
*la **reunión** meeting
reunir to amass, get together
reverente reverent, respectful
revocar to plaster
revolucionario, –a revolutionary
*el **rey** king
rezagarse to remain behind
***rezar** to pray
***rico,** –a rich
el **río** river
***rojo,** –a red
romano, –a Roman
romper to break
***ronco,** –a raucous, hoarse
*la **ropa** clothes
*la **rosa** rose
*el **rubí** ruby
Rusia Russia
la **ruta** route

S

*el **sábado** Saturday
***saber** to know, know how, can (*know how*); **— a** taste of
***sabroso,** –a savory; **ser —,** to taste good
***sacar** to take out
el **saco** bag

el **salario** salary, wages

****salir** to go *or* come out; rise *(the sun)*; — **de** leave

saludar to greet

el **saludo** salute, greeting

****santo, -a** holy, saint

la **satisfacción** satisfaction

****se** himself, herself, yourself, itself, oneself, themselves, yourselves; one, you, each other, one another; to him, to her, to it, to them, to you

****seco, -a** dry

la **sed thirst; **tener** —, to be thirsty

****seguida : en** —, immediately

seguir (i) to follow, continue, keep on

****segundo, -a** second

****seguro, -a** sure

****seis** six

la **selección** selection

la **semana week

****sentarse** (ie) to seat oneself, be seated, sit, sit down

****sentir** (ie) to regret, be sorry

la **señal** sign, indication

****señor** Mr., sir, gentleman; **señora** Mrs., mistress, madam (ma'am), lady; **señorita** Miss, young lady; **señorito** master, young man; **señores** Messrs., sirs, gentlemen, Mr. and Mrs.

****septiembre** *m.* September

****séptimo, -a** seventh

****ser** to be; **es que** the fact is that; **lo que es a ella** in her case

la **seriedad** seriousness; **con** —, seriously

serio, -a serious

el **sermón** sermon

el **servicio** service

****servir** (i) to serve; **no sirve para nada** it is good for nothing; **no sirve eso** that is not good

****sesenta** sixty

****setecientos, -as** seven hundred

****setenta** seventy

****sexto, -a** sixth

****si** if, whether

****sí** yes; *object of prep.* himself, herself, yourself, oneself, themselves, yourselves

****siempre** always; — **que** whenever, provided that

la **siesta** siesta *(afternoon nap or rest)*

****siete** seven

****siguiente** following

Silvestre Sylvester

la **silla chair

el **sillón armchair

la **simpatía** sympathy

simple simple

****sin** without

****sino** but

siquiera even; **ni** —, not (nor) even

el **sirviente** servant

el **sitio place

sobrar to exceed; *with indirect object* have too much (many)

****sobre** about, on

el **sobretodo** overcoat

la **sociedad** society

el **sofá sofa

el **sol sun; **hace** (**hacía,** *etc.*) —, it is (was, *etc.*) sunny, the sun is (was, *etc.*) shining; **hay** (**había,** *etc.*) —, it is (was, *etc.*) sunny

el **soldado** soldier

solicitar to seek, apply (for)

****solo, -a** alone

sólo only

el **sombrero hat

sonoro, -a sonorous

sonreír to smile

la **sopa soup

la **sopera** soup tureen

el **sorbete** sherbet

****sorprender** to surprise

el **sótano basement, cellar

****su(s)** his, her, your *(sing.)*, its, your *(pl.)*, their

****subir** to go, come *or* get up; bring *or* take up; amount to

sublime sublime

****suceder** to happen, follow, succeed

el **sucedido** happening

el **suelo** floor, ground

el **sueño sleep; **tener** —, to be sleepy

la **suerte** luck
el **sufrimiento** suffering
  *****sufrir** to suffer
  superar to excel
  superior superior
  suponer to suppose
  supremo, –a supreme
  suscitar to stir up
  *****suyo, –a** your, (of) yours, his,
  her, (of) hers, (of) its, their,
  (of) theirs; **el suyo, la suya,**
  etc. his, hers, yours, theirs

T

*****tal** such, such a; **con — que**
  provided that; **— vez** perhaps
*****también** also, too
*****tampoco** neither; no (= *not that
  either*); **no (ni) . . . —,** not
  (nor) . . . either
*****tan** as, so
*****tanto(s)** as (so) much (many);
  tanto . . . como both . . . and
*****la tarde** afternoon, evening; **por
  la —,** in the afternoon (evening); *adv.* late; **más —,**
  later
*****la taza** cup
  *****te** thee, to thee, you, to you,
  yourself (thyself)
 el **te** tea
*****el teatro** theater
*****el teléfono** telephone; **llamar por
  —,** to telephone
 la **telegrafía** telegraphy
*****el telegrama** telegram
*****el tema** theme, written exercise
  temblar (ie) to tremble
  *****temer** to fear, be afraid
  *****temprano** early
  ⃰**tener** to have; **— que** have to;
  **— calor (frío, hambre,
  miedo, prisa, sed, sueño)**
  be warm (cold, hungry, afraid,
  in a hurry, thirsty, sleepy);
  ¿qué tienes? what is the
  matter with you? **¿cuántos
  años tienes?** how old are
  you?
 la **tentativa** attempt
  *****tercer(o), –a** third

*****el tercio** third
  Teresa Theresa
  *****terminar** to finish; **se termina**
  is finished, is over
*****la tesis** thesis
*****ti** you (thee)
*****la tía** aunt
*****el tiempo** time, weather; **a —,** in
  time; **a un —,** at the same
  time, together; **hace (hacía,**
  etc.) **buen (mal) —,** the
  weather is (was, *etc.*) good
  (bad)
*****la tienda** store
 la **tierra** land
*****la tinta** ink
*****el tío** uncle
 el **tipo** type
  titular to entitle
  tocar to play (*a musical instru-
  ment*)
  *****todavía** still, yet
  *****todo, –a** all, every; *n.* every-
  thing; **todos los días** every
  day
  *****tomar** to take, drink
 el **total** total, whole
  *****trabajador, –ora** industrious
  *****trabajar** to work
*****el trabajo** work; trouble
 la **tradición** tradition
  *****traducir** to translate
  *****traer** to bring
  *****tranquilizar** to calm
  tranquilo, –a tranquil
  *****tratar de** to try (to)
 la **traza** appearance
  *****trece** thirteen; **plantarse en
  sus —,** to stand firm, stick to
  it
  *****treinta** thirty
*****el tren** train
  *****tres** three
 el **tripulante** sailor
  *****triste** sad
 el **trozo** selection
*****el trueno** (peal of) thunder
  *****tu(s)** your (thy)
  *****tú** you (thou)
 el (la) **turista** tourist
  *****tuyo, –a** your, (of) yours (thy,
  of thine)

U

*u (*before* o– *or* ho–) or
*un, una a, an
universal universal
*la universidad university
*uno, –a one; *pl.* some; *before
numerals* about
la uña (finger)nail
*usar to use; usado broken in
el uso use
*usted(es) you
*útil useful
*la uva grape

V

la vaca cow
el vagón (railroad) car
*valer to be worth; más vale it
is better
el valor value
*varios, –as several, miscellane-
ous
*el vaso (drinking) glass
vasto, –a vast
*veinte twenty
*veinticinco (veinte y cinco)
twenty-five
*veinticuatro (veinte y cuatro)
twenty-four
*veintidós (veinte y dos) twenty-
two
*veintinueve (veinte y nueve)
twenty-nine
*veintiocho (veinte y ocho)
twenty-eight
*veintiséis (veinte y seis)
twenty-six
*veintisiete (veinte y siete)
twenty-seven
*veintitrés (veinte y tres)
twenty-three
*veintiuno (veinte y uno)
twenty-one
*vencer to conquer, overcome
*vender to sell
*venir to come; — bien fit, be
becoming; la semana (el
mes, el año) que viene next
week (month, year)
*la ventana window

*ver to see; a —, let's see; tener
que — con have to do with
*el verano summer
*la verdad truth; es —, it is true;
¿ no es —? isn't it true?
isn't it so? don't you? *etc.*
*verde green
verdemar sea-green
el vestido dress, suit of clothes
vestir (i) to dress
*la vez time; una —, once; tal —,
perhaps
*viajar to travel
*el viaje trip; hacer un —, to take
a trip
el viajero traveler
*el vicio vice
*la vida life; en mi —, never
*viejo, –a old
*el viento wind; hace (hacía, *etc.*)
—, it is (was, *etc.*) windy
*el viernes Friday
*la villa town
la visita visit
*visitar to visit
visto *past part. of* ver: por lo —,
apparently
*vivir to live
vivo, –a keen
*el volumen volume
*volver (ue) to return, go *or* come
back; — a + *inf.* to . . . again;
—se be *or* become
*vosotros, –as you (ye)
*la voz voice; a media —, in a low
voice
la vuelta turn, return; darse —,
to turn around
*vuestro, –a your, (of) yours; el
vuestro, la vuestra, *etc.* yours

Y

*y and
*ya already, now, in due time, at
once; — no no longer, no more
*la yerba grass
*yo I

Z

*el zapato shoe
*zurcir to darn

VOCABULARY

English–Spanish

A

a, an un(o), una
able: be —, poder
about de, sobre
accompany acompañar
account cuenta; **on — of** por
acquainted: be —, conocer
address dirigir
advise aconsejar
aeroplane aeroplano
afraid: be —, tener miedo
after después de
afternoon tarde *f.*; **in the —,** por la tarde
afterwards después; **a short time (soon) —,** poco después
again: to ... —, volver a + *inf.*
aid ayudar
all todo, -a
allow dejar
almost casi
alone solo, -a
already ya
also también
although aunque
always siempre
amiable amable
among entre
and y, e (*before* i *or* hi)
angry enfadado, -a; **make —,** enfadar; **get —,** enfadarse
another otro, -a; **one —,** nos, os, se
answer contestar
any alguno, -a; **— (at all)** cualquiera (cualesquiera); **— one** alguien; **not — one** no ... nadie
anybody alguien
anything algo; **not ... —,** no ... nada
appear parecer, figurarse

appetite apetito
apply dirigirse
April abril *m.*
armchair sillón *m.*
arrive llegar
art arte *m.*
artist artista *m. & f.*
as como, que (*with* mismo), tan, tanto, -a
ask (for) pedir (i); **— questions)** preguntar
asleep: fall —, dormirse
assent: give —, otorgar
at en, a
August agosto
aunt tía
author autor *m.*
automobile automóvil *m.*
awake despertar (ie)
ax el hacha *f.*

B

bad malo, -a; **be too —,** ser lástima
badly mal
ball pelota
bank banco
basement sótano
be ser, estar; **— to** haber de
beach playa
beautiful hermoso, -a; bello, -a
because porque; **— of** por
become ponerse; **— acquainted** conocer; **— lost** perderse
becoming: be —, venir bien
bed cama
before (*in time*) antes de; *formerly*) antes; *conj.* antes de
begin empezar (ie); ponerse a
believe creer
beloved querido, -a
best mejor
better mejor; **it is —,** más vale

between entre
bicycle bicicleta
big grande
bill billete *m.*, cuenta
bird pájaro
birthday: reach one's —, cumplir
... años
black negro, –a
blue azul
book libro
bookstore librería
boss jefe *m.*
both ambos, –as; los (las) dos
box caja
boy muchacho; **small** —, niño
Brazil el Brasil
bread pan *m.*
breakfast almuerzo, desayuno; **have
(late)** —, almorzar (ue); **have
(early)** —, desayunarse
breakfast *(late)* almorzar (ue);
(early) desayunarse
bring traer; — **up** subir
brother hermano
build construir
building edificio
business negocio
busy ocupado, –a
but pero, mas, sino
buy comprar
by por, de

C

cage jaula
call llamar
can *(present of)* poder
Canada el Canadá
candy dulces *m. pl.*
capital capital *f.*
car coche *m.*
care cuidado
careful: be —, tener cuidado
carriage coche *m.*
carry llevar; — **away** llevarse
Castilian castellano, –a
catch coger
cellar sótano
cent centavo
certain cierto, –a
chair silla
chapter capítulo
Charles Carlos

cheese queso
child niño, –a; **children** niños,
hijos
church iglesia
city ciudad *f.*
class clase *f.*
classroom clase *f.*
clean limpiar
clear claro, –a
climate clima *m.*
clock reloj *m.*
close cerrar (ie)
clothes ropa
club club *m.*
coach coche *m.*
coffee café *m.*
cold frío, –a
color color *m.*
come venir; — **back** volver (ue);
— **out** salir; — **up** subir; —
upon dar con
comedy comedia
comet cometa *m.*
comfortable cómodo, –a
command mandar
common común
company compañía
condition condición *f.*
conquer vencer
construct construir
content contento, –a
continue continuar
contrary contrario, –a; **on the**
—, por el contrario
cool fresco, –a
cordially cordialmente
cost costar (ue)
costly costoso, –a
count contar (ue)
country campo; *(nation)* país *m.*
cousin primo, –a
crisis crisis *f.*
cry llorar
cup taza
custom costumbre *f.*
cut cortar

D

dahlia dalia
danger peligro
darn zurcir
daughter hija

day día *m.*
deal: a great —, mucho, -a
dear caro, -a; querido, -a
debt deuda
deceive engañar
December diciembre *m.*
decide decidir
delinquent: be —, delinquir
deny negar (ie)
depart partir
dessert postres *m. pl.*
develop explotar
die morir (ue)
difficult difícil
difficulty dificultad *f.*, pena
dine comer
dinner comida
diploma diploma *m.*
direct dirigir
distinctly distintamente
distinguish distinguir
divide dividir
do hacer
dog perro
doll muñeca
dollar dólar *m.*, peso
door puerta
doubt dudar
dozen docena
drink beber, tomar
drive pasearse, ir (pasearse) en coche
drop dejar caer; I dropped it se me cayó
drown ahogar(se)
dry seco, -a
duck pato
dust polvo
dusty: it is —, hay polvo
duty deber *m.*

E

each cada; — one cada uno (-a); — other nos, os, se
early temprano
earn ganar
easily fácilmente
easy fácil
eat comer
Ecuador el Ecuador
effect efecto

egg huevo
eight ocho
eighteen diez y ocho (*or* dieciocho)
eighth octavo, -a
﹅eighty ochenta
either: not (nor) ... —, no (ni) ... tampoco
eleven once
Emily Emilia
engine máquina
England Inglaterra
English inglés, -esa
Englishman (-woman) inglés (-esa)
enough bastante
enter (into) entrar (en)
equal igual
Europe Europa
evening tarde *f.*, noche *f.*; in the —, por la tarde (noche)
ever: not ... —, no ... nunca
every cada, todo, -a; — day (week) todos los días (las semanas)
everything todo
excellent excelente
exchange: in — for por
exercise ejercicio; written —, tema *m.*
exhausted: be —, no poder más
expect esperar
expense gasto
expensive caro, -a; costoso, -a
eye ojo

F

face cara
fall caer(se)
family familia
far lejos; as — as hasta
fast aprisa; as — as possible lo más aprisa (pronto) posible
father padre, papá
favor favor *m.*
fear miedo; *v.* temer
February febrero
fellow: young —, chico (*coll.*)
few pocos, -as; a —, algunos, -as
fifteen quince
fifth quinto, -a
fifty cincuenta
film película
find hallar, encontrar (ue), dar con
finger dedo
finish acabar, terminar

first primero, -a; *adv.* primero
fish (*after being caught*) pescado
fit caer (*or* venir) bien
five cinco
floor piso
flower flor *f.*
fog neblina
foggy: it is —, hay neblina
following siguiente
fond: be — of querer (a)
food comida
foot pie *m.*
for *prep.* para, por; *adv. or conj.* pues
forbid prohibir
forest bosque *m.*
forget olvidar(se) (de); I forgot se me olvidó
formerly antes
forty cuarenta
fountain pen plumafuente *f.* (pluma fuente)
four cuatro
fourteen catorce
fourth cuarto; *adj.* cuarto, -a
France Francia
Frances Francisca
French francés, -esa
fresh fresco, -a
Friday viernes *m.*
friend amigo, -a
frighten asustar
from de, desde
fruit fruta(s)
fulfill cumplir
fun: make — of burlarse de

G

garden jardín *m.*
gather coger
gentleman señor
George Jorge
German alemán, -ana
get conseguir, obtener; — angry enfadarse; — down bajarse; — lost perderse; — up subir, levantarse
gift regalo
girl muchacha, chica (*coll.*); small —, niña
give dar; — assent otorgar; — back devolver (ue)

glad contento, -a; be — (of) alegrarse (de)
glass (*for drinking*) vaso
glove guante *m.*
go ir, andar; — (to) dirigirse; — away irse, marcharse; — back volver (ue); — on foot ir a pie; — out salir; — up subir
gold oro
good bueno, -a; it is — for nothing no sirve para nada
goods bienes *m. pl.*
grandfather abuelo
grant otorgar
granted: — that dado que
grape uva
grass yerba
grateful agradecido, -a
great grande
greatly mucho
green verde

H

half medio, -a; *n.* mitad *f.*
hand mano *f.*
handsome hermoso, -a
happen suceder
happy feliz, contento, -a
hard mucho
harm daño; — oneself hacerse daño
hat sombrero
Havana la Habana
have haber, tener; — to + *inf.* tener que + *inf.*; — to do with tener que ver con
he él
hear oír; — (it said) oír decir; — (spoken of) oír hablar; hear! ¡oye! ¡oiga!
help ayudar
Henry Enrique
her le, la, ella; su, sus
here aquí
hers el suyo, la suya, *etc.*; of —, suyo, -a
herself se, sí; with —, consigo
high alto, -a
him le, lo, él
himself se, sí; with —, consigo
his su, sus; suyo, -a; *pron.* el suyo, la suya, *etc.*

historical histórico, –a
history historia
hit pegar
hoarse ronco, –a
holy san(to), –a
home casa; **at —**, en casa; **(to) —**, a casa
hope esperar; **I hope . . . !** ¡ ojalá !
horse caballo
horseback: be riding on —, ir a caballo
hotel hotel *m.*
hour hora
house casa
how *interrog.* cómo; **— much (many)** cuánto, –a (–os, –as)
hundred: one (a) **—**, cien(to); **five —**, quinientos, –as; **seven —**, setecientos, –as; **nine —**, novecientos, –as
hunger el hambre *f.*
hungry: be —, tener hambre
hurry prisa; **be in a —**, tener prisa
hurt oneself hacerse daño

I

I yo
ice hielo
idle haragán, –ana
if si
ill enfermo, –a; **be —**, estar enfermo (–a)
immediately en seguida
importance importancia
important: be —, importar
in en
industrious trabajador, –ora
ink tinta
inquisitive preguntón, –ona
intend pensar (ie)
interesting interesante
intimate íntimo, –a
introduce presentar
it lo, la, él, ella, ello
its su, sus; suyo, –a
itself se

J

jail cárcel *f.*
January enero
Japan el Japón
job empleo

John Juan
Joseph José
judge juez *m.*
July julio
June junio
just: have — + *past part.* acabar de **+** *inf.*

K

kind clase *f.*; *adj.* amable
king rey
kite cometa
knock llamar
know saber, conocer; **how** saber

L

lady señora; **young —**, señorita
lake lago
language idioma *m.*
large grande
last pasado, –a; **— night** anoche
late tarde
laugh (at) reírse (de)
lazy haragán, –ana
learn aprender
least menos; **at —**, por lo menos
leave dejar, partir, salir (de)
lecture conferencia
lend prestar
less menos; **— than** menos de
lesson lección *f.*
let dejar, permitir
letter carta
library biblioteca
lie mentira
lie down acostarse (ue); **lying down** acostado, –a
life vida
light luz *f.*
listen escuchar; **listen !** ¡ oye ! ¡ oiga !
little pequeño, –a; poco, –a; *adv.* poco
live vivir
long largo, –a; **as — as** mientras (que); **no longer** ya no
look mirar; **— for** buscar
lose perder (ie)
loud alto, –a
Louis Luis
love amar, querer (a)

low bajo, -a
lunch almorzar (ue)

M

madam señora
mail correo
majority mayoría
make hacer
mamma mamá
man hombre; **young —,** joven
manner manera, modo; costumbre *f.*
many muchos, -as; **so —,** tantos, -as
map mapa *m.*
Mary María
matter: **what is the —?** ¿qué hay?
May mayo
me me, mí; **to —,** me; **with —,** conmigo
meal comida
meat carne *f.*
meet encontrar (ue), dar con; (= *become acquainted*) conocer
meeting reunión *f.*
Messrs. señores
metal metal *m.*
meter metro
Mexico Méjico
milk leche *f.*
million millón *m.*
mine mina; *adj.* mío, -a; *pron.* el mío, la mía, *etc.*
minus menos
minute minuto
miscellaneous varios, -as
Miss señorita
mock burlarse (de)
modern moderno, -a
moment momento
Monday lunes *m.*
money dinero
month mes *m.*
moon luna; **the — is shining** hay luna
more más; **— than** más de; **no —** ya no
morning mañana; **in the —,** por la mañana
most más, la mayor parte
mother madre, mamá
move (away) mudarse

movies cine *m.*
Mr. don (*before given name*), señor; **— and Mrs.** señores
Mrs. doña (*before given name*), señora; **Mr. and —,** señores
much mucho, -a; *adv.* mucho, muy; **so —,** tanto, -a; *adv.* tanto; **too —,** demasiado
mud lodo
muddy: **it is —,** hay lodo
multiply multiplicar
must: **one —,** hay que
my mi, mis; mío, -a
mysteriously misteriosamente

N

name nombre *m.*; **his — is** se llama
near cerca (de)
necessary necesario, -a; preciso, -a; **it is — +** *inf.* hay que + *inf.*
need necesitar
neglect descuido
neighbor vecino
neither tampoco
never nunca, no . . . nunca
new nuevo, -a
news noticia(s)
newspaper periódico
next próximo, -a
night noche *f.*; **last —,** anoche
nine nueve
nineteen diez y nueve (diecinueve)
ninety noventa
ninth noveno, -a
no no; ninguno (ningún), -a
nobody nadie
none ninguno, -a
nor ni; **— . . . either** no (ni) . . . tampoco; **neither . . . —,** ni . . . ni
not no
notebook cuaderno
nothing nada, no . . . nada, cosa alguna, ninguna cosa
November noviembre *m.*
now ahora, ya
number número

O

object efecto, objeto
obliged agradecido, -a

October octubre *m.*
of de
office oficina
often a menudo
old viejo, –a
on en; — + *pres. part.* al + *inf.*
once una vez
one un(o), –a; **no** —, nadie; **not
. . . any** —, no . . . nadie; **the** —
of el (la) de
oneself se
open abrir
or o, u (*before* o– *or* ho–)
order mandar, pedir (i); **in** — **to**
para; **in** — **that** para que
other otro, –a; **each** —, nos, os, se;
—**s** demás
ought deber
our nuestro, –a
ours nuestro, –a; el nuestro, la
nuestra, *etc.*
outside fuera
overcome vencer
owe deber
owner dueño

P

package paquete *m.*
page página
pale pálido, –a
papa papá *m.*
paper papel *m.*
parcel paquete *m.*
parents padres *m. pl.*
park parque *m.*
part parte *f.*
pass pasar
past pasado, –a
Paul Pablo
pay pagar
peace paz *f.*
pear pera
pen pluma
pencil lápiz *m.*
people gente *f.*
per por
perfectly perfectamente
perhaps tal vez, quién sabe
permit permitir
person persona
Peru el Perú
Peter Pedro

Philip Felipe
physician médico
pick coger
picture película; **moving** —**s** cine
(cinematógrafo) *m.*
pity lástima; **be a** —, ser lástima
place sitio; *v.* poner
planet planeta *m.*
play jugar (ue)
played out: be —, no poder mas
please agradar, gustar, placer; **be
pleased** tener gusto
pleasure gusto
plus más
pocket bolsillo
poem poema *m.*
police policía
poor pobre
position empleo
possible posible; **as soon as** —,
lo más pronto posible
postpone diferir (ie)
potato papa (*Spanish America*);
patata (*Spain*)
pray rezar
precious precioso, –a
prefer preferir (ie)
present regalo
present presentar
pretty bonito, –a
priest cura *m.*
profoundly profundamente
program programa *m.*
promise prometer
proper: be —, convenir
property bienes *m. pl.*
provided that con tal que, siempre
que
public público, –a; — **square** plaza
punish castigar
put poner; — **on** (*clothes*) ponerse

Q

quantity cantidad *f.*
quarter cuarto

R

rain llover (ue)
rare raro, –a
raucous ronco, –a
read leer
ready listo, –a

recall recordar (ue)
receive recibir
red rojo, -a
reduce reducir
regret sentir (ie)
remain quedar(se)
remember recordar (ue)
rent alquilar
repair reparación *f.*
reply contestar
rest demás; *v.* descansar
rest. irant restaurant(e) *m.*
return volver (ue), devolver (ue)
rich rico, -a
ride pasearse, ir a caballo
rise levantarse
road camino
room cuarto, habitación *f.*
rose rosa
ruby rubí *m.*
run correr; (*as an engine*) funcionar

S

sad triste
saint san(to), -a
sake: for the — of por
salad ensalada
same mismo, -a
Saturday sábado
save ahorrar
savory sabroso, -a
say decir
scholarship beca
school escuela
scold regañar
seat: — oneself sentarse (ie)
second segundo, -a
see ver; let's —, a ver
seem parecer, figurarse
self mismo, -a
sell vender
send enviar, mandar
sentence frase *f.*
September septiembre *m.*
servant criado, -a
serve servir (i)
set poner; — the table poner la
    mesa; — (*the sun*) ponerse
seven siete
seventeen diez y siete (diecisiete)
seventh séptimo, -a

seventy setenta
several varios, -as
share acción *f.*
shareholder accionista *m. & f*
she ella
shine lucir
shoe zapato
should (= *ought to*) deber
shout gritar
show mostrar (ue), proyectar
shut cerrar (ie)
sick enfermo, -a
side lado
silver plata
since desde, pues
sir señor
sit sentarse (ie)
six seis
sixteen diez y seis (dieciséis)
sixth sexto, -a
sixty sesenta
sleep sueño; *v.* dormir (ue)
sleepy: be —, tener sueño
slip descuido
small pequeño, -a
snow nieve *f.*
so tan; — much tanto, -a; *adv.*
    tanto; — as (that) de manera
    (modo) que
sofa sofá *m.*
some alguno, -a; unos, -as
somebody alguien
some one alguien
something algo, alguna cosa
somewhat algo
son hijo
soon pronto, luego; — afterwards
    poco después; as — as luego que
sorry: be —, sentir (ie)
soul el alma *f.*
soundly profundamente
soup sopa
Spain España
Spaniard español, -ola
Spanish español, -ola; castellano, -a
speak hablar
spend gastar; (*time*) pasar
spoon cuchara
square (*public*) plaza
state estado; United States (los)
    Estados Unidos
station estación *f.*

steel acero
still todavía
store tienda
story historia
strange raro, -a
street calle *f.*; **Main Street Calle Mayor**
strike dar; pegar; **it is striking one (two)** da(n) la(s) una (dos)
stroll pasearse
struggle luchar
student alumno, -a
study estudio; *v.* estudiar
such (a) tal
suffer sufrir
suitable: be —, convenir
summer verano
sun sol *m.*; **the — is shining** hay (hace) sol
Sunday domingo
sure seguro, -a
surprise sorprender
sweet dulce
swim nadar

T

table mesa; **set the —,** poner la mesa
take coger, llevar, tomar; **— away** llevarse; **— out** sacar; **— up** subir
talkative hablador, -ora
tall alto, -a
taste: **— of (like)** saber a; **— good** ser sabroso (-a)
teach enseñar
teacher maestro, -a
telegram telegrama *m.*
telephone teléfono; *v.* llamar por teléfono, telefonar, telefonear
tell decir
ten diez
tenth décimo, -a
than que; de (*before numerals*); del que, de la que, *etc.* (*before clauses*)
thank you, thanks gracias
that *rel. pron. & conj.* que; *adj.* ese, -a; aquel, -ella; *pron.* ése, -a; aquél, -élla; *neut. pron.* eso, aquello; **— of** el (la) de; el (la)

que; **— which** lo que; **all —,** cuanto, -a
the el, la, los, las, lo
theater teatro
thee, to —, te
their su, sus; suyo, -a
theirs, of —, suyo, -a; el suyo, la suya, *etc.*
them les, los, las, ellos, ellas
theme tema *m.*
themselves se, sí; **with —,** consigo
then entonces, luego
there allí, allá; (*near the person addressed*) ahí; **— is ... to** hay que . . .
these *adj.* estos, -as; *pron.* éstos, -as
thesis tesis *f.*
they ellos, -as
thief ladrón *m.*
thing cosa
think creer, pensar (ie)
third tercero, -a; *n.* tercio
thirst sed *f.*
thirsty: be —, tener sed
thirteen trece
thirty treinta
this *adj.* este, -a; *pron.* éste, -a; *neut. pron.* esto
those *adj.* esos, -as; aquellos, -as; *pron.* ésos, -as; aquéllos, -as; **— of** los (las) de; **— who** los (las) que
thousand: one (a) —, mil
three tres
through por
thunder trueno; **peal of —,** trueno
Thursday jueves *m.*
time tiempo; vez *f.*; **in —,** a tiempo; **in due —,** ya; **a short — afterwards** poco después
tire neumático
tired cansado, -a
to a, por
today hoy
tomorrow mañana
tonight esta noche
too también, demasiado
town pueblo
train tren *m.*
translate traducir
travel viajar
tree árbol *m.*

trip viaje *m.*; **take a —**, hacer un
 viaje
trouble pena
truck camión *m.*
true: it is —, es verdad
truth verdad *f.*
try (to) tratar (de)
Tuesday martes *m.*
turn ponerse
twelve doce
twenty veinte
two dos

U

uncle tío
under debajo de
understand comprender, entender
 (ie); **now I —**, ya caigo
university universidad *f.*
unless a menos que
until hasta (que)
urge instar
us nos, nosotros, -as
use usar; **— up** gastar
useful útil
usually por lo común

V

very muy
vest chaleco
vice vicio
visit visitar
voice voz *f.*
volume volumen *m.*

W

waistcoat chaleco
wait (for) esperar
wake up despertar (ie)
walk andar, ir a pie, pasearse; *n.*
 paseo; **take a —**, dar un paseo
want querer (ie)
war guerra
warm: be —, tener calor
wash lavar
watch reloj *m.*
water el agua *f.*
way camino
we nosotros, -as

wear llevar; **— out** gastar
weather tiempo
Wednesday miércoles *m.*
week semana
weep llorar
weigh pesar
well bien, pues; **be —**, estar bueno,
 -a; convenir
what *interrog.* qué; *rel. pron.* lo que;
 — a qué
whatever cualquiera (*pl.* cualesquiera)
when cuando; *interrog.* cuándo
whenever siempre que
where donde; *interrog.* dónde;
 (= *whereto*) a dónde (adónde)
whether si
which que, cual, lo cual; *interrog.*
 cuál, qué; *rel. pron.* que, el (la,
 etc.) que; **that —**, lo que
while mientras (que)
white blanco, -a
who que, quien(es); *interrog.*
 quién(es); el (la, *etc.*) que *or* cual;
 he (she, *etc.*) —, el (la, *etc.*) que;
 all —, cuantos, -as
whoever quienquiera (*pl.* quienesquiera)
whom que, a quien(es), al que, *etc.*,
 al cual, *etc.*; *interrog.* a quién(es)
whose cuyo, -a; *interrog.* de
 quién(es)
why por qué; **that's —**, por eso
wife esposa
wind viento
window ventana
windy: it is (was, *etc.*) —, hace
 (hacía, *etc.*) viento
winter invierno
wish desear, querer; **I — he (she,
 etc.) . . . !** ¡ojalá que . . . !
with con
without sin
woman mujer; **young —**, joven
word palabra
work trabajo, obra; *v.* trabajar;
 (*a mine*) explotar; (*as an engine*)
 funcionar
world mundo
worried preocupado, -a
worse peor
worst peor

worth: be —, valer; it is not —
while no vale la pena
wrap envolver (ue)
write escribir

Y

year año
yellow amarillo, –a
yes sí
yesterday ayer

yet todavía
you tú, vosotros, –as; usted, ustedes;
ti, os; le, lo, la, los, las, se; with
—, contigo
your tu, tus; vuestro, –a; su, sus
yours tuyo, –a; suyo, –a; vuestro,
–a; el tuyo, *etc.*, el suyo, *etc.*, el
vuestro, *etc.*
yourself te, se, sí
yourselves os, se, sí

INDEX